FrontPage 2000

for Busy People

Import an Existing Web from the Internet

See "Importing a Web" in Chapter 3.

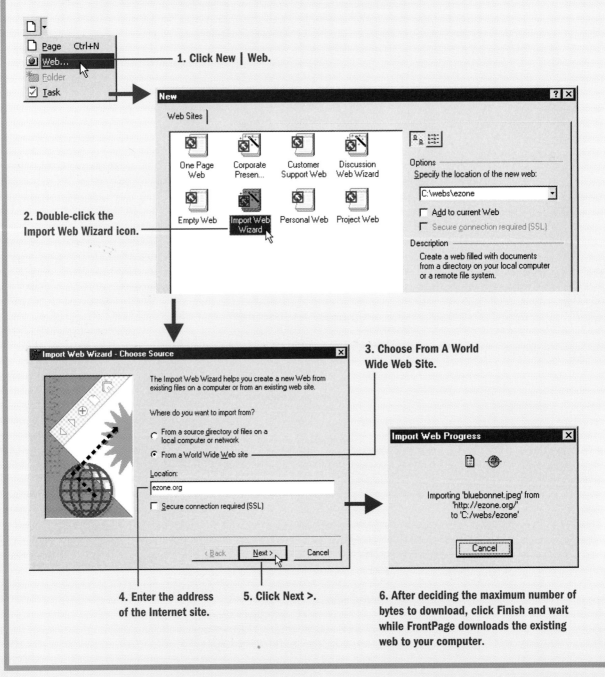

1. Click New | Web.

2. Double-click the Import Web Wizard icon.

3. Choose From A World Wide Web Site.

4. Enter the address of the Internet site.

5. Click Next >.

6. After deciding the maximum number of bytes to download, click Finish and wait while FrontPage downloads the existing web to your computer.

Create a New Web Page

See "Creating a New Page" in Chapter 4.

1. In Page view, select File | New | Page.

2. Click one of the page templates or wizards or choose one of the predesigned frames pages on the Frames Pages tab.

3. If the preview looks acceptable, click OK.

4. To save the page, press CTRL+S, type a name, give the page a title, and click the Save button.

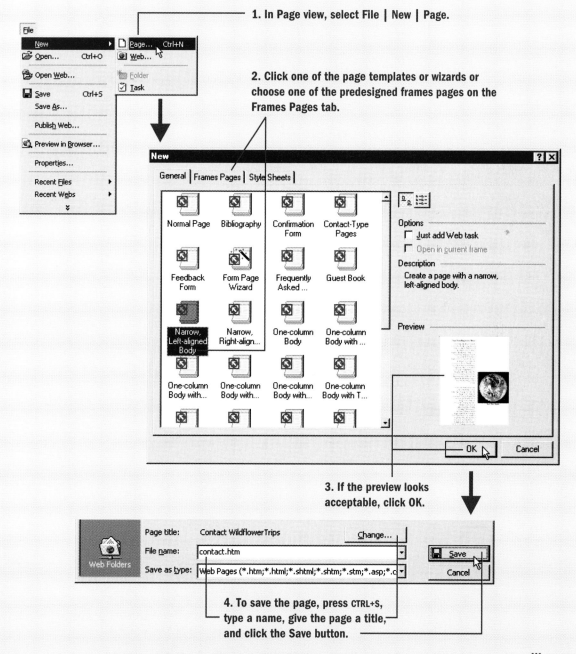

Lay Out Pages with Tables

See "Laying Out Pages with Tables" in Chapter 5.

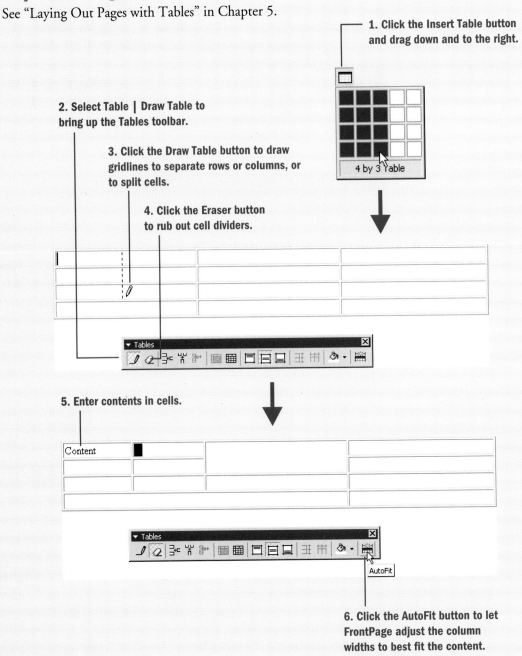

1. Click the Insert Table button and drag down and to the right.

4 by 3 Table

2. Select Table | Draw Table to bring up the Tables toolbar.

3. Click the Draw Table button to draw gridlines to separate rows or columns, or to split cells.

4. Click the Eraser button to rub out cell dividers.

Tables

5. Enter contents in cells.

Content

Tables

AutoFit

6. Click the AutoFit button to let FrontPage adjust the column widths to best fit the content.

Design Your Web with Style Sheets

See "Global Formatting with Style Sheets" in Chapter 5.

2. Select File | New | Page and click the Style Sheets tab in the New dialog box.

1. Make sure CSS (Cascading Style Sheets) is available on the Compatibility tab of the Page Options dialog box (Tools | Page Options).

3. Choose Normal Style Sheet.

4. Click OK.

7. Type a name for your new style.

5. Click the Style button.

8. Click the Format button | Font or Paragraph, select formatting, click OK, and repeat as necessary.

6. Click the New button.

11. To link a page to the style sheet, select Format | Style Sheet Links.

10. To save your style sheet, press CTRL+S, type a name, and click the Save button.

9. Click OK.

12. Click the Add button, double-click the style sheet, and click OK.

Insert and Format Pictures

See "Inserting Pictures into Your Web" and "Editing a Picture" in Chapter 6.

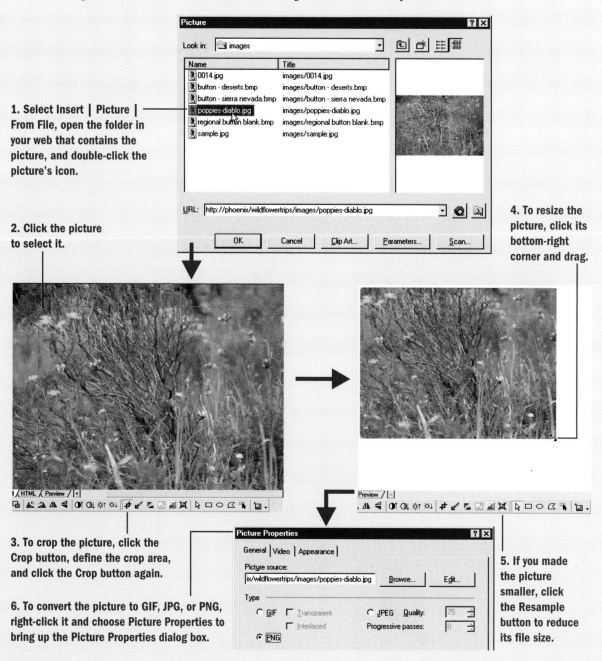

1. Select Insert | Picture | From File, open the folder in your web that contains the picture, and double-click the picture's icon.

2. Click the picture to select it.

4. To resize the picture, click its bottom-right corner and drag.

3. To crop the picture, click the Crop button, define the crop area, and click the Crop button again.

6. To convert the picture to GIF, JPG, or PNG, right-click it and choose Picture Properties to bring up the Picture Properties dialog box.

5. If you made the picture smaller, click the Resample button to reduce its file size.

Set Up Navigation Links

See "Setting Up Navigation Bars" in Chapter 7.

Switch to Navigation view.

To add a new page, click the New Page button.

To add an existing page, click its icon in the Folder list and drag it into the Navigation view.

To rename a page, select it, press F2, and then type the new name.

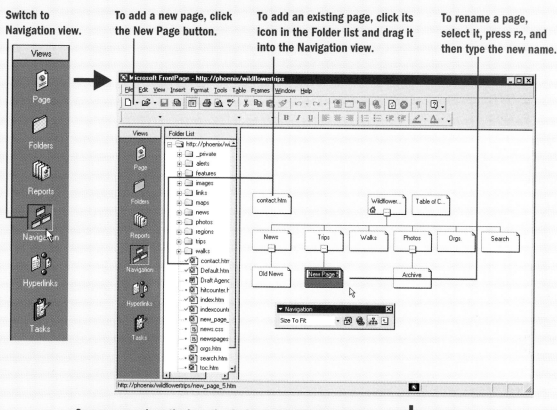

On any page, place the insertion inside a shared border and select Insert | Navigation Bar to bring up the Navigation Bar Properties dialog box.

Choose which types of links you want and click OK.

Make Your Web Searchable

See "Adding a Search Page" in Chapter 7.

1. Select File | New | Page to bring up the New dialog box, then choose the Search Page template, and click OK.

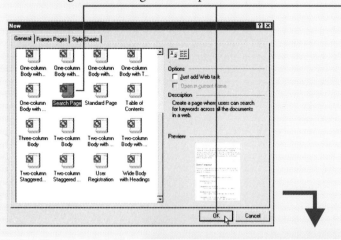

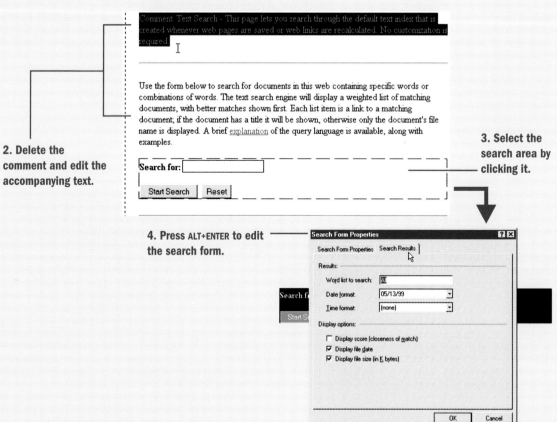

Comment: Text Search - This page lets you search through the default text index that is created whenever web pages are saved or web links are recalculated. No customization is required.

Use the form below to search for documents in this web containing specific words or combinations of words. The text search engine will display a weighted list of matching documents, with better matches shown first. Each list item is a link to a matching document; if the document has a title it will be shown, otherwise only the document's file name is displayed. A brief explanation of the query language is available, along with examples.

Search for:

Start Search   Reset

2. Delete the comment and edit the accompanying text.

3. Select the search area by clicking it.

4. Press ALT+ENTER to edit the search form.

Add Dynamic HTML Effects

See "Adding Dynamic HTML Effects" in Chapter 8.

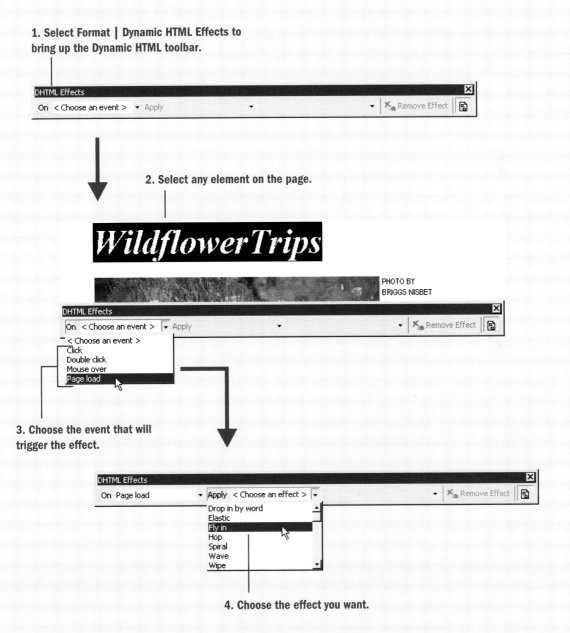

1. Select Format | Dynamic HTML Effects to bring up the Dynamic HTML toolbar.

2. Select any element on the page.

3. Choose the event that will trigger the effect.

4. Choose the effect you want.

Create a Discussion Group

See "Adding Discussion Groups" in Chapter 8.

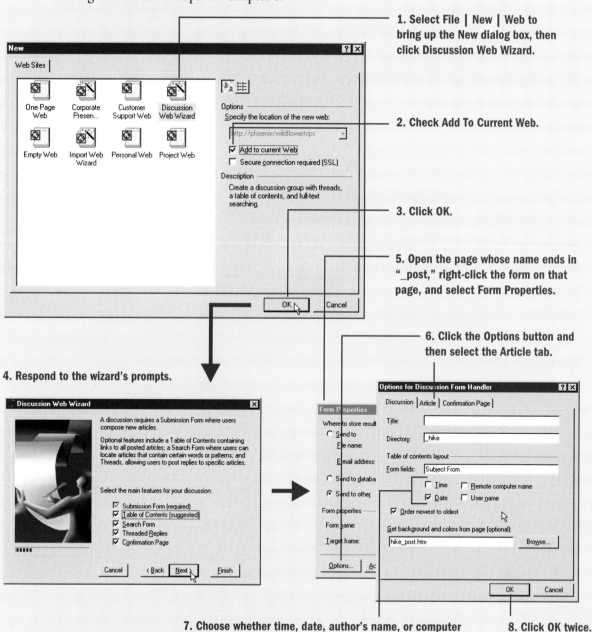

1. Select File | New | Web to bring up the New dialog box, then click Discussion Web Wizard.

2. Check Add To Current Web.

3. Click OK.

5. Open the page whose name ends in "_post," right-click the form on that page, and select Form Properties.

6. Click the Options button and then select the Article tab.

4. Respond to the wizard's prompts.

7. Choose whether time, date, author's name, or computer name (or any combination) will appear with posted articles.

8. Click OK twice.

Publish on an Intranet

See "Publishing Pages" and "Publishing on an Intranet" in Chapter 9.

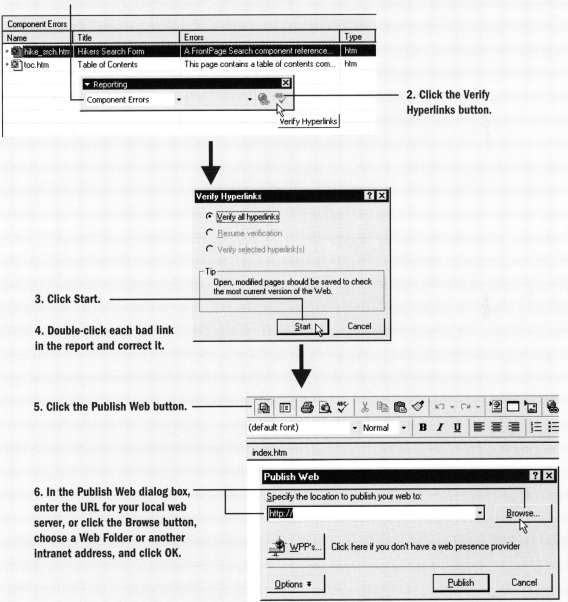

1. Select View | Reports | Component Errors to check for errors before publishing.

Component Errors			
Name	Title	Errors	Type
hike_srch.htm	Hikers Search Form	A FrontPage Search component reference...	htm
toc.htm	Table of Contents	This page contains a table of contents com...	htm

▼ Reporting

Component Errors

Verify Hyperlinks

2. Click the Verify Hyperlinks button.

Verify Hyperlinks

⦿ Verify all hyperlinks

○ Resume verification

○ Verify selected hyperlink(s)

Tip
Open, modified pages should be saved to check the most current version of the Web.

Start   Cancel

3. Click Start.

4. Double-click each bad link in the report and correct it.

5. Click the Publish Web button.

(default font)   Normal   **B** *I* <u>U</u>

index.htm

Publish Web

Specify the location to publish your web to:

http://   Browse...

WPP's...   Click here if you don't have a web presence provider

Options ▼   Publish   Cancel

6. In the Publish Web dialog box, enter the URL for your local web server, or click the Browse button, choose a Web Folder or another intranet address, and click OK.

Register Users of Your Web

See "Protecting Your Web with Permissions" in Chapter 10.

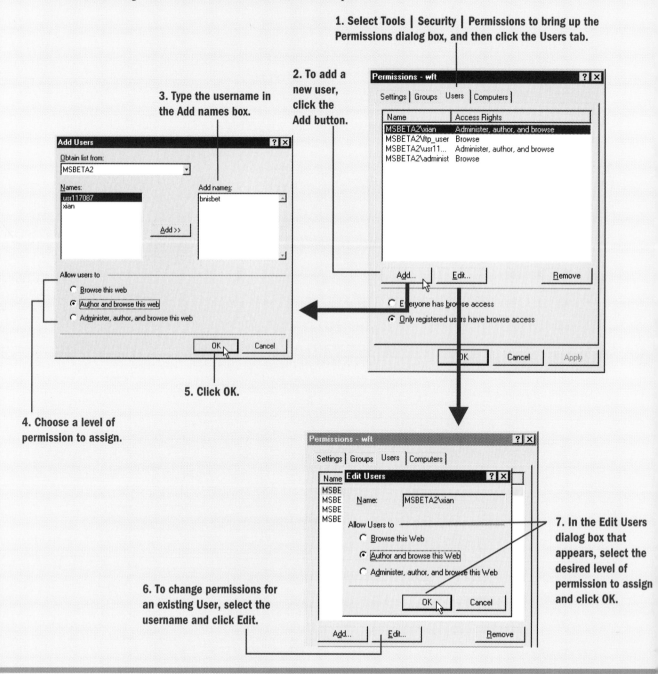

1. Select Tools | Security | Permissions to bring up the Permissions dialog box, and then click the Users tab.

2. To add a new user, click the Add button.

3. Type the username in the Add names box.

5. Click OK.

4. Choose a level of permission to assign.

6. To change permissions for an existing User, select the username and click Edit.

7. In the Edit Users dialog box that appears, select the desired level of permission to assign and click OK.

Check Pages Out and In

See "Site Maintenance and Project Management" and "Checking Pages Out and In" in Chapter 10.

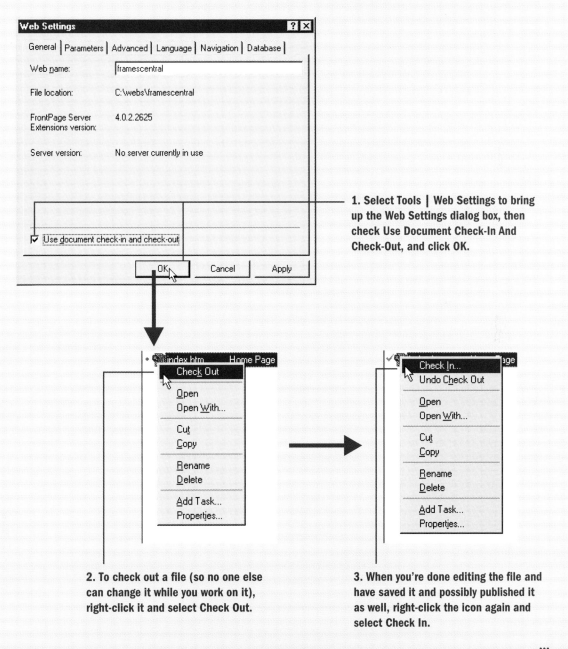

1. Select Tools | Web Settings to bring up the Web Settings dialog box, then check Use Document Check-In And Check-Out, and click OK.

2. To check out a file (so no one else can change it while you work on it), right-click it and select Check Out.

3. When you're done editing the file and have saved it and possibly published it as well, right-click the icon again and select Check In.

FrontPage 2000

for Busy People

The Book to Use When There's No Time to Lose!

Christian Crumlish

OSBORNE

Osborne/**McGraw-Hill**

Berkeley / New York / St. Louis / San Francisco / Auckland / Bogotá
Hamburg / London / Madrid / Mexico City / Milan / Montreal / New Delhi
Panama City / Paris / São Paulo / Singapore / Sydney / Tokyo / Toronto

A Division of The **McGraw·Hill** *Companies*

Osborne/**McGraw-Hill**
2600 Tenth Street
Berkeley, California 94710
U.S.A.

For information on translations or book distributors outside the U.S.A., or to arrange
bulk purchase discounts for sales promotions, premiums, or fund-raisers, please contact
Osborne/**McGraw-Hill** at the above address.

FrontPage 2000 for Busy People

234567890 DOC DOC 90198765432109

ISBN 0-07-211981-0

Publisher   Brandon A. Nordin
Associate Publisher and Editor-in-Chief   Scott Rogers
Acquisitions Editor   Joanne Cuthbertson
Project Editors   Heidi Poulin, Cynthia Douglas
Editorial Assistant   Stephane Thomas
Technical Editor   Jody Cline
Copy Editor   Sally Hancock
Proofreader   Mike McGee
Indexer   Valerie Robbins
Computer Designers   Gary Corrigan, Micky Galicia
Illustrators   Bob Hansen, Brian Wells, Beth Young
Series Designer   Jil Weil
Cover Design   Damore Johann Design, Inc.
Cover Illustration/Chapter Opener Illustration   Robert deMichiell

This book was published with Corel VENTURA.

To the folks of antiweb,
who make the World Wide Web sing...

About the Author

Christian Crumlish is a writer, editor, literary agent, book packager, and publisher. He co-founded the online magazine *Enterzone* and writes computer books for people who are as busy as he is. He is author of the best-selling *Internet for Busy People, Third Edition* and coauthor of *Web Publishing with Netscape for Busy People.*

CONTENTS

Acknowledgments . . . . *xxv*
Introduction . . . . *xxvii*

1   Planning Your Web **1**
Skip This Chapter If...   3
Designing Your Web on Cocktail Napkins   4
    Brainstorming: What Might You Want in Your Web?   5
    Prioritizing Potential Content for Your Web   7
    From Skeleton to Skin: How to Present Your Web   9
FrontPage Essentials   12
    Starting FrontPage   12
    Toolbars   13
    Views   14
    Exiting FrontPage   19
There's More   20

2   Stuff to Do Once to Make Your Life Easier **21**
Changing Your Toolbars   24
    Add or Remove Buttons   25
    Custom Toolbars   26
    Tweaking Toolbar Appearance   26
Getting FrontPage to Do Things Your Way   27
    Always Open Your Last Project?   27
    How Useful Is the Status Bar?   28
    Set Your Connection Speed   29
    View | Reveal Tags   30
    Turning Off Background Spell Checking   30
    Designing Your Web for a Specific Browser   31
    Default Fonts   34
    Other Options You Set for Each Web or Each Page   35
Putting FrontPage One Click Away   35
    Putting a FrontPage Icon on Your Windows Desktop   35
    Listing FrontPage on the Windows Start Menu   36
    Adding FrontPage to the Quick Launch Toolbar   37
There's More   37

3   Setting Up a New Web **39**
Creating a New Web   42
    Where to Put It   44
    Starting from Scratch   45
    Using FrontPage's Predesigned Webs   46
Importing a Web   52
    Importing from the Internet   53
    Importing from Your Own Computer or Network   55
    Importing More Files Later   57

Opening an Existing Web 59
Organizing Your Site 60
    Making New Folders 60
    Making Subfolders 62
    Deleting a Folder 64
Turning on Shared Borders 64
Naming Your Web 67
There's More 68

4   **Making Web Pages** **69**
Creating a New Page 72
    Starting with a New Blank Page 73
    Starting with a Blank Page in a Predesigned Web 74
    Starting with a Predesigned Page 75
Saving and Titling Your Page 77
    Saving a Page for the First Time 78
    Saving a Page Thereafter 81
Converting an Existing Document into a Web Page 82
Removing Pages from a Web 84
    Deleting a Page Completely 85
    Removing a Page from Your Web Without Deleting It 85
Opening an Existing Web Page 86
    Opening Any Web Page 87
    Opening a Page in an Open Web 87
    Reopening a Recent Web Page 88
There's More 88

5   **Developing Content** **89**
What Type of Page? 92
Working with Text 93
    Entering Text 93
    Making Corrections and Changes 94
    Formatting Text 98
Laying Out Pages with Tables 100
    Drawing a Table 100
    Changing the Structure of a Table 100
    Filling in Content 102
    Formatting Your Table 102
Repeating Elements in Shared Borders 104
Global Formatting with Style Sheets 107
    Changing an Existing Style 107
    Making a New Style 114
    Removing a Custom Style from a Page 115
    Making a Style for Your Whole Web 115
Editing HTML Directly 121
Previewing Your Work 122
    Quick and Dirty 122
    In Your Browser 122
There's More 124

6   Graphics and Multimedia **125**

Web Picture Formats: GIF, JPEG, and PNG 128
Inserting Pictures into Your Web 129
   Inserting Clip Art 130
   Inserting Original Artwork 131
   Inserting a Photograph 134
Editing a Picture 136
   Cropping a Picture 137
   Resizing a Picture 138
   Resampling a Picture 140
   Orienting a Picture 140
   Other Things You Can Do to a Picture Easily 141
   Creating a Thumbnail 142
   Positioning a Picture 143
   Converting a Picture to a Different Format 146
   Adding Text to a Picture 148
   Saving a Picture with a Page 150
Designing with Color Schemes and Themes 151
   A Color Scheme and More 151
   Choosing a Theme 152
   Changing a Theme 153
   Removing a Theme 154
Adding Sound or Video 154
   Inserting a Background Sound onto a Page 154
   Inserting a Sound (or Video) Clip 154
   Setting Video Properties 156
   The Web Is Not a CD 157
There's More 157

7   Making Your Site Navigable **159**

Hyperlinks, the Sinews of the Web 162
   Dragging Pages to Make Links 163
   Selecting the Link Anchor 164
   Inserting Links 164
   Deleting a Hyperlink 169
   Creating an Image Map 169
   Viewing Hyperlinks in Your Web 171
   Recalculating Hyperlinks 172
   Making Hyperlinks Roll Over 173
Setting Up Navigation Bars 175
   Planning in Navigation View 176
   Absolute and Relative Page Relationships 177
   Adding Top-Level Pages 177
   Adding Child Pages 177
   Inserting a Navigation Bar 180
   Editing Your Navigation Bar 183
   Removing a Navigation Bar 184
Inserting a Table of Contents 185
   Making a New Table of Contents Page 186
   Making a Site Map 188
Adding a Search Page 191

Making the Best of Frames 193
Creating a New Frames Page 194
Filling the Frames 194
Formatting the Frames 196
Hyperlinks Require Frame Targets 197
Setting Up Your No Frames Page 197
There's More 198

8   **Animating Your Pages** **199**

Inserting FrontPage Components 202
Inserting and Formatting a Marquee 202
Inserting a Hover Button 203
Scheduling a Picture 204
Inserting and Managing Banner Ads 205
Inserting Office Components 207
Inserting and Setting Up a Spreadsheet Component 208
Inserting and Setting Up a Chart Component 212
Inserting a Pivot Table Component 213
Adding Dynamic HTML Effects 213
Adding Page Transitions 215
Getting Feedback from Your Visitors 216
Using the Form Page Wizard 216
Saving the Results 218
Validating Form Information 221
Creating a Confirmation Page 222
Adding Discussion Groups 222
Create a Discussion Group 223
Set Properties for a Discussion Web 225
Registering Users 225
Moderating a Group 225
Incorporating Database-Generated Content 226
Registering Your Database 227
Importing the Database 228
Using the Database Results Wizard 228
There's More 234

9   **Publishing Your Web** **235**

Choosing a Server 239
Paying an ISP to Host Your Site 239
Hosting on Your Own Computer or Network 239
Ask About FrontPage Server Extensions 240
Preparing to Publish (Don't Go Off Half-Cocked) 241
Checking for Errors and Bad Links 241
Determining What Goes Public 244
Publishing Pages 247
Publishing Your Web for the First Time 248
Looking for an ISP at the Last Minute 248
Publishing via HTTP 248
Publishing via FTP 249

Publishing on an Intranet 251
This May Take a While 253
Publishing Changed Pages 254
Cleaning Up Orphaned Pages 255
Viewing Your Published Web 256
Tracking Access 257
Promotion and Findability 258
Register at Portals 259
Flag Your Home Page for Search Engines 260
Get Your Own Domain Name 261
There's More 262

10   **Maintaining and Administering Your Site** **263**
Who's Minding the Site? 266
Reorganizing Your Web 267
Sorting Your Files by Date 267
Moving Folders Around 268
Setting Up Subwebs 268
Protecting Your Web with Permissions 270
Permission to Browse, Author, or Administer 270
Add a User 272
Add a Group of Users 272
Change Permissions for a User or Group 272
Remove a User or Group 274
User Self-Registration 274
Change a Password 276
Site Maintenance and Project Management 277
Completing Tasks 277
Checking Pages Out and In 280
Tracking Review Status 281
Sharing Templates 281
Tending Your Web 283

A   **Installing FrontPage** **285**
Before You Begin 286
If You Are Upgrading 286
If You Are Installing with Office 2000 287
Performing the Installation 288
Entering Personal Information 288
Choosing a Location 290
Choosing Whether to Remove Previous Versions 290
Upgrading Internet Explorer 290
Choosing Components to Install 290
Registering the Product 294
If Something Goes Wrong 295
Uninstalling FrontPage 295

Index **297**

Acknowledgments

This book would never have occurred if Briggs Nisbet hadn't egged me on, helped me develop an influential web site (Enterzone at **http://ezone.org/ez/**), come up with the idea for the California WildflowerTrips site demo'd in this book, and put up with my work binges and sloughs of despair throughout this long and difficult (if ultimately satisfying) project. For that I thank her and acknowledge her unfailing support for me.

Even when the gang at Osborne had legitimate concerns about me making my deadlines, everyone there was always friendly and supportive, which made it a lot easier to get back on track, time after time. Heidi Poulin, a longtime colleague, pulled the whole project together smoothly, and Cynthia Douglas stepped in to cover for her admirably when she took a well-deserved vacation. Copyeditor Sally Hancock brought out the best in my writing while toning down my self-indulgent excesses and careless oversights. Technical Editor Jody Cline staved off a number of potential howlers, investigated confusing beta problems, and enabled me to focus on my drafts knowing that her keen eyes would assure the technical accuracy of my manuscript.

Gary Corrigan and Micky Galicia typeset the book with alacrity, executing a new design with aplomb. Stephanie Thomas managed the early stages of the project, buoyed me when I was feeling down, and restored my sense of humor when I was in danger of losing it completely. Gordon Hurd managed the concurrent revision of my *Word 2000 for Busy People*, enabling me to give this project the attention it deserved. Databases have never really been my bag, so I was pleased to have the help of Jonathan Kamin in preparing the most technical chapter in this book (Chapter 8). He put a lot of work into the database, component, and dynamic HTML parts of that chapter. He also prepared the very thorough installation appendix. To be honest, he saved my bacon at a time when this project threatened to overwhelm me.

I'd never have gotten the opportunity to write this or other Busy People books if it weren't for Joanne Cuthbertson. I'd also especially like to thank the sales, marketing, and publicity people at Osborne, who've really pulled out all the stops with these books and who deserve a lot of credit for the success of the series so far.

Thanks to the little elves at Microsoft for writing (and acquiring) software that needs some explaining. Thanks to my friends for feigning interest in my boring job. Thanks to my family for their love and patience.

Introduction

How busy have you become lately? Has your job mushroomed with sprawling layers of responsibility? Do you feel like you have almost no time for anything? This book is for people with only a night or a few lunch hours to learn the latest version of FrontPage. The digital revolution has given with one hand, creating all kinds of efficiencies and organizational wizardry, and taken away with the other, accelerating everyone's expectations and constantly moving the goalposts. The eruption of the Internet, the Web, and in-house intranets has, if anything, picked up the pace.

I Know You're in a Hurry, So

If you're sitting there with an as yet uninstalled copy of FrontPage, peel off that shrink wrap and flip to Appendix A, where you'll be taken effortlessly through the installation process. If someone has mercifully set up FrontPage for you already, you need not know the appendix is there.

Let's agree right now to dispense with the traditional computer book preliminaries. You've probably used a mouse, held down two keys at once, and know (or choose not to know) the history of Microsoft. So, we'll cut to the chase. After reading the first few chapters, you'll be able to:

- Plan and sketch out a web site
- Kick-start a new web in FrontPage
- Create blank or structured web pages
- Add content to your pages, format them, design them, and lay them out

Later chapters will show you how to add pictures and other media to your pages, how to link web pages together and establish a navigational infrastructure, how to add active or databased content to your web pages, how to publish your web to the Internet or to an intranet, and how to maintain a site and work with others to keep it up to date.

As long as you've picked up the basics of FrontPage, you shouldn't have to work your way through the book chapter by chapter. You'll also be able to skim through it, reading only the parts you need, when you need them. Remember: just because you can do something with FrontPage doesn't mean that you should. Simple is often best, particularly when you are busy. I'll try to remind you of that from time to time.

How FrontPage 2000 Differs from Earlier Versions

With FrontPage 98, Microsoft did away with the separate editing and site-management views in FrontPage. Now all the features of the program are available from a single standard type of window, and the View bar down the left side of that window gives you quick access to the program's various modes. Other improvements are piecemeal, identified throughout the book. Say what you like about Microsoft, they sure know how to improve a program each time around. They really do listen to their users and grant their wishes.

As with other Microsoft Office programs, the toolbars in FrontPage 2000 have been updated, and both the toolbars and the menus can now hide the features that you haven't been using (without making them inaccessible). The settings for the program are still scattered over a number of different dialog boxes, though, so I take you around the various furnace rooms and supply closets of the program in Chapter 2.

Things You Might Want to Know About This Book

You can read this book more or less in any order. I suggest cruising Chapter 1 and reading Chapter 2 first, but you'll be fine no matter how you go. Use the book as a reference. When you're stuck, not sure how to do something, and you know there must be an answer, just pick up the book, zero in on the solution to your problem and put the book down again. Aside from the clear, coherent explanations of this all-over-the-map software product, the book includes some special elements to help you get the most out of FrontPage. Here's a quick rundown.

Blueprints

The Blueprints at the front of the book depict and demonstrate key task and goals you can accomplish with FrontPage.

Fast Forward

Every chapter begins with a section called *Fast Forward*. Each of these sections is, in effect, a book within a book—a built-in quick reference guide, summarizing the key tasks explained in the chapter that follows. If you're a fast learner, or somewhat experienced, the Fast Forwards may be the only material you need. Written step-by-step, point-by-point, they even include page references to guide you to the more complete information later in the chapter.

EXPERT ADVICE

Timesaving tips, techniques, and worthwhile addictions are all reported under the rubric of *Expert Advice*. (Look for the know-it-all professor.) Force yourself to develop some good habits now, while it's still possible! These notes also give you the big picture and help you plan ahead. From time to time, for example, I'll suggest that you save your document before performing some magical automatic transformation that you might live to regret.

Shortcut

These are designed for the busy person—when there's a way to do something that may not be as full-featured as the material in the text, but is *faster*, it will show up in the margin, next to the leaping businessman.

Caution

Sometimes it's too easy to plunge ahead and fall down a rabbit hole, resulting in hours of extra work just to get you back to where you were before you went astray. This alarmed-looking guy will warn you before you commit time-consuming mistakes.

Definition

Usually, I'll explain computer or word processing jargon in the text, wherever the technobabble first occurs. But if you encounter words you don't recognize, look for this bookworm in the margin. Definitions point out important terms you reasonably might not know the meaning of. When necessary, they're strict and a little technical, but most of the time they're informal and conversational.

Upgrade Notes

If you've used early versions of FrontPage, such as 97 or 98, then be on the look-out for Upgrade notes. They will tell you when something has changed and make sure you don't miss any of the latest advances.

Let's Do It!

Ready? Let's dig into FrontPage before the millennium arrives!

Incidentally, I'm always happy to hear your reactions to this or any of my other books. You can reach me through Osborne, or on the Net (**fp2k@syx.com**).

CHAPTER 1

Planning Your Web

INCLUDES

- Thinking it through on paper
- Brainstorming and prioritizing content for the site
- Coming up with an internal structure for your web
- Mocking up the site on paper before putting it on your computer
- Starting FrontPage for the first time

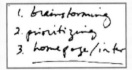

Plan Your Web on Paper ➡ pp. 4–8

1. Don't touch the computer until you've thought your web through.
2. Start by brainstorming; use free association—no criticism allowed.
3. Arrange content by priority; figure out which elements are essential before you go public.
4. For more complicated webs, think about the structure in advance.

Design the Front End ➡ pp. 9–12

1. Decide how to present the content of the site (what comes first, how things are connected).
2. Mock-up a home page on paper and see if it meets your needs.

Start FrontPage ➡ pp. 12–13

To start the program, select Start | Programs | FrontPage.

Exit FrontPage ➡ pp. 19–20

1. Click the Close box in the upper-right corner of the FrontPage window.
2. Repeat for any additional open webs.

As a busy person, you don't have a lot of time to study the niceties of whatever computer programs you have to use. You've got to be able to get the gist of them quickly and start getting work done right away. With FrontPage, though, there's one step you have to take before you can really plunge in. Believe me, I'd spare you any preliminaries if it were possible, or advisable, but it's not.

First, you must think through your website (or "web," as FrontPage prefers to call it) on paper, away from the computer. Think of it first as an object with an appearance and a function. I'll help you do this. Paper napkins and oozy felt-tip pens are recommended for this first step.

When you have a plan ready (and plans were made to be revised, so don't feel married to your sketchy ideas), I'll have you start FrontPage for the first time. With a little guidance, you'll get your bearings with the program's basic interface (the way the window is laid out, what the main buttons do, where the useful commands are hidden in the menus).

If you already know your way around FrontPage, feel free to skip ahead to whatever chapter discusses your specific goals for today. You can always come back here if you need a refresher.

Skip This Chapter If...

You can skip this chapter if it's too late for you to design your web site from scratch (that is, you're using FrontPage to work with an existing site), and you already know how to start and run FrontPage (or how to start programs in general with Windows). Chapter 2 shows you a handful of things you can do once to customize FrontPage and make

DEFINITION

Web page: (also webpage) A document on the Web or on an intranet.

it easier to use forever after, *and* shows you how to establish your web's organization and structure in FrontPage right away so that you don't end up having to revise a lot of links and embedded images later. If you'd rather just get started cranking out web pages with the tools FrontPage provides, skip directly to Chapter 3.

Designing Your Web on Cocktail Napkins

To get your ideas flowing, start by thinking about the purpose of your web, the goal of the site, and what benefits your web presence will offer you and your visitors.

I really think it's important to conceptualize your web *away* from a computer, at first. There's something paralyzing about the blank screen. Pen (or pencil) and paper feel more flexible and open to scribbling. I recommend the following steps to facilitate planning a web:

1. Start by brainstorming. You can do this by yourself, but the more people involved the better. Without vetoing or criticizing any suggestions, just start yelling out ideas for what the site should offer.

2. Once you have a fairly comprehensive list, you have to sort it by importance. Try to distinguish three categories of content: Must Have, It Would Be Nice, and Wish List.

3. Work out a skeletal structure for the site, planning ahead by assigning folders to any section of the site that's bound to grow.

4. Put yourself in the shoes of visitors to your web; ask yourself what they should see on the first page and which contents should be reserved for those who specially request them. Sketch out a home page that shows what visitors will see first.

5. Reconsider the first draft of the "back-end" structure in light of your presentation ideas, and repeat steps 3 and 4 until you have a solid back-end and front-end plan.

In the rest of this section, I will illustrate what I've just outlined with a specific web-project example: a guide to wildflower trips (hikes) in California. All the doodling my partner Briggs and I did to get started fit onto a single page of a blank-book journal, shown in Figure 1.1.

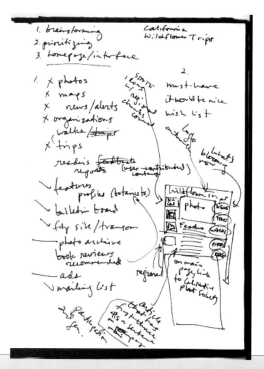

Figure 1.1: A little bit of brainstorming, sketching, scribbling, and doodling now will save you a lot of wasted time in front of your computer later.

Brainstorming:
What Might You Want in Your Web?

First we sat down to think about what we wanted to put at the WildflowerTrips web site. "Photographs!" we both said. That one was obvious. "Maps," said Briggs, who'd already spent some time thinking about wildflower trips. "You'll need a place for news or 'What's New'," I said. "Alerts," said Briggs, "to tell people when flowers in a given region are about to bloom." At this point we were rolling.

"How about links to useful organizations?"

"A guide to specific walks or trips."

"User-contributed content is always good. You know, feedback…"

"Reader's Reports!"

"Feature articles? Maybe profiles of botanists?"

"Great. OK, how about a bulletin board?"

"We need a way for people to send us their pictures. You know, over the transom…"

"In the long run, we'd want a photo archive."

"What about book reviews? Or recommended books and references?"

"Will we have ads?"

"Why not?"

"A mailing list so people can get the alerts even if they don't check the site."

At this point we were exhausted, but we had a pretty good list (see Figure 1.2).

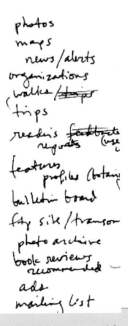

Figure 1.2: A list of unprioritized content brainstormed for the California WildflowerTrips web.

Prioritizing Potential Content for Your Web

Next, we had to sort our ideas into three categories: Must Have, It Would Be Nice, and Wish List. The Must Haves—the bare essentials—were those elements without which there'd be no point in publicizing the site at all. It Would Be Nice is all the stuff we'd hope to have working by the time we're ready to unveil the web, but the category also implies that we could, without any shame, add some of these features as we go along, after the web's "debut." The third category, Wish List, is all those items that we honestly may never have time to include, but which we want to bear in mind as we plan and start building the site. If we gain the resources, time, or other impetus for adding one of these more ambitious elements, we can do so without redesigning the site from scratch.

First we marked the Must Have's with x's:

1. Photos
2. Maps
3. News/alerts
4. Organizations
5. Walks and Trips

Without all of the above content categories, we didn't think the WildflowerTrips web would fly. Then we marked the It Would Be Nice items with checkmarks:

1. Features and Profiles
2. Bulletin Board
3. FTP site (transom)
4. Mailing List

The features and profiles would require time and preparation, and we couldn't be sure to have a ready supply of them in time to go "live" at the site. The bulletin board, FTP site, and mailing list features would all be relatively easy to set up, but not essential.

That left the rest for our Wish List, which we marked with dashes:

1. Reader's Reports
2. Photo Archive
3. Book Reviews and Recommended References
4. Ads

The first three would take time to accumulate and an effort to organize. It's too early to tell whether the web would support advertisements (or any other revenue stream). Figure 1.3 shows the prioritized list.

Figure 1.3: We sorted our original list into Must Haves (x), It Would Be Nice (check mark), and Wish List (—).

From Skeleton to Skin: How to Present Your Web

Once you've assembled a conceptual grab-bag of content for your web, you have to think a little about how to organize your offerings. There are two levels to organization in the web universe: the back end and the front end. The back end is the bare-bones file-structure tech-y view of the site where all the raw files actually sit on a specific computer. The front end is the cosmetic appearance of the site: the home page, the design, the navigation, and so on. The back end is something like the way inventory is organized in the storeroom behind a store. The front end is the way the items are displayed for customers. In a clothing store, for instance, customers look for articles of clothing, styles, and certain sizes, not SKU numbers and inventory dates.

The back end and front end of a web are interdependent. It's impossible to design them separately (or at least highly undesirable). Trouble is, you can stymie yourself with the fear of making a false move in the front or back. Get used to the idea that designing a web is an "iterative" process:

1. Sketch out an organization structure for the web's back end.
2. Come up with a home page and apparent structure for users of the web's front end.
3. Review the back-end structure to make sure it supports the design properly.
4. Review the front-end structure to make sure it reflects the contents of the site adequately.
5. Repeat steps 3 and 4 (this is the iterative part) until the front- and back-end designs are in sync.

Sketching a Skeleton

For the WildflowerTrips web, we'll want to set up a separate folder (directory) for every item category that might end up needing to hold many files. If we call the directory containing the web's home page the "root," then we need the following subdirectories:

```
Root--+
     |-photos
     |     |-archive
     |-maps
     |-news
     |-alerts
     |-links
     |-walks
     |-trips
     |-features
     |     |-profiles
     |     |-readersreport
     |     |-books
     |     |-refs
```

(The potential bulletin board, FTP site, and mailing list features might require folders, but we don't know what to call them yet, and we'll end up generating them automatically, so we can ignore them for now. Same story for ads.)

Any other incidental files we need will live in the root directory with the home page. Now it's time to think of the cosmetic side of things.

Mocking Up a Home Page on Paper

For your home page, you need to brainstorm again. Don't be afraid to err on the side of including too much content in your home-page design. For now, you're just sketching a mock-up on paper, and there's plenty of time to revise and refine your ideas. For the Wildflower Trips web, we threw together a sketch of an ideal home page after spending a little time kicking ideas around (see Figure 1.4).

Massage the Structure and the Design

Right away, you may have noticed, we've invented a new organizational need by including a set of links to various California regions (the links all have different weather and different wildflowers

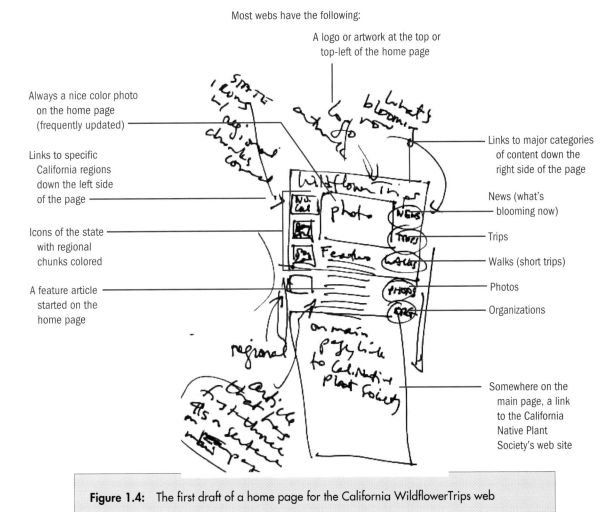

Most webs have the following:

A logo or artwork at the top or
top-left of the home page

Always a nice color photo
on the home page
(frequently updated)

Links to specific
California regions
down the left side
of the page

Icons of the state
with regional
chunks colored

A feature article
started on the
home page

Links to major categories
of content down the
right side of the page

News (what's
blooming now)

Trips

Walks (short trips)

Photos

Organizations

Somewhere on the
main page, a link
to the California
Native Plant
Society's web site

Figure 1.4: The first draft of a home page for the California WildflowerTrips web

blooming on different schedules). Going back to the original folder
tree, we'd add a new subdirectory, with further subs below that one:

```
|-regions
|      |-bayarea
|      |-sierras
|      |-valley
|      |-etc
```

We now have a reasonably forward-looking and flexible back-end plan and the beginning, at least, of a front-end plan as well. (We really need to think about how people will navigate the web to complete that task.)

You're Going to Change Things as You Go

Don't overwhelm yourself trying to anticipate everything about your web. Your idea of what's possible and what you're attempting to do will evolve naturally as you develop your web and become capable of using FrontPage to produce sophisticated results. Bear in mind that some content takes time to develop. Now that I've encouraged you to prepare a skeleton plan before diving in, I'm going to get you started with FrontPage. Meanwhile, I've reminded Briggs to get some scans made of her color slides of wildflowers, so the digitized files will be available when the time comes to produce the home page.

In the long run, you may have to change your back-end structure, and your home page and the rest of your front end will inevitably change with fashion. You can't anticipate every future aspect of your web, but it will be easier to track the changes as your web evolves after you've taken a little time to think about your plan.

FrontPage Essentials

With any new program (or even an update of an old, somewhat familiar program), you must give yourself a little time to become accustomed to the *interface*: the layout of the windows on the screen, the options and the menu names that disguise them, and so on. In the rest of this chapter, I will give you a tour of the FrontPage interface, so you can start using the program and get used to the feel of it as smoothly as possible.

If FrontPage 2000 is not yet installed on your computer, jump now to the Appendix A for basic installation instructions. Then come back here once everything's hunky dory. The first time you start FrontPage, you may be prompted for information about the name of your "server." Again, see Appendix A for help with this simple setup procedure.

Starting FrontPage

Starting FrontPage 2000 is as easy as clicking on the Start button and pointing to Microsoft FrontPage on the Programs submenu. (If you don't have a FrontPage option on your Programs menu, read down the menu to see if there's a Microsoft Office submenu or another option that might lead to FrontPage. If you still can't find it, go get whoever installed FrontPage for you and make them show you where it is!) You also can make a shortcut (an icon on your desktop) for FrontPage or add FrontPage to the main Start menu. For more on these two options, see Chapter 2.

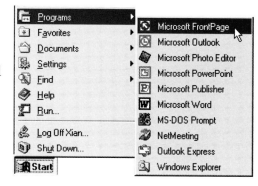

The first time you start FrontPage, it checks to see whether it's registered with the Windows 98 operating system as your default HTML editor. If not, it prompts you, asking if you want to give it that default status.

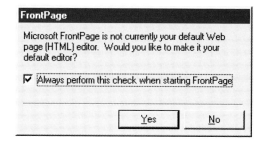

To make FrontPage your default HTML editor (as opposed to Netscape Composer or some other program), click Yes. To leave things as they are, click No.

Whenever FrontPage starts, it comes up with no web open and a blank document showing. If the FrontPage window does not fill up the whole screen, click on the Maximize button:

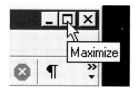

If you're sure you'll never change your mind again, check Always Perform This Check When Starting FrontPage to uncheck it before clicking No.

Toolbars

Let's take a look at the basic FrontPage screen (see Figure 1.5). You can see the normal elements typical of every program that runs under Windows 98 on the screen, such as the Taskbar at the bottom of the screen and the title bar and menu bar at the top. In addition, you'll

Standard toolbar

Formatting toolbar

Views bar

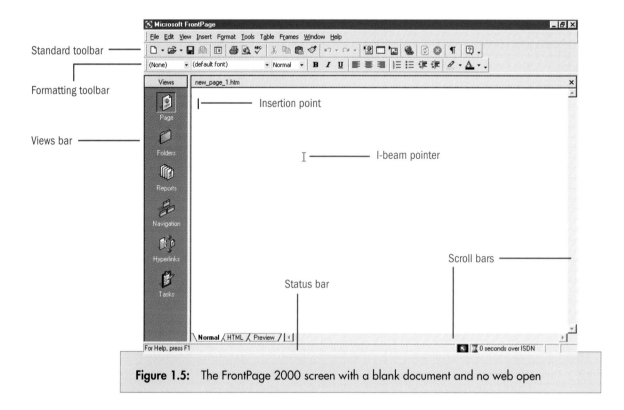

Figure 1.5:   The FrontPage 2000 screen with a blank document and no web open

see many specific FrontPage elements, which are there either to give you information or to make certain procedures automatic.

- The Standard and Formatting toolbars help you create, edit, and format your web pages.
- The Views area makes it easy to jump from one aspect of the web to another.
- The HTML and Preview tabs show the codes or the visual appearance of the current page.

Views

What you're looking at is FrontPage's Page view. The View bar shows you the other views available: Folders, Reports, Navigation, Hyperlinks, and Tasks. If you click the Folders button, a new frame appears, called the Folder List, but since you haven't created a web yet, the Folder List is empty, and the larger area of the screen contains the message "When a FrontPage web is open, this view lets you organize its files and folders."

Quickly click the other view buttons and you'll see more helpful, generic messages, or simply blank work areas.

To help you visualize how these different views are used, I whipped up a dummy web with a FrontPage wizard (as I'll explain in detail in Chapter 3) called Corporate Presence. By the way, if you wish to follow along on your own computer, select File | New | Web, select Corporate Presence Wizard, specify a location on your hard drive (use C:*blah-blah* or D:*etc.* instead of the suggested Web-style address, starting with http://), and click OK. As the Wizard quizzes you for the type of content you wish to include, check off as many options as possible to create a web similar to the one I threw together for the rest of the figures in this chapter. Don't feel obliged to do this, though. You can simply view the screen shots in the book to save yourself time.

Figure 1.6 shows the Page view of my Corporate Presence web, with the web's home page showing as the open page. As with any

Figure 1.6: The home page of a pre-fab Corporate Presence web, generated by a wizard (see Chapter 3)

word processor, you can simply select and type over any text or graphics you wish to replace.

When I click the Folders view, the Folder List shows a few directories, the first two of which FrontPage creates automatically for its own housekeeping purposes (see Figure 1.7). Double-click on any page in the file listing to have FrontPage open it in Page view. You'll be using Folders view from Chapter 3 on in this book.

At first you won't have to worry about FrontPage's reporting capabilities, but once your web gets complicated and you find yourself revising it, the reports FrontPage can generate automatically may come in handy, particularly the Broken Links report (which tells you which links are currently not working correctly). Figure 1.8 shows the

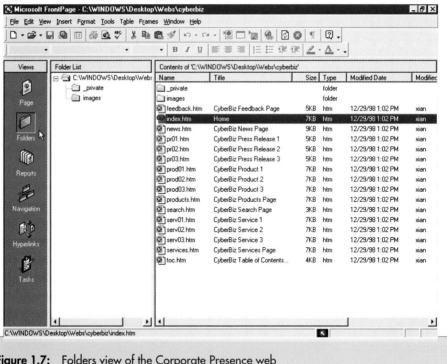

Figure 1.7: Folders view of the Corporate Presence web

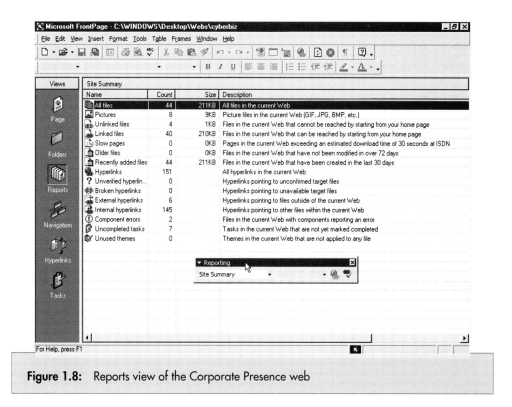

Figure 1.8: Reports view of the Corporate Presence web

reports generated automatically for the Corporate Presence web, in Reports view. You can select a report in the Reporting toolbar (the one floating in the Site Summary area) to see its details displayed.

As I mentioned in the first half of this chapter, the visual appearance of the home page of your web is only one part of the site's front end. The most important component of that interface is the navigational structure. FrontPage's Navigation view shows you the automatically generated navigation links among pages in your web, in a schematic diagram form (see Figure 1.9).

Besides the helpful navigation links for going to the Next or Previous page, or to Search, Home, Forward or Back, you will probably link together various pages in your web using hyperlinks.

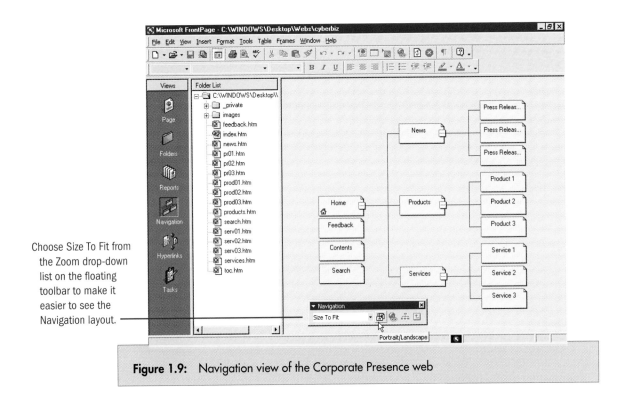

Choose Size To Fit from the Zoom drop-down list on the floating toolbar to make it easier to see the Navigation layout.

Figure 1.9: Navigation view of the Corporate Presence web

Hyperlinks view shows the links that can be reached from any starting page you choose. By clicking on the little plus signs, you can expand a particular branch of the tree of hyperlinks (see Figure 1.10). We'll cover Navigation view and Hyperlinks view in Chapter 7.

The last view, Tasks, helps you keep track of what still needs to be finished, how far along various tasks are, and who's responsible for them. With a dummy web like the one I generated for these figures, the tasks are all along the lines of "replace generic text with something more specific to your company" and "add your own public relations text," but the potential for this feature as an organizational tool is promising. We'll discuss Tasks view more fully in Chapter 10.

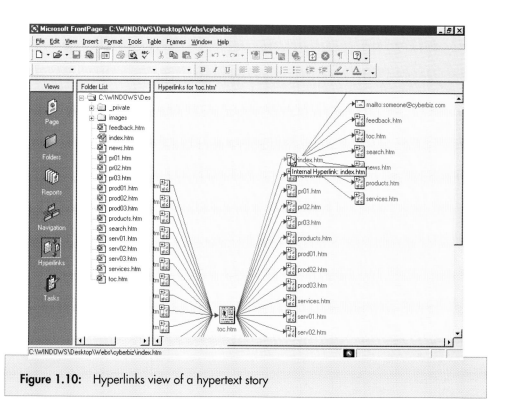

Figure 1.10: Hyperlinks view of a hypertext story

Exiting FrontPage

You can't work (or even window-shop) forever. Eventually, the time comes to quit FrontPage. To do so, pull down the File menu and select Exit, or just click the Close button in the upper-right corner of the FrontPage window (repeat for any other open webs).

If you try to exit FrontPage after having made unsaved changes to a web document, FrontPage will first ask if you want to save your changes before exiting. Generally, you will want to save the changes, and should click on Yes. If you're not sure about saving changes, it's usually safer to click Cancel and review things instead of clicking No and possibly losing important work. No matter how busy you are, rushing and accidentally losing your work will ruin your day. Unsaved work is harder to recover than deleted work.

There's More . . .

Chapter 2 explains some simple things you can do (and you'll only have to do them this one time) to make FrontPage easier and more comfortable to use. If you're so busy that you can't even spare a little tinkering time, you can skip ahead. Chapter 3 elaborates on how you can set up your first web (or open an existing web).

Stuff to Do Once to Make Your Life Easier

INCLUDES

- FrontPage's new self-customizing toolbars
- Tweaking the FrontPage setup
- Tuning FrontPage for a specific browser
- Setting default fonts
- Adding a FrontPage icon to your Windows desktop
- Listing FrontPage on your Start menu

Customize a Toolbar ➡ pp. 24–25

1. Click the More Buttons button at the right edge of the toolbar you wish to customize.
2. Click the Add or Remove Buttons button.
3. Select a button you want to add or remove from the toolbar.
4. Repeat step 3 until the toolbar looks the way you want.
5. Click somewhere outside the menu to finish.

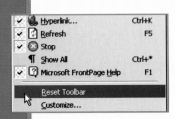

Return a Toolbar to Its Original Settings ➡ p. 25

1. Click on the More buttons button at the right end of the toolbar.
2. Select Add Or Remove Buttons | Reset Toolbar.

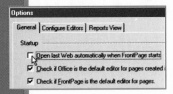

Always Start with Your Last Project ➡ pp. 27–28

1. Select Tools | Options.
2. Select the General tab (if it is not already in front).
3. Click Open Last Web Automatically When FrontPage Starts.
4. Click OK.

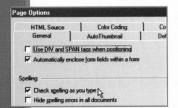

Turn Off Background Spell Checking ➡ pp. 30–31

1. Select Tools | Page Options.
2. Select the General tab.
3. Click Check Spelling As You Type to de-select it, or click Hide Spelling Errors In All Documents to check it.
4. Click OK.

Tune FrontPage for a Specific Browser ➥ pp. 31–33

1. Select Tools | Page Options.
2. Select the Compatibility tab.
3. Choose the type of browser you wish to focus on in the Browsers drop-down list box.
4. Choose the version of the browser whose features you want to support.
5. Click OK.

Put a FrontPage Icon on Your Desktop ➥ pp. 35–36

1. Right-click on the Start button and click Open.
2. Double-click the Programs folder.
3. If necessary, scroll until you see the Microsoft FrontPage icon.
4. Right-drag the FrontPage program icon onto the desktop, and select Copy Here.
5. Select the icon's label, press F2, type **FrontPage** (or select and delete the word Microsoft), and press ENTER.

List FrontPage on the Start Menu or the Quick Launch Toolbar ➥ pp. 36–37

1. Right-click on the Start button and click Open.
2. Double-click the Programs folder.
3. If necessary, scroll until you see the Microsoft FrontPage icon.
4. Click the FrontPage program icon and drag it onto the Start button or the Quick Launch toolbar area of the taskbar.

Honestly, FrontPage works pretty well straight out of the box. You can safely skip this chapter and not lose any sleep, but if you're willing to take ten minutes to make FrontPage easier to use from now on, stay with me. It will save you time in the future.

I'll take you step by step through the few FrontPage options you may want to think about and set up in advance. You'll only have to do these things once.

Changing Your Toolbars

One of the best new features of FrontPage is the way the toolbars can now be folded up into a small space on the screen, with their buttons still easily accessible (you can just click on the left edge of the bottom toolbar and drag it into the same row as the top one, or you can choose to have them appear this way automatically on the Customize menu, as I'll explain later). You can always click the More Buttons button at the right end of any toolbar and choose any currently hidden buttons:

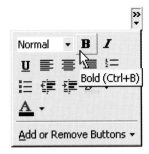

When sharing a row like that, each toolbar will tend to show the buttons used most frequently although it's easy to take buttons off the toolbar or put them back on.

Add or Remove Buttons

If you do want to take buttons clean off a toolbar (not just hidden one click away), that's also very easy to do now. Again, start by clicking that More Buttons button. Then choose the button called Add Or Remove Buttons at the bottom of the menu that appears. This will bring up a new menu showing all the likely buttons for this toolbar, with included buttons checked (see Figure 2.1).

To add or remove a button, select it. Repeat this for each button you want to add or remove. When you're done, click somewhere outside the menu. To return a toolbar to its original state, click More Buttons, then select Add Or Remove Buttons and click Reset Toolbar.

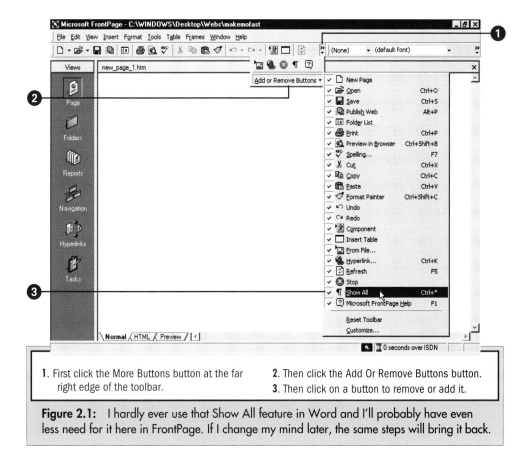

1. First click the More Buttons button at the far right edge of the toolbar.

2. Then click the Add Or Remove Buttons button.

3. Then click on a button to remove or add it.

Figure 2.1: I hardly ever use that Show All feature in Word and I'll probably have even less need for it here in FrontPage. If I change my mind later, the same steps will bring it back.

EXPERT ADVICE

Removed buttons won't show up when you click More Buttons, but they'll remain, unselected, on the Add Or Remove Buttons menu in case you ever want to add them back.

Custom Toolbars

If you want to add a FrontPage feature to a toolbar, select Tools | Customize, select the Commands tab, scroll through the Categories box for the menu the command appears on, then scroll through the Commands box for the command itself, and finally drag the command's icon onto the toolbar you want to add it to.

To create your own toolbar (I don't really recommend this), select Tools | Customize, select the Toolbars tab, click the New button, type a name for the toolbar, and press ENTER. Then click the Commands tab and follow the instructions I just gave for adding commands to your new toolbar.

Tweaking Toolbar Appearance

To exert fine-tuned control over the appearance of your toolbars, select Tools | Customize, and select the Options tab.

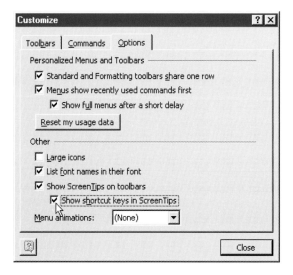

Here, you can control the following: see that the Standard and Formatting toolbars stay as small as possible; overrule FrontPage's way of hiding menu commands you haven't used recently (or clear its record of what commands you've been using); set the toolbars to display large icons (useful at high resolutions); overrule the way font names are displayed using their own fonts; eliminate the little sticky labels that appear when the mouse pointer hovers over a toolbar button, or, (as I prefer) require that the Screen Tips (that's what they're called) include keyboard shortcuts when they exist.

Getting FrontPage to Do Things Your Way

The settings described in this section are somewhat a matter of personal preference, so I won't dictate to you exactly what to do. I'll just lay out the options (and their ramifications) and let you decide for yourself. The title of this chapter promises that you will only have to do these things once (set it and forget it), but of course you might change your mind later, in which case you'd need to perform these actions again.

FrontPage's customization options are scattered over a number of different dialog boxes. One reason for this is that there are settings for the program itself (like the toolbars options just discussed), the currently open web, or the currently open page. Still, it's needlessly complicated. Mark my words: as soon as you've adapted to their inconsistent system, a new version of the program will come out with all the menus changed around to suit some new look and feel theory.

We'll start with the Options dialog box. Select Tools | Options.

Always Open Your Last Project?

By default, FrontPage starts with no web or web page open, but you can change it so that FrontPage automatically opens the last web you (or someone) had open. If you want FrontPage to work that way, make sure the General tab is in front on the Options dialog box and check Open Last Web Automatically When FrontPage Starts in the FrontPage startup options area (see Figure 2.2).

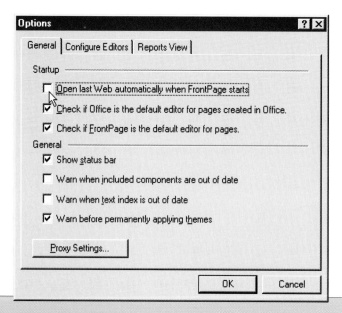

Figure 2.2: Make FrontPage open your last web whenever you start it to save yourself a few mouse-clicks each time, or leave things the way they are if you don't want to wait for the last web to open every time you start.

EXPERT ADVICE

The other two options in this area permit Office and FrontPage to check and make sure some competing program has not usurped their association with their particular file types. Uncheck them only if you have other programs with which you prefer to edit Office or web documents.

How Useful Is the Status Bar?

All Windows programs are supposed to have a status bar, but some make better use of it than others. Word, for example, has a weird bunch of shortcuts down there. FrontPage is still really an infant in the Microsoft Office family, and its status bar has not reached Word's baroque level of complication (or usefulness) yet. You can easily eliminate the status bar from the screen if you never find yourself looking there. If you end up missing it, bringing it back is just as easy.

Just uncheck Show Status Bar in the General FrontPage options area of the General tab of the Options dialog box.

Set Your Connection Speed

From time to time, FrontPage will display your progress in opening or publishing a document across your Internet connection (in the status bar, naturally). For FrontPage to provide you with accurate information, it needs to know the speed of your Internet connection (this is used in some reports as well). To tell FrontPage your connection speed (ask your provider or network administrator if you are unsure), select the Reports View tab of the Options dialog box, click the Assume Connection Speed Of drop-down list, and select the correct speed or type of connection (see Figure 2.3).

Click OK when you're done making changes in the Options dialog box.

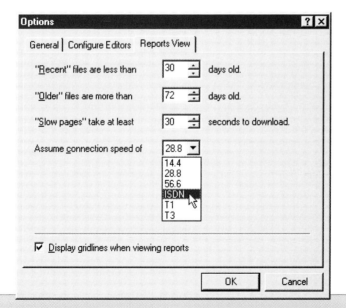

Figure 2.3: For FrontPage to report accurately on the speed of page downloads and transfers, I need to tell it that I'm connecting the Net via ISDN (a fast, digital, modem-like thing—you probably connect at 56K or 33.6).

View | Reveal Tags

If you ever used WordPerfect, you're familiar with the concept of revealing hidden codes.

Unless you have some interest in understanding HTML, the formatting language used on the Web, you can skip this section. Any time you want to see the HTML coding underlying a specific page, you can click the HTML tab near the bottom of the FrontPage window, but there is another option. If you want to continue to view your pages in the ordinary FrontPage interface (showing formatting, color, placeholders, and so on), but you'd like to see the formatting tags surrounding text, then select View | Reveal Tags. Instantly, you'll see at least the <BODY> and </BODY> tags embedded into your document, along with tags for any other formatting you've applied.

Turning Off Background Spell Checking

Whether to allow automatic background spell checking to go on is for you to decide, based on how you prefer to work. Do you prefer to correct typos as they occur, or does that break your concentration? If you fall into the latter category, you can turn off automatic spell checking on the General tab in the Page Options dialog box.

FrontPage sticks the control of this feature over on the Page Options dialog box, so start by selecting Tools | Page Options, and then select the General tab (Figure 2.4).

Then uncheck Check Spelling As You Type. Alternatively, you could check Hide Spelling Errors In This Document, which instructs FrontPage to continue to check your spelling as you type, but to hide the wavy underlines. When you're ready to fix any spelling errors that may have accumulated, you can return to the Options dialog box and uncheck the Hide Spelling Errors option.

EXPERT ADVICE

If you turn off automatic spell checking and later turn it back on, FrontPage then points out any suspicious words it finds, so from the user's point of view, there's no real difference between the two approaches.

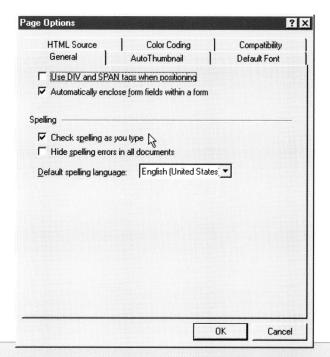

Figure 2.4: Both options on the Spelling tab of the Page Options dialog box have about the same effect.

Designing Your Web for a Specific Browser

Because the two major web browsers, Microsoft Internet Explorer and Netscape Navigator, are in a features war, they offer different levels of support for different web-development technologies, from various versions of HTML to dynamic stylesheets, Java, and Visual Basic. If you design your web for the widest possible audience, you'll want to stick with the features that a majority of your audience can handle. If you know what browser most (or all) of your visitors will be using (say you are setting up your web on an intranet whose users have standardized on one browser or the other), you can tune FrontPage menus to offer just the features that one browser supports.

To meddle with these settings, select the Compatibility tab of the Page Options dialog box. To change from the browser you're developing for, click the Browsers drop-down list box and choose Microsoft Internet Explorer Only, Netscape Navigator Only, or Both Internet Explorer And Netscape Navigator (see Figure 2.5).

Both Internet Explorer and Netscape Navigator have undergone several major revisions. At the 3.0 level, both browsers supported frames and tables. At the 4.0 level, each supported its own concept of style sheets and dynamic HTML. To set FrontPage to one of these

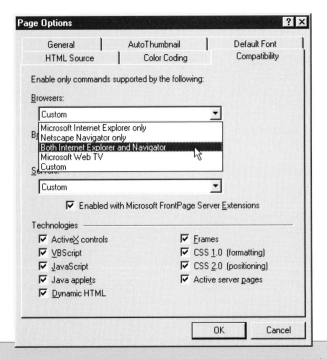

Figure 2.5:   Click the Browsers drop-down list box in the Compatibility tab of the Options dialog box if you only want to address the features that one or both of the two major web browsers can handle.

two levels, click the Browser Versions drop-down list box and choose
4.0 Browsers And Later or 3.0 Browsers And Later.

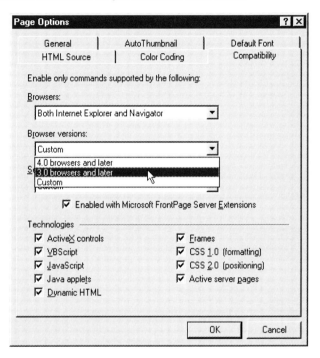

So, for example, if you choose 3.0 Browsers And Later, you'll see
that some of the specific features listed in the Technologies section at
the bottom of the Compatibility tab become automatically unchecked.

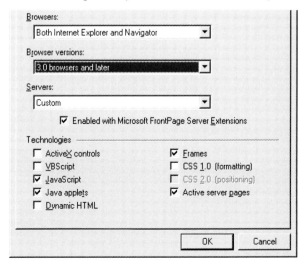

EXPERT ADVICE

You can choose your own custom set of features by checking or unchecking any of the items listed under Technologies.

Default Fonts

Another setting that FrontPage lumps with other page options is the default fonts your web pages will display. This is something that you don't have to change if you don't want to. Each web page has two basic fonts, a proportional font (used for text and headings) and a fixed-width font (used for program code, typewritten text, and so on). By default, the proportional font is Times New Roman and the fixed-width font is Courier New. To change either of these, click the Default Font tab of the Page Options dialog box. Then click the Default Proportional Font or Default Fixed-width Font drop-down list box and choose one of the alternative fonts listed (see Figure 2.6).

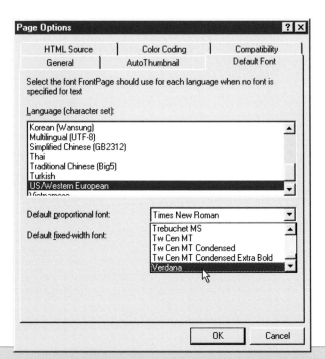

Figure 2.6:   Many people feel that Microsoft's Verdana font is clearer and easier to read on the screen than Times New Roman.

When you're finished with the Page Options dialog box, click OK.

Other Options You Set for Each Web or Each Page

As mentioned earlier in this section, FrontPage scatters its options over a number of dialog boxes. Some of these commands are grouped separately because they apply to just the current web or just the page you've got open at the moment. For setting properties of a specific web, there's the Tools | Web Settings command. (We'll cover creating and setting up a new web in Chapter 3.) For an open page, there are the other tabs of the Page Options dialog box, and there's the File | Properties command. (We'll cover creating and setting up a new web page in Chapter 4.)

Putting FrontPage One Click Away

If you use FrontPage all the time, you shouldn't have to fumble around with two or three levels of submenus just to get the darn thing started. Two convenient places to stow shortcuts to FrontPage are your desktop and your Start menu.

Putting a FrontPage Icon on Your Windows Desktop

If you use FrontPage all the time, you may want to have a FrontPage icon live on your desktop to make the program easy to start. First, exit FrontPage, or at least minimize the window. Then, to find a shortcut you can borrow, follow these steps:

1. Right-click the Start button and choose Open.
2. Double-click Program Files (or single-click if you have Windows 98 set up to work that way).
3. Scroll through the Program Files window to find the Microsoft FrontPage icon.
4. Right-drag the FrontPage program icon onto the desktop, and select Copy Here.

5. Select the icon's label, press F2, type **FrontPage** (or select and delete the word *Microsoft*), and press ENTER.

Now you've got a handy desktop icon for FrontPage. You can also make desktop shortcuts for important documents using the same method described here. Just search for the filename of the document you want.

Listing FrontPage on the Windows Start Menu

Don't right-click—just click and drag normally.

Another convenient place to put a FrontPage shortcut is directly on the Start menu. You can snag the program icon shortcut from the Start menu's Programs folder, and once you've got your FrontPage icon visible, drag it onto the Start button to add it to the menu.

EXPERT ADVICE

If you ever want to double-click a desktop icon that's obscured by several open windows, click the Show Desktop icon on the Quick Launch portion of the Windows 98 taskbar, or right-click on the taskbar first and select Minimize All Windows to get a clear shot at the desktop.

Adding FrontPage to the Quick Launch Toolbar

Perhaps the most convenient place to put a FrontPage shortcut is on the Quick Launch toolbar of the Windows 98 taskbar. Once you find the program icon, add it by clicking and dragging it onto the Quick Launch toolbar.

There's More . . .

What do you want to do now? You're ready to roll. You've got a basic plan for your web. Your copy of FrontPage is set up for your convenience, and you know your way around the program (at least a little). From here on, you should be able to skip through the book, picking out only the information you need as you need it.

CHAPTER 3

Setting Up a New Web

INCLUDES

- Making an empty web
- Making a one-page web
- Starting with a predesigned web
- Importing an existing web
- Reopening a web
- Adding folders to your web
- Turning on shared borders
- Naming a web

Start with a Blank Web → pp. 45–46

1. Select File | New | Web.
2. Double-click Empty Web or One Page Web.

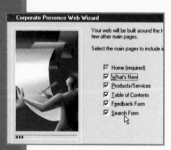

Start with a Predesigned Web → pp. 46–52

1. Select File | New | Web.
2. Double-click Corporate Presence Wizard, Customer Support Web, Project Web, or Personal Web.
3. Respond to all the wizard's prompts.

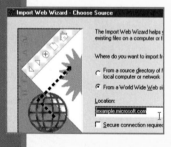

Import a Web from the Net → pp. 53–55

1. Select File | New | Web.
2. Double-click Import Web Wizard.
3. Enter the Internet address of the web site you are importing and click Next >.
4. Choose a limit to the maximum size of the web and click Next >.
5. Click Finish.

Import a Local Web → pp. 55–56

1. Select File | New | Web.
2. Double-click Import Web Wizard.
3. Check From A Source Directory Of Files On A Local Computer Or Network.
4. Press TAB.
5. Type (or browse to find) the location of the local web.
6. Check Include Subfolders and click Next >.
7. Exclude any files you don't want to import and click Next >.
8. Click Finish.

Reopen an Existing Web → pp. 59–60

1. Select File | Open Web.
2. Browse to and double-click the web's root folder.

Add a Folder to Your Web → pp. 60–62

1. Click the Folder View button.
2. Select the root folder, or select an existing folder to create a subfolder.
3. Select File | New | Folder.
4. Type a name for the new folder and press ENTER.

Turn On Shared Borders → pp. 64–67

1. Select Format | Shared Borders.
2. Click All Pages.
3. Check Top, Left, Right, Bottom, or any combination.
4. Click Include Navigation Buttons if you want them.
5. Click OK.

Because a web generally contains multiple pages, starting a new project involves two major steps. First you have to create the new web, which includes assigning a location for it on your computer's hard disk (or network). After that you can create the individual new web pages that the web will comprise. In this chapter, I'll show you FrontPage's essential commands for creating and opening webs. In Chapter 4, we'll get down to the page level.

By the way, you should know that what FrontPage calls a "web," most of the rest of the world (or at least most of the rest of the Web) calls a "web site." The terminology FrontPage uses is not wrong, per se. Just as the World Wide Web can be thought of as an enormous far-reaching interconnected web of pages and resources, so, also, can any small collection of pages be referred to as a "web." I'm using Microsoft's terminology throughout this book because I don't want to make things any more confusing inside FrontPage than they need to be, but you should be aware when communicating with other folks about Web matters that you may have to refer to your web as a "web site" or even just a site, to be understood.

Creating a New Web

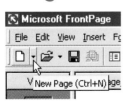

The first step in creating a new web, after starting FrontPage if it's not already running, is simple. Click the little down-arrow strip on the right side of the New Page button (don't be fooled by the button's name as it pops up—the same button works for new pages, webs, folders, and tasks). This pops down a menu.

If the Web choice is not visible, point to the chevrons at the bottom of the menu, or just leave the pointer hovering over the menu for a moment, and any hidden choices will appear. Click Web. The

New dialog box will appear with its only tab (for the moment), Web Sites, showing (see Figure 3.1). See, even FrontPage isn't perfectly consistent about referring to web sites as webs.

The dialog box offers you eight choices of templates and wizards for starting a new web. A template is a predesigned document containing placeholders for content and sometimes more elaborate interactive elements, such as forms. A wizard is a miniature question-and-answer program that walks you through a process step-by-step. In this case, the process is that of creating some more elaborately structured webs. The icons for the templates and wizards are similar, but the wizards are the ones with the magic wands and pixie dust floating about.

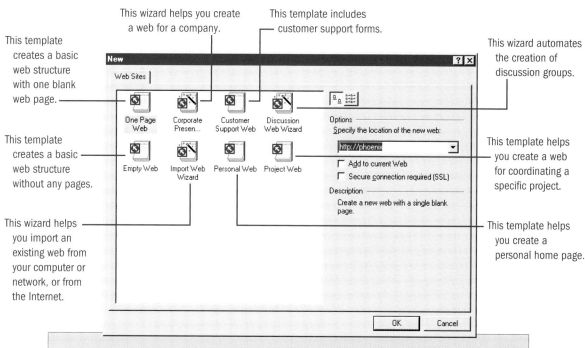

Figure 3.1: FrontPage provides templates and wizards for an assortment of basic web types.

The five templates offered include

1. One Page Web, a dummy web with one blank page to start on.

2. Empty Web, a dummy web with no pages in it.

3. Customer Support Web, a web for interacting with customers and tracking their requests and problems.

4. Personal Web, a template for an individual's home page.

5. Project Web, a web for tracking an ongoing project.

The three wizards are

• Corporate Presence Wizard, which creates a fairly elaborate company web.

• Discussion Web Wizard, which creates a searchable discussion group web (see Chapter 8 for more on this topic).

• Import Web Wizard, which creates a web from documents (web pages or otherwise) already existing on your computer or network, or on the Internet.

But before you go ahead and choose one of these templates or wizards to work from, you have to decide where you're going to be putting your webs. Over on the right side of the New dialog box, you'll see a section called Options. Under the primary option, Specify The Location Of The New Web, you'll need to type a location on your computer's hard disk (or possibly on your network), where you will place this web.

Where to Put It

Think for a moment before you proceed. If there's any chance that you'll be creating other webs in the future, you'll probably want to establish a main folder (directory) for *all* your webs, and to keep them clear of each other, you'll have to put each web in its own subfolder. I recommend something simple, such as putting a web folder, C:\webs\, on the main volume of your hard drive.

UPGRADE NOTE For those who've used previous versions of FrontPage, you'll notice that you're no longer required to run a web server just to design and set up a site. If you do already have a server running, you can still locate your new webs on it.

Remember then to include a folder name for this particular web. If you want to experiment with the different templates and wizards, specify a location like C:\webs\test\ for your first web.

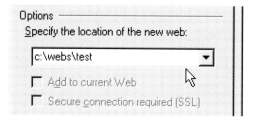

Starting from Scratch

If the type of web you're trying to create isn't similar to any of the predesigned webs offered in the New dialog box, then the easiest thing to do is create an empty or blank web and start from scratch.

Empty Web

To create an empty web, double-click the Empty Web template icon in the New dialog box. A dialog box called Creating New Web appears (briefly, in this case), and voila, your first web is created (although it's completely boring and contains nothing besides the folders FrontPage creates for itself automatically in every web). Whatever page (probably a blank one) that was already showing in Page View will remain. The only sign that you've created a new web is the appearance of the web's location in the program's title bar.

One Page Web

The only apparent difference between the Empty Web template and the One Page Web template is that one page, a blank starter home page. I'll use this template for starting the WildflowerTrips site whose planning I discussed in Chapter 1. I follow these steps:

1. Click the New Page button's little down-arrow thingie again.
2. Choose Web again.
3. Type a new location (**C:\webs\wildflowertrips**, in this case).
4. Double-click the One Page Web icon.

A new FrontPage window opens showing the one blank page in the new web in Page View. I'll continue to work on this WildflowerTrips web when it serves as a useful example of the techniques covered, but let's first take a look at a few of the more elaborate web templates and wizards.

Note that the Add To Current Web check box becomes usable as soon as you have one web open. This is used to create a new section of an existing web, which is not what we're doing right now.

Using FrontPage's Predesigned Webs

Whether or not you end up ever using any of FrontPage's predesigned webs, you still may find it helpful, even (dare I say it?) educational, to create one or two of them just to see how it's done. The entire Web was built by people cribbing from each other's pages and designs, so even a somewhat hokey, canned web may offer some ideas you can "borrow" or adapt for your own specific project.

Customer Support Web

To create a customer support web, assign a new test location and double-click the Customer Support Web. To see the pages FrontPage has created and inserted into the new web, switch to Folders view (see Figure 3.2).

To see the predesigned page in Page view, just double-click its file name in Folders view. Figure 3.3 shows the page called feedback.htm, which will eventually display content generated by a customer suggestion form (we'll discuss forms and related kinds of interactive elements in Chapter 8).

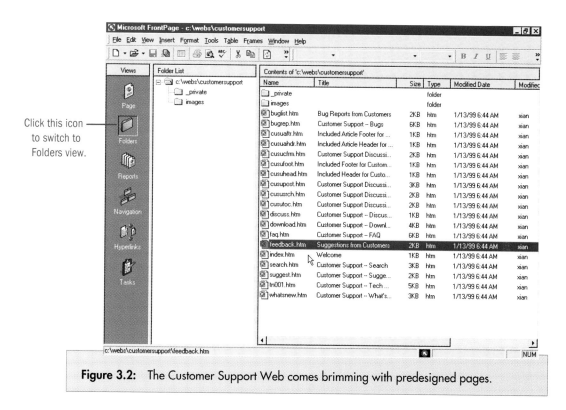

Click this icon to switch to Folders view.

Figure 3.2: The Customer Support Web comes brimming with predesigned pages.

To look at another page, switch back to Folders view and double-click the file called faq.htm (see Figure 3.4).

Continue poking around the pages to get a feel for thumbing through a site.

Corporate Presence Web

I used the Corporate Presence wizard to create the dummy site used as an example in Chapter 1. You can try it now yourself to see how the wizard questions you about what elements you'd like to include in your web. To start the wizard, choose a new location and double-click the Corporate Presence Wizard icon in the New dialog box.

The Corporate Presence Wizard dialog box appears. It will stay on the screen until you've completed the Q&A process, but its content

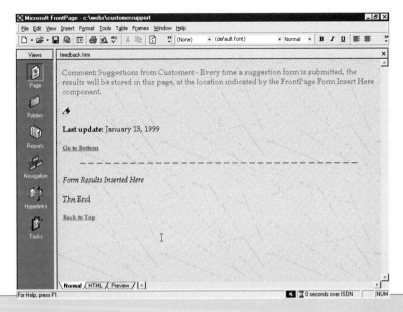

Figure 3.3:   The feedback.htm contains placeholders for now.

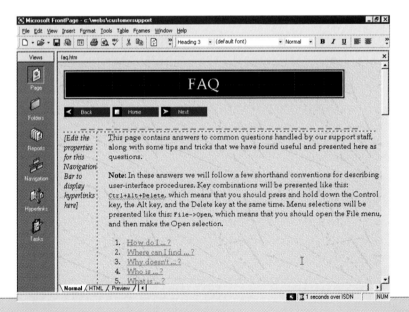

Figure 3.4:   A Frequently Asked Questions page for a customer support page, containing a banner, navigation buttons, and even hints at types of questions. (We'll get to navigation techniques in Chapter 7.)

will shift for each new question or set of questions. Click Next > to begin. The first panel explains the process. The second panel asks you to check off which types of main pages you wish to include in your web (see Figure 3.5).

I don't believe in filling up this type of book with shot after shot of wizard dialog boxes. The wizards provide sufficient hand-holding themselves, and I don't want to waste your time (or paper), but I'll quickly run through the remaining steps in this wizard's sequence.

1. Choose topics to be placed on the corporate web's home page.

2. Select topics to be placed on the What's New page.

3. Indicate the number of products and services covered.

4. List items to display for each product and service.

5. Choose items of information to collect from customers on the feedback page.

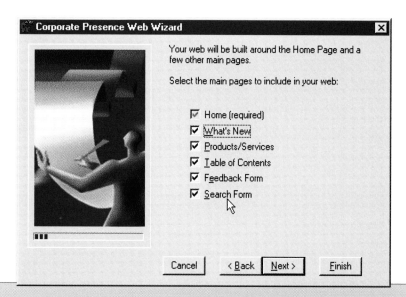

Figure 3.5: Every time you click the Next > button, the wizard will produce a new panel of questions for you to answer. When you're through the process, you'll click Finish, and the wizard will assemble a web to your specifications.

6. Decide whether you'll want your feedback archive to be compatible with standard database and spreadsheet programs (such as Access and Excel).

7. Customize the Table Of Contents page.

8. Decide which repeating elements should appear at the top and bottom of each page in the site.

9. Add an Under Construction icon or not. (I say not—they look tacky!)

10. Give the company's full name, short name, and address.

11. Enter contact information.

12. If you wish, you can choose a design theme for the site (see Chapter 6 for more on stylesheets and themes).

13. Choose to see outstanding tasks when you're done.

And that's it. The wizard creates the pages to your specification and makes a list of tasks that still need to be performed to complete the web (or at least a presentable draft of the web). It leaves you in Tasks view (see Figure 3.6).

Project Web

The Project Web template helps you put together a web for a collaborative project; that is, a web that lists the goals and status of the project, the participants, and discussions among participants. (The discussions involve forms, which we'll get to in Chapter 8). From the dummy text supplied, you can see that the model for this type of web is a software development project, but you can easily adapt it to other purposes.

Figure 3.7 shows a project web's Schedule page.

Personal Web

On the chance that you're using a fancy-schmancy program like FrontPage just to put together a personal page for yourself (you know the kind I mean: Here's a picture of my cat, etc.), start with the Personal Web template. Figure 3.8 shows the home page of the personal web.

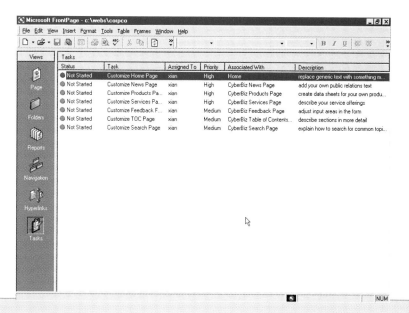

Figure 3.6: The Corporate Presence wizard reminds you of the tasks that still need to be fulfilled to finish the web.

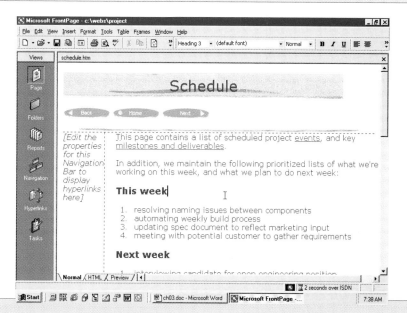

Figure 3.7: Replace this elaborate dummy text with information about the actual schedule of your project. (The italicized bracketed instructions are comments that won't show up when the web is viewed in a browser.)

Right-click on any page element to edit its properties (for example,
I personalized this banner in the Page Banner Properties dialog box).

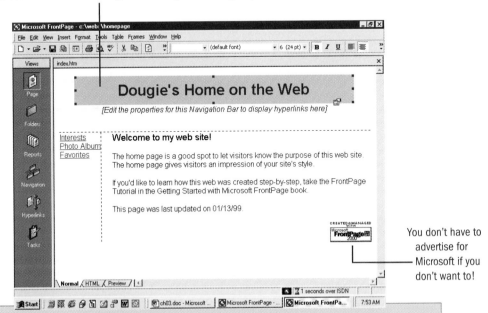

Figure 3.8: If you want a kick in the pants getting started with a personal site (a site about yourself), the Personal Web template may do the trick.

Importing a Web

CAUTION

A frequent complaint about FrontPage from people who don't use it is that web sites imported into FrontPage and then republished are converted entirely to FrontPage's way of doing things, and that makes it difficult for collaborators to contribute to the web site if they themselves use different software.

There are two alternatives to starting your web from scratch, both of which fall under the general rubric of importing. You can assemble a new web from documents you've already created (both web pages or other types of documents), or you can import an existing web (even one created with different software) either from your local network or computer, or from the Internet.

There's no real difference between these two approaches from FrontPage's point of view. Either way, you tell it to grab a bunch of files and it gets them and copies them into one of its standard folders-and-subfolders deals. FrontPage doesn't really care if the existing documents are linked web pages or scattered word-processing documents.

Importing from the Internet

Let's say you've been assigned to update or manage an existing web site, and you want to use FrontPage as the tool. You'll have to import the web as it currently exists into FrontPage, manage the web on your own computer, and then publish your updates and changes to the external web site. (See Chapter 9 for the nitty-gritty of publishing your web.) To import the web, choose a new location and double-click the Import Web Wizard in the New dialog box. The first thing the wizard wants to know is whether you'll be importing the web from a directory on your own computer or network, or from an existing site on the World Wide Web (see Figure 3.9).

1. Make sure From A World Wide Web Site is checked.

2. Press TAB.

3. Type the web address of the site you wish to import.

4. Click Next >.

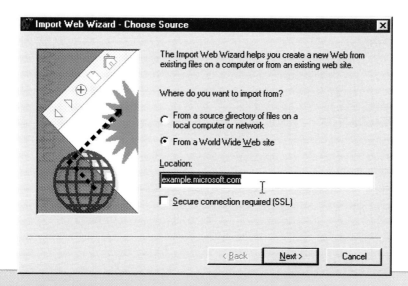

Figure 3.9: Choose the From A World Wide Web Site option and enter the public site's address option to import your web from the Internet.

The second panel of this wizard addresses the amount of material you will import. This may seem like a strange thing to ask. If you're going to work on an existing web site, you want the whole thing, right? That's probably true for any small site, but some sites are enormous, containing many interlinked layers of information. To keep the importing process under control, you can limit the wizard to any number of levels of pages below (meaning linked from) the root page at the site you're importing. The wizard suggests five levels, which is more levels than many small webs have.

The wizard also offers to limit the import by how much storage space it will require on your hard disk or network. It suggests limiting the download to 500K. Thirdly, the wizard gives you the option of only importing text and image files (this would be most or all of the files in many web sites), but leaves that option unchecked by default. Make your decisions, click Next >, and then click Finish. FrontPage will report to you on the progress of the import as it grabs file after file.

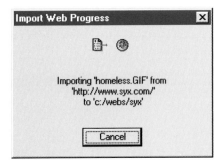

If the web address you gave the wizard is incorrect (even a simple typo will mess it up), FrontPage will report an error. Click OK, double-check the address you typed, and then start the process over from the beginning.

EXPERT ADVICE

If you're not sure of the precise address of the web site you're trying to import, visit a site with a web browser and copy its address from the browser's address box.

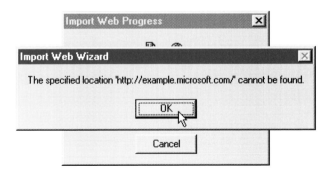

The wizard will tell you when it has completed the import (or reached the maximum number of levels or raw kilobytes of data you specified as a ceiling).

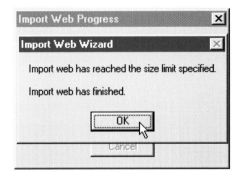

Click OK. Figure 3.10 shows the home page of a real web site (**www.syx.com**) that I just imported into FrontPage.

Importing from Your Own Computer or Network

To import a local web, you still start by choosing a new location and double-clicking the Import Web Wizard in the New dialog box.

1. Check From A Source Directory Of Files On A Local Computer Or Network.

2. Press TAB.

Figure 3.10: I created this web site by hand a few years ago, but now I've imported it into FrontPage.

3. Type the location of the directory, or if you can't remember it exactly, click the Browse button, root around on your computer or network, find the directory, and click OK.

4. Check Include Subfolders (see Figure 3.11).

5. Click Next >.

The next panel of the wizard lists all the files available from the location you specified. Left as it is, the wizard will import all the files listed. To remove one from the list, select it and click the Exclude button. If you remove one by mistake or otherwise change your mind, click Refresh. Unfortunately, that will restore the entire original list

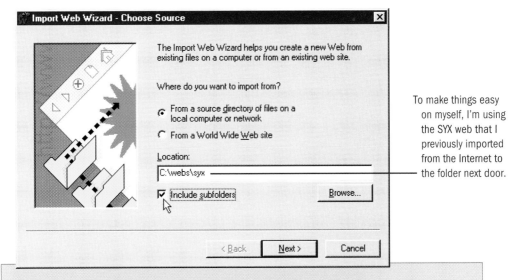

To make things easy on myself, I'm using the SYX web that I previously imported from the Internet to the folder next door.

Figure 3.11: Type the location or use the Browse button to import a local web from elsewhere on your computer or network.

and you may need to exclude some files again. When you are satisfied, click Next >, and then click Finish. FrontPage will report to you on the progress of the import as it grabs file after file.

Importing More Files Later

You can always import additional web pages or other documents or files into an existing web. To do so for the first time, you need to dig into the File menu for the hidden Import command (unless you didn't tell FrontPage to show only the most used menu choices back in Chapter 2, in which case, you can just select File | Import, no problem).

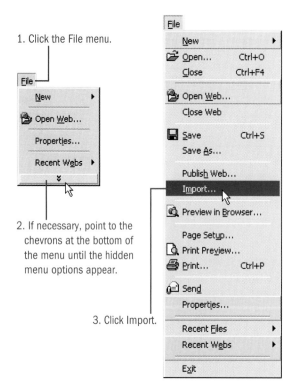

1. Click the File menu.

2. If necessary, point to the chevrons at the bottom of the menu until the hidden menu options appear.

3. Click Import.

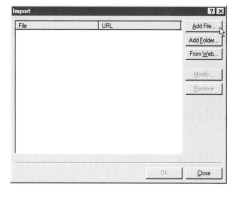

4. Click the Add File or Add Folder button in the Import dialog box that appears.

- Add File brings up an Open dialog box focused on your desktop, so you can root around for a specific file.

- Add Folder brings up the Browse window, so you can indicate any folder on your computer or network.

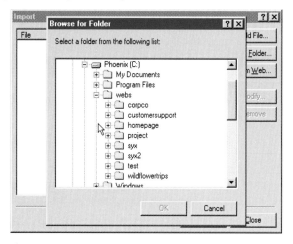

- From Web starts the Import Wizard.

When you have selected a file or folder, click OK. To add additional files or folders, click Add File or Add Folder again. When you are satisfied with the list of files and/or folders to import, click the OK button. FrontPage will report to you on the progress of the import as it grabs the files.

Opening an Existing Web

To open an existing web (that is, one you've already created in or imported into FrontPage), select File | Open Web.

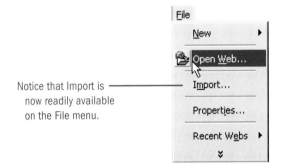

Notice that Import is now readily available on the File menu.

This brings up the Open Web dialog box (Figure 3.12).

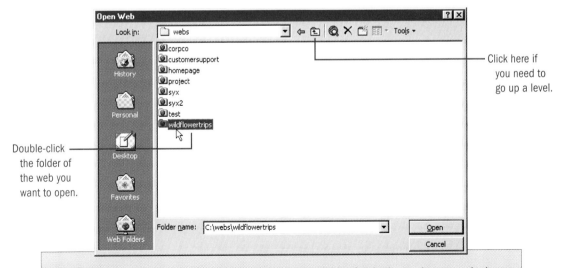

Double-click the folder of the web you want to open.

Click here if you need to go up a level.

Figure 3.12: You'll probably start out looking in the folder for the last web you worked on. You may have to go up one level to look for your other webs if you have more than one already.

EXPERT ADVICE

To reopen a FrontPage web you worked on recently, select the File | Recent Webs and then choose one of the most recent webs.

The new web will open in its own window (adding a new button to your Windows task bar). You may want to switch to the old FrontPage window and close it now.

Organizing Your Site

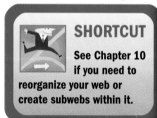

SHORTCUT

See Chapter 10 if you need to reorganize your web or create subwebs within it.

You can't organize your site all at once, especially not at the beginning of the process, before you've assembled any of the content. It's an ongoing process, and fortunately, FrontPage takes a lot of the sting out of changing your mind about folders and subfolders, hyperlinks, or other navigation issues. You can rearrange just about anything later on in the project. FrontPage will help you make sure that pages don't get orphaned, links continue to point to the correct destinations, and so on. (Don't worry if you find talk of links and navigation confusing—there's a whole chapter on this subject in your immediate future if I read these lines on your palm correctly.)

There is one thing you can do right away, and that's set up the folders inside (or "below," in a hierarchical sense) the root folder of your new web. If you don't remember, the root folder is the main one. One thing you can do is set up folders for sections you know you'll need. To demonstrate, I'm going to add the folders I figure I'd need for the California WildflowerTrips site back in Chapter 1 (see "Sketching a Skeleton" in that chapter).

Making New Folders

To make new folders, first choose Folders view in the View bar (see Figure 3.13).

FrontPage creates these folders automatically.
Don't mess with them.

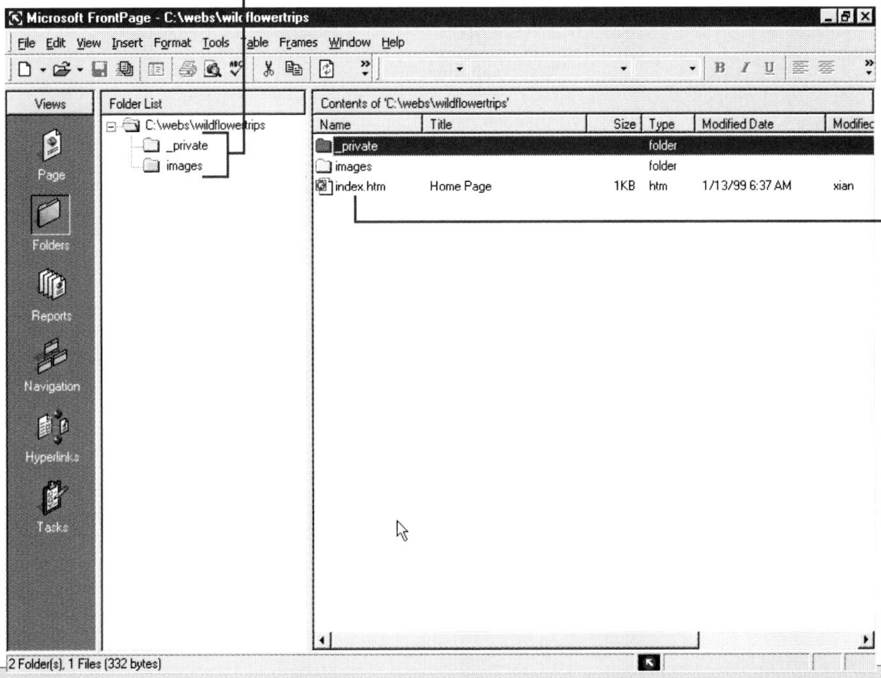

So far, the web only has one page—its home page.

Figure 3.13: Folders view resembles a Windows Explorer window, showing you the folder structure of your site and the files within the selected folder in the Folder List.

1. Choose the thingie on the right side of the New Page button.

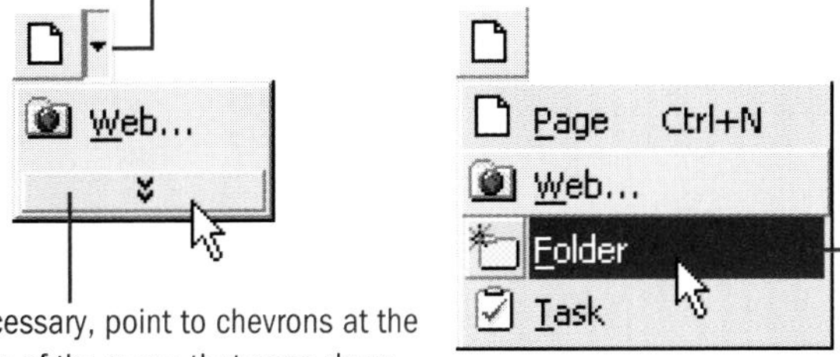

2. If necessary, point to chevrons at the bottom of the menu that pops down.

3. Select Folder.

This creates a new folder called New_Folder, with its label already selected. Type a new name for the folder (see Figure 3.14) and press ENTER.

My original web skeleton for the site includes some subfolders inside of folders, such as an archive folder inside the main photos folder. I'll create subfolders now.

Making Subfolders

To make a subfolder:

1. Double-click the folder in the Folder List.

2. Click the thingie on the right side of the New Page button.

3. Choose Folder (it's now visible immediately).

4. Type a name for the new subfolder.

To expand the subfolder contents of a folder in the Folder List, click the plus-in-a-box next to the folder's icon (it will turn to a minus-in-a-box as it expands to show subfolders).

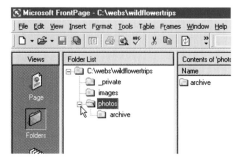

To create more subfolders, repeat the steps above. When you are ready to continue creating ordinary folders within the root, be sure to select the root folder again at the top of the folder list (to avoid adding subfolders when you want to add folders).

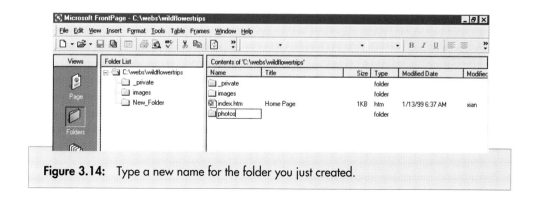

Figure 3.14: Type a new name for the folder you just created.

Figure 3.15 shows the set of folders I used as a base for the WildflowerTrips web.

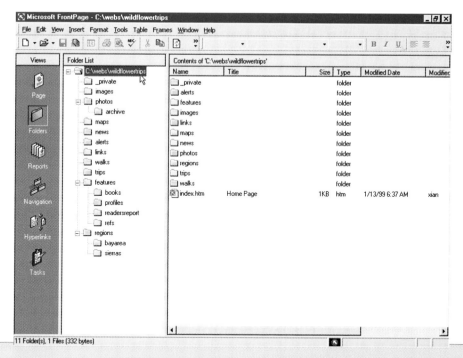

Figure 3.15: I've now created all the folders I envisioned when planning this site with my partner. We'll probably have to create more and we may end up getting rid of some as well in the long run, but it's a start.

Deleting a Folder

If you create a folder in the wrong place, create one too many folders, or simply decide to delete a folder, it's easy to do. Select the folder and press DELETE. FrontPage will ask you to confirm the deletion. (This becomes more important when the folders aren't empty!)

Click Yes to delete.

Turning on Shared Borders

DEFINITION

Shared Border: FrontPage permits you to designate any or all of the four page borders (top, left, bottom, and right) as "shared borders," whose contents may appear on every page in the web.

Many of the predesigned web templates, such as the Customer Support web, have something called *shared borders* turned on, usually with a dummy-text banner on the top border, a place for navigation buttons or links on the left border, a copyright statement and perhaps authorship or contact information on the bottom border, with the right border left off (see Figure 3.16).

You can turn on shared borders in any web, even a blank one. Most navigation schemes rely on at least one shared border (usually the top or left border of each page, frequently both). See Chapter 7 for more on navigation. Turning on at least one shared border can make it easier for you to maintain a uniform look for your web, especially when you decide to change something on every page. If it's part of a shared border, you can change it once and FrontPage will update the rest of the pages.

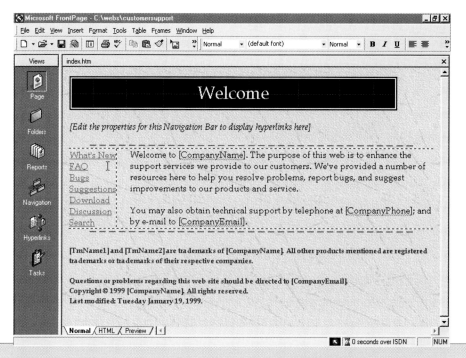

Figure 3.16: This generic customer-support web uses three shared borders (top, bottom, and left side), set off by dashed lines.

To turn on shared borders, select Format | Shared Borders. This brings up the Shared Borders dialog box (see Figure 3.17).

1. Click All Pages.

2. Check Top, Left, Right, or Bottom, or any combination of the four borders.

3. Click Include Navigation buttons if you want them on the top or left border, or both (see Figure 3.18).

When you're ready, click OK. FrontPage will update all the pages in your web (or just this page, if you did not select Click All Pages). Figure 3.19 shows a page in the WildflowerTrips web with shared borders down the left side and across the bottom.

To change a page back to the borders shared by the rest of a web, click Reset Borders For Current Page To Web Default.

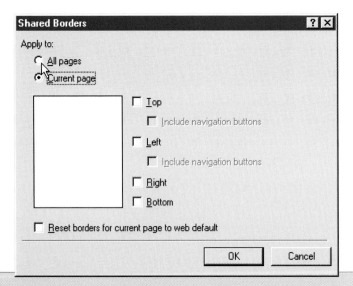

Figure 3.17: You can give a common look to all the pages in your web at once with the Shared Borders dialog box.

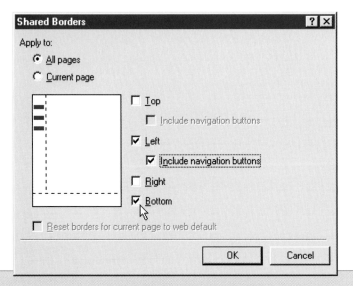

Figure 3.18: FrontPage only enables you to put navigation links in the top and left borders.

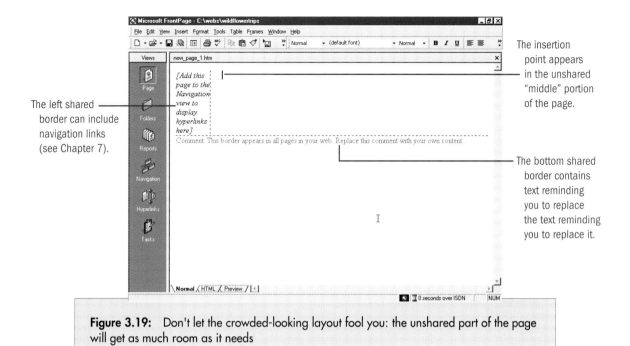

The left shared border can include navigation links (see Chapter 7).

The insertion point appears in the unshared "middle" portion of the page.

The bottom shared border contains text reminding you to replace the text reminding you to replace it.

Figure 3.19: Don't let the crowded-looking layout fool you: the unshared part of the page will get as much room as it needs

After you learn more about creating new pages in Chapter 4, we'll come back to shared borders in Chapter 5, so you can start adding meaningful content to these important parts of your web.

Naming Your Web

The last step in setting up a new web is naming it. To do so, select Tools | Web Settings and make sure the General tab is selected (see Figure 3.20).

I called this web "California WildflowerTrips," and clicked OK.

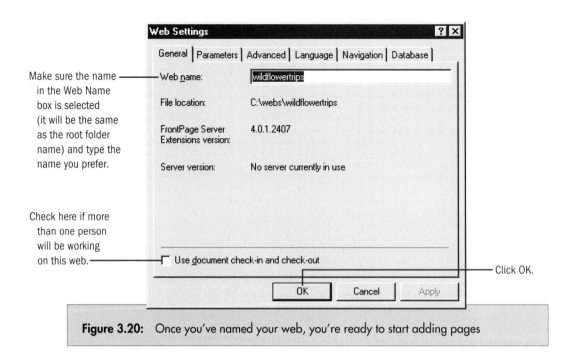

Make sure the name in the Web Name box is selected (it will be the same as the root folder name) and type the name you prefer.

Check here if more than one person will be working on this web.

Click OK.

Figure 3.20: Once you've named your web, you're ready to start adding pages

There's More . . .

Once you've set up your new web, you can start adding pages to it. Chapter 4 will tell you all about how to create new pages, set up the properties for a page, and reopen old pages. Then, over the next few chapters, you'll learn how to add content to your pages (and edit and format it), how to add graphics and visual themes, and how to link pages together.

Making Web Pages

INCLUDES

- Making a blank page
- Making a page with a wizard or template
- Converting documents into web pages
- Removing a page from a web
- Preventing a page from being published
- Opening existing pages

Start with a Blank Page ➡ p. 73

- Click the New Page button.

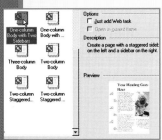

Start with a Predesigned Page ➡ pp. 75–77

1. Select File | New | Page.
2. Select a template to preview it.
3. Click OK.

Save a Web Page ➡ pp. 78–79

1. Press CTRL+S.
2. Type a file name.
3. Click the Change button.
4. Type a title.
5. Click OK.
6. Click Save.
7. If the page has one or more embedded files, click OK again
   (or change the setting for each file in the Save Embedded Files
   dialog box, and *then* click OK).

Convert an Existing Document
into a Web Page ➡ pp. 82–84

1. Select Insert | File.
2. Choose the type of file you're looking for.
3. Select a folder to look in for the file.
4. Select the file you wish to insert.
5. Click Open.

Remove a Page from a Web ➥ p. 85

1. Click the Folder View button in the View bar or the Folder List button on the toolbar.
2. Select the file you want to remove.
3. Press DELETE.
4. Click Yes.

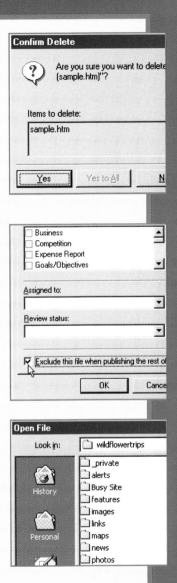

Prevent a Page from Being Published ➥ p. 86

1. Select a file's icon.
2. Select File | Properties.
3. Choose the Workgroup tab.
4. Click Exclude This File….
5. Click OK.

Open an Existing Web Page ➥ p. 87

1. Press CTRL+O.
2. Browse to and double-click the file's icon.

If you've worked your way through Chapter 3, then your web right now is either a big empty shell or the equivalent of one of those slightly too-cheerful prefab store formats you find in strip malls. Now, as George Carlin used to say, you have a "place" for your "stuff." Every page that will appear in your web will be stored in the web's root folder or one of the subfolders. In the long run, you have to work out how all the pages will relate to each other, but for now, you've got to throw all your stuff into the web (whether that means creating new pages from scratch, adapting existing documents and artwork, or both).

This chapter's simple, covering just the mechanics of making, closing, reopening, and setting up web pages. I'll leave writing, editing, formatting, designing, linking, and presenting the web pages to the next few chapters.

Creating a New Page

First, run FrontPage and open your current web. (See Chapters 1 and 3 respectively if you haven't yet and just said to yourself, "Run who and open your what now?") If you just want an empty document to work with, then a blank new page will do. You can use the one FrontPage starts with (if you haven't told it to open the last web and the last web you opened was made with a template or wizard or has a theme), or you can use the one that appears whenever you open a web (but you didn't really want to know that much at this point, did you?).

Just as with webs, FrontPage also offers templates and wizards to help you in the creation of individual web pages. To take this analogy a step further: just as you can import existing web sites into FrontPage, so can you import or open individual documents—both web pages and other types of documents—into an existing web. First things first—how to make a new blank page.

Starting with a New Blank Page

This only works with webs that lack themes. If you used a wizard or template to create your web in the first place, then your new pages will probably not be blank (they'll be devoid of meaningful content but fully designed with tips and placeholders), and you can skip to the next section. For the rest of us, to create a new, blank page,

- Click the New Page button (*not* the little thingie on its right side), or press CTRL+N.

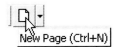

FrontPage automatically switches you to Page view and creates a new blank page named new_page_2.htm or new_page_3 or a higher number (depending on how many new pages you've already created since you last started FrontPage), as shown in Figure 4.1.

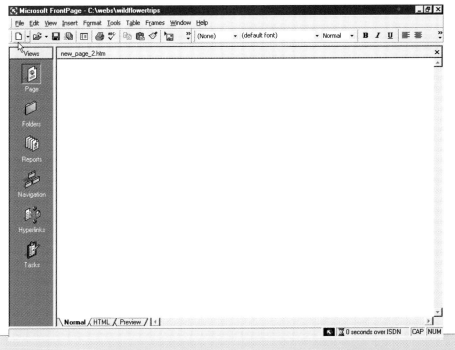

Figure 4.1: A new blank web page, a blank slate of a screen, a veritable tabula rasa of your mind.

To confront that empty blank space, skip to the next section to save and title your page, and then proceed directly to Chapter 5.

Starting with a Blank Page in a Predesigned Web

This is similar to but different from starting with a predesigned *page* in a web (either a blank web or a predesigned web), which comes up next.

If you click the New Page button after opening a web you originally created with a wizard or template, then the new page will come with the thematic elements of the web, the design elements (relax—we'll get to these in Chapter 6), the placeholders with their vaguely condescending advice, and so on (see Figure 4.2).

All three of these messages refer to how FrontPage can automatically insert navigation buttons into all the pages in your web, as I'll explain in Chapter 7.

These dotted lines section off shared borders, as explained in Chapter 3.

The soothing background graphic comes with the web's theme (which I'll explain in Chapter 6).

You can rewrite this dummy copyright statement just once here to change it throughout the web.

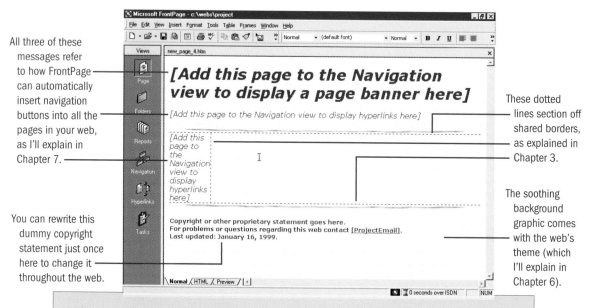

Figure 4.2: This doesn't look like a blank page, but in a way, it *is* blank, since it contains only dummy text and boilerplate.

Starting with a Predesigned Page

To get a leg up with the design and layout of your new page, you have the option of using one of FrontPage's web page wizards or templates. To do it this way, select File | New | Page. This brings up the New dialog box (see Figure 4.3).

Click a template icon to see a preview of its design, as shown in Figure 4.4.

If it's close enough to how you'd like your new page to look, double-click the icon (or just click OK). The new page that appears will be laid out as in the preview, with dummy text (Latin, no less—it gives the spell checker fits!) and photos (see Figure 4.5).

We'll discuss frames in Chapter 7.

To see all the options, scroll down or switch the dialog box from Large Icons view to List view.

If you don't have time to work on this page today, you can opt just to create the blank file and add a reminder to the web's task list that you have to finish the page some day (I'll discuss tasks in Chapter 10).

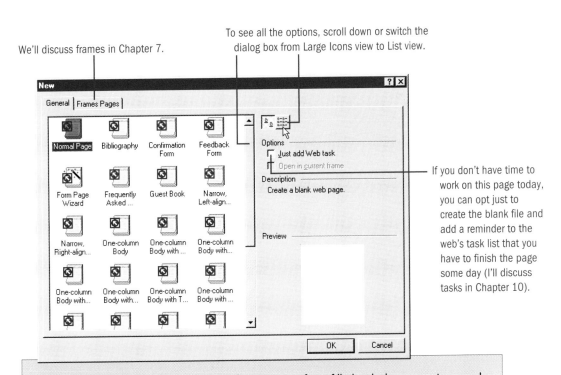

Figure 4.3: Starting with a predesigned page (even if it is filled with dummy text) can make the design job easier even if you end up changing things around. You still have to write your own copy, though, as we'll discuss in Chapter 5.

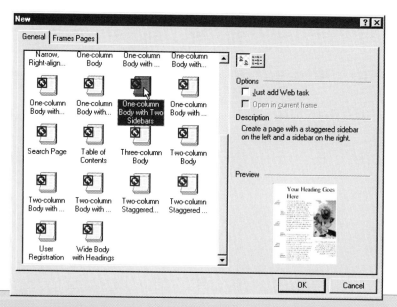

Figure 4.4: The Preview area in the bottom-right corner of the New dialog box gives you some idea of what design you're buying into.

You can erase this reminder or follow its suggestions and replace it with a link (see Chapter 7) related to the content of the page.

Replace the dummy text with your own headline.

You'll almost certainly want to replace this photograph and its caption with something more suitable (see Chapter 6).

These gridlines tell you the page is laid out this way with a table (see Chapter 5).

Replace this gibberish with real content.

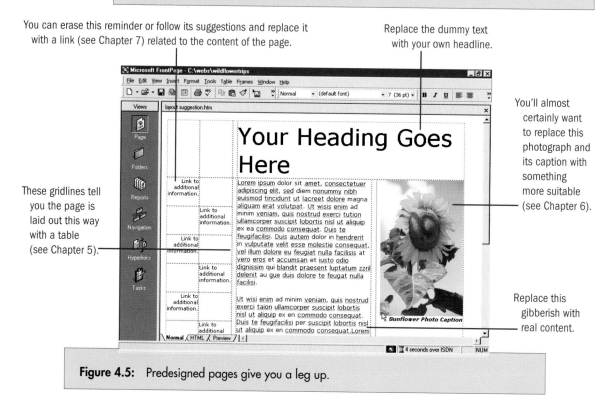

Figure 4.5: Predesigned pages give you a leg up.

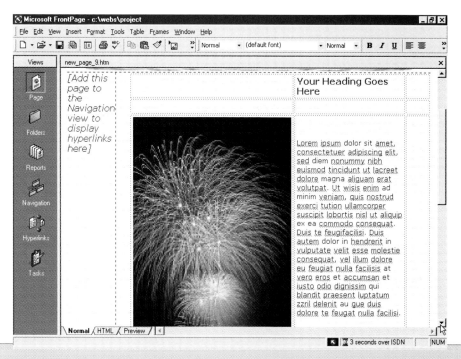

Figure 4.6: As part of the project web, this page has shared borders in addition to the layout samples that came with its template.

If you make a new page of this sort in a predesigned web, the elements of the web template (the theme, the shared borders, the boilerplate text) and the page template (the layout, more dummy text, forms, dummy art) get mixed together (see Figure 4.6).

Saving and Titling Your Page

Whether you start with an empty page or a template-designed page full of nonsense (a pretty face with nothing upstairs), you can see that working on the page will requiring entering some real text at the very least. Chapters 5 through 8 will help you do so. First, though, you must save the page you've created before you take a step further.

Saving a Page for the First Time

To save a page for the first time, select File | Save or press CTRL+S. This brings up the Save As dialog box (see Figure 4.7).

You can do this in any order really, but it's easiest to enter the file name first and assign your page a title second.

1. Type a file name for your page in the File Name box.
2. Click the Change button. This brings up the Set Page Title dialog box.

1. Type an informative title (*New Features of Our Widget* says more than just *Features*).

2. Click OK.
3. Click Save (back in the Save As dialog box), to close the deal.

Saving a Blank Page

If you just created a blank page, or if your page contains text only—no embedded graphics or other file formats—then that's all you do (so you can skip the next section).

EXPERT ADVICE

If people end up bookmarking your page, the text of the title is what will appear in their bookmark (or favorites) menu, so it's the real name of the page from the point of view of the Web.

By default, FrontPage will save this page in the current web.

Double-click a folder to save your page in it.

Click here to go up one level.

Your page's title is important. Click the Change button to give your page a meaningful title.

Type a file name for your page. One word is best (you don't have to type the .htm).

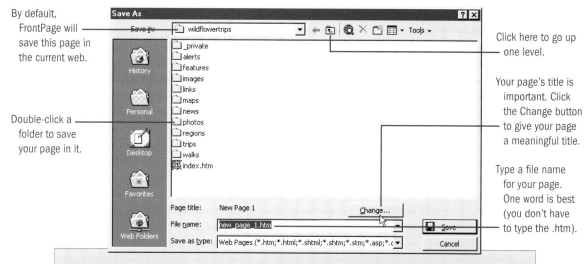

Figure 4.7: FrontPage's Save As dialog box is similar to that of other Office programs, such as Word. The differences are the suggested file type and the opportunity to set the page's title before saving.

Saving a Page with an Embedded File

If the page has an embedded file (such as an image), there's one more step. After you click the Save button in the Save As dialog box (Figure 4.7), the Save Embedded Files dialog box will appear, listing any and all embedded files and showing a preview of the first (or only) file on the list.

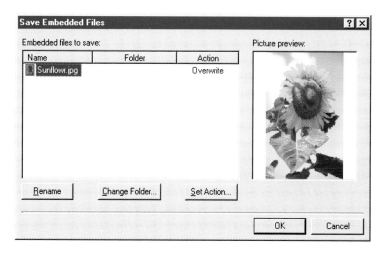

If you want to give an embedded file a new name, select it if it is not currently selected (the Picture Preview area will show the selected file) and click the Rename button. This highlights the file icon's title, much as when you press F2 anywhere in the Windows Explorer interface.

Then type a new name and press ENTER. To save the image in a different folder from the page's (such as the common "images" folder the FrontPage automatically set up for you), click the Change Folder button. This brings up the Change Folder dialog box, which has the folder-selection features of an ordinary Save As dialog box.

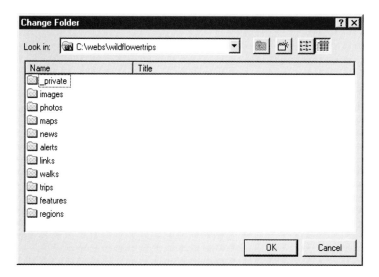

Double-click the folder you want to change to.

If an embedded file is used in more than one place, you don't need to save a new copy of it for each file; instead, select it, and click the Set Action button. Then choose Don't Save in the Set Action dialog box that appears.

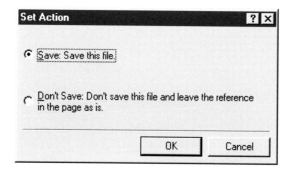

When all the embedded-file settings are as you wish, click OK. Depending on the actions you prescribed for any files, FrontPage will save them or remember in the future that they do not need to be saved each time.

Saving a Page Thereafter

After saving a page for the first time, you can save it again whenever you've made changes you want to keep without having to go through all the naming and specifying that complicate the first time you save.

Saving Repeatedly as You Work

There's probably nothing more frustrating in the world of computers than losing an afternoon's (or a day's) work. It's infuriating! The only way to prevent this is to save your work frequently. Not just every time you make a major change, but every time you make any change at all. Turn it into a habit you don't think twice about. Recently my 'puter crashed and I thought I'd lost a lot of writing, but it turns out I had saved my work at the end of the last paragraph I'd written and I lost not a word. I wouldn't be smug if I hadn't been very badly burned in the past too many times to admit.

The fastest way to save repeatedly is to use the keyboard shortcut: CTRL+S, although the Save button works about as well. It depends on whether you prefer pressing keys or pointing with your mouse.

Saving a Copy of a Page with Save As

Often you'll base new pages on existing pages (something like an informal, personalized version of the predesigned templates that come with FrontPage), and the easiest way to do that is to save a copy of the original right away, so you don't accidentally change it! To do so, select File | Save As. This brings up the Save As dialog box shown in Figure 4.7. Type the new file name, assign a new title, change the location if need be, and save the copy (and, if necessary, any embedded files). Then you're ready to change the text or layout to develop the new page, as discussed in Chapter 5.

Converting an Existing Document into a Web Page

Few webs are created completely out of thin air, as it were. Often, there is an archive of existing documents (press releases, product specifications, catalog pages, published stories, and so on) that you can adapt to your new web instead of creating them from whole cloth. Most of the time, these documents will not yet be in the web's format (HTML), so you'll need to convert them somehow to get them there.

If you're working with Microsoft Office files, such as Word documents, Excel worksheets, or an Access database, see Chapter 8 for more on how these different programs should be used together.

The easiest way to get a single file into your web is to insert it directly into a blank web page. To adopt a group of files, use FrontPage's Import feature (as explained in Chapter 3).

To insert an existing document into a blank file, select Insert | File (you may have to point to the chevrons at the bottom of the menu or wait for the File option to appear). This brings up the Select File dialog box (a simplified version of the Open dialog box).

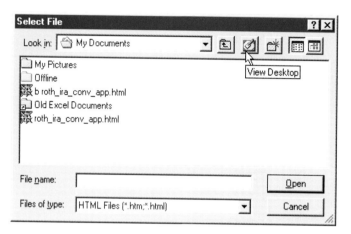

You'll have to navigate your computer or desktop via this dialog box to find the file you want to insert.

In the Files Of Type box, you can widen or specify the types of files the box should list. If you're not sure of the file format you're looking for, choose All Files (*.*). For plain text files, try Text Files (*.txt), and for Word files, choose one of the Word documents options (*.doc).

In the Look In area of the dialog box you can change the folder you're looking in for the file to insert, or you can click the Up One Level or View Desktop button to hunt around. Double-click folder icons in the main window to open folders or delve into subfolders. When you've opened the right folder and found the file you want to insert, click the Open button.

EXPERT ADVICE

If inserting or importing an existing file somehow fails to preserve the content or formatting of the source document the way you had hoped, you can try converting the document to HTML format in the original application with which you created it (assuming you still have that program handy).

EXPERT ADVICE

You can also insert other types of files into a web page this way.

If you're importing a text file, FrontPage will ask you how to format the text (that is, how to handle line breaks and paragraphs).

Click here to treat the entire file as one preformatted block (of fixed-width text).

Click here to treat the file as a series of preformatted paragraphs.

Click here to code the file as paragraphs of unformatted (variable-width) text.

Click here to keep the existing line breaks with unformatted paragraphs.

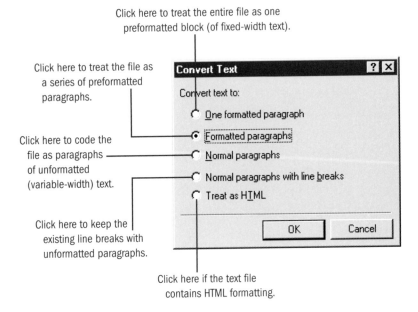

Click here if the text file contains HTML formatting.

Remember to save your page after you've inserted the file. To massage the original contents to suit your web, see Chapter 5.

Removing Pages from a Web

If I tell you how to create new pages in a web, I also have to tell you how to remove them. You will inevitably remove pages from your web whether it's because you added a page by mistake or because you'll want to change your web's design sometime down the road. When you delete a page from a web, you delete it entirely. FrontPage assumes that a file with its own reason for existing besides being in your web will already exist in some other folder (and you'll probably have imported it into the web), so it doesn't give you the option of removing a file from the web without deleting it.

You can prevent a page from being published with the web without deleting it, though (and you can always move the file from the web's folder in the ordinary Windows Explorer interface).

See Chapter 9 for more on publishing your web to a Web or intranet server.

Deleting a Page Completely

To remove a page from your web, first switch to Folder view or click the Folder List button in the toolbar to see your web's files regardless of the current view. Double-click a folder icon if you want to delete a file in a subfolder. Select the file you want to get rid of and press DELETE. FrontPage will ask you to confirm the deletion, referring to the page by its title and its file name.

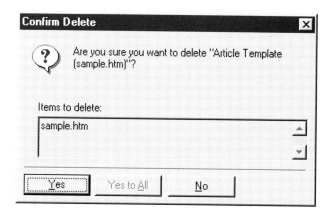

Removing a Page
from Your Web Without Deleting It

If you merely want to move the page to a different location on your computer or network for safekeeping but remove it from the current web, the easiest way is to open the web's folder in the Windows Explorer (one way to do this is to select Start | Run, type the folder's location, such as **c:\webs\wildflowertrips**, and press ENTER). Click the file's icon and drag it (or cut and paste it) to a different location. This will remove the page from the web without deleting it.

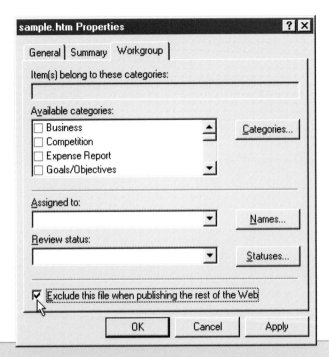

Figure 4.8:   The Workgroup tab is mostly useful for collaboration (which I'll explain more about in Chapter 10).

CAUTION

The page you removed will still appear to be part of the web until the next time you open it.

Another approach is to keep the page in the web but simply prevent it from being published along with the other pages when you make the web public (see Chapter 9 for a discussion of publishing your web). To do this, right-click on a file's icon and choose Properties in the menu that pops up (or open the page or even just highlight the page's file icon, and then select File | Properties). In the Properties dialog box that appears, choose the Workgroup tab (see Figure 4.8).

Click the checkbox item Exclude This File When Publishing The Rest Of The Web at the bottom of the dialog box, and then click OK.

Opening an Existing Web Page

After you've created (or imported) a page, saved it, and maybe even worked on its content (which I'll tell you how to do in Chapter 5), at some point you'll close the page (using File | Close) or more likely simply quit FrontPage (File | Exit). The next time you want to work on that page, you'll have to open it again. Even though the page is part of a web, you don't have to open the web itself first. Opening a page automatically opens the web it's in.

Opening Any Web Page

To open a web page, press CTRL+O (or click the thingie next to the Open button and choose Open—unless the last thing you opened was a web; you can also just click the Open button directly). This brings up the Open File dialog box (see Figure 4.9).

Choose a folder to look in and then double-click a web page's icon to open it. If you already have a web open, FrontPage will open the web you chose in a new window.

Opening a Page in an Open Web

If you simply want to open another page in a web that's already open, switch to Folder view or click the Folder List button in any other view, and then double-click the icon of the page you want to open.

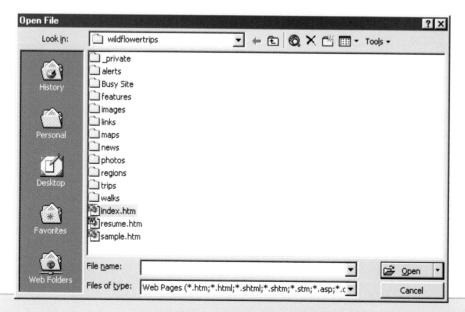

Figure 4.9: Look for and open web pages with the Open File dialog box.

Reopening a Recent Web Page

To reopen a web page you were working on recently, select File |
Recent Files | *the file name of the web page you wish to open.*

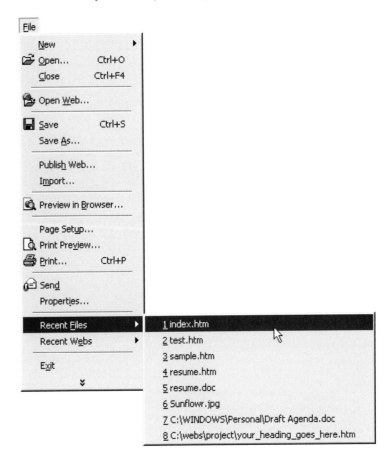

There's More . . .

You've now completed your FrontPage orientation. The next four
chapters will tell you how to create, edit, and design pages, how to add
graphics and other multimedia elements to your pages, how to link
the pages of your web together and make them navigable, and how to
make the most of other Office programs and documents in your web.

CHAPTER 5

Developing Content

INCLUDES

- Working with different types of pages
- Entering and editing text
- Formatting text
- Laying out pages with tables
- Working with shared borders
- Standardizing your web with style sheets
- Previewing your pages

Enter and Edit Text ➡ pp. 93–97

- Click the area you want to type in.
- Type the text, leaving only one space after each sentence.
- Press ENTER to start a new paragraph.
- Select text, and then cut (CRTL+X) or copy (CTRL+C), and paste (CTRL+V) to edit.
- Use Replace (CTRL+H) to make across-the-board changes.

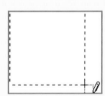

Format Text ➡ pp. 98–99

1. Select the text to which you wish to apply formatting.
2. Apply formatting (such as bold and italic) from the Format toolbar.
3. Choose headings and other styles from the Styles drop-down list on the Format toolbar.

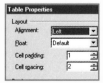

Draw a Table ➡ pp. 100–102

1. Choose Table | Draw Table.
2. Click where you want the upper-left corner of the table and drag to where you want the lower-right.
3. Draw in row and column dividers.

Edit and Format a Table ➡ pp. 102–103

- Select Table | Insert | Rows Or Columns *or* Cell.
- Select Table | Delete | Cells (or Rows Or Columns, depending on your selection).
- Select Table | Merge Cells.
- Select Table | Split Cells.
- Select Table | Properties | Table (or Cell).

Edit Shared Borders ➡ pp. 104–106

1. Click in the border area.
2. Select the text you want to replace.
3. Type and format your own content.

Modify Existing Styles → pp. 107–113

1. Make sure CSS is available on the Compatibility tab of the Page Options dialog box (Tools | Page Options).
2. Select Format | Style to open the Style dialog box.
3. Choose All HTML Tags, select the style you want to change (for Normal, choose P), and click the Modify button.
4. Click the Format button | Font *or* Paragraph.
5. Select the formatting you want to apply, click OK, and repeat step 4 if necessary.
6. Click OK.

Make New Styles → pp. 114–115

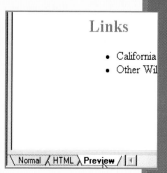

1. Select Format | Style, and click the New button.
2. Type a name for your new style.
3. Click the Format button | Font *or* Paragraph.
4. Select the formatting you want to apply, click OK, and repeat step 4 if necessary.
5. Click OK.

Preview Your Page → pp. 122–124

- Click the Preview tab to preview in FrontPage.
- Select File | Preview In Browser, select a browser, and click OK to preview the page in a real web browser. (Click OK to save the page if asked.)

The hands-on work involved in building a web is the creation, editing, and formatting of the individual pages in that web. A page can contain text, graphics, and other media. In this chapter I'll tell you how to type, edit, and format the text contents of a page (we'll discuss graphics and other page embellishments in Chapter 6).

I'll also explain techniques for designing and laying out a web page, such as using a table as a design grid, developing style sheets to formalize a design, and how to make best use of shared borders. The last thing I'll cover in this chapter is how to preview a page in FrontPage or a web browser.

What Type of Page?

Regardless of the type of page you're working on, the techniques you'll use to enter, edit, format, and position text are essentially the same. Nevertheless, you should still take some time to clarify the different types of pages you'll be using in your web before you plunge in. The web's home page, for example, is unique. You won't need any other pages at the site to look just like the first one. To use mixed, insectoid metaphor, it's the "queen," the oversized cornerstone from which the rest of the hive (or web, to use the more usual arachnid metaphor) springs.

Most of the other pages at your site will be the workers or drones. Designwise, they're interchangeable. Once you have a design you like,

---

EXPERT ADVICE

Webs that are so complicated as to require subwebs (see Chapter 10) may have special needs, such as multiple home pages, one for each subweb.

you can replicate it endlessly for each new specific page. Finally, there will be some pages with special functions, like soldier ants—catalog pages, or form-pages for taking orders or comments, and so on. These special categories of pages may have particular layout requirements, but their designs will still be replicable, within their own category.

Working with Text

There's an aspect of creating web pages that's just like word-processing (except with emphasis more on web-publishing than on printing as an end result). You still have to type and edit text, and then format the text and lay it out in a presentable manner. Microsoft has deliberately evolved FrontPage to work more and more like Word (and other Office programs), so if you are already familiar with Word, or really any what-you-see-is-what-you-get word processors, then you'll find FrontPage easy to get the hang of. Trust your intuition. One thing you can say for Microsoft; they put a lot of effort into making sure their software works the way users expect it to.

We'll start with these word-processing type tasks: entering, editing, and formatting text.

Entering Text

You have probably typed before, so there most likely won't be any surprises here for you. First, make sure the insertion point is in the correct part of the page (for example, on a page with shared borders, the unique content of the page goes in the middle area).

As with a word processor, don't press ENTER when you get near the end of a line (as you would with a typewriter). Don't try to line up or format text as you type it. Save that for later. One other difference from old typewriter-based touch-typing is that you don't add two spaces after the end of a sentence.

Figure 5.1 shows some sample text I typed to get started on the home page of the WildflowerTrips site.

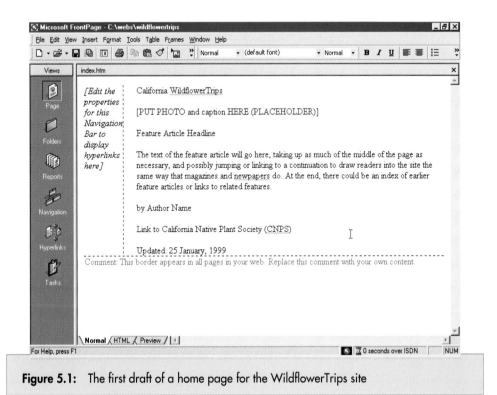

Figure 5.1: The first draft of a home page for the WildflowerTrips site

Making Corrections and Changes

It's natural to make some mistakes while entering text. Typos and other lapses are especially common. Fortunately, it's easy to correct mistakes (one of the good things about computers), and FrontPage even helps by proofreading for spelling errors.

Proofreading as You Go

In Chapter 2, I showed you how to turn off background spell and grammar checking when you don't want to deal with it.

FrontPage notices words it doesn't have in its dictionary and marks them with a squiggly red line. When you notice FrontPage calling your attention to a suspect word with its squiggly underline, either edit (or retype) the word yourself manually or right-click on the word. This will cause a menu to pop up, offering suggested spellings, along with the options to ignore the unusually spelled word or add it to the dictionary. Choose the correct spelling.

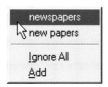

For a proper noun, or commercial trademark, such as WildflowerTrips, choose Add so that you won't have to explain the word to FrontPage again.

The same goes for acronyms, such as CNPS.

Undoing Big Mistakes

FrontPage keeps track of the state of your document as you work on it and can restore your work to a previous state (most of the time). If you realize you've done something you really want to undo, just click on the Undo button on the Standard toolbar:

SHORTCUT
You can always press CTRL-Z to undo your last action without having to take your hands away from the keyboard.

To undo several actions at once, click the thingie to the right of the Undo button, and then choose the series of actions you want to undo from the menu that pops down.

Editing Text

If you catch a mistake immediately after typing it, the easiest way to correct it is to press the Backspace key. The Backspace key erases the character to the left of the insertion point.

If you notice a mistake later, you can either move the insertion point to the right of the error and press BACKSPACE, or move the insertion point to the left of the error and press DELETE. DELETE erases the character to the right of the insertion point.

To erase an entire word at once, you can hold down CTRL as you press the Backspace key or as you press DELETE. Here's a rundown of when to use Backspace and when to use DELETE:

To Erase	Press
A character to the left of the insertion point	BACKSPACE
A character to the right of the insertion point	DELETE
A word (or portion of a word) to the left of the insertion point	CTRL+BACKSPACE
A word (or portion of a word) to the right of the insertion point	CTRL+DELETE

If you're working with a predesigned page or a new page from a predesigned web, then you'll probably be replacing the dummy text with your own real content. Select the text you want to replace and simply type over it.

Welcome to [CompanyName] The p
support services we provide to our ʒ
resources here to help you resolve p
improvements to our products and s

You may also obtain technical suppɔ
and by e-mail to [CompanyEmail].

Welcome to Blueline Repro The p
support services we provide to ou
resources here to help you resolve
improvements to our products anɔ

You may also obtain technical sup
and by e-mail to [CompanyEmail]

Cutting, Copying, and Pasting

As with Word, and most other Windows programs, you can use Cut, Copy, and Paste to move selections around in FrontPage:

- Cut a selection with CTRL+X to remove it for later pasting.
- Copy a selection with CTRL+C to leave the original in place.
- Paste a cut or copied selection with CTRL+V.

EXPERT ADVICE

Searching and replacing throughout your entire web (with All Pages) can be a lifesaver when last-minute changes come down "from on high."

Finding and Replacing All at Once

If you discover you've been misspelling a word throughout your web page (or throughout your entire web), or if you change the name of a product or service, or if you want to make a systematic change throughout the page for any reason, press CTRL+H or select File | Replace to bring up the Replace dialog box (see Figure 5.2).

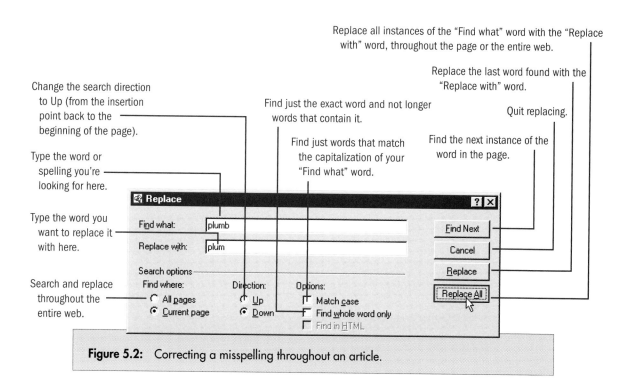

Replace all instances of the "Find what" word with the "Replace with" word, throughout the page or the entire web.

Replace the last word found with the "Replace with" word.

Change the search direction to Up (from the insertion point back to the beginning of the page).

Find just the exact word and not longer words that contain it.

Quit replacing.

Type the word or spelling you're looking for here.

Find just words that match the capitalization of your "Find what" word.

Find the next instance of the word in the page.

Type the word you want to replace it with here.

Search and replace throughout the entire web.

Figure 5.2: Correcting a misspelling throughout an article.

Formatting Text

The basic hand-motions involved in formatting text are simple. Generally, you select the text you want to affect and then click a button or choose an option from a dialog box to apply some kind of formatting to the selection. The trickier aspect of formatting is understanding the different levels of it. Some kinds of formatting appear only occasionally, such as italics to emphasize a word or phrase. Others apply to a category of content, whether pre-existing in HTML (the formatting language web documents are coded with), such as paragraphs, headings, lists, captions, addresses, and so on, or invented by you for your own purposes, such as by-lines, blurbs, reviews, addresses, pull quotes, or really anything you care to name.

Formatting by Hand

You may want to drag the Formatting toolbar so that all of its buttons become visible.

Select text by clicking and dragging your mouse pointer or by double-clicking to select a word. Then use the Formatting toolbar for most common types of formatting:

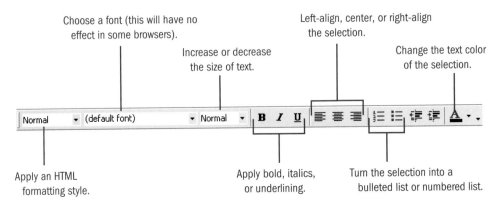

Choose a font (this will have no effect in some browsers).

Increase or decrease the size of text.

Left-align, center, or right-align the selection.

Change the text color of the selection.

Apply an HTML formatting style.

Apply bold, italics, or underlining.

Turn the selection into a bulleted list or numbered list.

Text size on the web, for example can be hard on some folks' eyes, so one design approach is to put long swatches of text in a larger than ordinary font size, such as 14 point.

Applying a Style

To apply a standard HTML formatting style to a selection, choose it from the Style drop-down list box in the Formatting toolbar (see Figure 5.3).

To change the formatting of an existing style or create a new style element, see "Global Formatting with Style sheets," later in this chapter.

For now, the site doesn't have a logo, so I've formatted the banner text as Heading 1, added italics, reduced the size of the introductory word, and inserted a line break (SHIFT+ENTER) to stack the words.

I upped the size of the running text to 4 (14 pt) to make it easier on the eyes.

I'm applying the Heading 2 style to the headline of the feature article (actually just an existing article by my partner, pasted in to aid the design process).

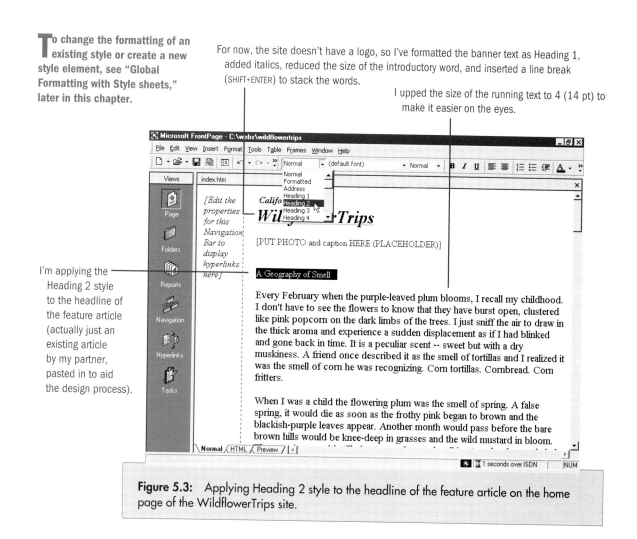

Figure 5.3: Applying Heading 2 style to the headline of the feature article on the home page of the WildflowerTrips site.

To copy formatting from one area of your page to another, select the text with the formatting you want to copy, click the Format Painter button on the Standard toolbar, and then (scroll to, if necessary, and) click and drag across the text to which you want to apply the formatting.

Removing Formatting

To remove character formatting, such as bold and italics, select the text you want to "unformat," and then press CTRL+SPACEBAR. To remove an HTML style from text, select it and then choose the Normal style in the Style drop-down list in the Formatting toolbar.

Laying Out Pages with Tables

Web designers use tables much more often as page-layout grids than for the display of tabular material (such as a bus schedule), although you work with tables the same way regardless of how you intend to use them.

If you're familiar with Word's table-making tools, then you'll recognize FrontPage's technology as the same.

EXPERT ADVICE

If you're using a table to display tabular material, then you'll probably want to have visible borders between table rows and columns, or you might want to use background color to distinguish sections of a table. If you're using a table as a layout aid, you'll want to have invisible borders.

Drawing a Table

To make a simple table of two or more columns and any number of rows, click the Insert Table button and drag down and to the right until the grid that appears matches the number of rows and columns you want (you'll always be able to change these things later).

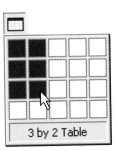

3 by 2 Table

Changing the Structure of a Table

To modify a table or draw a new one with a number of rows, columns, and cells wherever you like, select Table | Draw Table to bring up the Tables toolbar (see Figure 5.4).

With the Draw Table button "pushed in" you can draw gridlines to separate rows or columns or to split cells.

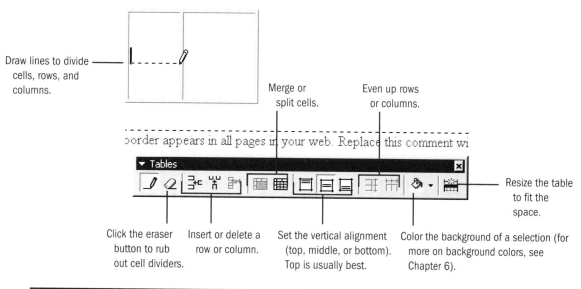

Draw lines to divide cells, rows, and columns.

Merge or split cells.

Even up rows or columns.

Resize the table to fit the space.

Click the eraser button to rub out cell dividers.

Insert or delete a row or column.

Set the vertical alignment (top, middle, or bottom). Top is usually best.

Color the background of a selection (for more on background colors, see Chapter 6).

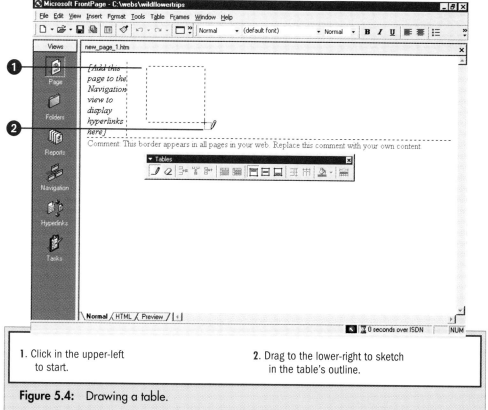

1. Click in the upper-left to start.

2. Drag to the lower-right to sketch in the table's outline.

Figure 5.4: Drawing a table.

To change the relative height or width of columns or rows, simply click and drag the dividers. (You can do this whether or not the table-drawing feature is on).

When you are done, click the Draw Table button on the Tables toolbar to turn off the table-drawing tool, and then close the toolbar or push it out of the way.

EXPERT ADVICE

You can also insert or delete cells or even tables within tables with the Table | Insert menu.

Filling in Content

To enter content into a table, click in the cell you want to fill in, and then type as you would normally. Press TAB to jump to the next cell. If you are designing a page with tables, then you may need to cut (CTRL+X) existing content and paste (CTRL+V) it into a cell in your table.

Formatting Your Table

You format the contents of a table the same way you do ordinary text. That is, you make selections (you can click and drag to select a swath of cells or entire rows or columns), and then click buttons on the Formatting toolbar or apply styles from the Style list box.

If you want to control the exact dimensions and features of your table, select Table | Properties | Table to bring up the Table Properties dialog box (see Figure 5.5).

To control the exact dimensions or other aspects of a cell, a selection of cells, a row, or a column, first make the selection, and then choose Table | Properties | Cell (see Figure 5.6).

To make the column widths or row heights even, click the Distribute Rows Evenly or Distribute Columns Evenly button on the Tables toolbar.

To let FrontPage adjust the column widths to best fit the table's content, click the AutoFit button on the Tables toolbar.

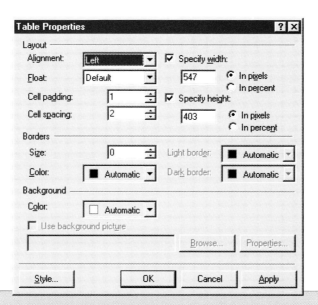

Figure 5.5: It's easier to smoodge the table rows and columns around by clicking and dragging, but if all else fails, you can confront this control panel.

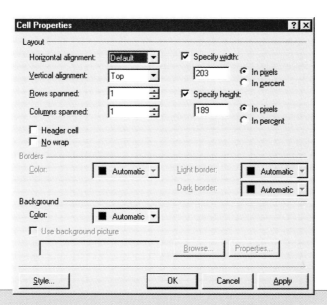

Figure 5.6: Cell properties are similar to table properties in devilishly fascinating (no, wait, I meant hopelessly boring) ways.

Repeating Elements in Shared Borders

See Chapter 7 for how to insert page banners and navigation bars into shared borders.

In Chapter 3, I showed you how to turn on shared borders. At the time, I promised that in Chapter 5 I'd show you how to replace the comments and dummy text in the borders with your own content that will show up on each page that shares the borders. By now, you could probably figure it out for yourself. Figure 5.7 shows the bottom of the WildflowerTrips home page, with a little bit of formatting.

First, click in the shared border area to select it. The text within it will also be selected.

I used the Address style to put this byline in italics.

I put this line in with Insert | Horizontal Line.

This is a Heading 2.

You need to select this comment, and then replace it (or, in predesigned pages, select and replace the sample dummy text).

These items are in a bulleted list.

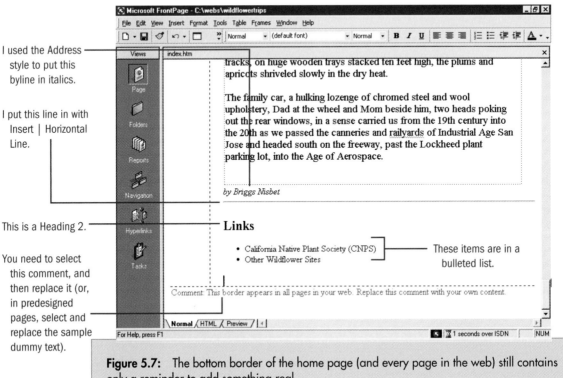

Figure 5.7: The bottom border of the home page (and every page in the web) still contains only a reminder to add something real.

Then just start typing. Press CTRL+ENTER to start a new line without starting a new paragraph. To insert symbols such as the copyright symbol, select Insert | Symbol, choose the symbol, click Insert (see Figure 5.8), and then click Close.

Some people like to inform their web visitors when the page was last updated. FrontPage can stamp a date into your page and then change it automatically the next time you update the page. To insert a date this way, select Insert | Date and Time. This brings up the Date and Time Properties Dialog box.

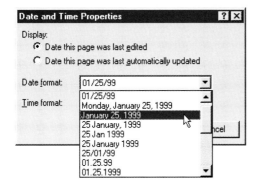

Choose the date format you prefer and then click OK. When you're done entering text in the border area, you can edit it if necessary and format it the usual way. For the WildflowerTrips web, I've tentatively decided to make the trademark and last-updated

Figure 5.8: Copyright law might be confusing, but it never hurts to put that little C-in-a-circle symbol on your work.

statements bold and smaller than ordinary Normal text, and I'm right-aligning them as well as the copyright notice.

Borders shared by the pages in your web can be changed at any time. Consulting our original mockup of the home page, I realized that the links to sections will have to wait for me to set up a navigation bar (see Chapter 7), but that the links to state regions were supposed to run down the left margin. I'll reverse them, and since FrontPage doesn't permit a navigation bar in the right margin, select Format | Shared Borders to turn on the right-side border as well. This brings up the Shared Borders dialog box. Click Right (or any unchecked border) to add it, or click a checked border to uncheck and remove it from the web.

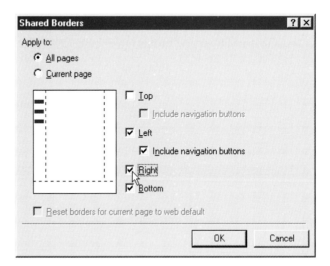

When you are done, click OK. For now, I'll just put a little table in that right border with some placeholders for the state-regional buttons I'd like to have there eventually.

Global Formatting with Style Sheets

Just as shared borders provide a way for you to create standard page elements and have them repeat throughout your web, style sheets (also known as cascading style sheets or CSS) permit you to create your own styles for use in a single page or throughout your entire web. In this section, I'll first explain how you change existing HTML styles or create new styles in an embedded style sheet within a single page. In the second half of this section, I'll show you how to create your new styles in a separate style sheet file, making them available to all the pages on your web.

   If you wish to create such a stand-alone style sheet, be sure to read through the sections before "Making a Style for Your Whole Web" (later in this chapter) because you'll need to understand the same techniques either way.

   CSS was not implemented in Netscape or Internet Explorer until they each released their version 4, and even then there are differences of interpretation, so consult the Compatibility tab of the Page Options dialog box, as discussed in Chapter 2, if you want to enable or disable CSS.

Changing an Existing Style

FrontPage displays the standard HTML formatting styles the way most web browsers do to give you some idea of how your page will look, but you can change the font, size, color, spacing, indentation, and so on of any style element just as easily as you can format specific text. The difference is that changing the formatting of a style changes the results everywhere that style has been (or will be) applied. It also makes it easier later to change your mind and reinvent the display of a style. Change again and all the text formatted as that style changes to reflect your new choices.

   To change an existing style, select Format | Style. This brings up the Style dialog box. Choose All HTML tags in the List drop-down box, if they aren't selected already. You may need to scroll down through the Style list to find the HTML code for the style you want to change (see Figure 5.9).

World Wide Web Consortium (W3C) specifications on cascading style sheets are at *www.htmlhelp.com/reference/css/*.

DEFINITION

CSS (Cascading Style Sheets): A Web-standard coding format for describing how various web elements should be displayed. FrontPage combines the style and style sheet terminology and tools of Word with the Web's CSS standard to automate the creation of style sheets.

Cascading: Style sheets are called cascading because you can apply multiple style sheets to the same page, and the various style definitions will be combined for the page in question, with more "local" styles superseding in cases of conflicts.

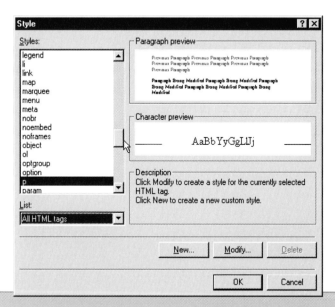

Figure 5.9:   You'll notice there are many more styles listed here than in the Style drop-down list box. FrontPage was trying to shelter you from the ever-more complex reality of HTML, but you just wouldn't stop prying, would you?

When you find the style you want, select it and click the Modify button. This brings up the Modify Style dialog box. Click the Format button, and choose Font (see Figure 5.10).

This brings up the Font dialog box (see Figure 5.11).

In the Font dialog box, you can

- Choose a preferred typeface in the Font list box if you want. Browsers will use that font if they find it available on the viewer's system.
- Apply italics or bold or both in the Font-style list.
- Enter or choose a font size in the Size list box.

EXPERT ADVICE

There is a much longer list of syles shown here than in the Style list box; also it's HTML, which you've avoided so far. The main things you'll be working with at first are headings, which are h1 through h6, and normal paragraphs, indicated by p.

If you want to have more than one type of paragraph, you can add a period and a name for this type of paragraph (such as p.first or p.indented).

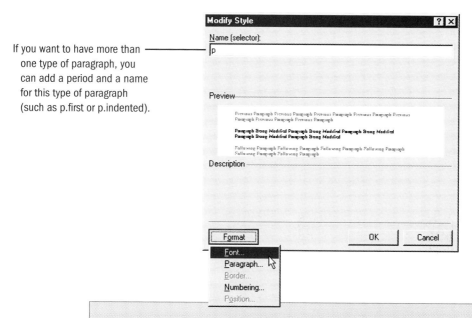

Figure 5.10:   Click the Format button and choose an aspect of the style to format, to keep slogging through these many dialog boxes.

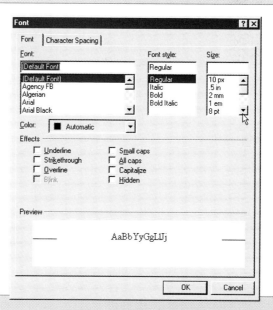

Figure 5.11:   Choose a preferred font, add italics or bold to a style, choose a font size (in a variety of possible units), add a color, or add the other usual Word-style character formatting (not all of which will appear in most browsers).

- ˙Add one of the other Word-style text effects.
- Change character spacing, if you really care about that kind of thing.

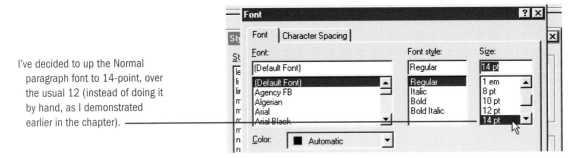

I've decided to up the Normal paragraph font to 14-point, over the usual 12 (instead of doing it by hand, as I demonstrated earlier in the chapter). ————

When you're done in this dialog box, click OK. This returns you to the Style dialog box, where you'll see the choices you've made, now listed as part of the style's description. Click the Format button and choose Paragraph this time.

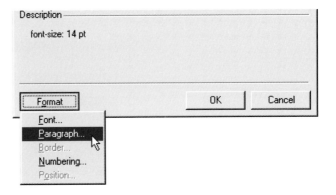

This brings up the Paragraph dialog box (see Figure 5.12). In the Paragraph dialog box you can

- Set the alignment for a style.
- Indent the left side, right side, or first line of text formatted with the style.
- Change the spacing before or after a paragraph.
- Change the word spacing.
- Change the line spacing.

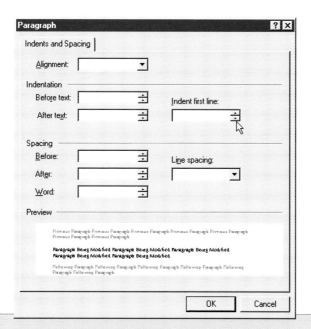

Figure 5.12: If you're tired of all the paragraphs on the web having spacing before and after and no indentation, you can change all that and more (such as alignment, and word and line spacing) right here.

When you're satisfied, click OK. Then click OK again to save the changes to the style. Text already formatted with the original style will change to reflect the new formatting. You can also apply the style the way you normally would, from the Style list in the Formatting toolbar.

I've changed the Normal (p) style on the WildflowerTrips home page to 14 pt. text with indented (24 units) paragraphs (see Figure 5.13).

When I look at the page now, though I like the paragraph indentation, it somehow doesn't look right on the first paragraph, so I'll make a special version of the Normal style, just for the first paragraph of a feature.

EXPERT ADVICE

If you change a paragraph style and it doesn't seem to affect the first paragraph of text inside a table cell, select the first paragraph and apply the Normal paragraph style to it in the Formatting toolbar.

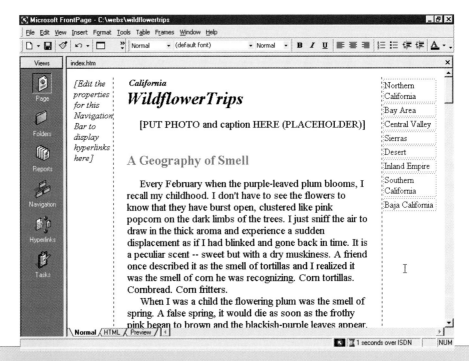

Figure 5.13: With the headline set to that woodsy green and the font size a little larger, this home page is starting to look a little more presentable. Still, maybe the first line of the feature article *shouldn't* be indented.

To make a variation of a style, select Format | Style. In the Style dialog box, choose All HTML Tags to make a variation on a style you haven't modified yet or User-defined Styles to make a variation on a custom style. Then choose a style and click the Modify button. Since I've already modified the Normal style, I'll choose User-defined Styles, select the p style, and click Modify (see Figure 5.14).

This brings up the Modify Style dialog box. Type a dot (.) and then a name onto the end of existing style code (turning p into p.first or h1 into h1.red, for example).

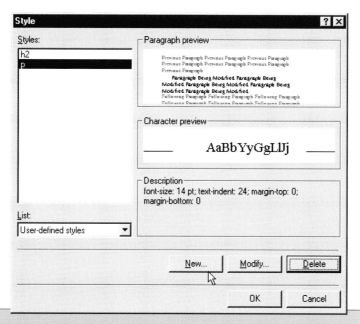

Figure 5.14: Choose the existing custom *p* (Normal) style as a basis for an unindented first-paragraph style.

Then click the Format button and choose Font or Paragraph. To remove the indentation, I'll choose Format | Paragraph, change the indentation back from 24 to 0, click OK, and click OK again.

To apply the new variation of the Normal style, I'll select the first paragraph and then choose Normal.first in the Style list, giving the first paragraph no indentation and leaving the other (Normal) paragraph alone:

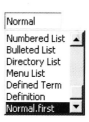

A Geography of Smell

Every February when the purple-leaved plum blooms, I recall my childhood. I don't have to see the flowers to know that they have burst open, clustered like pink popcorn on the dark limbs of the trees. I just sniff the air to draw in the thick aroma and experience a sudden displacement as if I had blinked and gone back in time. It is a peculiar scent -- sweet but with a dry muskiness. A friend once described it as the smell of tortillas and I realized it was the smell of corn he was recognizing. Corn tortillas. Cornbread. Corn fritters.

When I was a child the flowering plum was the smell of

Making a New Style

You can create your own style from scratch. The technique is much the same as with modifying an existing style or making different variations. You still start with Format | Style, but you then click the New button instead of the modify button. This brings up the New Style dialog box (which looks exactly like the Style dialog box but has nothing in the Name (selector) box). Type a name for your new style there. I'll create one for the author's byline, so I don't have to "borrow" the standard HTML address style, which is really for contact information.

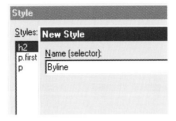

You choose Font and Paragraph formatting the same as with modified styles, as explained in the previous section. I'll make the byline 14 point, with italics. When you have chosen the formatting you want, click OK. FrontPage automatically appends a period before the name of user-defined styles, and lists them at the bottom of the Style list in the Formatting toolbar. Figure 5.15 shows me applying the new .Byline style to the selected byline.

Ordinary HTML styles and custom styles can coexist in one selection, with the custom style superseding when there is a conflict. If you point to a selection formatted with both an HTML style and a custom style, the Style list will display a hybrid, in the form of the HTML style code followed by the *.name* of the custom style (such as Normal.byline). You can't select this item in the Style list, but you can remove the custom style by selecting another choice in the list.

EXPERT ADVICE

For a page with an external style sheet, any styles described in an embedded style sheet will combine with (if possible) or supersede (if there's a conflict) equivalent styles in the external style sheet.

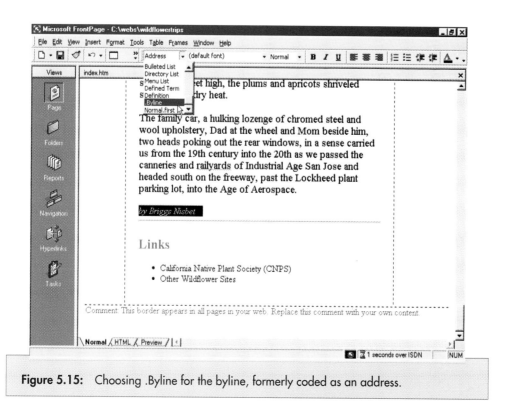

Figure 5.15: Choosing .Byline for the byline, formerly coded as an address.

Removing a Custom Style from a Page

You can easily remove any custom style from a page:

1. Select Format | Style.

2. Choose User-defined Styles.

3. Select the style you want to delete.

4. Click the Delete button.

5. Click OK.

You can't remove the standard HTML styles!

Making a Style for Your Whole Web

FrontPage's predesigned web templates and wizard (discussed in Chapter 3) all make use of external stylesheets to enforce consistent formatting throughout the web. This consistency of design is one of the things that distinguishes professional or "serious" web sites from haphazard "here is my cat" yearbook pages. You can achieve that same level of consistency by creating your own external style sheets.

You can start using an external style sheet with three easy steps:

1. Create an external style sheet.
2. Add styles to it (you already know how to do that).
3. Link one or more pages to the new style sheet.

Create an External Style Sheet

Creating a new style sheet starts much like creating any new FrontPage web page:

1. Select File | New | Page.
2. Click the Style Sheets tab in the New dialog box (see Figure 5.16).
3. Choose Normal Style Sheet to start with a blank.
4. Click OK.

This opens up a blank style sheet (see Figure 5.17).

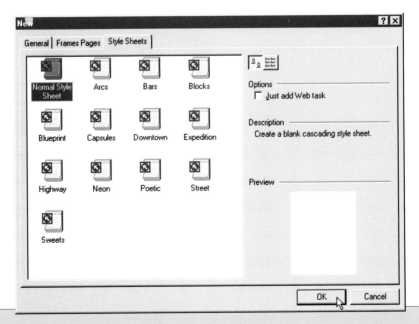

Figure 5.16: Unless you want to start with a predesigned style sheet and modify it, click Normal Style Sheet and then click OK.

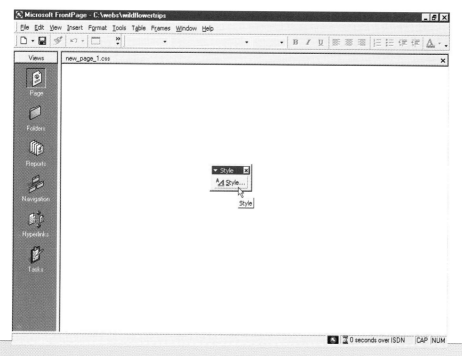

Figure 5.17:   Not much to look at, an external stylesheet can save you lots of re-formatting down the road.

Add Styles to a Style Sheet

To start adding styles to your new style sheet, click the Style button. This brings up the Style dialog box. Follow the same steps explained in the earlier part of this section to select Font and Paragraph formatting. When you are done customizing styles (for now), click OK in the Style dialog box. FrontPage will convert your instructions into CSS code and insert it into the style sheet.

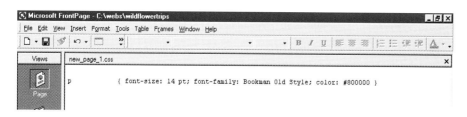

When you're done adding styles to your stylesheet, click the Save button on the Standard toolbar (or press CTRL+S), which brings up the Save As dialog box with the HyperText Style Sheet (*.css) file type already selected. Type a name for your style sheet and click Save (see Figure 5.18).

Later, if you want to revise the style sheet further, you can find it in the web's folder list (see Figure 5.19).

Just double-click the CSS file to open it, and click the Style button again to continue working with the styles in the style sheet.

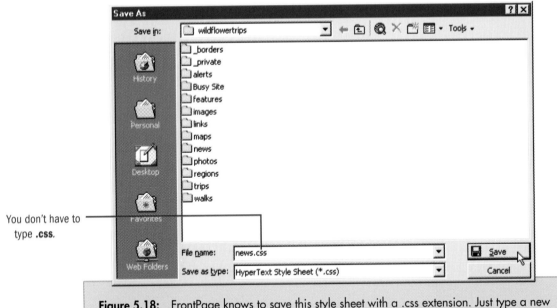

Figure 5.18:   FrontPage knows to save this style sheet with a .css extension. Just type a new name, and click the Save button (style sheets don't get titles).

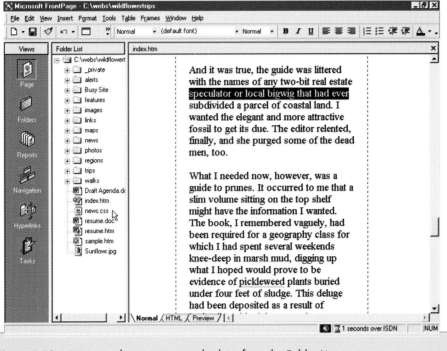

Figure 5.19: You can always open a style sheet from the Folder List.

Link a Page to a Style Sheet

You can make the styles in an external style sheet available to one or more pages in the Web. In CSS parlance, this is called linking the page or pages to the style sheet. (This is an unfortunate choice of terms, since link already has a much more common meaning in the world of web pages; namely, the hypertext links folks use to get around web sites.)

EXPERT ADVICE

To link multiple pages at once, select them in the Folder List first.

Select Format | Style Sheet Links. This brings up the Link Style Sheet dialog box.

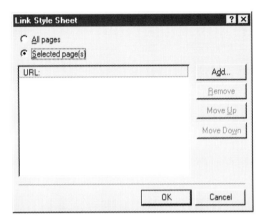

To link just the open pages or the pages selected in the Folder List, make sure Selected Page(s) is selected. To link all the pages in the web to the style sheet, click All Pages. If the file name of the style sheet is not listed in the URL list, click the Add button. This brings up the Select Hyperlink dialog box.

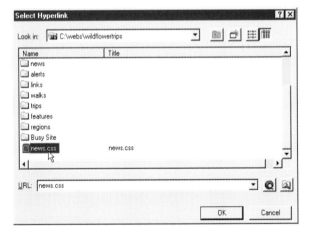

Double-click the icon of the style sheet you want to add to the URL list. Then click OK in the Link Style Sheet dialog box. Now that the page is linked, all the styles in the external stylesheet are available, and any new styles or modifications you invent will be stored with the external stylesheet.

Editing HTML Directly

Like any good web page editor, FrontPage gives you direct access to the HTML if you want it. Most people are relieved to be excused from learning HTML, so I would not judge you for showing no interest in this. Others learned how to make web pages with HTML and would find it frustrating if FrontPage did not permit this kind of tinkering under the hood.

You can see (and edit) the HTML underlying any open page just by clicking the HTML tab at the bottom of the FrontPage window. Sometimes, when you can't figure out where you went wrong applying formatting, the HTML view might make it easier for you to disentangle misapplied codes. Figure 5.20 shows the WildflowerTrips home page in homely HTML.

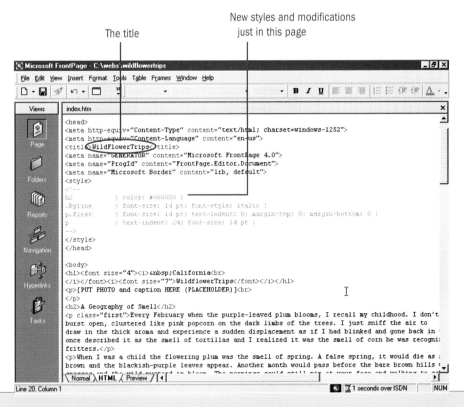

Figure 5.20: Why you'd want to mess with this stuff at this stage, I don't know.

You can search and replace in here just as you would in the normal view of the page. Speaking of which, to return to the Normal view, just click the Normal tab at the bottom of the window.

Previewing Your Work

There are two ways to preview your page. Why would you want to do this at all? Isn't FrontPage already showing you how things will look? Well, yes and no. FrontPage is designed to help you create, edit, and do page layout (among other things), so it errs on the side of placing visible grids on the screen so you can see what you're doing. Also, the View bar and other interface elements take up a significant amount of the FrontPage window.

The first way to preview your page keeps you within FrontPage, so the window proportions won't be just right, but it's quick. The second way to preview your page literally opens a real web browser with the height and width you choose, so it takes a little longer, but it's more accurate.

Quick and Dirty

The quick way to preview your page (it's actually not that dirty), is to click the Preview tab at the bottom of the window (see Figure 5.21). Click back to Normal view when you are ready to continue working on your page.

In Your Browser

To preview your page in any of the web browsers available on your system, select File | Preview In Browser. This brings up the Preview In Browser dialog box.

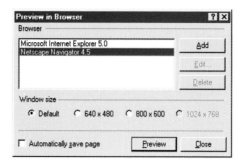

1. Choose the browser you want to preview with (or click Add and browse your computer or network to add additional browsers to the list).

2. Choose the proportions of the browser window (for example, many people still view the Web with a 640 × 480 screen resolution, so you can preview how it looks for them, even if you are working at a higher resolution).

3. Check Automatically Save Page.

4. Click Preview.

Figure 5.22 shows the WildflowerTrips home page in Netscape Navigator, in a 640 × 480 window.

If you don't check Automatically Save Page, FrontPage will still automatically prompt you to save the page (just click OK).

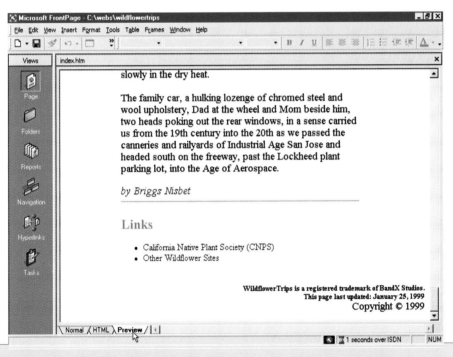

Figure 5.21:   Click the Preview tab for a decent idea of how the page will look (you might want to hide or minimize the View bar too).

Figure 5.22: Here's the page as it currently stands in a 640 × 480 Netscape window (OK, I upped the "trademark" text at the last minute—a good thing about FrontPage is you can always keep tweaking your page; it's also a bad thing).

There's More . . .

You've now completed your FrontPage orientation. The next four chapters will tell you how to create, edit, and design pages, how to add graphics and other multimedia elements to your pages, how to link the pages of your web together and make them navigable, and how to make the most of other Office programs and documents in your web.

CHAPTER 6

Graphics and Multimedia

INCLUDES

- Adding pictures to a page
- Working with photographs
- Cropping and resizing pictures
- Positioning a picture
- Choosing a color scheme for your web
- Adding a predesigned theme to your web
- Adding other media (sound and video, mostly)

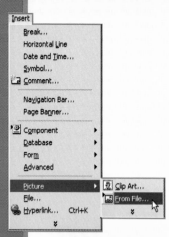

Insert a Picture ➥ p. 129

1. Place the insertion point where you want the picture to appear.
2. Select Insert | Picture | From File.
3. Open the folder in your web containing the picture, or look on your computer or on the Web for the picture.
4. Double-click the picture's icon.

Crop a Picture ➥ pp. 137–138

1. Click once on the picture to select it.
2. Click the Crop button on the Picture toolbar.
3. Define the border between the area of the picture you want to preserve and the part you want to crop away by clicking in the upper-left corner of that area and dragging to the bottom-right.
4. Click the Crop button again.

Resize and Resample a Picture ➥ pp. 138–140

1. Click the bottom-right corner of the picture and drag it toward the upper-left to reduce the size of the picture or away from the upper-left to increase it.
2. If you made the picture smaller, click the Resample button to reduce the picture's file size.

Convert a Picture to GIF, JPEG, or PNG Format ➥ pp. 146–147

1. Right-click on the picture and choose Picture Properties from the menu that pops up.
2. On the General tab, choose the file format to which you'd like to convert the file.
3. Click OK.

Change the Color Scheme of a Page ➥ pp. 151–152

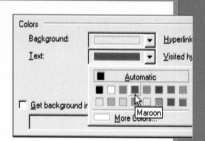

1. Select File | Properties.
2. Click the Background tab.
3. Choose a background color.
4. Choose a text color.
5. Choose a color for Hyperlinks, Visited (used) Hyperlinks, and Active (while they're being clicked) Hyperlinks. (See Chapter 7 for more on links.)

Apply a Theme to Your Page or Web ➥ pp. 152–153

1. Select Format | Theme.
2. Choose All Pages to apply the theme to your entire web or Selected Page(s) to apply it to the current page or to all pages selected in the folder list.
3. Click Themes in the list box to preview them in the Sample Of Theme box.
4. When you find a theme you like, click OK.

Insert a Sound Clip or Video Clip ➥ pp. 154–155

1. Select Insert | Picture | Clip Art (or Insert | Picture | Video).
2. In the Clip Art dialog box, choose the Sounds or Motion Clips tab.
3. To add clips to the gallery from your computer or from the Net, click the Import Clips or Clips Online button.
4. Double-click a clip to insert it.

Part of what makes the Web so appealing is that it permits the combination of text and graphics, lending it more of the feel of a glossy magazine than, say, a gray newspaper page. There's no obligation to include artwork or graphics on your pages, but they liven up the web, invite readers in, and help you develop truly pleasing designs. Even if you can't draw at all and won't be involved in the creation of graphic images for your web, you can still learn how to insert pictures onto pages, position, crop, and edit them. FrontPage makes it easy.

Web Picture Formats: GIF, JPEG, and PNG

Before we delve into the nitty-gritty of "how to do it," let me take a moment to tell you how images are displayed on the Web and what formats are permitted. (Skip the next section if you couldn't care less).

There are three standard image formats for the Web, all of which involve some form of compression: GIF, JPEG, and the newest format, PNG.

You can convert files to any of the web formats within FrontPage (I'll explain how to do that later in the chapter), or you can let FrontPage convert them automatically

DEFINITION

GIF: Graphics Interchange Format, a compression format all browsers can display for 256-color graphic images with areas of solid color, developed by CompuServe, the online service now owned by America Online. GIF is pronounced with a hard or soft g.

JPEG: Joint Photographic Experts Group (named for the Internet committee that developed the standard), a compression format all browsers can display for photographs and other graphic images with subtly blended color tones. Pronounced jaypeg.

PNG: Portable Network Graphic (but sometimes jokingly spelled out as "PNG's Not GIF"), a compression format not all browsers can display that combines the best features of GIF (such as interlacing, so that the image appears to load more quickly, and transparent background colors, so that graphics appear to float instead of looking rectangular) and JPEG (a compression formula that works well with continuous-tone images such as photos, and the ability to choose the level of compression as a trade-off with image quality). Explicitly developed for the Web; pronounced ping.

when you save your web page. FrontPage converts images with up to 256 colors to GIFs, and images with higher color to JPEGs.

Inserting Pictures into Your Web

Regardless of the type of image you're inserting, whether it's a photograph, a drawing, or a computer graphic, FrontPage calls it a picture, and the techniques for first inserting and then editing and tweaking the picture are the same.

To insert a picture, first place the insertion point where you want the picture to appear (at least roughly—you'll be able to move it later). Then select Insert | Picture. A submenu pops up.

To learn how to use graphics as hyperlinks in your web and how to insert recurring page banners, see Chapter 7. For pictures that appear on schedule, animated pictures that change when the mouse pointer hovers over them, and banner advertisements, see Chapter 8.

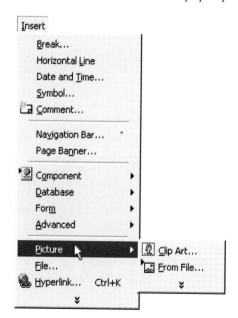

EXPERT ADVICE

You can also select a picture file in any Explorer window in Windows 98 and drag it directly into the FrontPage window to insert a picture directly into the open web page.

Inserting Clip Art

If you have no source of original art, FrontPage offers you some adequate quality commercial art organized into a number of categories (and Microsoft offers more to download from its Office web site). To see what's available, select Insert | Picture | Clip Art. The Clip Art Gallery window appears (see Figure 6.1). Click a category to see sample art of specific types. If you see a graphic you'd like to use, double-click it to insert it.

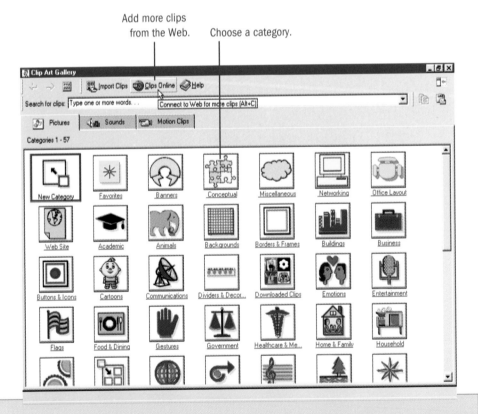

Figure 6.1:   Moderately cheesy clip art... cheap!

Inserting Original Artwork

If you're an artist, or if your site has a budget that covers graphic art, or if you need fairly simple graphic images, then you can insert your own custom art into your page. For the WildflowerTrips site, we wanted links to various California regions. The linking part will have to wait till Chapter 7, but I put together the images in a few hours one morning. I worked in Paintbrush, the simple paint program that comes with Windows 98. The trick with tiny little iconic art is to zoom in till the grid is 600 or 800% of its true size. It's a lot less frustrating that way!

I made a simple hand-drawn base map of California in drab colors and saved it, and then I colored in a different bright red area on each new copy of the original image to create my regional buttons. Figure 6.2

If your original artwork is on paper, then you can scan it, as explained in the next section, "Inserting a Photograph."

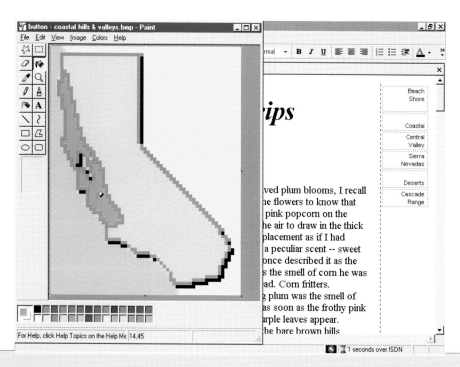

Figure 6.2: The Coastal Hills and Valleys region highlighted in a variation of my base map

shows the regional button for California's Coastal Hills and Valleys I made from the base map.

When you have your art files ready, you can either move them *en masse* to your Web (or to a subfolder or the images folder in your web, depending on whether you want to keep all the art in one place or organize it by category), or leave the originals where they are and permit FrontPage to copy them to your web when you save the page you're working on.

Then place the insertion point where you want the first image to appear and select Insert | Picture | From File. This brings up the Picture dialog box (see Figure 6.3).

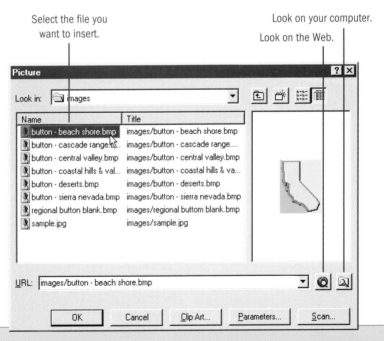

Figure 6.3: Select a picture to insert into your web page in the Picture dialog box.

Browse through the folders in your web in the Look In drop-down list box, or click the Search Your Computer button to look elsewhere on your computer or network for the picture you want to insert.

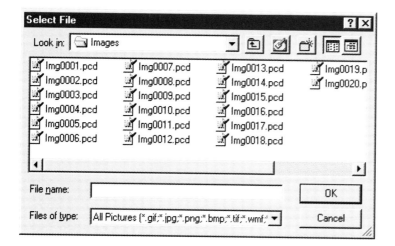

EXPERT ADVICE

If you want to select an image from the Web, enter its address in the URL box (you can click and scroll through the URL list box to choose from web addresses you've entered before), or click the Search the Web button, browse to the page or image you're looking for in your browser, and then return to FrontPage (the address you browsed to will appear in the URL box).

Figure 6.4 shows the regional buttons I inserted into the right-side shared border of the WildflowerTrips web.

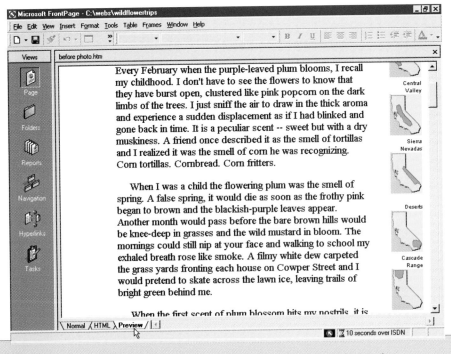

Figure 6.4: My graphics representing regions of California may not be utterly sophisticated, but they'll do the job.

Inserting a Photograph

Probably the best forum for discussions of photography and particularly how pictures are rendered on the Web is Phil Greenspun's Photo.net site (*http://www.photo.net/*). You can also preview his book chapter on this subject (at *http://www.photo.net/wtr/ thebook/images.html*).

To insert a photograph into a web page, you must first make an electronic version of it by scanning it. Photographic prints can be scanned adequately with an ordinary flat-bed scanner (and if you don't have one, most copy centers these days generally do), but you'll get the highest quality by starting with slides or negatives. Unfortunately, slide scanners are very expensive and you'll probably have to hire this work out. Kodak has a number of centers around the country for processing negatives into Photo CDs. (Photo CD is a format invented and promoted by Kodak.) There are also many independent service bureaus that can turn your slides into Photo CDs, often for no more than $2.50 or $3.00 a slide, depending on how many you have done. A Photo CD can hold 100 slides, and you don't have to fill it all up at once.

If you have your own scanner, you can now scan photos and other forms of artwork directly into FrontPage. To do so, click the Scan button on the Picture dialog box (Figure 6.3). The first time you do this, FrontPage will ask you to identify the type of scanner driver you have installed (usually TWAIN). Once you've done this, you can "acquire" (that is, scan) the image.

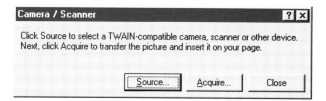

If you insert a large scanned source file, it may appear larger than you expected, overwhelming your page (see Figure 6.5)

Don't worry. You can wrestle the picture under control quite easily.

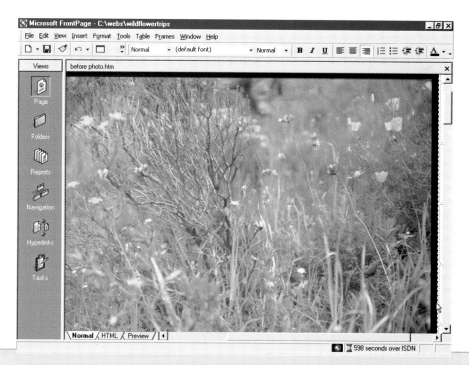

Figure 6.5: This is the highest resolution version of this image on the Photo CD. It hasn't erased the existing contents of the page—just pushed it off the screen.

Editing a Picture

Most of the things you'll want to do to your picture, you can do within FrontPage. To edit a picture, click it once to select it. This will make the Picture toolbar appear at the bottom of the FrontPage window.

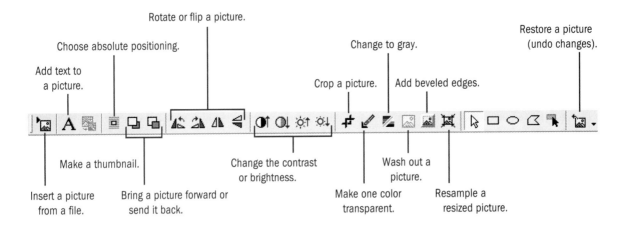

Cropping a Picture

One way to reduce a picture is to crop it. This means clipping out a subsection of the picture and discarding the rest. To crop a picture, first click on it once. On the Picture toolbar, click the Crop button. Then click and drag to describe the portion of the picture you'd like to preserve (see Figure 6.6).

If you don't get it right the first time, you can click and drag again until you are satisfied with the area you've described. Then click the Crop button again to execute the crop (see Figure 6.7).

Figure 6.6: Click in the upper-left corner of the area you want to keep, and drag to the lower-right.

Figure 6.7:   The cropped portion of the picture I inserted fits the page a little better.

Resizing a Picture

You can also reduce or increase the size of a picture without cropping any of it away. When you select a picture, you'll notice that handles appear on each corner and in the middle of each side. To change the size of a picture, just click on one of those handles and drag the picture larger or smaller (see Figure 6.8).

Resizing a picture does not change the file size of the original picture. You may feel that you are preserving disk space or bandwidth by reducing the size of your image, but unless you "resample" the picture, as explained in the following section, you won't save any space at all.

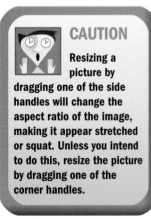

CAUTION

Resizing a picture by dragging one of the side handles will change the aspect ratio of the image, making it appear stretched or squat. Unless you intend to do this, resize the picture by dragging one of the corner handles.

Drag a corner handle to resize without changing the height-to-width proportion (aspect ratio).

Figure 6.8: Resize a picture by dragging one of the handles that appear when you click on it.

EXPERT ADVICE

To resize a picture to some precise height or width, right-click on it and choose Properties from the menu that pops up. Then click the Appearance tab of the Picture Properties dialog box, check Specify Size, and enter the height or width of the image in terms of pixels (dots on the screen) or as a percentage of the original size. You can also increase the horizontal or vertical spacing around a picture here if you find your text or other content running too close to the picture.

Resampling a Picture

You may notice the image changing as FrontPage reduces the resolution of the original image to match the number of pixels across the height and width.

If you've resized a picture smaller, FrontPage is merely displaying a reduced image of the still-large picture file. To obtain the benefits of displaying a smaller picture, you need to resample the picture, which will reduce the height and width of the original source image. To do this, just click the Resample button on the Picture button.

Orienting a Picture

Often, when you scan a picture, the scan is not oriented correctly at first. Photo CD scans, for instance, are oriented with the longer dimension as the width and the shorter as the height. For some images, this means they will appear at first on their sides (see Figure 6.9).

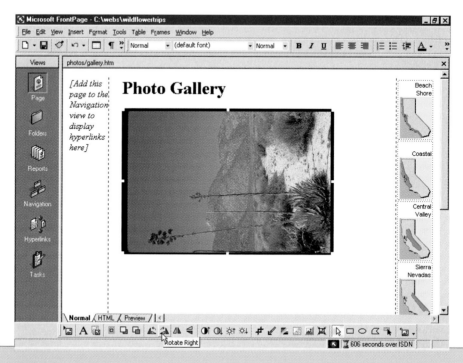

Figure 6.9: This picture of an agave plant in bloom in the Anza Borrego desert appears on its side when I first insert it.

Click the Rotate Right button to rotate the picture clockwise (see Figure 6.10) or click the Rotate Left button to rotate the picture counterclockwise. To rotate a picture 180 degrees, click either the Rotate Right or the Rotate Left button twice.

Similarly, slides being transparent, their scans sometimes come out flipped; that is, mirror images of the original scene. To reverse the orientation of a picture, click the Flip Horizontal or Flip Vertical button on the Picture toolbar.

Other Things You Can Do to a Picture Easily

Many of the other buttons on the Picture toolbar activate features that web publishers frequently need to fine tune their images. You can increase or decrease a picture's contrast or brightness (experiment all you want—you can undo a single change with Undo or restore a picture to its original state with the Restore Picture button at the right

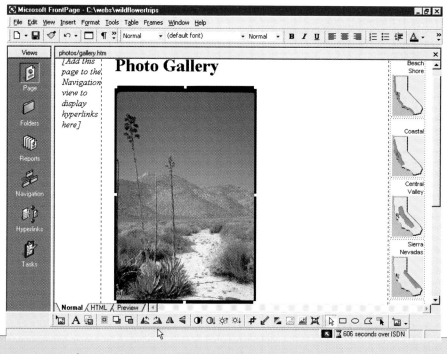

Figure 6.10: The same picture rotated to the right.

end of the Picture toolbar). Photo CD scans sometimes look hazy or dingy compared to the original, so increasing the brightness might help alleviate this.

For GIFs and PNGs, you can select a color to be transparent, meaning it will show through whatever is behind it, most likely the background color of the page (more on that later in this chapter). To do so, click the Set Transparent Color button, and then click a color in the selected picture. If the picture is currently in a format that does not permit transparent colors (such as JPEG), then FrontPage will warn you that it will convert the file to GIF format. Click OK to agree or Cancel to decline.

There can only be one transparent color in any picture.

You can easily convert a picture to black and white by clicking the Black And White button. (You can use a black and white version of a picture as the low-resolution alternative that will load first, by choosing it in the Picture Properties dialog box shown in Figure 6.14, later in this chapter.) Similarly, you can wash out an image to make it faded—this is most useful when you want to put legible text over the picture, as explained in "Adding Text to a Picture," later in this chapter—by clicking the Wash Out button. Finally, you can add the ever-popular beveled edges to a picture by clicking the Bevel button.

Creating a Thumbnail

If you want to display a large image at your site, it's customary not to force readers to download it but to offer a smaller version of the picture, called a "thumbnail," as a link to the larger version of the picture. (We'll explain all about links in Chapter 7.) To create a thumbnail version of an original picture, click it, and then click the Thumbnail button on the Picture toolbar (see Figure 6.11).

To control exactly how FrontPage creates your thumbnails for you, select Tools | Page Options and select the Auto Thumbnail tab.

- To specify the height or width of your thumbnails, click the Set drop-down list box and choose Width or Height (see Figure 6.12), and then enter a number of pixels in the first Pixels box.

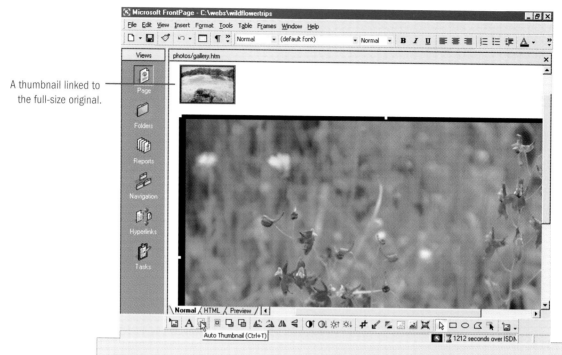

A thumbnail linked to the full-size original.

Figure 6.11: FrontPage replaced the original picture with a smaller thumbnail linked to it. (The larger photo below is still at full size.)

- To make the link border of the thumbnail invisible, replace the number 2 with 0 in the second Pixels box.
- To give your thumbnail the ever-popular beveled edge, check Beveled Edge.

Positioning a Picture

The easiest way to position a picture is simply to click it and drag it into position. To position a number of images, you may want to create a table with invisible borders (see Chapter 5), and click and drag or cut and paste the pictures into the table cells.

To fix a picture's position precisely as a distance down and to the right from the page's edge or from some other object on the page,

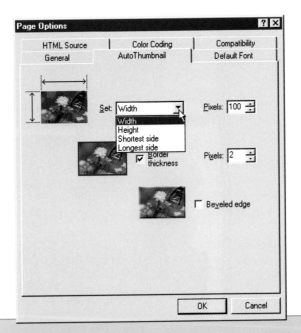

Figure 6.12: To create uniform thumbnails, FrontPage lets you specify that the length, height, or shortest or longest side be set to some precise number of pixels (regardless of the height and width of the original).

select Format | Position. This brings up the Position dialog box (see Figure 6.13).

- If you want text to wrap (flow) around your picture, click the Left or Right examples under Wrapping style.
- To position your picture absolutely (from the edge of the page) instead of relative to other objects (such as text) on the page, click the Absolute button under Positioning style. To position your picture relative to some object on the page (so that if the shape of the window changes, the picture will stay associated with the right text or other content), click the Relative button.
- To change the picture's position from the left and top edge of the page (or the page contents relative to which the picture is

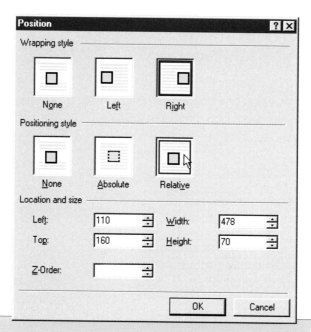

Figure 6.13:   You can control how a picture is positioned here.

positioned), enter different pixel values in the Left and Top boxes in the Location And Size area.

- For pictures positioned absolutely, one on top of another (this is not as silly as it sounds if the pictures are partially transparent), you can change the stacking order of the selected picture in the Z-Order box. A lower number is closer to the "front."

You can also change the positioning style of a picture from relative to absolute by clicking the Position Absolutely button on the Picture toolbar.

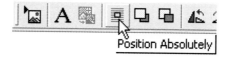

Converting a Picture to a Different Format

If you want to change the format of a picture or overrule FrontPage's ordinary rubric of converting 256-color (and less) images to GIFs and greater to JPEGs, right-click on the picture and choose Properties from the menu that pops up.

This particular graphic is in a table and a shared border, so there are some extra options on the menu.

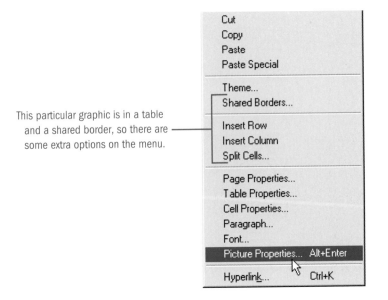

This brings up the Picture Properties dialog box. Make sure the General tab is clicked (see Figure 6.14).

- To convert your picture to a GIF, click the GIF radio button, and then check Transparent if you want the GIF to have a transparent color, and Interlaced if you want the GIF to appear to load more quickly.

- To convert your picture to a JPEG, click the JPEG radio button, and then choose the percentage of the original file size to which you'd like to compress the image—the lower the number, the lower the quality. Increase the number in the Progressive Passes box if you want the JPEG to seem to appear more quickly (at the cost of more downloading overall for your viewers).

- To convert your picture to a PNG, click the PNG radio button.

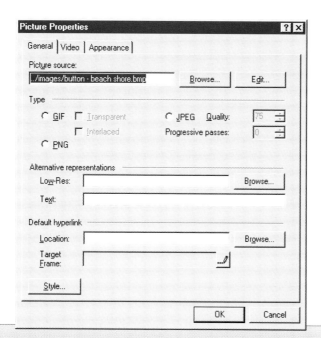

Figure 6.14: You can convert your picture to any of the three Web picture formats here.

While you've got this dialog box open, take a look at the Appearance tab, on which you can specify the picture's alignment, the thickness of the (invisible, unless it's a link) border around the picture, and the horizontal and vertical spacing around the picture; or specify a size in terms of pixels or percentage of original height or width.

When you are done, click OK.

Adding Text to a Picture

There are three different ways to associate text with a picture. You can create captions or photo credits as ordinary text directly adjacent to the picture. With GIFs, you can place text directly over the image, and for any picture you can associate alternative text that will be displayed when pictures are not shown (or read aloud for sight-deprived readers by their browsers, and so on).

Adding Captions and Credits

Typing a caption or credit for a picture is easy, but you may have to play around a little with the layout tricks explained in Chapter 5 to get the text to look the way you want. If you have text wrapping turned on, then you may have trouble getting the caption or credit to stay put under or next to the picture. For the cover photo on the WildflowerTrips site, I've put a photo credit in tiny type to the right of the photo, but then I need to get the caption down underneath the picture, and I don't want to have to insert a bunch of arbitrary paragraph breaks to get the caption in *roughly* the right place. To deal with this, all I need to do is insert a break that clears the page to the bottom of the picture. To do so, select Insert | Break. This brings up the Break Properties dialog box.

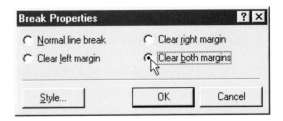

- If you choose Normal Line Break, you get the same result as if you had pressed CTRL+ENTER, but this doesn't help with clearing to the bottom of the picture.
- To get to the bottom of any pictures aligned along the left margin, choose Clear Left Margin.
- To get to the bottom of any pictures aligned along the right margin, choose Clear Right Margin.

Figure 6.15 shows the WildflowerTrips home page cover photo with a photo credit to its right and a caption below.

Putting Text on the Image Itself

To cover an image with text, select it and click the Text button on the Picture toolbar. If the picture is not a GIF, FrontPage will warn you that it will have to convert the picture to GIF format.

Click OK and then type your text in the box that appears over the picture. You can format the text as you ordinarily would.

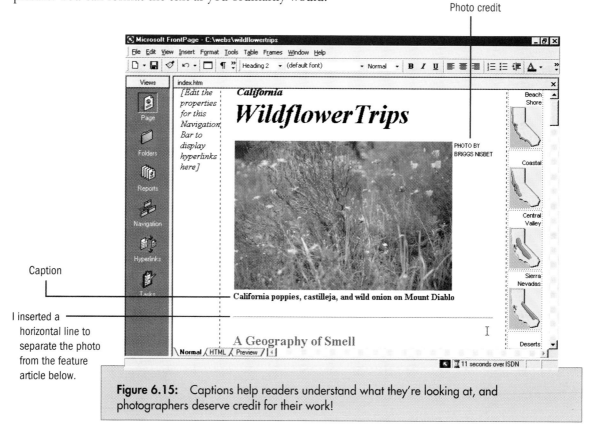

Figure 6.15: Captions help readers understand what they're looking at, and photographers deserve credit for their work!

Adding Alternative Text for People Not Viewing Images

To offer substitute text to explain what images look like to those not displaying them (or even to make sure nothing is displayed, instead of [IMAGE]), right-click the picture and select Properties, make sure the General tab is selected on the Picture Properties dialog box (shown in Figure 6.14), and type your alternative text in the Text box in the Alternative Representations area.

Saving a Picture with a Page

As mentioned briefly in Chapter 4, when you save a page with pictures in it, you must save the pictures to your web as well. Press CTRL+S to save the page. If you haven't saved the page before, you'll need to name, title, and save it as explained in Chapter 3. Then FrontPage will display the Save Embedded Files dialog box (see Figure 6.16).

Click the Rename button to give your photo a one-word name you can remember easily, click the Change Folder button to change where in the web the picture will be saved, and then click OK.

FrontPage will convert this Photo CD image to JPEG format.

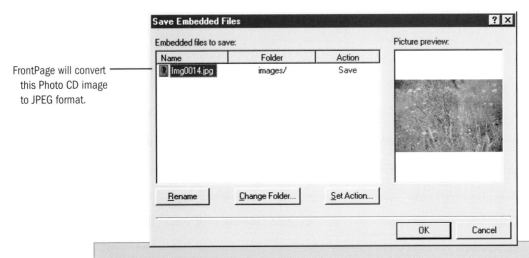

Figure 6.16: When you save a web page with embedded pictures, you have to save the pictures as well.

Designing with Color Schemes and Themes

The standard web page has black text, a white (or gray, depending on the browser) background, and blue links. Links appear red when you click them and purple when you've clicked them recently. (We'll get to links in Chapter 7.) With FrontPage you can change the color scheme on your page if you want. Some people recommend using the Web's standard color scheme, so that people will recognize a link when they see one, but others suggest that as long as you are consistent within your web, you'll be fine. There's a lot to be said for making your links red, which is a much easier color than blue to pick out from black.

FrontPage also comes with a number of themes that incorporate color schemes along with background tiles, styles for standard headings, graphics for bullets and horizontal lines, and predesigned navigation buttons. I'll show you how to choose your own colors and how to apply a theme to your web in this section.

You can also insert a background image onto your page, which will supersede the background color. Such an image needs to "tile" (fit together smoothly as it repeats across and down the page) unless it's very large, and it should also be washed out so that it doesn't make any text appearing on top of it illegible.

A Color Scheme and More

To choose a color scheme for or add a background image to your page (or for all the pages selected in the Folder list), select File | Properties, and choose the Background tab of the Page Properties dialog box.

To add a background image, check Background Picture, and then enter the file name of the picture, or click the Browse button and select it that way. If you want the background image to stay static even when the viewer scrolls the page, then check Watermark as well.

To choose a new color scheme, one-by-one click the drop-down lists in the Colors area and choose a color from the menu that pops up. If you want to choose a color different from the sixteen listed on the menu that pops down (see Figure 6.17), click the More Colors button, choose a color, and click OK.

EXPERT ADVICE

You can add different background colors or images to a table or even a single cell in a table in the Background area of the Table Properties (Table | Properties | Table) or Cell Properties (Table | Properties | Cell) dialog box.

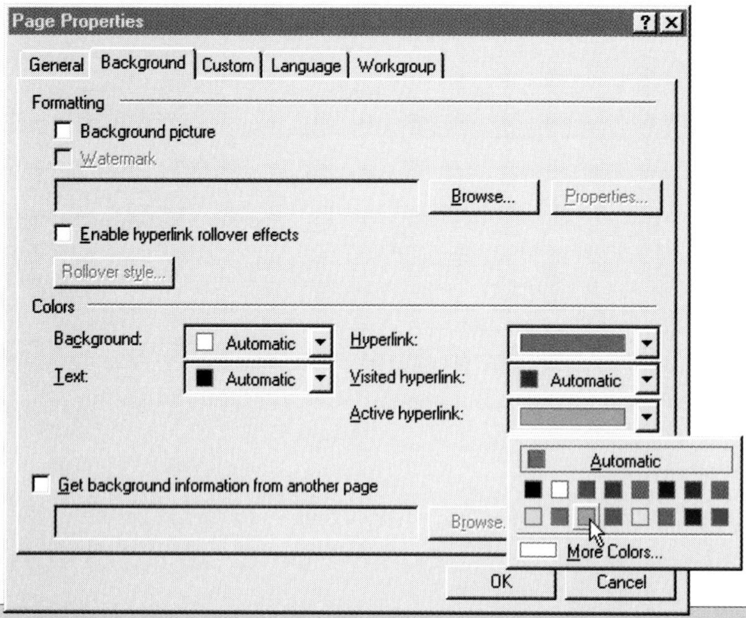

Figure 6.17: Choose your color scheme in the Page Properties dialog box.

You can also copy the color choices of an existing page by checking Get Background Information From Another Page, at the bottom of the Page Properties dialog box, and then entering the location of the example page (or you can click the Browse button to find it that way).

When you're done, click OK.

Choosing a Theme

To go beyond just a color scheme and add a coherent design to your page, select Format | Theme. This brings up the Themes dialog box. Scroll through the choices in the list box on the left side of the dialog box to see how each theme looks in the Sample Of Theme box (see Figure 6.18).

To apply a theme to your entire web, check All Pages. When you've found a theme you want, click OK.

If you did not install all available themes when first setting up FrontPage (see Appendix A), then click Install additional themes in the list box to add the rest.

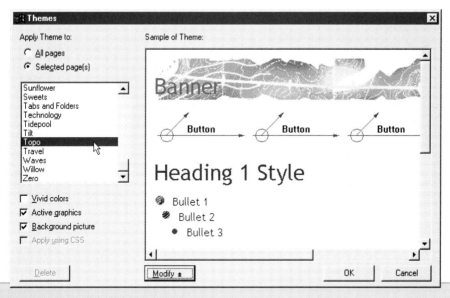

Figure 6.18: Add one of FrontPage's canned themes to your page for instant graphic design consistency.

Changing a Theme

To modify an existing theme, click the Modify button just below the Sample Of Theme box in the Themes dialog box. FrontPage offers you the choice of choosing alternative colors, graphic elements, or text formatting styles.

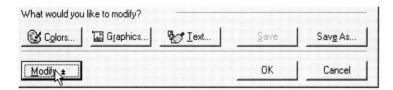

Click the Colors, Graphics, or Text button to change that aspect of the theme. When you've made changes to your satisfaction, click OK to return to the ordinary Themes dialog box.

Removing a Theme

To remove a theme from a page or web, select Format | Theme, choose All Pages if you want to remove the theme from the entire web, choose No Theme in the list box, and then click OK.

Adding Sound or Video

The various forms of page animation that FrontPage can help you create are discussed in Chapter 8.

Working with sound and video is a little trickier than working with pictures, but FrontPage can help you with some of that. For example, you can insert a background sound into pages, or you can insert a video clip, but it won't help you edit sound or video files.

CAUTION

If the Background Sound option is grayed out, you need to go to the Compatibility tab of the Page Options dialog box (Tools | Page options) and choose Internet Explorer Only, as Netscape does not support Microsoft's standard for embedded background sounds.

If there are no sound or video clips in your clip art categories, try reinstalling to add clip art.

Inserting a Background Sound onto a Page

To insert a sound file into a page, select File | Properties and make sure the General tab is selected. In the Background sound area in the middle of the tab, type a location (or click the Browse button to find your sound clip that way). If you want the sound to repeat a set number of times, uncheck forever and enter a number in the Loop box (see Figure 6.19).

Inserting a Sound (or Video) Clip

To insert a sound or video clip into a location on a page, select Insert | Picture | Video. This brings up the Video dialog box, more or less exactly like the Picture dialog box. Select the video (or sound) clip file or click the Search the Web or Search Your Computer button to seek the clip outside this immediate web. If the video clip you want to add is from your clip art collection, click the Clip Art button, and then choose an option in the Motion Clips tab. If you see a clip that looks interesting, click it to preview it or insert it into your page.

To add a sound clip from the Clip Art Gallery, select Insert | Picture | Clip Art, and then choose the Sounds tab (see Figure 6.20).

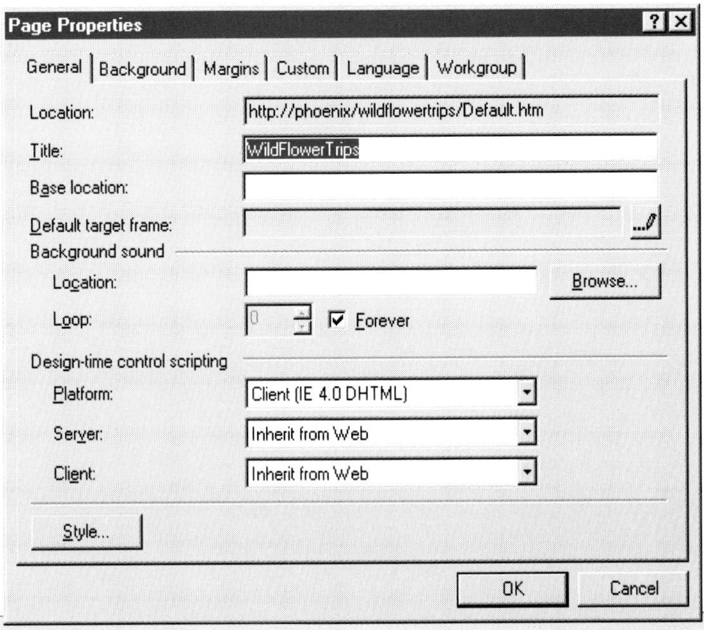

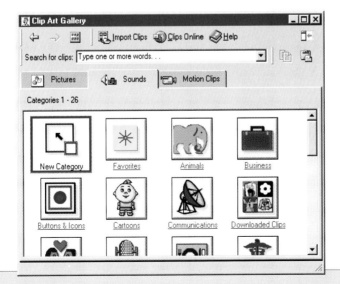

Figure 6.19: I don't necessarily recommend forcing your viewers to listen to a music or sound clip when they first arrive at the page, but here's how you do it.

Figure 6.20: Choosing sound clips from the Clip Art Gallery

Setting Video Properties

Once you've inserted a video into a page, there are a number of settings you can control. Right-click on the video and choose Picture Properties, and then choose the Video tab (see Figure 6.21).

You can enter a different location or use the Browse button to choose a different video clip. Check Show Controls In Browser if you want the user to be able to control the playback of the video clip. You can choose to have the clip loop a set number of times or forever, and you can set the delay time between repeat showings of the video. Lastly, in the Start area, you can determine whether the video clip should start playing when the user reaches the page or when the user moves the mouse pointer over the video.

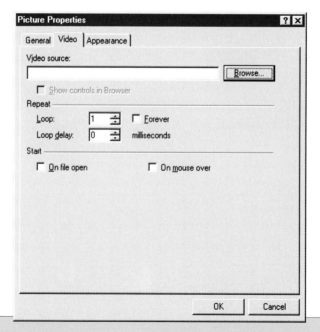

Figure 6.21:   Control the looping of your video, and when it should start playing.

The Web Is Not a CD

Just because FrontPage can insert all these doodads into your page and Microsoft Internet Explorer can play them back is no reason to go hog wild. A few snazzy elements, well chosen, go a long way toward making the experience of your web more pleasant, but if you pile on the bells and whistles, all you will do is slow things down to a crawl and chase away potential viewers. Things that seem to load quickly and play back promptly when they're located on your hard disk may be an entirely different story over the Internet or even a busy local network.

There's no substitute for taste, but at least you don't have to give away the game all at once!

There's More . . .

You now understand the nuts and bolts of web page creation. You can set up a web, make a page, add text to it, lay it out, and add artwork. That's really quite a lot and you should be proud of yourself for your progress so far. The next chapter is *crucial*, because it covers how to insert the hyperlinks that weave web pages together, and how to establish a navigation system so that your viewers don't get lost in your web.

CHAPTER 7

Making Your Site Navigable

INCLUDES

- Inserting local links
- Inserting external links
- Making an image map
- Working in navigation view
- Inserting navigation bars
- Making a table of contents
- Adding a search page to your web
- Structuring a web with frames

Insert a Local Link ➥ p.163

1. Open the Folder list.
2. Click the icon of the page to which you want to link and drag it onto your page.
3. Select the link text (the title of the page you're linking to) and replace it, if you wish.

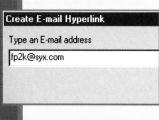

Insert an E-Mail Link ➥ pp. 164, 166

1. Type the link text or insert the link picture.
2. Select the link text or picture.
3. Select Insert | Hyperlink.
4. Click the E-mail Link button.
5. Type the e-mail address.
6. Click OK, and then click OK again.

Insert an External Link ➥ pp. 164, 167

1. Type the link text or insert the link picture.
2. Select the link text or picture.
3. Select Insert | Hyperlink.
4. Type the address of the external page in the URL box or click the Search The Web button to browse to the page to which you want to link.
5. Click OK.

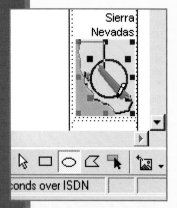

Make an Image Map ➥ pp. 169–171

1. Insert and select the link picture.
2. Create the Rectangular Hotspot, Circular Hotspot, or Polygonal Hotspot button.
3. Draw the hotspot shape on the image.
4. On the Create Hyperlink dialog box that appears, type or browse to the link destination.
5. Repeat steps 2–4 to create as many hotspots as you need.
6. Set a default link destination for the picture by right-clicking on it, and entering the destination in the Location box in the Default Hyperlink area of the General tab of the Picture Properties dialog box.

Add Pages to the Navigation View ➡ pp. 177–180

- To add an existing page, click its icon in the Folder list and drag it into the Navigation view.
- To add a new page, click the New Page button.
- To add a destination outside your web, right-click the page Select External Hyperlink, and then enter the link's address in the URL box.
- To rename a page, select it, press F2, and then type the new name.

Insert a Navigation Bar ➡ pp. 180–183

1. Place the insertion inside a shared border or in the main area of the page, depending on whether you want this same navigation bar on every page or not.
2. Select Insert | Navigation Bar.
3. Choose which types of links you want to appear in the navigation bar.
4. Click OK.

Generate a Table of Contents ➡ pp. 186–187

1. Click the New Page button.
2. Choose the Table Of Contents template and click OK.
3. Delete the comment and edit the introductory text.
4. Double-click the table of contents to edit it.

Make Your Web Searchable ➡ pp. 191–193

1. Click the New Page button.
2. Choose the Search Page template and click OK.
3. Delete the comment and edit the accompanying text.
4. Select the search area and press ALT+ENTER to edit the search form.

A web doesn't really function as a unit until it's bound together with hyperlinks and a navigational structure. A hyperlink, or link, is a connection between an anchor in one web page and some other page, either inside your web or from the external World Wide Web. When the link is clicked or otherwise selected, the user is transported to the destination. You can insert links anywhere in web pages and I'll show you how in the first part of this chapter.

It's one thing to link together arbitrary pages to provide ways for readers to jump around your web, and it's another thing entirely to provide your viewers with a coherent navigation system so they always know where they are and can get to key pages, such as the home page. After you've gotten the gist of hyperlinks in general, I'll show you how to establish a navigation structure for your web and how to insert navigation bars into web pages to enable users to easily take advantage of the relationships established in the navigation structure.

After that, I'll show you how to add two types of pages to your web that can help your viewers get around: a table of contents page, and a search page. Finally, I'll give you the basics of designing with frames, even though I don't especially recommend using them. They seem to be declining in popularity as the years pass since they subdivide each screen and can sometimes be very confusing for users.

Hyperlinks, the Sinews of the Web

Hyperlinks are the essence of the web interface. The Internet got a lot easier to use when the World Wide Web came along in 1991 (and especially when graphical browsers, such as Mosaic, first appeared in

1994). Suddenly, instead of having to know the precise location, file name, and protocol for downloading resources from the Internet, a user could simply click on a highlighted link and get access to the resource directly. FrontPage makes it easy to insert hyperlinks anywhere you want.

See Chapter 6 for how to change the colors of hyperlinks, both before and after they've been visited.

Dragging Pages to Make Links

The quickest way to insert (into an open web page) a link to an existing page, is to open the Folder list (View | Folder List), and then drag the page's icon onto the open web page.

To create picture links, as opposed to text links, you must use the method explained in the next section.

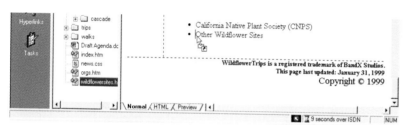

A text hyperlink appears highlighted, its content the title of the page to which the link refers.

- California Native Plant Society (CNPS)
- Wildflower SitesOther Wildflower Sites

To change the text of the hyperlink, type *inside* existing text, even if that will require a little more tweaking (or the new text will not be part of the hyperlink).

- California Native Plant Society (CNPS)
- WOther Wildflower SitesOther Wildflower Sites

Then, if necessary, delete any extra text, either in the hyperlink or in the original text where you inserted the new link.

- California Native Plant Society (CNPS)
- Other Wildflower Sites

Use Ctrl+Click to follow a hyperlink ——————— CTRL+CLICK on a hyperlink in Normal view to open the page to which it refers.

Selecting the Link Anchor

The thumbnails you learned how to create in Chapter 6 are one specific type of picture hyperlink.

You can also create hyperlinks by first typing the text (see Chapter 5) or inserting the picture (see Chapter 6), which will function as the clickable anchor linked to the destination. Then select the text or picture.

Inserting Links

To associate a hyperlink destination with a selection, choose Insert | Hyperlink (or press CTRL+K or right-click on the selection and choose Hyperlink). This brings up the Create Hyperlink dialog box (see Figure 7.1).

There are three main types of hyperlinks: links to other parts of your own web, links to the external Web, and e-mail links.

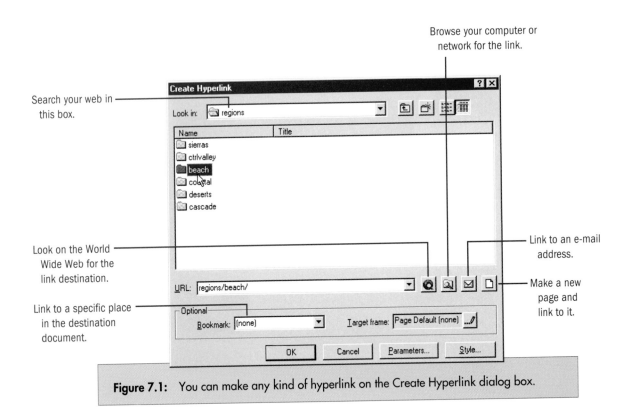

Figure 7.1: You can make any kind of hyperlink on the Create Hyperlink dialog box.

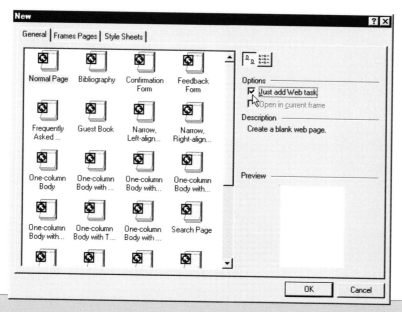

Figure 7.2: FrontPage lets you create pages as you link to them.

Link Within Your Web

To link to a page within your own web, choose its folder in the Look In box, click it in the main list, and then click OK.

To link to a page you haven't created yet, you can create it on the fly. Just click the New Page button. In the New dialog box that appears, choose a template, and click Just Add Web Task (see Figure 7.2).

Click OK. This brings up the Save As dialog box (see Figure 7.3).

Sometimes, FrontPage inexplicably asks you to reconfirm the save:

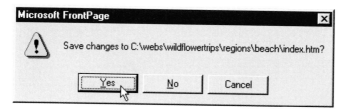

If it does, click Yes.

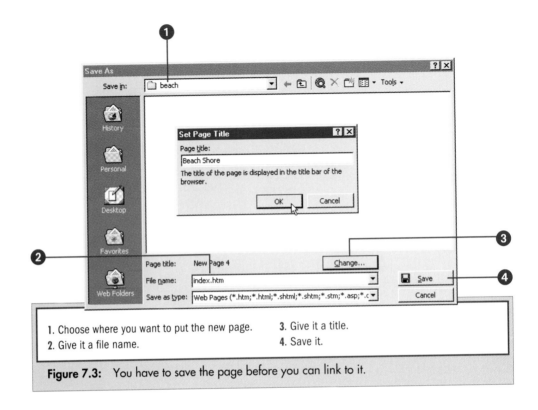

1. Choose where you want to put the new page.
2. Give it a file name.
3. Give it a title.
4. Save it.

Figure 7.3: You have to save the page before you can link to it.

Link to an E-Mail Address

To make it easier for readers to reach you, or contributors to your web, you may want to make e-mail hyperlinks available. To do so, select the link text (or picture), press CTRL+K, click the E-mail Link button, and type the e-mail address to which you want to link.

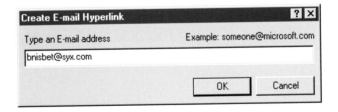

Then click OK, and click OK again.

CAUTION

Some e-mail spammers use software to scoop e-mail addresses and e-mail links off public web pages for the purpose of sending unsolicited e-mail. Therefore, you might not want to expose your primary e-mail address on a web page in this way.

Link to an Address on the World Wide Web

To insert an external link (a link to a site on the Web), select the link text (or picture), press CTRL+K, and type the destination's address in the URL box, if you know it.

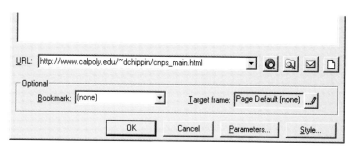

If you're not sure of the address, click the Search The Web button. This brings up Microsoft Internet Explorer (or possibly some other browser), with a message inviting you to browse your way to the page you're looking for.

Since you don't know the address, try typing a plain-language description of the page you're looking for in the Address box.

(I like to keep my toolbars all scrunched up as little as possible.)

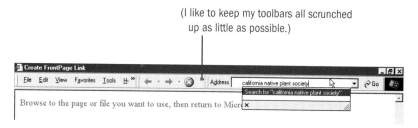

For the WildflowerTrips' link to the California Native Plant Society, typing the organization's name into MSIE's search box yielded some pretty helpful results (see Figure 7.4).

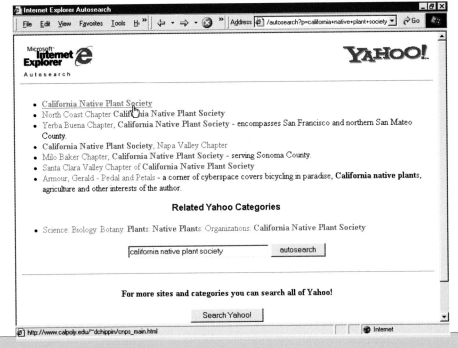

Figure 7.4: The first link on this search results page is the one I'm looking for, but they're all relevant to the subject of the WildflowerTrips site, and I may save their addresses for my own web's eventual link page.

It's important to click the link leading to the page you want, or you'll end up linking to the search results page. When you're there, switch back to FrontPage (or close MSIE window). The URL of the page you found will automatically be inserted in the URL box of the Create Hyperlink dialog box.

Click OK.

Deleting a Hyperlink

To delete a hyperlink (but not the text anchor), select the link, press
CTRL+K, select the text in the URL box (of the Edit Hyperlink dialog
box—it's identical to the Create Hyperlink dialog box except for its
title), delete it, and click OK.

Creating an Image Map

An image map is a picture that points to more than one destination,
depending on what part of it is clicked. Each clickable area on an
image map is called a hotspot. To turn a picture into an image map,
first select it. This brings up the Picture toolbar.

Draw a circle center-to-edge.

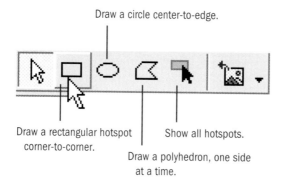

Draw a rectangular hotspot
corner-to-corner.

Show all hotspots.

Draw a polyhedron, one side
at a time.

After that, it's easy.

1. Click one of the Hotspot buttons.
2. Draw a shape on the picture (see Figure 7.5).
3. Enter the hyperlink and click OK in the Create Hyperlink
   dialog box that appears.
4. Repeat for each hotspot on the image map.

You can select a hotspot and then drag its handles to alter its size or
boundaries. After you've drawn a number of hotspots on an image, it
may be hard to see all the boundaries. Click the Highlight Hotspots

Figure 7.5: FrontPage takes all the pain out of making an image map (believe me, it used to be much harder).

button to blank out the picture and show the hotspots, with the selected hotspot, if any, colored in (see Figure 7.6).

It's a good idea to assign a default hyperlink to an image map. That's the destination the viewers will be taken to if they click the map outside of all the hotspots. Right-click on the picture and enter the default destination in the Location box in the Default Hyperlink area of the General tab of the Picture properties dialog box. Then click OK.

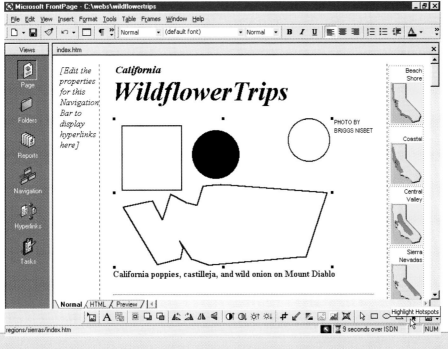

Figure 7.6: These four hotspots each link from a different flower or plant in the original photo.

Viewing Hyperlinks in Your Web

After you've started linking pages in your web, you may lose track of exactly which pages point to what. FrontPage's Hyperlinks view shows you those relationships. To view your web this way, click the Hyperlinks button in the Views bar (see Figure 7.7).

You can go directly to any page in Hyperlinks view by double-clicking it.

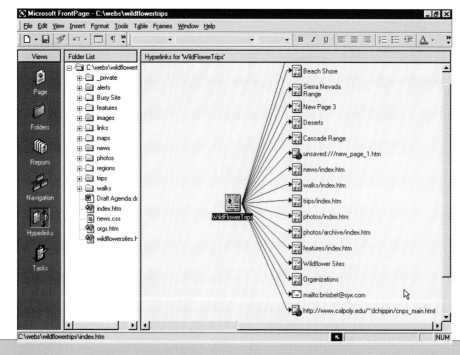

Figure 7.7: I added a lot of links to the main body of the WildflowerTrips home page, as you can see.

Recalculating Hyperlinks

One of the really nice things about FrontPage is that it keeps track of your hyperlinks for you, and if you move a page referred to by links from other pages, FrontPage can make sure those links don't get

EXPERT ADVICE

Before you publish your web, it's a good idea to verify the hyperlinks and check them for errors, as I'll explain in Chapter 9.

broken. Any time you want to update all the hyperlinks in your web, select Tools | Recalculate Hyperlinks. FrontPage will warn you that this might take a little time.

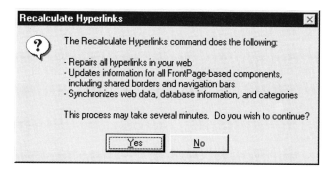

Click Yes.

Making Hyperlinks Roll Over

FrontPage offers an MSIE-only feature for hyperlinks called a "rollover." What this really means is that you can assign a different style (font, size, color, and so on, as explained in Chapter 5) that the link will turn to when the mouse pointer floats over it. You can use this feature to make links appear to leap at the opportunity of being clicked. Whether or not this makes the links more desirable I will leave to your discretion.

"To add such an effect to the links on a page, select File | Properties, Background Tab and check Enable Hyperlink Rollover Effects. Then click the Rollover style button (see Figure 7.8).

This brings up the Font dialog box. Choose a typeface if you want, font styles, a font size, and a color (see Figure 7.9).

Then click OK, and click OK again. Figure 7.10 shows a hyperlink rolling over in Preview view.

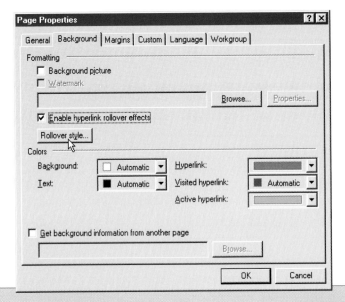

Figure 7.8: Rollover effects make hyperlinks change when you point to them, at least in Microsoft's browser.

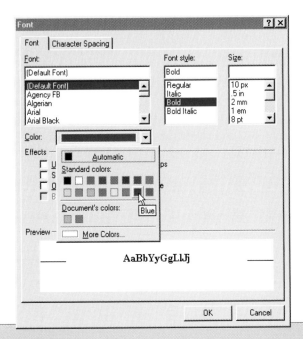

Figure 7.9: Links will turn bold and light blue if I have my way.

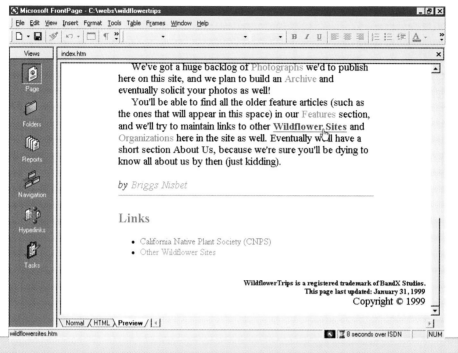

Figure 7.10: The link to other wildflower sites turns light blue and bold when I point to it.

Setting Up Navigation Bars

In order to enable FrontPage to generate navigation bars on pages in your web, you must first set up a navigation tree, which is a diagram showing how the pages in your web relate to each other. This is different from the Folder view of your site and from the Hyperlink view. The Folder view shows the internal, skeletal structure of your site. There's no reason to assume that the content must be presented within that same structure, since visitors bring an entirely different perspective to a web from those "engineering" the site from behind the scenes. Likewise, the Hyperlink view shows every hyperlink in the web, but it doesn't show the logical relationships of the pages in your web.

Once you've established the navigation tree for your web, any page represented in the tree can be given a navigation bar with links to related pages. The benefit of automatically generated navigation bars is that FrontPage will maintain the links, updating them as you move or add pages.

CAUTION

A navigation bar is only useful if it repeats throughout the site, appearing always in the same place and with the same types of links. If a navigation bar changes throughout the web, it must change in an intuitively understandable way. Inconsistent navigation aids are worse than none at all!

EXPERT ADVICE

Right-click anywhere in Navigation view to quickly zoom in or out, rotate the view, expand all subtrees, assign a new top page (home page), or to control web settings; particularly how standard navigation buttons to home, parent, previous, and next pages are labeled (by default, the choices are Home, Up, Back, and Next), on the Navigation tab of the Web Settings dialog box.

Planning in Navigation View

To establish a navigation tree for your site, first click Navigation in the Views bar. FrontPage switches to Navigation view, showing at first only the web's home page and the Navigation toolbar (see Figure 7.11).

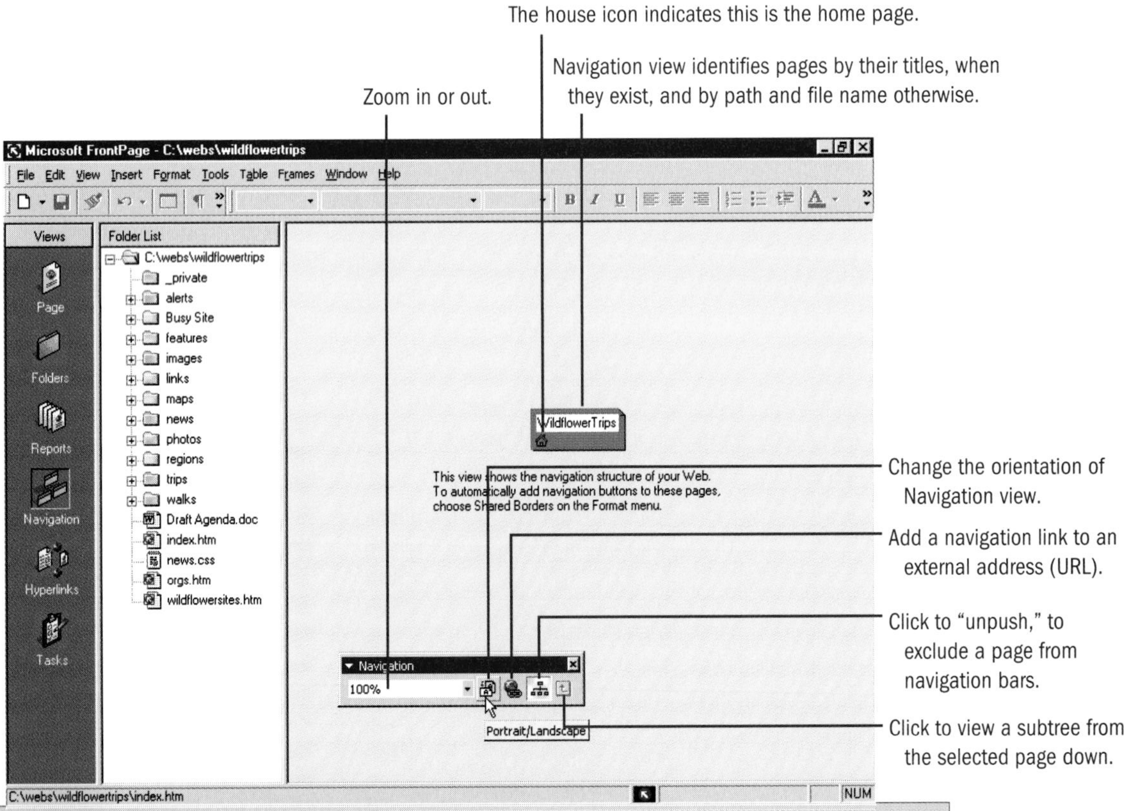

The house icon indicates this is the home page.

Navigation view identifies pages by their titles, when they exist, and by path and file name otherwise.

Zoom in or out.

Change the orientation of Navigation view.

Add a navigation link to an external address (URL).

Click to "unpush," to exclude a page from navigation bars.

Click to view a subtree from the selected page down.

Figure 7.11: Navigation view starts you with a clean slate, regardless of the existing hyperlinks in your web.

Absolute and Relative Page Relationships

Navigation view provides for two types of page positions. First there are some absolute positions, namely the web's home page (or top page), and other top-level pages. Top-level pages are conceptually at the same level as the home page, and they may have subtrees of their own. You can refer to a home page or to all top-level pages from anywhere in the web and you will always be talking about the same pages.

The relative positions describe relationships between any page and the pages directly connected to it in the tree. Every page except for the home page and other top-level pages has a parent page, one step higher in the tree than itself. Some pages also have child pages extending from them, representing the first echelon of a subtree. Pages may also be said to have same-level pages, which are essentially "siblings" or "cousins" depending on whether they share parents. All the top-level pages are considered to be at the same level as each other.

Adding Top-Level Pages

To add a page to the top level of the Navigation tree, click it in the Folder List and drag it into the Navigation window, so that it lands next to the home page (see Figure 7.12).

When you release the mouse button, the page will land next to the home page, with no connector (since they do not technically share a parent). The page appears labeled with its path and file name, if it does not yet have a title.

Adding Child Pages

To add a child page to the tree, drag it into position beneath the parent page until you see a connector appear. You can also move existing pages around the tree to change their relationships.

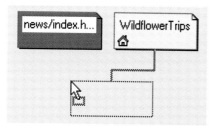

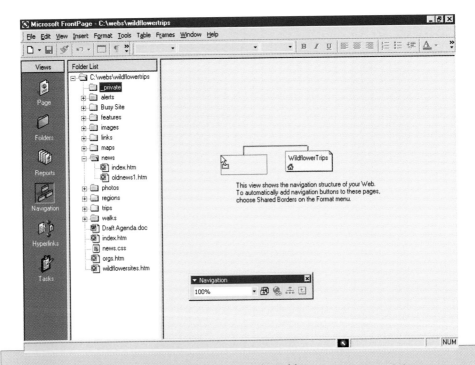

Figure 7.12: When you drag a page icon from the Folder List next to an existing page, FrontPage suggests a sibling relationship between the new page and the closest page to the new location.

When you release the mouse button, the page will land beneath its parent page, connected by a line showing the relationship (and a little minus-sign button you can click to collapse the subtree from that point down).

To relabel a page, press F2 and then type a new label for the page.

To jump directly to a page from Navigation view, simply double-click it.

   To add a new page under an existing page, right-click the page, and choose New Page from the menu that pops up. To add an external page (a page that is not in your web) under an existing page, right-click the page, select External Hyperlink, and enter (or browse to) the destination in the URL box.

   To exclude a page from the navigation bars (but leave it visible in the tree), right-click on it and uncheck Include In Navigation Bars on the menu that pops up. To remove a page from the navigation structure, select it and press DELETE, and then click Remove This Page From All Navigation Bars and OK on the dialog box that appears.

   Figure 7.13 shows the navigation tree for the WildflowerTrips site in progress (as with anything in FrontPage, you can tinker with a navigation tree to your heart's content—you are not locked into your initial ideas).

EXPERT ADVICE

You can print your navigation tree to retain a paper copy of your web's navigation structure. To do so, just select File | Print in Navigation view, and then click OK.

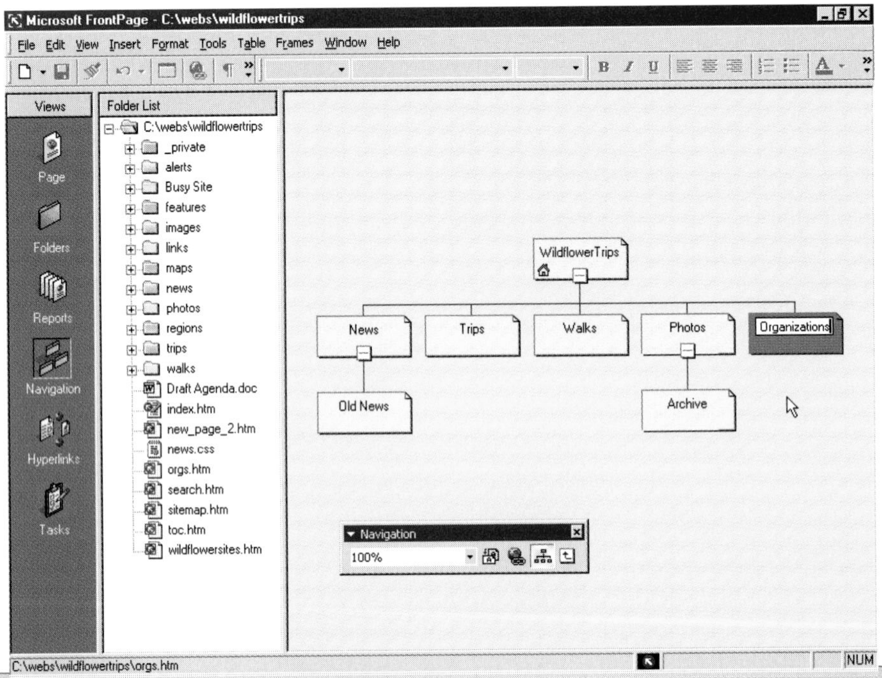

Figure 7.13: The navigation tree for the WildflowerTrips shows pages representing the major sections of the site as children of the home page.

Inserting a Navigation Bar

Once you've established a navigation tree, you can start placing Navigation bars on pages. There are two steps involved in creating a navigation bar. One is to insert the bar itself into a page (or shared border). The second is to add the page in question to the navigation tree (if it is not already there). If you do the first step but not the second, the navigation bar will consist only of a reminder to add the page in question to the navigation tree (as you've seen in the left shared border of the WildflowerTrips home page in the past few chapters).

Before you start plopping nav bars into pages, though, spend a moment thinking about whether you want them in shared borders or not. The benefit of placing a nav bar in a shared border is that you automatically insert it into all pages sharing that border the moment you insert it into one. The downside is that the nav bar will feature the same elements on every page (that is, the same relative elements, such as parent, child, or same-level pages).

Some webs have a shared navigation bar for the top-level pages (which stay in the same absolute relationship to each page, regardless of where the individual page is located in the navigation tree), and another navigation bar in the ordinary part of the page (which has links to parent pages, child pages, same-level pages, or all three).

To add a navigation bar to a page, first place the insertion point where you want the bar to appear, and then select Insert | Navigation Bar. This brings up the Navigation Bar Properties dialog box (see Figure 7-14).

If a page lacks some related pages (such as child pages) chosen for the nav bar, then the bar will leave them out.

- If you choose Parent Level, the nav bar will include links to the page's parent and all the other pages on the same level as the parent.

- If you choose Same Level, the page's nav bar will include links to all the other pages on the same level.

- If you choose Back And Next, the nav bar will include links to its next and previous sibling pages.

- If you choose Child Level, the nav bar will include links to the page's child pages, if any.

- If you choose Top Level, the nav bar will include links to the home page and any other pages at the top level.

- If you choose Child Pages Under Home, the nav bar will include links to the home page's child pages.

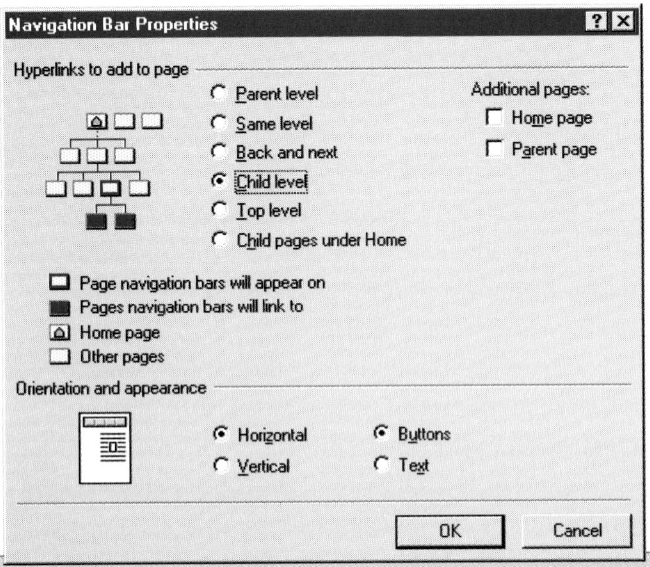

Figure 7.14: The diagram in the Hyperlinks To Add To Page area of the Navigation Properties dialog box shows which pages will appear in the bar depending on which type of relationships you choose.

Regardless of what linking scheme you choose for your nav bar, you can also check Home Page and/or Parent Page to add the home page or the current page's parent to its nav bar.

In the Orientation And Appearance area of the Navigation Bar Properties dialog box, you can choose whether the nav bar will appear across the width of the page or down the length of it. You can also choose whether the links will appear as graphical buttons or as text (the buttons choice only works if you have a theme associated with your page).

For the WildflowerTrips site, I've chosen the Child Pages Under Home scheme, plus the home page and parent page, with vertical text buttons, in the left-side shared border (with Colonel Mustard, in the

Figure 7.15:　These text links appear after I've inserted a nav bar into the WildflowerTrips home page.

pantry, with the candlestick…). Figure 7.15 shows the navigation links that FrontPage inserts into the shared border on the left side of the home page.

Editing Your Navigation Bar

To change the link text in a navigation bar, edit the page labels for the pages in question in Navigation view. For example, notice that the word "Organizations" sticks out in the nav bar in Figure 7.15, since it's so much longer than all the other link names. To edit it, I'll switch back to Navigation view, select the Organizations page, press F2, and type **Orgs.** to shorten it.

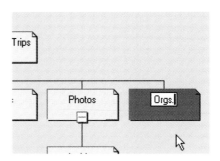

You can format text links in a nav bar just as you would ordinary text, by applying formatting from the Formatting toolbar or by imposing styles (as explained in Chapter 5). To make the links in the WildflowerTrips nav bar more visible without taking up too much space, I've formatted the text as Arial Narrow, bold, and size 4 (14 pt).

You're also not locked into any choices you made when you first inserted the nav bar. To reconsider a nav bar's properties, select it and press ALT+ENTER (or right-click on it and choose Navigation Bar Properties). This brings up the Navigation Bar Properties dialog box shown in Figure 7.14. Change the link scheme, orientation, or button type, and click OK.

Removing a Navigation Bar

To remove a nav bar from a page, switch to Navigation view, right-click on the page in question, and select Include In Navigation Bars to uncheck it.

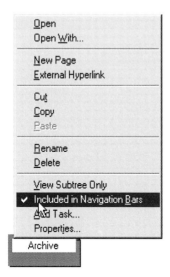

This will also remove the nav bar from all pages in the subtree below the page you just changed. You can add any of those pages back to nav bars by right-clicking on them and rechecking Included In Navigation Bars.

In Page view, you can remove a Navigation bar from a page by selecting the Navigation bar contents and pressing DELETE.

CAUTION

If you delete a navigation bar in a shared border, the nav bar will disappear from every page sharing that border.

Inserting a Table of Contents

Another way FrontPage can help you make your web easy for readers to navigate is by creating a table of contents page showing all the pages linked from the site's home page. FrontPage can keep this table of contents up to date for you, even as you add new pages, add or change links, or rearrange pages in the navigation view.

There are two sorts of table of contents you can make: one is the default type the FrontPage generates by listing the home page and then listing all pages linked from it, and all pages linked from those pages, and so on. The other is a "site map," a listing of pages in your web, organized by category.

Making a New Table of Contents Page

The easiest way to create a table of contents is to start a new page. Switch to Page view, select File | New | Page, and choose the Table Of Contents template (see Figure 7.16) and click OK.

FrontPage generates your initial table of contents on a page with a comment explaining a bit about the TOC, and some dummy text with a sample introduction before the table of contents, and sample footer afterward (See Figure 7.17).

To alter the setting of a table of contents, double-click it or select it and press ALT+ENTER. This brings up the Table of Contents Properties dialog box.

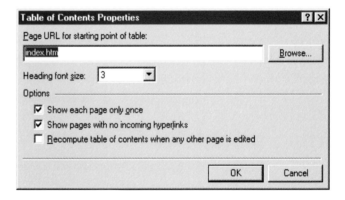

- Enter a different file name or browse to choose a starting page besides your web's home page.
- Change the heading font size, if you wish.
- If you want the table of contents updated every time you add or change a new page, click Recompute Table Of Contents When Any Other Page Is Edited, although this will slow down the editing process somewhat. (You can always force a TOC page to be recomputed by closing and then reopening it.)

Finally, save the TOC page.

You can also insert a table of contents into any existing page by selecting Insert | Component | Table Of Contents.

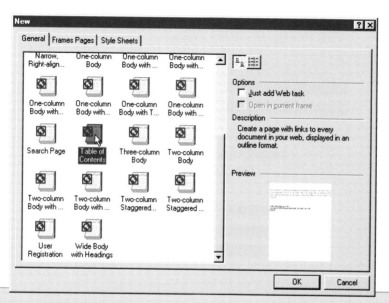

Figure 7.16: Make a new table of contents (TOC) page using this template.

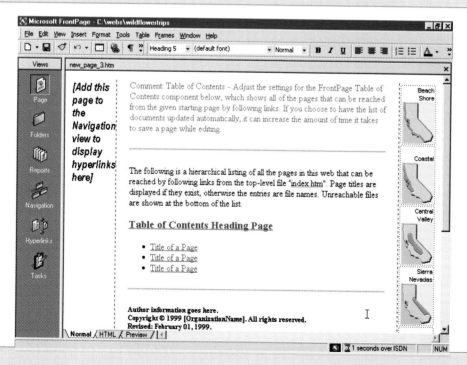

Figure 7.17: The table of contents contains dummy text until it is published.

Making a Site Map

If you want a table of contents organized by category instead of a straight hierarchical listing of pages from the home page down, then you need to invent categories to define the different aspects of your web, and then assign each page you want to appear in your site map to one of those categories.

Creating Categories

To create a category, select File | Properties, and click the Workgroup tab (see Figure 7.18).

If any of the business-oriented existing categories works for your page, select it from the Available Categories list box (scroll to see the whole list). If not, click the Categories button to invent a new

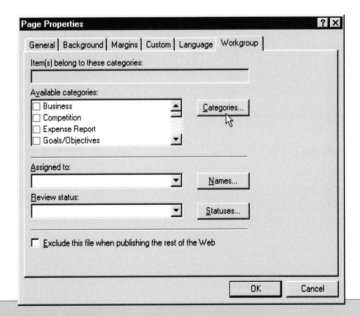

Figure 7.18:   Choose one or more of the existing categories in the Available Categories list box, or click the Categories button to create a new category.

category. This brings up the Master Category List dialog box. Type a new category name and click the Add button.

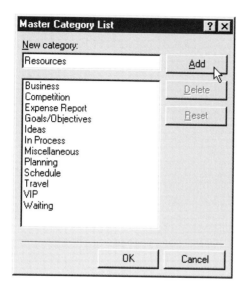

Repeat to create additional categories. When you are done, click OK.

Assigning Pages to Categories

To assign the current page to a category, select File | Properties, click the Workgroup tab, click a category, and then click OK. Repeat this for each page you want to appear in your site map. To see the categories all your pages are assigned to, switch to Reports view (click Reports in the View bar), and then click Categories in the Reports toolbar (see Figure 7.19).

EXPERT ADVICE

To list only the files in a single category, click the drop-down list that reads "(all categories)" and choose the category you want.

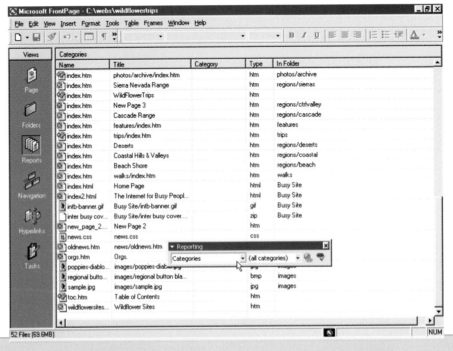

Figure 7.19:   I've got a lot of work ahead of me assigning pages to categories.

Adding Lists of Categories to the Site Map

Finally, to create the site map, first start a new blank page. Type a name for the page (such as **Site Map**) and make it a Heading 1. Then type the name of the first category you'd like to list on the site map and format it (perhaps as a Heading 2).

Select Insert | Components | Categories. In the Categories Properties dialog box that appears, choose the first category you'd like to list, decide how you want the files in that category sorted (alphabetically by document title or chronologically by when updated), and decide if you want to list the date the page was last modified (this is useful for repeat visitors to your web).

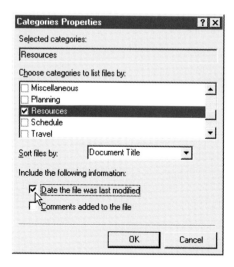

Then click OK. Repeat this process for each category you want to list in your site map. The map will be dynamic, in that FrontPage will update it whenever you add a file to or remove a file from a category. Remember to save the page when you're done, and add it to the navigation tree, perhaps as a top-level page.

Adding a Search Page

Another type of page that can make your web more accessible to users is a search page. Without having to know anything about programming or database queries, you can easily insert a search page into your web and let FrontPage do the hard work of indexing the site and responding to requests from the search form.

To add a search page to your web, select File | New | Page, and select the Search Page template and click OK (see Figure 7.20). FrontPage creates a new page headed by a comment you can delete and some explanatory text that you may find overly dry (see Figure 7-21).

Edit the text of the page to make it more inviting. For the search page in the WildflowerTrips site, I added a heading, reduced the basic explanation to something a lot simpler (and made the text a little larger), and added the page to the navigation tree as a child of the home page. Figure 7.22 shows the search page in the Preview window.

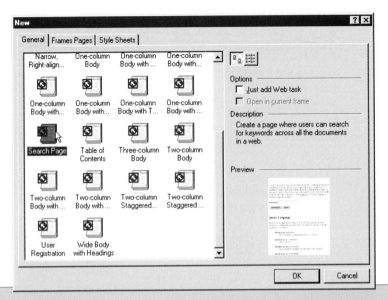

Figure 7.20: FrontPage takes the pain out of making your web searchable.

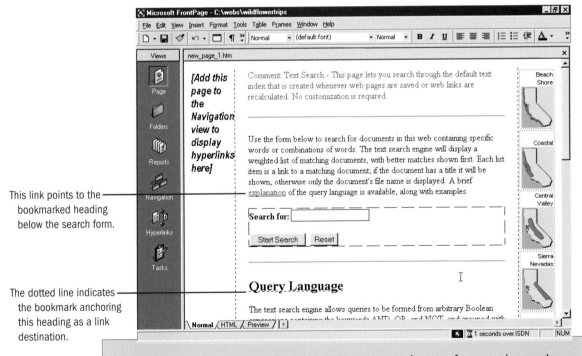

This link points to the bookmarked heading below the search form.

The dotted line indicates the bookmark anchoring this heading as a link destination.

Figure 7.21: The search page features a comment, an explanation for users, the search form itself, and a further explanation.

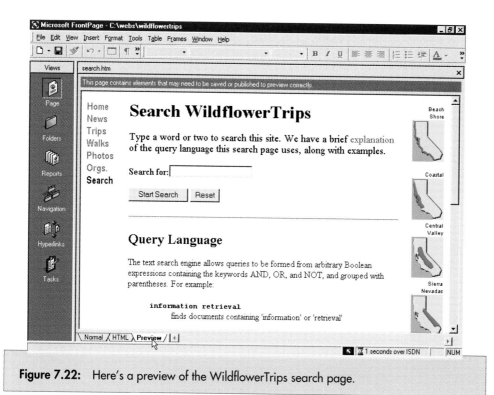

Figure 7.22:   Here's a preview of the WildflowerTrips search page.

Making the Best of Frames

A few years back, frames were the "cool new thing" on the web. Frames are dividers in the web browser's window that can scroll separately and link to new pages without changing the contents of the other frames. Frames have been most popular as a way to keep a nav bar constantly on the screen, but FrontPage's automation of the navigation design process does away with the need for frames, at least for that purpose. The downside of frames is that they can confuse a user, which makes a site harder to navigate. They can also make it more difficult for readers to save pages in their bookmarks (or as favorites) because the browser thinks of the overarching frames page as the one currently in view; not any of the pages that are displayed within the frames themselves.

Still, if you must use frames, FrontPage makes it very easy to set up your pages.

Creating a New Frames Page

To start working with frames, create a new page. Select File | New | Page and click the Frames Pages tab in the New dialog box. Click the various template icons once to see how each one's frames are laid out in the Preview (see Figure 7.23).

Choose the frames layout you like and then click OK. FrontPage opens a new page divided into empty frames (see Figure 7.24).

Filling the Frames

To select a frame to fill, just click anywhere inside it. A thick blue border will jump to the frame you clicked (if it wasn't there already). To fill a frame with a blank new page, click the New Page button. To insert a page you've already created into the frame, click the Set Initial

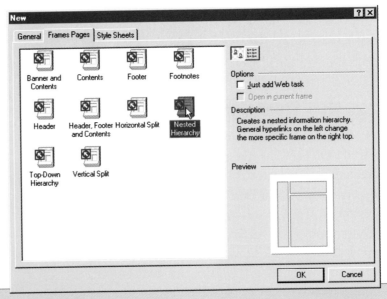

Figure 7.23: FrontPage's frames templates cover all of the most common configurations for frames pages.

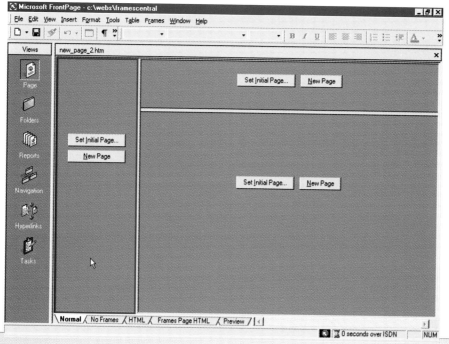

Figure 7.24: Into each frame you can insert an existing page or create a new blank page.

Page button. This brings up the Create Hyperlink dialog box. Choose the page you want to insert in the frame, and click OK.

Top and left-side frames can contain navigation bars that work the usual way (as explained earlier in this chapter).

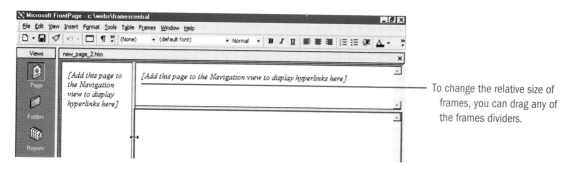

To change the relative size of frames, you can drag any of the frames dividers.

Formatting the Frames

To change the properties of a frame, right-click within the frame and select Frame Properties. This brings up the Frame Properties dialog box (see Figure 7.25).

- To change the frame's name to something you'll remember, type in the Name box.
- To change the page that will appear initially in the frame when this page is loaded, enter a new file name or click the Browse button and select the page you want.
- To change the width or height of the frame, choose units of measurement and enter numbers in the Column Width and Height boxes.
- To set (or reduce) margins in frames, change the numbers in the Width or Height boxes.
- To prevent users from resizing the frames (by dragging the borders), click Resizable In Browser to uncheck it.
- To change how browsers should decide whether to show scroll bars, choose Always, Never, or If Needed in the Show Scrollbars list box.

When you're done, click OK.

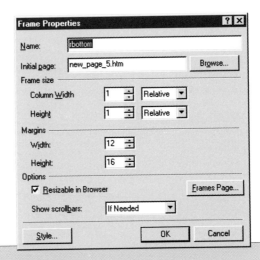

Figure 7.25: Change the properties of a frame in this dialog box.

Hyperlinks Require Frame Targets

When you create hyperlinks in a frames-based web, you have to identify the target frame where the destination page should appear (especially if it is a different frame from the one containing the hyperlink). To do so, click the Change Target Frame button in the bottom-right corner of the Create Hyperlink dialog box, and then choose one of the frames, Whole Page, or New Window (to open the link in an entirely separate browser window), and click OK. Otherwise, the process is the same as outlined in the earlier part of this chapter.

EXPERT ADVICE

Even in webs that don't use a frames-based design, you can direct a hyperlink to open a new window. This is a good way to link to other sites without losing your visitor.

Setting Up Your No Frames Page

Not all browsers can interpret frames pages, so part of the frames standard is to incorporate "no frames" content for such browsers. Traditionally, this has been a very unhelpful message encouraging the user to get a browser with frames capability. To see the "no frames" content for the page you just created, choose the No Frames tab at the bottom of the window.

Then change it to something more helpful (such as actual content, or alternative links to pages in your web).

There's More . . .

Now that you know how to insert hyperlinks into pages and how to set up navigation aids for your web, you've got the essential ingredients of web design under your belt. In the next chapter, we'll discuss some of the frills: namely, animations and other "juiced up" web content that FrontPage can help you create. If you're disinclined to mess around with animations and other fancy-schmancy content, consider skipping directly to Chapter 9 to learn how to publish your web once you've created enough of the key pages.

CHAPTER 8

Animating Your Pages

INCLUDES

- Inserting FrontPage and Microsoft Office Components
- Adding animation through DHTML and page transitions
- Creating forms for user response
- Creating and managing discussion groups
- Adding database connectivity to your web

Insert Buttons That Change
When You Point at Them ➡ pp. 203–204

1. Select Insert | Components | Hover Button.
2. Type the button text and the link target.
3. Choose formatting for the button.
4. Choose an effect for the button.
5. Click OK.

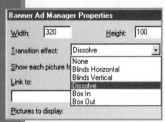

Schedule a Picture ➡ pp. 204–205

1. Select Insert | Component | Scheduled Picture.
2. Select the starting and ending dates and times for the picture to appear.
3. Enter the filename of the picture or browse to select it.
4. Schedule any other pictures to alternate in the same space.
5. Click OK.

Sell Your Soul to the Adman ➡ pp. 205–207

1. Select Insert | Component | Banner Ad Manager.
2. Enter the width and height of your banner ads.
3. Choose a transition effect.
4. Click the Add button and choose the first ad.
5. Click OK and repeat step 4 for any other ads you want to appear in the same space.
6. Use Move Up and Move Down to change the order of the ads, if need be.
7. Enter or browse to the filename of the page to which the ads should link.
8. Click OK.

Add Dynamic Effects to
Any Page Element ➡ pp. 213–215

1. Select Format | Dynamic HTML Effects to bring up the Dynamic HTML toolbar.
2. Select any element on the page (such as text or an image).
3. Choose the event that will trigger the effect in the toolbar.
4. Choose the effect you want in the toolbar.
5. Click the Preview tab to see the effect in action.

Add Cinematic "Wipes" to Page Transitions ➥ pp. 217–218

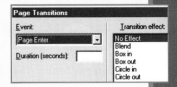

1. Select Format | Page Transition.
2. Choose an event to trigger the transition (entering or exiting the current page or the entire web site).
3. Choose a short duration.
4. Choose a transition effect.

Make Your Web Interactive with Forms ➥ pp. 216–221

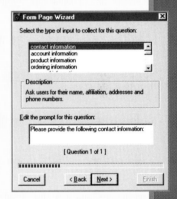

1. Select File | New | Page.
2. Double-click the Form Page Wizard.
3. Let the wizard take you through the form-building process.
4. Right-click on the form to determine where the results will be saved.

Create a Discussion Group ➥ pp. 223–224

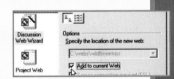

1. Select File | New | Web.
2. Click the Discussion Web Wizard icon.
3. To add the group to your existing web, click Add To Current Web.
4. Let the wizard take you through the process of building a discussion web.

Hook Up Your Web to an Existing Database ➥ pp. 226–229

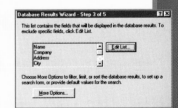

1. Install the Active Server Pages extensions (or make sure they are installed at your provider's site—see Chapter 9 for more on server extensions).
2. Register your database with the Open Database Connectivity Driver in the Control Panel.
3. Select File | Import, click Add File, find the database file you want to import, and click Open to import the database.
4. Use the Database Results Wizard to insert database forms onto a page in your web.

If you're tired of web pages that just lie there, then you can use some of the components built into FrontPage to juice up your pages. Most of these features depend on you publishing your web at a site with FrontPage server extensions installed (see Chapter 9 for more information). You should be careful not to overload any one page or your web as a whole with too many fancy doohickeys. Remember that the content is the most important part of your site. That said, anything that engages your readers— or, better yet, involves them interactively in the site—will make your web more compelling.

There's a lot to cover in this chapter. Don't be discouraged if you find parts of it confusing—it's some of the most technical material presented in the book. As you're a busy person, you may well have better things to do than teach your web pages a few of these dog and pony tricks. For those who want to persevere, we'll start with the easier, virtually automatic components, such as those that make pictures move or change at specified times or intervals, and work our way up to content that responds to a user query.

Inserting FrontPage Components

FrontPage comes with a number of components that you can insert easily by choosing them from the Component menu.

Inserting and Formatting a Marquee

A *marquee* is essentially moving text, much like a stock ticker. I personally don't find marquees particularly compelling, but it's not for me to make your design decisions for you. To create a marquee, select Insert | Component | Marquee. This brings up the Marquee Properties dialog box, shown in Figure 8.1. Enter the text you want to animate in the Text field. Then choose options so that the text behaves as you wish.

CAUTION

Marquees created by FrontPage 2000 appear in Netscape browsers as plain (unmoving) text in the browser's default font.

Inserting a Hover Button

A *hover button* is a button that responds in some way when the mouse pointer passes over it and can be used anywhere you might otherwise use a button. FrontPage 2000 includes a tool that creates hover buttons with a variety of effects.

EXPERT ADVICE

Once you've created your marquee, you can recall the Properties dialog box by selecting the marquee and pressing ALT+ENTER, or by right-clicking and choosing Marquee Properties from the context menu, or double-clicking the component on the page. The same is true for all FrontPage components.

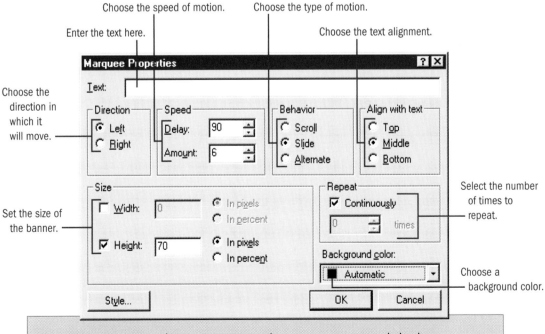

Figure 8.1: Format a tickertape marquee on the Marquee Properties dialog box.

To create one, choose Insert | Components | Hover Button. This displays the Hover Button Properties dialog box, shown here. Enter the text to appear on the face of the button, and enter, or browse for, the page (or bookmark) to which the button should link.

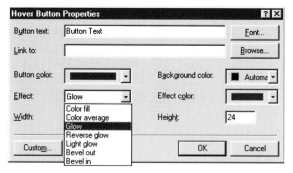

To choose a font, click the Font button. This displays a simplified Font dialog box, in which you can choose one of four fonts—Arial, Courier New, Times New Roman, or MS Sans Serif (the default). You can also choose a font style, a size, and a color.

Next, choose an effect (or keep Glow, the default effect, which makes the middle of the button glow in the effect color):

TIP

The bevel effects don't show up very well in dark colors.

- **Color Fill**   The effect color fills the entire button.
- **Color Average**   A color between the background and effect colors fills the button.
- **Reverse Glow**   The button glows at its edges.
- **Light Glow**   The button glows with a washed-out color.
- **Bevel Out**   The button appears to pop out.
- **Bevel In**   The button appears to pop in.

Scheduling a Picture

Sometimes you may want to call attention to a particular event. Your group may have a meeting scheduled on the last Wednesday of every month, for example, or you may need to warn everyone of an

---

EXPERT ADVICE

Be aware that the font size interacts with the button height, determined in the main Hover Button dialog box. Your button height has to be great enough to hold the text size you choose, and your button width has to be great enough to hold all the text you want to appear on it. Generally, you'll want to limit the text on buttons to a word or two.

efficiency expert's impending visit. Who knows, you may even want to announce a special sale on a new product.

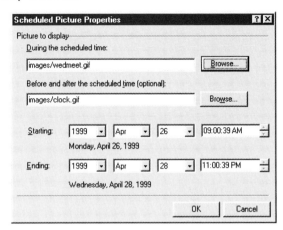

To insert a scheduled picture, choose Insert | Component | Scheduled Picture. This brings up the Scheduled Picture Properties dialog box shown here. To insert a picture at a specified time, click the Browse button and select the picture file, and then set the starting and ending dates and times.

If you want a different picture to appear in the same space at other times, enter its location as well. Click OK when you are done.

Inserting and Managing Banner Ads

The Banner Ad Manager is used to display a set of images in a series, all in the same space. You've no doubt seen such displays on commercial web sites. You can use them for any series of images—they don't have to be ads, but they *should* all be the same size.

To begin, you must create your images using a graphics program. I suggest that you create one image as a template and use the File | Save As command to create as many copies as you want images, which will ensure that they are all the same size. You can then fill the templates with whatever content you want.

Before you close your graphics program, use whatever feature will tell you your image's height and width in pixels because you'll need this information later on.

EXPERT ADVICE

Make the scheduled image the same size as the one it is to replace so you don't have to worry about reformatting the page.

All set? Click on the screen where you want the banner ads to appear. Then choose Insert | Component | Banner Ad Manager and you'll see this dialog box:

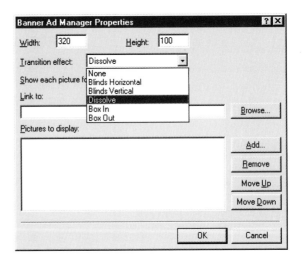

Enter the correct dimensions in the Width and Height fields. If you don't, the space not filled by your image will be gray.

1. Choose a transition effect. Here are your choices:

- **None**   The new image simply replaces the old one.
- **Blinds Vertical**   The new image appears with a "venetian blinds" effect.
- **Blinds Horizontal**   The same as Blinds Vertical, only with horizontal blinds.
- **Dissolve**   The new image appears to come up in speckles through the existing one. This is the default.
- **Box In**   The new image grows from the edges toward the center.
- **Box Out**   The new image grows from the center toward the edges.

You may have to experiment to decide which effect you like best. Fortunately, you can see the effects in the Preview window.

2. Click the Add button. You'll see a standard image-file dialog box. Choose one of the images that's to be part of your display. Click OK.

3. Repeat step 2 for each image you want to rotate.

4. Use the Move Up and Move Down buttons to get them in the order you want them to appear.

5. If you want your banner to be clickable, enter, or browse for, the page to display when the image is clicked.

6. Click OK.

That's all there is to it!

Inserting Office Components

FrontPage 2000 includes a set of three *Office components*—a spreadsheet, a chart, and a pivot table. These are all roughly equivalent to the same features of Excel, but somewhat stripped down. It is important to note that they are all ActiveX controls, which means that they are viewable only in Internet Explorer 4.0 and later. If you've set up your system for compatibility with Netscape, or with earlier browsers, you can't use them, and they will not appear on your menus. If you can be sure that your audience uses only Internet Explorer 4.0 and later (which is most likely to be true on an intranet), spreadsheets and pivot tables can be used as a tool for the interactive management and analysis of data. However, they can also be used to display read-only data, if formatted correctly.

EXPERT ADVICE

If you want to use these components for those who can view them, but also provide an alternative for those who can't, select a component and press ALT+ENTER to bring up the ActiveX Component Properties box. Here you can enter the URL of an alternative page to be displayed in place of the one containing the ActiveX component.

Inserting and Setting Up a Spreadsheet Component

To insert a spreadsheet component, click at the point where you want it and choose Insert | Component | Office Spreadsheet. As you can see in Figure 8.2, it has many of the elements of a standard Excel spreadsheet. Although there's no menu in the usual sense, and only a limited toolbar, there's quite an extensive toolbox.

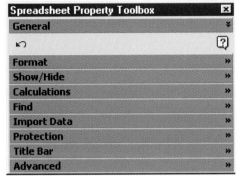

These are the tools most necessary for analysis. There are many tools in the Toolbox that let you disable various elements to protect the data, if you wish.

You can use this spreadsheet as you would an Excel spreadsheet—enter data, enter formulas, sort, and filter, but the functionality doesn't extend much beyond that. For what you *can* do, you need to look at the Spreadsheet Property Toolbox, shown on the left.

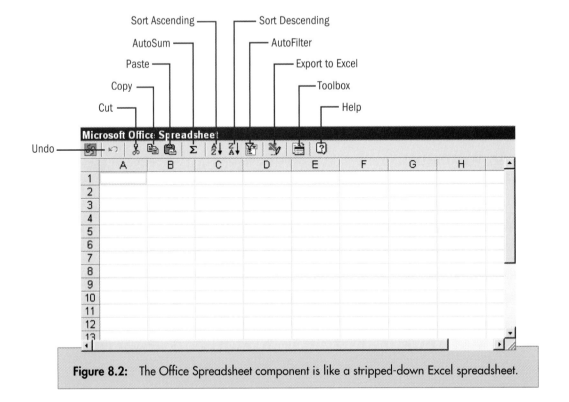

Figure 8.2: The Office Spreadsheet component is like a stripped-down Excel spreadsheet.

To display the Toolbox, either click on the Toolbox icon on the toolbar, or select a cell and right-click it. As with most spreadsheets, commands affect what is selected, so when you're actually creating a spreadsheet, you should select the target area before you open the Toolbox.

The first step is to enter the data, and this is done here the same way you would in an Excel spreadsheet. (You can see the spreadsheet with the data entered in Figure 8.3.)

Next, select the numeric cells, open the Toolbox and click on Format. You see the Format section of the Toolbox, shown next:

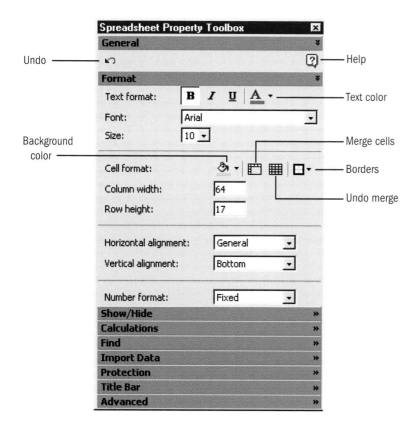

Formatting the Spreadsheet

In the Format toolbox, you see a subset of the usual spreadsheet formatting tools. Use the Number Format drop-down list to change the format to Fixed. (That's a fixed number of decimal places, in this

	A	B	C	D	E	F	G	H
1		Billy	Dot	Jim	Bob	Mary	Yolanda	Sarah
2								
3	Phone	2.25	0	3.75	1.75	4	5.8	0.3
4	Travel	0	0	0	23.86	194.16	0	
5	Office Supplies	8.23	16.32	0.67	14.08	2.3	4.27	
6	Entertainment	0	0	0	0	85.36	27.12	
7	Tools	0	0	0	0	0	19.42	67.0
8	Misc.	4.12	0.47	13.26	1.38	0	0	7.2
9								
10	Total	14.6	16.79	17.68	41.07	285.82	56.61	74.8
11	GRAND TOTAL	507.19						
12								
13								

Figure 8.3: I placed column totals at the bottom of each column using the QuickSum button and entered a formula to calculate the grand total.

instance: two. You don't have the option of any other fixed number.) With the toolbox still open, you can click in the A column label to select the first column and click the bold icon to boldface the row titles. Then click the row label 1 to select the column titles and click the bold icon twice (because the first cell has already been made bold by the column selection, and you have to turn it off to work on the whole row). You can do the same with the rows showing the totals.

To right-justify cells, rows, or columns, make a selection, click the Horizontal Alignment drop-down list, and choose Right.

To add colors, select column or row labels and click the Background Color icon, which displays a pallette.

To add a bottom border, select the bottom row and click the Borders icon, which displays a mini-window shown on the left.

EXPERT ADVICE

You can select multiple rows or columns by placing your pointer in the label at one end of the range to be selected and dragging to the other end.

Showing or Hiding Parts of the Spreadsheet

To control what parts of the spreadsheet are displayed on your web page, click the Show/Hide button on the Spreadsheet Property Toolbox to expand its section and display its options shown here.

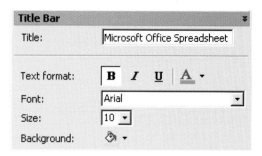

You can hide the toolbar, the grid lines, and (or) the column headers. You won't need the toolbar if you're just displaying data, nor would you probably need row headers. You may also choose to hide the grid lines for a cleaner look. (Borders you placed deliberately will still appear.)

Formatting the Title Bar

Keep the title bar, but replace its unhelpful title ("Microsoft Office Spreadsheet"). To change it to something more relevant, open the Title Bar section of the Toolbox. Change the title here and change the background color to a shade that goes with your color scheme, if you wish.

Protecting the Data

To prevent the values in your spreadsheet from being edited or erased, go to the Protection toolbox.

Here you see five check boxes:

- **Enable Protection** Prevents cells that have been locked from being changed, either in FrontPage or in a browser.
- **Lock Cells** Selects the cells on which protection will be in effect if you enable it. This selection is chosen by default.
- **Allow Property Toolbox At Run Time** Gives visitors to your site access to this very toolbox and is turned on by default. This is appropriate when data is posted on the web for input, analysis, and collaboration, but not when it's posted for display.
- **Allow Sorting** and **Allow Filtering** Should require no explanation.

You definitely don't want anybody to undo all your hard work, so click Allow Property Toolbox to prevent access. Then select the entire spreadsheet and click Enable Protection twice. (You have to do it twice because some of the cells are already protected and the first click turns off all protection.)

Finishing Touches

Just two more steps, and you're done. Open the Advanced toolbox. Just change the Vertical Scroll Bar setting to False, since all the data can easily fit on the screen vertically. To tweak the final shape of the component, click its bottom edge and drag it up or down a little.

Inserting and Setting Up a Chart Component

Once you've set up a spreadsheet, you can make a chart from it. First, take note of the cell addresses containing the data you want to chart because you won't be able to reach this information very easily once you've started. Next, choose Insert | Component | Office Chart. This brings up the Microsoft Office Chart Wizard, which takes you

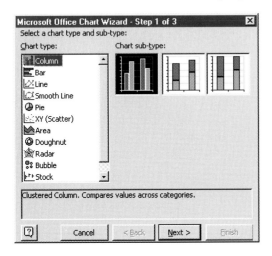

through creating the chart in five steps. You see Step 1, choosing a type of chart to display, in the illustration on the left. We're going to make a bar graph of the totals in the spreadsheet, so you can accept the default. A blank chart has meanwhile been placed on your page. Click Next without further ado.

The next step gives you a choice of data sources. Just click Next again to use your spreadsheet. For the third step, you can click Set This Chart's Data In One Step and enter a spreadsheet range (a range of cells) into the dialog box that appears, or click the Add button, and set up the chart manually. To do so, type a name for the chart and enter the cell range containing the data you

---

EXPERT ADVICE

If you made a mistake entering the range, it should be clear in the dummy window, so you can correct it in the Values field.

EXPERT ADVICE

You can grab the handles on the edges of the chart and stretch or shrink it in either direction. If you shrink it far enough vertically, the interval between the horizontal scale points will double.

want to chart in the Values box (such as "=**B10:I10**") and the cell range containing the column labels in the Category (X-Axis) Labels boxes (such as "=**B1:I1**").

The Wizard will then preview your chart, as shown in the illustration on the right.

Click Finish to complete the Wizard process. The completed chart will appear on your web page.

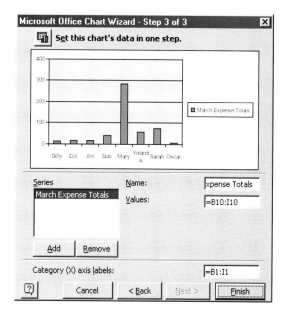

Inserting a Pivot Table Component

A pivot table is an interactive table that lets you analyze data dynamically from within your browser. It's really a cutting-edge spreadsheet feature that's available because of FrontPage's compatibility with other Office programs (in this case, Excel). To add a pivot table, select Insert | Component | Office Pivot Table.

Adding Dynamic HTML Effects

Another tool that can animate your page is Dynamic HTML (called DHTML for short). With DHTML, you can animate any portion of your page—a word, a picture, a paragraph, or virtually any other element. To use DHTML effects, choose Format | Dynamic HTML Effects. This displays the following toolbar:

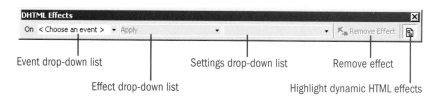

The basic formula for a DHTML effect is

`ON event APPLY effect [WITH settings]`

The effects you apply can all be viewed in the Preview window.

The effects you can apply depend on the object selected. If you select a picture, the only effect you can apply is to swap the picture with another. However, there are many effects you can apply to text. You can choose the following events to trigger an effect:

- **Page Load**   Allows a variety of effects, to be described later in this chapter.
- **Mouse Over**   Allows only the Formatting effect.
- **Click**   Allows the effects Fly Out or Formatting.
- **Double Click**   Allows the effects Fly Out or Formatting.

The effects are as follows:

- **Drop In By Word**   If text is selected, the words in the selection drop from the top of the window, one at a time.
- **Hop**   The selected items appear one at a time, in sequence, flying in a graceful curve above the resting line. If the effect were applied to a graphic and a heading, the graphic would appear first, followed by the words of the heading, with each word in turn hopping out of the previous object.
- **Elastic**   The object enters from the one direction, lands gently, and appears to bounce off the opposite border. Choose settings of From Right or From Bottom.
- **Spiral**   The object falls from the upper-left corner, swinging below and to the right of its final position before settling.
- **Wave**   Similar to Hop, except that the objects alternate swinging under and over the resting line.

EXPERT ADVICE

DHTML effects will appear in versions 4.0 or later of both Internet Explorer and Netscape, but not in earlier versions of either browser.

- **Wipe**　Best used on a graphic. The image fades in. From the Modifier drop-down list choose Left To Right, Top To Bottom, or From Middle.
- **Zoom**　This supposedly can zoom your object in or out, but it happens so fast that I couldn't really see anything.
- **Fly Out**　On a click or double-click event, the object leaves the screen in any of eight directions selectable in the Settings drop-down list.
- **Formatting**　On a mouse event, different formatting is applied to the object. From the Settings drop-down list, you can choose either font settings or border settings to change, or both.

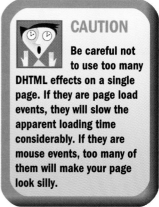

CAUTION
Be careful not to use too many DHTML effects on a single page. If they are page load events, they will slow the apparent loading time considerably. If they are mouse events, too many of them will make your page look silly.

If you're not happy with an effect after previewing it, click the Remove Effect button on the DHTML toolbar. The rightmost button highlights the areas to which effects have been applied. The effects you have assigned show up in a tool tip if you let the mouse pointer hover over the affected object in FrontPage.

Adding Page Transitions

Page transitions are like DHTML effects, but they affect an entire page, or site. With page transitions, you specify the way pages replace each other when visitors enter or leave them. The effects are very simple to use, and there are a lot of them, so I won't describe them in very much detail.

To apply a page transition, choose Format | Page Transition. You'll see the dialog box shown here.

Here are the events that can trigger a page transition:

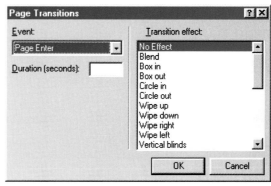

- Page Enter
- Page Exit
- Site Enter
- Site Exit

Be sure to enter a duration for the event in the duration box. Keep it short if you don't want to lose your visitors' interest. I've found that about five seconds is usually long enough to see the transition without its becoming boring.

Finally, choose your effect from the Transition Effect list box at the right of the dialog box, and that's all there is to it. You can preview the results either in the Preview window or a browser. If you decide you don't like the effect, open the page, open the dialog box, and choose No Effect.

Getting Feedback from Your Visitors

To enable visitors to contribute content to your web, volunteer information about themselves, or even order merchandise, you'll need to create a form. The easiest way to do this is to use FrontPage's Form Page Wizard, so we'll start with that.

Using the Form Page Wizard

To use the Form Page Wizard, choose File | New | Page and select Form Page Wizard. The wizard takes you through a series of questions about what you want on your form and creates the form to your specifications. The first page simply introduces the process. On the second page, click Add, then on the third page, choose a topic you want information about.

These are the choices:

- Contact Information
- Product Information
- Account Information
- Ordering Information

EXPERT ADVICE

If you use any of FrontPage's form handlers, your web *must* reside on a server that has the FrontPage Server Extensions installed. You can find out whether your server has them by calling your ISP. If it doesn't, you must either find a different ISP or write your own scripts to process the information. See Chapter 9 for more on servers and server extensions.

- Personal Information
- One Of Several Options (a radio button group or a check box group)
- Any Of Several Options (a check box group)
- Boolean (radio buttons or a check box)
- Date
- Time
- Range
- Number
- String (one word)
- Paragraph

Click an option, such as Contact Information, and an editable prompt will appear (such as "Please provide the following contact information:"). Edit it now, or later when it appears on the page. Click Next, and choose which items should be requested on your form, as shown in the illustration on the right.

Other input types yield similar forms, but with different items. When you click Next, the prompt appears in a box with an Add button so you can add additional items to the form. You might, for example, add a couple of Boolean questions: "I would like to become a volunteer?" and "Would you like to subscribe to our monthly e-mail newsletter?" Choose input types, such as a check box or Yes/No "radio" buttons (True/False buttons are also available). You can also modify the names of the variables that will pass the answers to the form handling software (such as Volunteer or Newsletter).

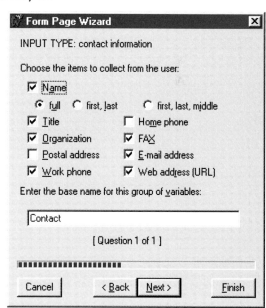

On these screens, you also have the options of modifying and deleting questions. When you click Finish, the wizard creates a new page for you, containing the form nicely laid out in a table, like the one in Figure 8.4.

The form area is enclosed in broken lines. The wizard has taken care of assigning variable names to all the fields it created, and

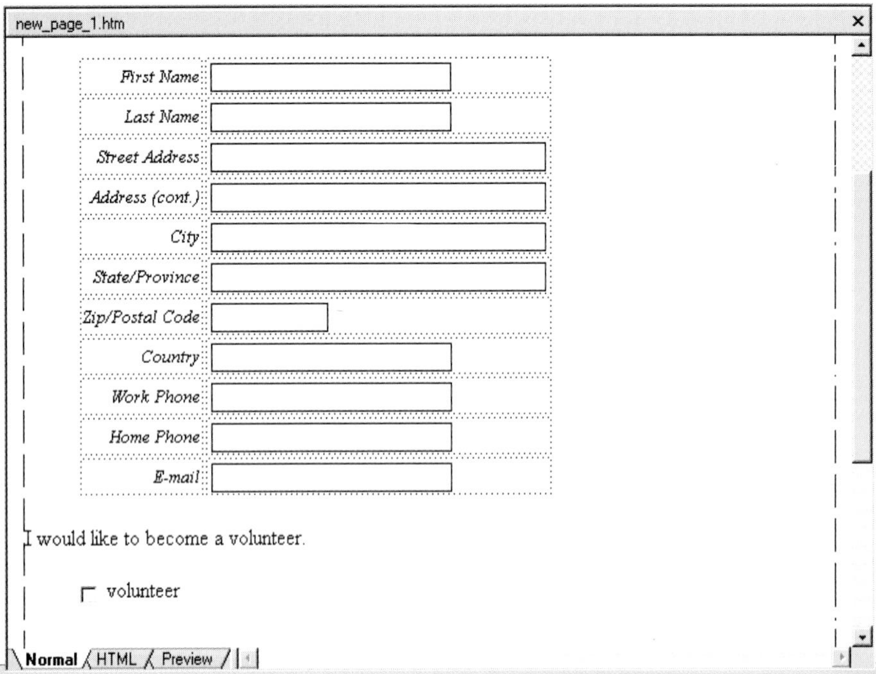

Figure 8.4: A basic contact-information form with a check box for volunteers.

assigning appropriate lengths to the fields, so you don't have to worry about that; but you may want to make some changes. I'll tell you how later in this chapter.

Before we copy the result to a page in our web, there's quite a bit more work to be done. We need to:

1. Set up a procedure for saving the results.
2. Make sure the visitors enter valid information.
3. Create a confirmation page, so the visitor can verify that the answers are correct.

Saving the Results

To take the remaining steps, we need to work with the form's properties. Right-click anywhere in the form (but outside the table) to bring up the Form Properties sheet.

You have several options on where to save the information, as the illustration on the right shows.

- Send the results to a file.
- Have the information sent to an e-mail address.
- Save the information in a database.
- Write a custom script to process the information.

This is also the page where you can give your form a name, and, if you want it to appear in a frame, specify the frame. Notice that you can save the results both to a file and to an e-mail address, but if you choose either of the other options, the first two become unavailable. In this section I'll show you how to save the results to a file and to e-mail, plus a few other options. Later in the chapter, I'll show you how to save the results to a database. (Ultimately a database is by far the handiest form in which to have the results, because you can search and sort the data, but it's also the hardest to set up.)

The first choice offered appears to be an HTML file, but you can actually save the results to any of a wide variety of file types, as you'll see momentarily. To proceed, choose Send To, then click the Options button. This brings up a tabbed dialog box, which we'll go over carefully because you need it all. The first page, File Results, is shown on the right.

EXPERT ADVICE

Whether to include the field names depends to some extent on what type of file you're saving the results to. In an HTML format it might be useful, but you don't want to clutter up a text database by inserting multiple instances of the field names.

The Form Properties dialog box offered to save the results to a page called formrslt.htm. Let's change the filename to refer to it as a Members page. As you can see on the File Results tab, there's a File

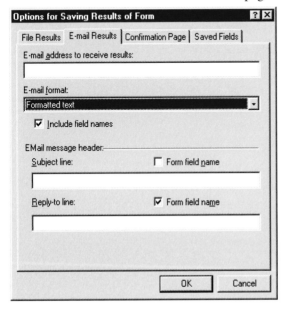

Format drop-down list from which you can choose any of several file types (all of which are either HTML formats or text databases). By default, you can include the field names in the file and place the latest results at the end. Optionally, you can save the results to a second file, perhaps of a different type.

Next, click the E-Mail Results tab, shown on the left.

Here you enter the e-mail address to which results are to be sent, the format (you have the choice of formatted text, as well as the same options listed earlier in this section), and whether field names should be included.

Most important, you can also enter the text for the subject line of the e-mail (or have FrontPage include the information from a form field) and for the From (Reply-to) line. It's great to have FrontPage place the sender's e-mail address in the form line, so check Form Field Name. However, you may not know the exact name of the field, so you'll need to turn to the Saved Fields tab, shown on the left.

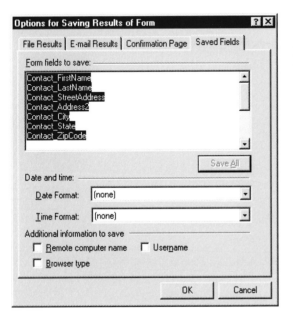

To pass all the form data along, click Save All. The field you want is Contact_Email, so go back to the E-Mail Results page and enter that information. Note, however, that on the Saved Fields tab, you can ask to have the following other types of information saved (in addition to those you asked for in the form):

- The date, in a format you can choose
- The time, in a format you can choose
- The name of the computer from which your visitor is logging in

- The type of browser being used (useful if you want to direct the user to appropriately formatted pages)
- The username

Click OK twice to exit. Now you're done with saving the results for the moment. There'll be more to do later (such as customizing the confirmation page your users will see when they submit a form entry).

Validating Form Information

You can save yourself (and your users) grief if your form validates data as it's entered, rejecting invalid or erroneous data. To enable the form to validate a field, right-click on it, and choose Form Field Validation. What you see depends on what type of information you've asked for. For example, I've chosen the Zip Or Postal Code field, and FrontPage has displayed a Text Box Validation dialog box, shown here.

Notice the Data Type drop-down list. It applies No Constraints by default, but you can choose Text, Integer or Number. You might think otherwise, but we should choose Text for the Zip Or Postal Code field. British Commonwealth postal codes contain letters and spaces as well as numbers, while U.S. Zip codes contain numbers and hyphens. When you choose Text, the Text Format options become available. To make sure you cover all your bases, check all of them, and add a hyphen to the Other field. (If you had chosen Number type, the Numeric Format options would have become available.)

We need to have Zip codes to send mail to new members, so check the Required box and enter a minimum length of 5. (It's customary to place a red asterisk on the field names of required fields and include a note of explanation.) If you want to restrict the input to a range, you can check the Data Value boxes at the bottom of the page, choose an operator, and enter a value.

Now that the form is complete, all that's left is to copy it to a page in the web. (But rest assured, there are more surprises to come.)

Creating a Confirmation Page

To set up the confirmation page, first create a new page to be used for the purpose. I recommend starting by choosing File | New | Page and selecting Confirmation Page because it gives you some instruction and examples. Save the page as confirm.htm. Now go back to the page that contains the form and right-click in it to bring up the Form Properties dialog box, click Options, choose the Confirmation Page tab, and enter the filename.

Before you close the box, click the Saved Fields tab, and press CTRL+C to copy the field names. You'll need them. Now click OK twice to get out of the dialog boxes and go back to the confirmation page.

On the confirmation page, you'll enter a series of confirmation fields. First, however, paste the field names onto this page so you can see them. If you don't enter the field names exactly right, they won't be processed.

TIP

To enter a confirmation field, choose Insert | Component | Confirmation Field. This brings up a dialog box that simply asks for the name of the field to confirm. The easiest way to confirm all your fields is to cut each one from this page with CTRL+X, one at a time, and paste them into the dialog box with CTRL+V. Some of the fields will need explanatory labels, so you can add them here. You should also format the address.

Adding Discussion Groups

One of the best ways to foster interactivity at a web site is to enable your visitors to congregate and discuss topics with one another. If you build it, they will come. Reader-contributed content can keep a web lively even when you don't have time to update it. Like most of the other components discussed in this chapter, the discussion group tools offered with FrontPage work only with FrontPage server extensions. If you don't have access to a server with the extensions installed, you may want to investigate some of the free services on the Web that offer discussion groups or chat rooms (usually supported by advertising, if you can stomach it).

EXPERT ADVICE

The quick way to step through the fields is to press DOWN ARROW, then press SHIFT+HOME to highlight the field, then press CTRL+X, I, O, F, CTRL+V, and ENTER.

In FrontPage, a discussion group is actually a complete web within your existing web (called a "subweb"—more on that in Chapter 10), and includes any of the following features:

- A table of contents that lists topics and articles within each topic
- A search form so your readers can search for articles using keywords
- An entry form readers use to submit new articles
- Threaded replies, so that other readers can follow up an article all within the same topic
- A confirmation page, which tells readers their articles have been posted successfully
- A registration form, in case you want to limit who can contribute to the discussions (such as only people from within your company)

Create a Discussion Group

To create a new discussion area, select File | New | Web. On the Web Site tab of the New dialog box, choose Discussion Web Wizard, check Add To Current Web, and click OK.

Choose which elements you wish to include in your discussion web in the second panel of Discussion Web Wizard, shown here.

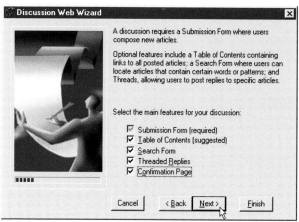

As you proceed, the wizard suggests a name for your web, the prosaic "Discussion," and a folder name, "_disc1," which doesn't matter as much. Enter a more relevant name for your discussion and change the folder name to match, if you like.

Determine which input fields you want to include in your discussion:

- Subject, Comments (the default)
- Subject, Category, Comments
- Subject, Product, Comments

FrontPage asks you whether the discussion takes place in a protected web. If you choose Yes, only registered users will be allowed. If you choose No, then anyone will be able to post articles (this is the default).

Select a sort order, either oldest to newest or newest to oldest (I prefer to see the newest articles first, but that's just me), and decide whether the table of contents for the discussion will also be the subweb's home page.

Then decide whether searches will return just the subject of each article found; the subject and size of each article; the subject, size, and date; or the subject, size, date, and score (meaning how relevant to the search terms the article appears to be).

Finally, decide whether you want to use a frames-based layout, one that involves ordinary pages, or both, tailored to the user's browser (Figure 8.5). See Chapter 7 for more on frames.

Even when the wizard is finished, you'll have more tweaking to do. Visit all the pages the wizard created and replace any dummy content you find with the actual categories or other information you intend to use.

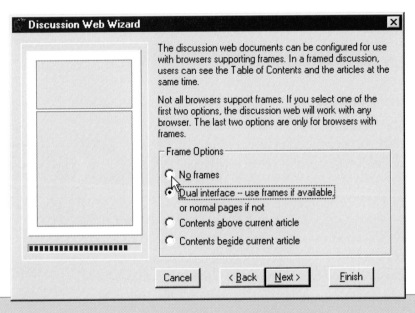

Figure 8.5: Choose how your discussion will appear to your visitors.

Set Properties for a Discussion Web

There are a number of discussion web properties you can control or change even after the wizard is done, including, among others:

- Table of contents format
- Background scheme
- Headers and footers

To fiddle with these settings, first open the page that contains the form for posting articles (its filename will end in "_post"). Right-click the form and select Form Properties on the menu that pops up. Click the Options button and then select the Discussion tab.

To set or change properties for articles in the discussion group web, click the Article tab on the same dialog box. I wouldn't play around with the URL options, but you can change the date and time format and choose whether an article's author's name or computer name will appear with his posts here.

Registering Users

If you chose to create a protected (private) discussion web, you'll have to register site visitors. The wizard created a registration form for you, but you'll have to open it and customize it as needed, save it to the root web (that is, the primary web, not the subweb) where the discussion group is located, and then make the page available to visitors.

Moderating a Group

Depending on your web's article, you may find it wise to moderate the group, meaning to monitor the content and remove or alter offensive posts. To do so, first select Tools | Web Settings, and then click the Advanced tab on the Web Settings dialog box. Then select Show Documents In Hidden Directories and click OK.

Click Yes in the confirmation dialog box that appears to refresh the web.

Then, click Folders view and select the folder containing the discussion group articles. Articles will have unhelpful names like

0001.htm or 5877.htm, etc. Open the page in question in Page view (that is, double-click it). Do not delete any articles, as that will make the navigation links to and from that article stop working. Instead, replace any offensive text with an explanation, a reminder of the rules of civility for your discussion, or simple boilerplate, such as [Removed by Moderator].

Incorporating Database-Generated Content

First, a few words of caution: FrontPage 2000 has special extensions for displaying, searching, and adding to databases. These extensions fall under the rubric of *Active Server Pages* or ASP. In order to use any database elements constructed with the Database Results Wizard (FrontPage's tool for creating ASP), you must have the ASP server extensions installed, and then log onto your computer from Internet Explorer 4.0 or later and open the page as if it were a web site. (The syntax for doing so is http://localhost/*drive:/local path/file*.asp.)

Moreover, if you want your pages to be viewable on an intranet or web site, the server hosting the ASP pages must also have the ASP extensions installed. Since ASP is a proprietary technology of Microsoft, nobody can view ASP pages with Netscape products. That being said, you may prefer to create your database access using one of the many other database technologies available for web pages.

There are basically four steps to using FrontPage's database connectivity tools. The first step need be done only once; the others must be repeated for each database you want to use. The steps are as follows:

1. Ensure your ISP supports Active Server Pages.
2. Register your database with the Open Database Connectivity Driver in the Control Panel.
3. Import the database to be used into your web.
4. Use the Database Results Wizard to create the appropriate database forms on one of your pages.

Ready? Let's begin.

Registering Your Database

The basic procedure for registering a database is the same regardless of the application used to create the database. However, if you want to use an Excel database, you must take an extra step before you begin. If you're planning to use an Access database, you can skip this step entirely because FrontPage does it for you.

Setting Up an Excel Database for Use with FrontPage

Before you register your Excel database:

1. Open the worksheet containing the database in Excel.
2. Select the area containing the data to be regarded as a database.
3. Choose Insert | Name | Define.
4. Type a name for your database. (Remember the name you just entered. You'll need it again very soon.)
5. Click Add.
6. Make sure the range displayed at the bottom of the dialog box matches the area to be defined as a database.
7. Click Close.
8. Close the worksheet. (This is very important! Nothing from here on will work if you don't.)

Registering an Excel Database

This procedure also takes a very precise series of steps.

1. Open the Control Panel by selecting Start | Settings | Control Panel.
2. Open the applet called ODBC Data Sources (32 Bit). This opens the Data Source Administrator.
3. Choose the System DSN tab.
4. Click Add.
5. Choose Microsoft Excel Driver (*.xls).
6. Click Finish. This displays the ODBC Microsoft Excel Setup dialog box, shown next.

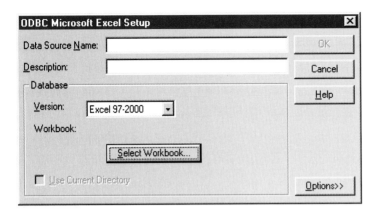

7. From the drop-down list, choose the version of Excel you're using.

8. Click Select Workbook. This opens an Open File browse window.

9. Find the copy of your workbook that's in your web folder.

10. Click Open.

11. In the Data Source Name field, enter the name you gave to the database range.

12. Enter a description in the description field if you want.

13. Click OK. If the data range name you entered doesn't match a named range in the worksheet, you will get an error message. Correct the name and click OK.

14. Click OK again.

Importing the Database

The basic procedure for importing a database is the same regardless of the application used to create the database.

1. Choose File | Import.

2. Click Add File. An Open File browse window opens.

3. Find the file you want to use.

4. Click Open.

The easy part's over now.

Using the Database Results Wizard

To demonstrate the use of the Database Results Wizard, I'm going to take you through two separate installations—one using an Excel database and one using an Access database. When everything works, the process should result in a set of table headings, or a single-record form, with space for the results of a search to appear. There should also be a search form.

Because many of the procedures are the same for all databases, I won't repeat them all, but by the time I'm done, you should have a good idea of what's available to you. We'll start with an Excel database.

Using the Wizard with an Excel Database

To begin, start with a new page, then choose Insert | Database | Results. This opens the Database Results Wizard, and on its first page you must create a database connection. You have three choices:

- Use The Sample Northwind Database.
- Use An Existing Connection.
- Create A New Connection.

Because you don't have a connection yet, select Create A New Connection, then click Create. This opens the Web Settings sheet. Click Add. This opens the New Database Connection dialog box, shown here.

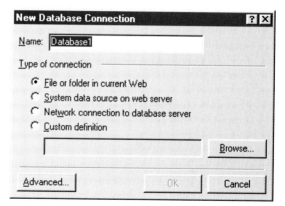

As you can see, FrontPage gives Database 1 as the default name for your connection. Change this to the name of the range you established in Excel. Since you've already imported the file to your web, the default connection type—File Or Folder In Current Web—is correct. Click Browse.

In the browse window that opens, go first to the Files Of Type drop-down list and choose Microsoft Excel Driver (*.xls). Click your workbook file and click OK. When you return to the Web Settings sheet, click Verify. If all is well, the question mark in the Status column should change to a check mark. If it hasn't, click Modify and verify that you typed the range name correctly.

Click OK. When you return to the Database Results Wizard, click Next. Here you must specify the record source containing the data you want to use. You have two choices. You can use the named range (the default choice), which appears in the Record Source drop-down list, or click Custom Query, click Edit, and write a SQL query, if you know SQL. For now, accept the default and click Next. FrontPage

CAUTION

The range name must be the same in Excel, the ODBC Settings applet, and the Web Settings sheet, otherwise FrontPage won't be able to connect to the database.

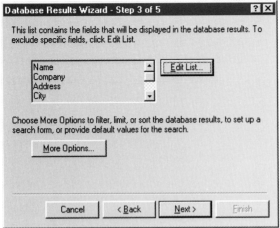

will test the connection and display either an error message or the dialog box shown on the left.

You'll see a scrollable list of field names. If you want to use only some of the fields in the database, click Edit List. This opens a box in which you can remove fields from those to be displayed, or change the order in which they appear. When everything is satisfactory, click Next.

On this page, you choose how your data will be formatted for display. You have three basic choices, which are in a drop-down list:

- **Table - One Record Per Row**   This creates a standard table in which you may edit the column heads, but can make no other changes.

- **List - One Field Per Item**   This creates what's known as a form in database parlance. You can rearrange and edit this form, as long as you do not make changes to the fields where the data will appear which are indicated like this: *<<fieldname>>*.

- **Drop-down list - One Record Per Item**   Your data is displayed one record at a time, depending on which record you choose in a drop-down list.

If you choose Table, you have three other choices, with check boxes:

- **Use Table Border**   Places a raised border around the table.
- **Expand Table To Width Of Page**   Is self-explanatory.
- **Include Header Row With Column Labels**   Places the field names in boldface at the top of the columns. This is very useful.

We'll choose Table - One Record Per Row for this example. Click Next when you've made your formatting choices.

You're now on the last step. Choose whether to display all records together or split them into groups. If you choose to split them, you can choose how many are in a group.

Also on this page is a check box for Add Search Form. Since the database will be useless without it, you should check it, unless you want to build one by hand.

Figure 8.6 shows the completed page, with a search form. I've edited the column heads (which would otherwise match the field names in the row below) to make them more human-friendly, and added a prompt to the search form.

Using the Wizard with an Access Database

Access databases are easier to use than others because FrontPage's database handler includes some special connections for Access. When you open an Access database in the Database Results Wizard, as soon as you create its database connection, FrontPage fills in the necessary details in the ODBC Data Sources applet. When you click Next, FrontPage supplies a record source name automatically. From that point on, the steps are the same as for an Excel database. FrontPage doesn't create a search form, but it does create a browse bar.

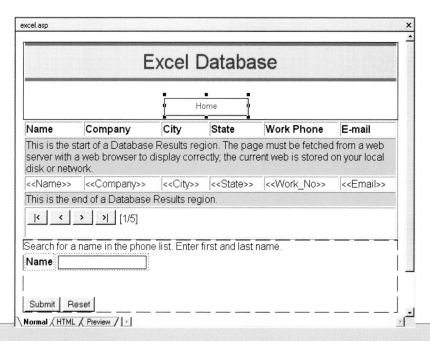

Figure 8.6: This database results page includes a search form at the bottom so users can refine a search.

EXPERT ADVICE

As the resulting page indicates, be sure to save with the file extension .asp. The page must be on a web server to be displayed correctly.

Using Advanced Features

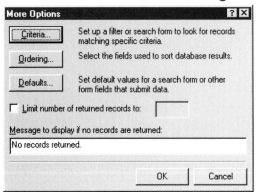

To use advanced features, click More Options, on page 3 of the wizard, which opens the dialog box shown on the left.

You can start here to enter search criteria, indexes, and/or default values. You can also limit the number of records returned from the database or change the default message FrontPage should display if no matches are found. We're going to add a sort feature and a couple of search criteria.

Sorting the Database

Start by clicking Ordering. Because this is a database of jazz recordings, the sort criteria should be artist's last name, artist's first name, and album title. Choose the fields containing that information, in that order. (You can change the order of the selected fields once you select them.)

Entering Search Criteria

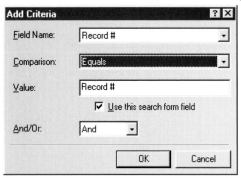

Next, set up search criteria for the search form. Click Criteria, then click Add, and you will see the dialog box shown on the left.

The upper drop-down list contains the field names, from which you can choose one to search on. The middle drop-down list contains a group of operators such as Equals, Is Greater Than, Contains, and so on. The third field is a space to enter a value. The default entry here is the name of the field you select. Leave it alone. Finally, a box lets you choose between And and Or. *And* means that this criterion and the one following it must be met. *Or* means either may be met.

You want people to be able to search by artist or title, so first choose Artist's Last Name Contains and set the And/Or choice to Or. Click OK, and the criterion is added to the list. Click Add again to add the Title field, and click OK. The Criteria list now looks like this:

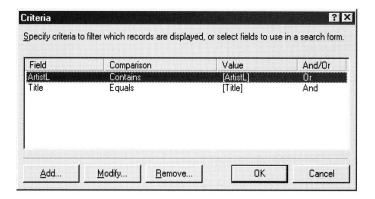

Next, choose the List format. If you choose List, the options change. These are the check boxes:

- Add Labels For All Field Values
- Place Horizontal Separator Between Records

In addition, there's a huge List Options drop-down list of styles for the data display . Choose Paragraph format because it's the most flexible. The resulting display form is rather ugly, and you'll want to edit it.

When it's finished, group various fields on single lines (such as first and last name), and change some of the labels to make them more meaningful. On the search form, add a prompt, and also change the labels. Right-click the Submit button, choose Form Field Properties, and change the button label to Search. Finally, center the buttons.

But there's one more step. The search fields have strange default values, such as <%=Request("ArtistL")%>. Double-click the form field, and delete those values. Figure 8.7 shows the finished page.

Now you know what you need to know to set up functional databases on the web, given the limitations of the technology.

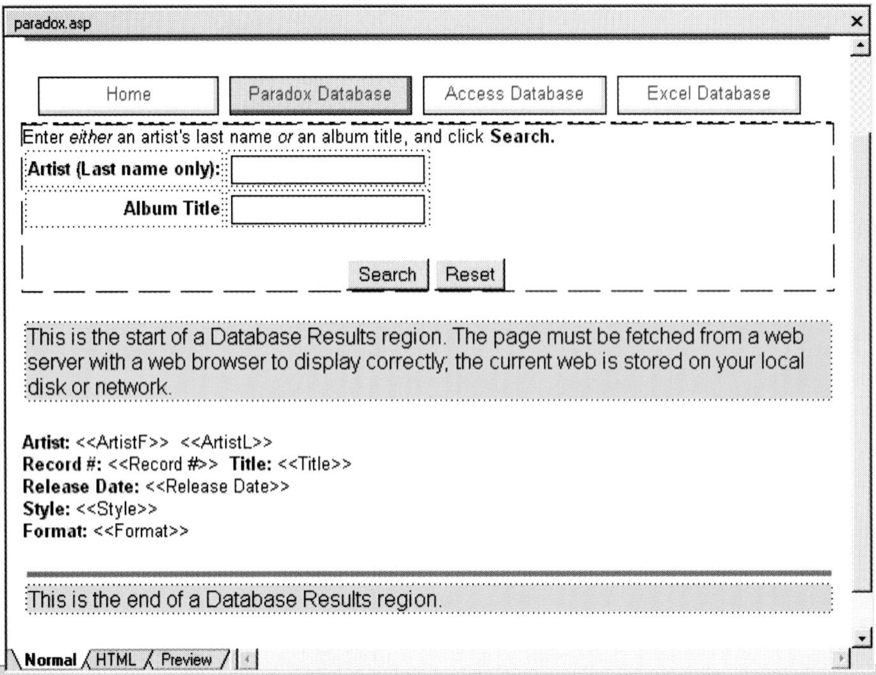

Figure 8.7: The database results page for a searchable database

There's More . . .

Whew! If you made it through this chapter then you have more time on your hands than I realized. Would you like to change the oil in my car? (Just kidding.) You should pat yourself on the back. You've now mastered far more of the elusive world of web development than many of the self-styled "webmasters" out there today. The last two chapters in this book deal with publishing your web somewhere where people can find it, and then maintaining and updating the web so it doesn't grow stale.

CHAPTER 9

Publishing Your Web

INCLUDES

- Finding a host for your web
- FrontPage server extensions
- Intranet publishing
- Checking for errors
- Publishing your web
- Deleting pages from a published web
- Tracking hits on a web page
- Promoting your web

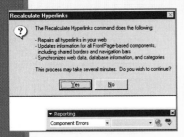

Check for Errors and Bad Links ➡ pp. 241–244

1. Click Reports in the Views bar.
2. Choose Component Errors in the list box on the Reporting toolbar.
3. Fix any errors reported.
4. Click the Verify Hyperlinks button on the Reporting toolbar, and then click Yes.

Flag Pages Not to Publish ➡ pp. 244–245

1. In Reports view, choose the Publish Status report on the Reporting toolbar.
2. Click in the Publish column to select a page.
3. Click the drop-down list that appears and choose Don't Publish.
4. Repeat steps 2 and 3 for each page you don't want to publish.

Publish Pages to a Server ➡ pp. 247–251

1. Select File | Publish Web.
2. Enter (or browse to) the address of your HTTP or FTP server, or the location of a server on your computer or intranet.
3. Click the Publish button.

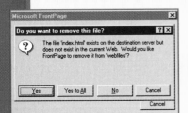

Remove Pages from a Server ➡ p. 255

1. Delete the pages from the local copy of your web.
2. Click the Publish button.
3. Click Yes to All.

Insert a Hit Counter ➥ pp. 257–258

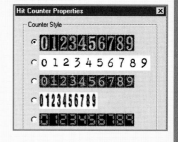

1. Select Insert | Components | Hit Counter.
2. Choose a style for your numbers.
3. Click OK.

Assign Keywords to
Promote Your Web ➥ pp. 260–261

1. Select File | Properties, and choose the Custom tab of the Page Properties dialog box.
2. Click the Add button and type **keywords**.
3. Press TAB and then type keywords, separated by commas, to help searchers find your web.
4. Click OK, and click OK again.

Everybody talks about publishing on the web, but what do they really mean? For example, my dad sells printing. Growing up, I understood publishing to mean something done with printing presses, on paper. Writers try to get their books published. Professors must publish or perish. In fact, the Web part of the Internet was originally conceived as a cheap and efficient way for academic folks to share their data and results. But material published on the Web is not printed on paper (or, rather, it *can* be printed on paper, but its paper existence is not the essence of its publication); it appears on computer screens—or on TVs, pagers, or other electronic media—and is considered published as soon as it is made available to the public. On an intranet, by analogy, web pages are considered published when they are made available to the intended audience.

Publishing comes after saving, and you don't publish everything you save. That is, you may save a partially finished draft of a web page, but you shouldn't publish it.

Throughout the book so far, I've had you save your web pages in a web folder on your computer or somewhere on your network. When you publish your web, FrontPage will copy your pages and files to a server, either on your computer or network, or elsewhere on the Internet. So before you can publish your web for the first time, you must choose a server, as I'll explain in the first section of this chapter.

EXPERT ADVICE

If you already had a web server installed on your computer or network, then you may have created your new web on that server, in which case pages saved directly to the server may be considered already published.

Choosing a Server

You might be wondering *where* you're supposed to publish your web. This is a good question. You'll need a web server, either one on the Internet or one on your network (on an intranet). Now, you might be wondering where you're going to find a server. This depends on the approach you take.

Perhaps the easiest solution (if not necessarily the cheapest) is to work with a service provider (or ISP, for Internet Service Provider) that offers web site-hosting among its other services. It's also possible to set up your own server (although keeping it up and running and connected to the Internet 24 hours a day, 7 days a week is another matter), or to make use of a server already installed on your network.

If your ISP, network, or local server is using Microsoft products, then it will support the FrontPage server extensions that make some of the groovier automatic features of your web work the way FrontPage implies they will. If you end up publishing your site on one of the other types of servers, then you will most likely not have access to those same server extensions and will have to look for alternative methods to add such dynamic elements to your site.

In this section, I'll discuss all of these considerations in further detail.

A great resource for anyone trying to manage web publishing on the cheap is Poor Richard's Web Site at *http://www.poorrichard.com/*. (Click the Free Information link in the upper-left corner.) You can buy his excellent book there as well.

Paying an ISP to Host Your Site

If you have an e-mail account with an ISP, then you may well already have access to a web server as part of your basic service. Check your provider's home page (inevitably, **http://www.***providerdomainname.* **com***or*.**net/**) and read up on available services. If web hosting is not included, you can look for a different ISP, either just to host your web site or to take over all your service-provider needs.

Hosting on Your Own Computer or Network

If you've already got a server on your computer or your network and FrontPage knows about it, *and* you created your web on the server (see Chapter 3), then you're already hosting your web, although the audience may be only your computer or the other people on your network. Possible FrontPage-compatible servers already installed include the following:

- **FrontPage Personal Web Server** came with earlier versions of FrontPage only, and is obsolete now. It supported FrontPage's old server extensions.
- **Microsoft Personal Web Server** comes with Windows 98, but you may have to install it separately from the CD (or have your network administrator install it for you). It supports the new FrontPage server extensions.
- **Microsoft Internet Information Server (IIS)** comes with Windows NT, and supports the new server extensions, as well as FrontPage's security features (see Chapter 10).

Even with MS IIS running on an NT system, you can install the MS Personal Web Server (PWS) from the Windows CD.

Ask About FrontPage Server Extensions

Regardless of whether you (or your system administrator) hosts your web or an outside ISP does this for you, you'll need to make sure FrontPage server extensions are installed with the host server, or many of the components covered in Chapter 8, for example, will not work. If you're looking for an ISP, make sure it offers FrontPage server extensions, or don't expect to be able to use any of those components.

To make sure FrontPage knows you'll be publishing on a server with FrontPage extensions (or if you're having trouble accessing some features), select Tools | Page Options, and choose the Compatibility tab of the Page Options dialog box. Then check Enabled With Frontpage Server Extensions (see Figure 9.1).

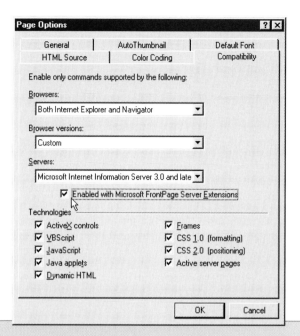

Figure 9.1: To take advantage of FrontPage server extensions, you have to let FrontPage know your server's got them, or the features that depend on them will not be available.

Preparing to Publish (Don't Go Off Half-Cocked)

Before you expose your web to the harsh glare of publicity, double-check to make sure you're not going to be publishing anything that's "not ready for prime time." You can give your web the once-over for obvious errors and omissions, and you can also mark which files you don't want published (yet, or ever) with the rest of the web.

Checking for Errors and Bad Links

You should check your web both for errors and for bad links (links that don't go anywhere or that contain errors). To check for errors in any and all components you've inserted into your web before publishing, select View | Reports | Component Errors.

FrontPage's Reports view lists all pages with errors and describes the specifics in the Errors column. Double-click any item to edit the page in question.

The errors can be hard to read even when you expand the window. Components that are based on FrontPage server extensions will show errors until published, if you're not editing the site on a local server with extensions installed.

To verify and update the hyperlinks in your web (see Chapter 7 for more on links), click the Verify Hyperlinks button on the Reporting toolbar.

This brings up the Verify Hyperlinks dialog box.

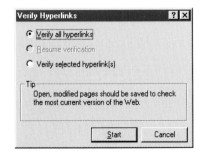

Click the Start button. Figure 9.2 shows some broken links in my WildflowerTrips web.

You can open any pages containing bad links and correct them the ordinary way or you can highlight a row reporting a bad link and click the Edit Hyperlink button on the Reports toolbar (see Figure 9.3).

Just retype the hyperlink's URL if you know what's wrong, or click the Browse button to look for the link's target somewhere within your web.

Replace hyperlink with:

news/index.htm   Browse...

When you've corrected the URL, click the Replace button.

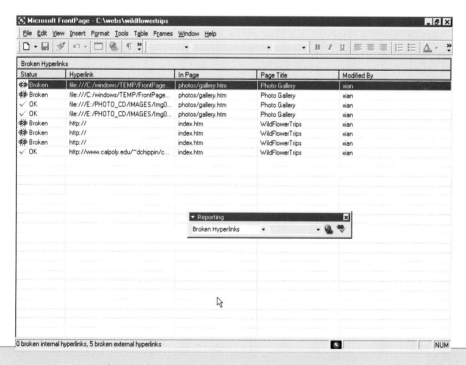

Figure 9.2: Most of the bad links reported here come from hyperlinks I didn't finish typing while showing you examples in Chapter 7.

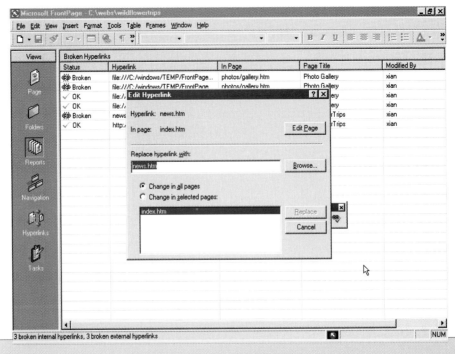

Figure 9.3: You can correct bad links from within Report view.

Determining What Goes Public

One final step before publishing your web is to identify what parts of the web are *not* ready for public consumption and marking them as such. To begin with, select View | Reports | Publish Status. The Publish Status lists all the files in your web, indicating in the Publish column either Publish or Don't Publish (see Figure 9.4).

To change the status of a single file (either from Publish to Don't Publish or vice versa), click the Publish cell in that file's row, and then

EXPERT ADVICE

Before you put your web out there, make sure any outstanding tasks have been completed. See Chapter 10 for more on tracking the progress of various tasks.

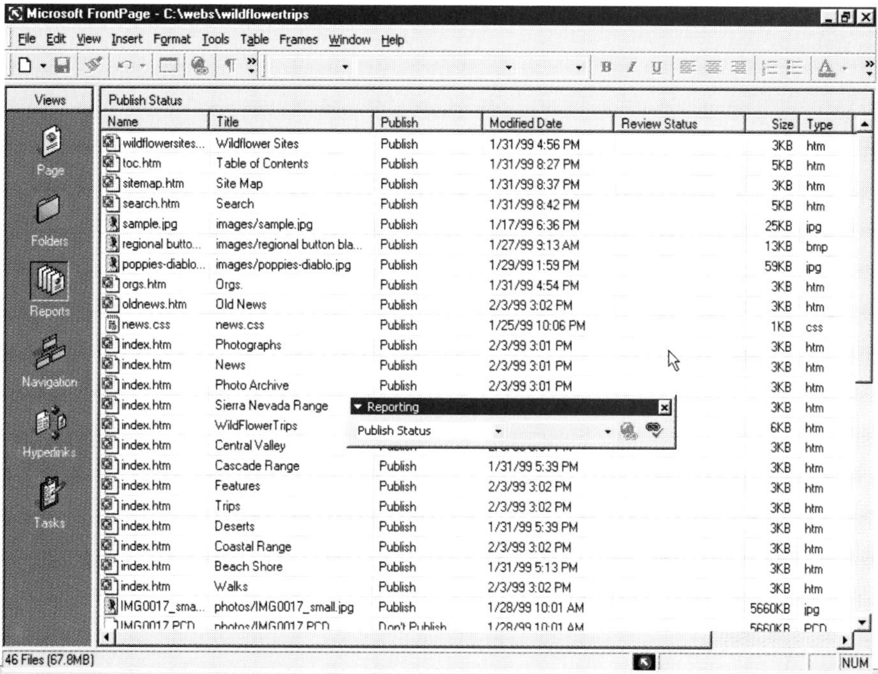

Figure 9.4: The Publish Status report gives you an overview of which pages in your web will be published. Click the Publish button at the top of the third column to sort pages by publish status.

choose the new setting you want from the listbox that drops down. (I had to click to highlight the row first, then click again to choose the row – at first I thought it wasn't working because when I just clicked on the cell it simply chose the row.)

FrontPage will change the status of that file.

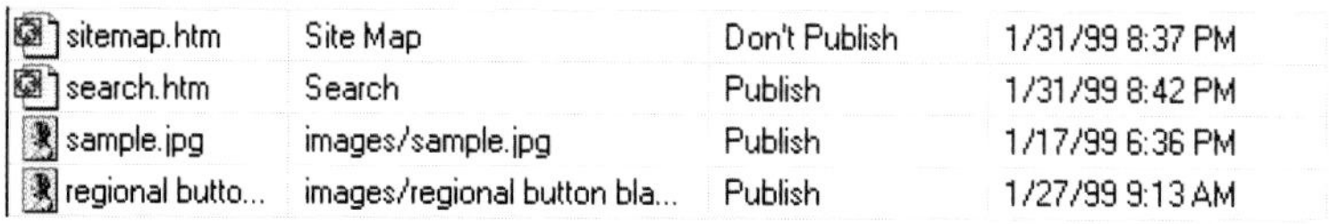

EXPERT ADVICE

Click on the Publish button at the top of report to sort your files by publishing status; click it again to reverse the sort order.

To change the publish status of a number of files at once, first select them in the Reports view (you may use Shift-click to select them all if they are contiguous or CTRL-click to add noncontiguous files to your selection). Then right-click on any of the selected files and choose Properties (see Figure 9.5).

This brings up a multiple-files Properties dialog box. Click the Workgroup tab (see Figure 9.6).

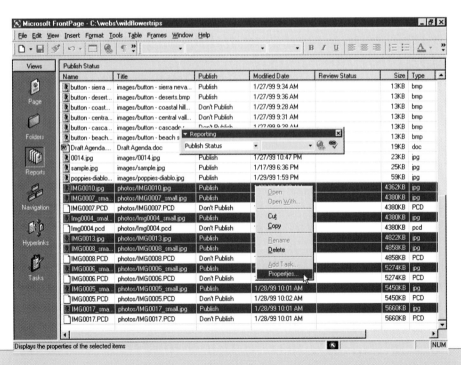

Figure 9.5: I made a bunch of huge thumbnail files while messing around, and I don't want to burden my Internet connection or my server by publishing them for no reason.

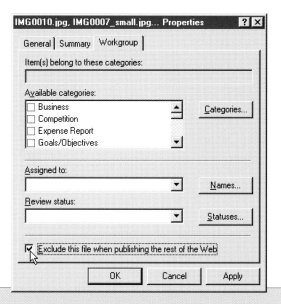

Figure 9.6: Click the checkbox at the bottom of the Workgroup tab of the Properties dialog box to exclude all selected files when publishing your web.

EXPERT ADVICE

Any hidden files in hidden folders in your web will not show up in this report. To include files in hidden folders, select Tools | Web Setting, click the Advanced tab, click Show Documents In Hidden Directories, and click OK.

Publishing Pages

Most web design or content-management programs brag about their "one button" publishing or some other such thing. Generally, this just means that the command for publishing your site is on a toolbar, or easily accessible from a menu. It's not a one-step process by any means, certainly not the first time. Once you've worked out the URL of the server to which you want to publish, and published the site once, updates might be accomplished in one step, but don't get frustrated if it doesn't seem as easy as advertised the first time around.

Publishing Your Web for the First Time

Anytime you want to publish some or all of a web, select File | Publish Web (or click the Publish Web button on the Standard toolbar). This brings up the Publish Web dialog box:

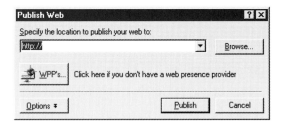

If you've published this same web before and just want to update anything that has changed since last time, skip ahead to "Publishing Changed Pages."

Looking for an ISP at the Last Minute

Even if you have no server and have put off searching for an ISP to host your site, the folks at Microsoft have thoughtfully provided for you by maintaining a web resource that lists the ISPs that install their server software. If you've got a server already installed or lined up, skip to the next section.

To choose from one of these Microsoft-friendly providers, click the WPP button. FrontPage will launch your web browser and take you to a Microsoft.com page with links to eligible providers. You can come to terms with an ISP and have a trial account set up nearly instantaneously. When you are ready, you'll have to continue from the Publish Web dialog box (where you left off).

Publishing via HTTP

For servers with FrontPage extensions installed, you can publish directly to a URL beginning with http:// (generally the same URL you'd give out for visitors). Your provider will tell you the URL to use. If you try publishing via HTTP to a server that cannot handle that form of upload, you'll get an error message, and you'll need to find out what FTP address you should be using (FTP always works).

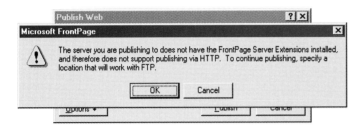

Publishing via FTP

If you want to make sure FrontPage remembers the FTP address to which you publish your web, type it in the Publish Web dialog box.

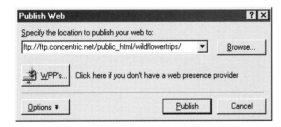

If you'd rather set up the FTP site in a way that other programs can access, click the Browse button. In the Open Web dialog box that appears, pull down the Look In list and choose Add/Modify FTP Locations (see Figure 9.7).

This brings up the Add/Modify FTP Locations dialog box (see Figure 9.8).

1. Type the domain of the FTP site.
2. Click User and type a username if it's different from the one suggested.
3. Press TAB and then type your password.
4. Click the Add button.
5. Click OK.

Figure 9.7: If you go through this rigamarole once, you can open from or save to this FTP site from numerous Windows programs.

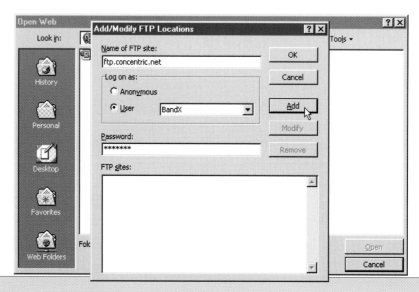

Figure 9.8: Add an FTP site to your permanent list here.

Then choose your FTP site in the Open Web dialog box.

Browse more if necessary, to get to the correct subfolder, and then click the Publish button.

Then skip ahead to "This May Take a While."

Publishing on an Intranet

From the point of view of FrontPage, publishing on an intranet is not much different from publishing on *the* Internet. It may be a little easier for you to find the right address the first time, since you can click the Browse button in the Publish Web dialog box and search around your network for the host server to which you have permission to publish your web.

EXPERT ADVICE

If Microsoft Word and other Office programs are standard issue on your intranet, then you can include Office documents "as is" in your web without worrying that folks with web browsers won't be able to open and read them.

On the other hand, you may find it more difficult if the server is down (not running) or not where you expect it—in which case you'll need to confer with your network administrator.

The URL for a local web server need not include any domain name information:

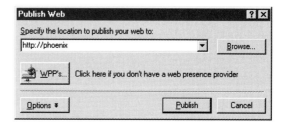

Windows 98's Web Folders feature can make publishing on an intranet much easier. Web Folders are server addresses that can be reached from anywhere within Windows, though naturally Microsoft's newest software, such as FrontPage and other parts of Office 2000, may be the first to take advantage of this feature.

If you click the Browse button, you can root around on your network for the location of your web server (see Figure 9.9).

Then FrontPage will remember the address you selected using Windows (or DOS, really) network syntax, starting with two backward slashes:

EXPERT ADVICE

If you're working on a server-based web, you can check the type of server software and whether FrontPage server extensions have been installed by selecting Tools | Web Settings and clicking the General tab.

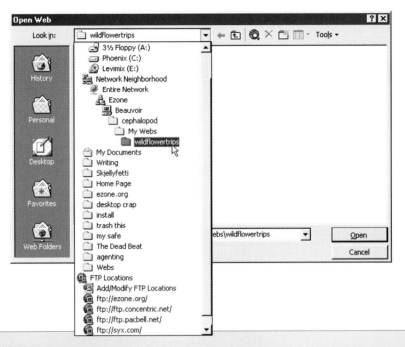

Figure 9.9: I'm going to publish my WildflowerTrips site across my network to this web server on my backup computer.

This May Take a While

If you try to publish a web that contains components to a server without the extensions to support them, FrontPage will warn you about the features that will not function as advertised.

Once FrontPage starts publishing your web, it may take some time to complete, especially as there are many large new files to upload. Meanwhile, the program will report to you on its progress...

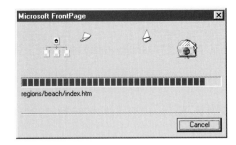

...and brag to you when it's done.

Click the underlined hyperlink on the dialog box to visit your published web in your default web browser.

Publishing Changed Pages

After the first time you publish your web, you won't need to republish every page in it every time you make a change (that is, unless you change them all, of course). One of the benefits of a program such as FrontPage over hand-coding web sites is its ability to keep track of what has changed in your staging area and what therefore needs to be updated at the public (published) site.

To update your published web, click the Publish Web button (ALT+P).

To make sure FrontPage will handle the update the way you want, click the Options button on the Publish Web dialog box. The dialog box will expand to include a few more choices.

CAUTION

Some dynamic (changing) pages in some webs should only be published once since they are updated by the server after that. These include guestbook files, hit counters, and discussion webs. Be sure to change the publish status of such pages after you've published them once.

If multiple people work on a web, you need to check pages in and out so that FrontPage doesn't accidentally overwrite them. See Chapter 10 for more on checking pages in and out.

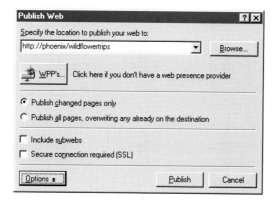

The Publish Changed Pages Only option should be selected. (Click it if it's not.) Click the Options button again to hide this area. You won't need to do this each time unless you have reason to think that you or someone else might have changed this setting since the last time you checked.

Then click the Publish button.

Cleaning Up Orphaned Pages

If you no longer use certain pages in your web, but you once published them, then they will linger at the public site, eating into your storage quota, for no good purpose. Instead, to remove pages from the published site, remove them from the staging web (the one you keep on your own computer or network). It's safer to move the specific files to a separate folder outside the web's hierarchy than to delete them outright, in that you can reverse the process if you change your mind.

Then, the next time you publish your web, FrontPage will offer to remove any files from the site that are absent from the local web:

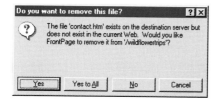

Click Yes (or Yes to All if you are feeling cavalier). Click Cancel if you think you've made a mistake.

Viewing Your Published Web

Since I was eager to see the first draft of my site published (and to try out a few of the components that require server extensions), I poked around for a while and then ran a search at the search page to test the actual site (see Figure 9.10).

If you notice anything not working right, you can fix it now before publicizing the site.

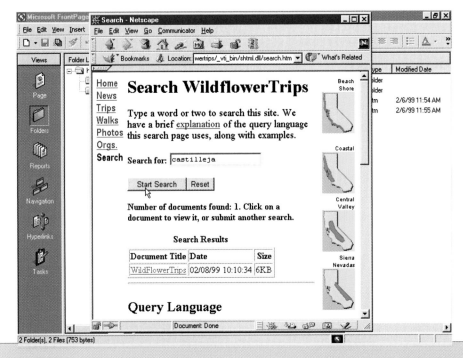

Figure 9.10:   The search page managed to find the one page at the site that contains the word "castilleja."

Tracking Access

A good ISP should give you access to your web's server logs, showing who hit what pages when and from where. A great ISP will provide some sort of analysis or charting to help you understand the raw data. In absence of such useful free services, you can at least get a handle on your web's traffic by inserting a hit counter.

Let me say right off the bat that I personally don't like hit counters because, for one thing, I think they look tacky. It's fine if the numbers shown are incredibly high, but most hit counters sport pitifully low numbers, and these could be generated by the site owner's nervous visits to the page. Other pages feature broken images produced when the provider offering the hit-counter service hiccups. Others have the lame "You are the *nth* visitor since the last time this hit counter broke down" type disclaimer. On the other hand, a hit counter on a hidden or secret page tracking the hits on another page might be useful. That's not the way most of them work, though.

Having said all that, I will bow to the fact that people love to put hit counters on their pages, and you have every right to do so if you like. If you're going to put one anywhere, stick it way at the bottom of your home page, as that's the one likely to get most of the traffic.

To insert a hit counter, position the insertion point where you want the counter to appear, and then select Insert | Component | Hit Counter. This brings up the Hit Counter Properties dialog box (see Figure 9.11).

Click the type of numerals you want to use. Consider clicking Reset Counter To and typing a nonembarrassing high number such as 5555 to start with (just kidding). Then click OK. On your page, you'll see that FrontPage has inserted [**HitCounter**], a placeholder.

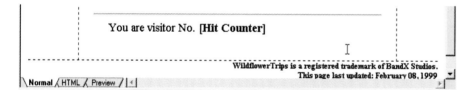

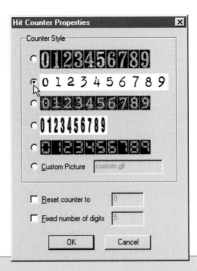

Figure 9.11: Choose a hit counter style with tasteful choices ranging from Tin Pan Alley to '70s era calculator.

To get a peek at how it will really look, view it on the Preview tab, or preview the page in your web browser.

You are visitor No. **0 0 0 0 0 0 0 3**

Promotion and Findability

If you're publishing your web on *the* Web, and you'd like to drum up traffic (as opposed, for example, to simply wanting to provide information to interested parties), then there are some basic things you can do to promote your site and make it easier for folks wandering the electronic byways to find.

EXPERT ADVICE

Once again, I'd like to direct readers to Peter Kent's incredibly useful Poor Richard site (*http://www.poorrichard.com/*) for a wealth of advice on web site promotion from a master of the art.

There are two grassroots-level steps you can take to build word of mouth for your web:

1. Trade links (with related sites).
2. Start an announcement list (to keep visitors apprised of new developments at your site).

To trade links, hunt for related sites (search for unique words or phrases that relate to your topics at any of the major portal or search sites—such as Yahoo.com or Altavista.com), and send e-mail messages individually to the responsible parties, inviting them to visit your site and consider trading links. If they agree, you're on your way.

An announcement list would be more tricky for a novice to manage if the resourceful Philip Greenspun hadn't built a free service at his **http://www.greenspun.com/spam/**, which enables you to add a free announcement list to any page by filling out a simple form. (Greenspun also offers a similar service to automate the adding of related links to your pages—and a number of other wonderful conveniences—accessible from **http://photo.net/wtr/ collaboration.html**.)

There are three other, slightly more complicated, things you can do to help build your site's presence on the Web:

1. Register your web at the major portal (search) sites.
2. Help those sites' search engines (programs) identify and categorize your web properly.
3. Register your own unique domain name.

I'll take them briefly one at a time (but, to be candid, not exhaustively).

Register at Portals

All search sites (including the search modules of major portals such as Yahoo.com, Netscape.com, Microsoft.com, etc.) actively search the Web for new content and try to index and list it, but talk about a moving target! Instead of just sitting around waiting for all the web spiders and search programs to wander by and find your site, you can go to the major sites and register your URL with them. There are also services that offer to add your address to numerous search sites at once, but I've heard reports that they are not dependable. I'd recommend doing the registering yourself unless your time is so valuable that you can afford to delegate that work.

Flag Your Home Page for Search Engines

Many web portals use a common method of indexing listed sites by their keywords. If someone goes looking for your web or something like it from a search page, they'll have an easier time finding it if you are able to anticipate the key search terms they are likely to employ and embed them into your home page.

To do so, select File | Properties, and then click the Custom tab on the Properties dialog box (see Figure 9.12). Make sure you are in normal view: I got confused the first time I tried this because I was in Preview mode and a different Properties dialog box came up.

CAUTION

Not all search engines use the same meta-tag conventions for flagging keywords. If you want to make sure your web will show up easily at a specific portal site, look for the help or advance information available from the search page for tips.

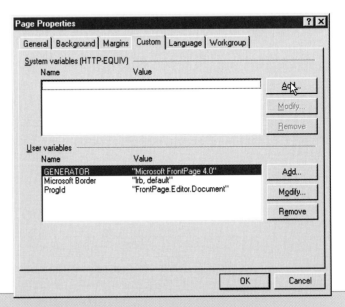

Figure 9.12:   Add keywords to your web in the User Variables area of the Custom tab.

Click the lower Add button (in the User Variables area). In the User Meta Variable dialog box that appears, type **keywords** in the Name box and press TAB.

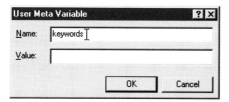

In the Value box, type the index keywords for your site, using commas to separate words.

In the Value box, type your keywords, separated by commas, with phrases in quotation marks. Here are the keywords I'm using for the WildflowerTrips site:

```
california,wildflower,flower,trip,fieldtrip,hike,walk,
botany,botanize,nature,"native plants"
```

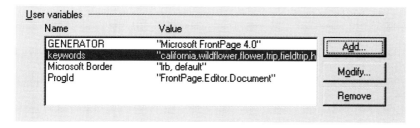

Then click OK twice.

Get Your Own Domain Name

The easiest URLs to remember are simple domain names without long trailing bits that look like

```
.../~something/morestuff/starthere.html
```

To position your web at a more simple address, such as **http://www.** *unique*.**com/**, first visit the Internic site at **http://rs.internic.net/** and search for the domain name you wish to register. If it's still available, the site will tell you so. If not, go back to the drawing board till you find something you like that is available.

Next, you'll need a host for your domain name. Unless you run your own network with two nameservers on the Internet, or have a friend or employer who does, then you'll probably have to pay an ISP for the domain name hosting. Your ISP will give you the addresses of their name servers and they should also be willing to coach you through Internic's forms (considering they're charging you a recurring fee for listing your address one time in two places) for claiming and registering the domain. Internic will charge you $35 a year ($70 right away for the first two years) for the registration service.

There's More . . .

You've just worked your way through one of the most important steps in web creation: publishing. You're now over the threshold from experiments and rehearsal to live performance, perhaps in front of the whole world; at least in front of your colleagues or co-workers. In the final chapter, you'll learn how to keep a web site running, even as it changes and evolves, and how to work with multiple collaborators on a site without creating inconsistencies or conflicts.

CHAPTER 10

Maintaining and Administering Your Site

INCLUDES

- Sorting files by date
- Rearranging folders in your web
- Setting up subwebs
- Using password protection
- Collaborating on tasks
- Checking pages in and out
- Sharing templates

Sort Your Files by Date ➥ pp. 267–268

1. Select View | Reports | Recently Added Files.

2. When ready, click the Report list in the Reporting toolbar and choose Recently Changed Files.

3. When ready, choose Older Files.

Reorganize Your Folders ➥ p. 268

1. If the Folder List pane is not visible, select View | Folder List to open it.

2. Click and drag any file or folder into a new folder.

3. FrontPage automatically corrects the changed hyperlinks for you.

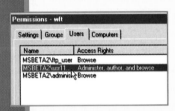

Set Permissions for a User or Group ➥ pp. 270–274

1. Select Tools | Security | Permissions.

2. To set unique permissions for a subweb, click Use Unique Permissions For This Web, and click Apply.

3. Select the Users tab.

4. To make the web "browsable" by anyone, click Everyone Has Browse Access (otherwise, leave Only Registered Users Have Browser Access selected).

5. To add a new user, click the Add button, select or type a user name in the Names box and click Add.

6. Select the type of access to give to the new user or users (browse, author, or administer access), and then click OK.

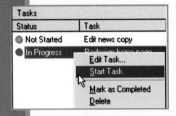

Track a Task to Completion ➥ pp. 277–279

1. To add a task to a file, right-click on the file, and choose Add Task; then type a task name, assign it, set a priority, enter a description, and click OK.

2. To start working on an existing task, enter Task view, right-click on a task and choose Start Task (this will open the file in question for editing).

3. When you close or save the file, FrontPage will ask you whether the task has been completed, and then will mark the task as In Progress or Completed depending on your answer.

Check a Page Out and Back In ➡ p. 280

1. Switch to Folder view.
2. Right-click on a file and select Check Out.
3. When you're done editing the page and have published it or saved it back to the server, right-click on it again and select Check In.

List Files by Review Status ➡ p. 281

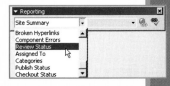

1. Switch to Reports view.
2. Click the Report drop-down list box in the Reporting toolbar.
3. Select Review Status.

Create a Shared Template ➡ pp. 282–283

1. Create an ordinary FrontPage page with whatever boilerplate text, formatting, or links you wish.
2. Select File | Save As.
3. Choose FrontPage Template (*.tem) in the Save As Type drop-down list box.
4. Type a file name and click Save.
5. In the Save As Template dialog box that appears, give the template a title, press TAB twice, and enter a description.
6. Click Save Template In Current Web.
7. Click OK.

You've built your web, created and formatted the pages, strung them together with links and other navigation aids, spruced them up with active content, and published them at a suitable host. So are you done? Not quite. Web publishing is different from the nonelectronic forms of publishing we're all familiar with that preceded it. When you publish a book or magazine or newspaper, you really are done, at least until the time comes to put out the next edition or issue. Publishing in the web medium is a bit more fluid. You're never really completely done. There's always an opportunity to correct niggling little errors, make major or minor changes, reorganize or redesign a site, add entirely new sections to your web, and so on.

Even if you don't go out of your way to look for more stuff to do with your web site, you're still going to have to maintain it. Links to other sites on the Web may change. User feedback from visitors may tell you that some of your navigation choices are confusing. Perhaps the topic of your web (whether that's yourself, your business, your obsession, or something else) will evolve, requiring you to change your web site to reflect new developments.

Who's Minding the Site?

Ideally, the responsibility for maintaining an ongoing web site won't fall entirely on your back. At best, you'll have colleagues or other collaborators to help you with day-to-day upkeep and periodic updates. Even then, you'll have to confront the problems of working in a group and making sure that one person's corrections don't inadvertently undo someone else's work. In this last chapter, I'll show you how to maintain a web site, changing or reorganizing it as needed, and how to work with others without jeopardizing the integrity of your web.

Reorganizing Your Web

There are two different ways in which you may want to reorganize your web. The first is trivial and involves just rearranging your view of the site. This is easily done with no trouble at all. More significantly, you may want to re*structure* your web at some point. Sites change and evolve. Old sections die off, losing their usefulness, and new ones come into being in response to evolving demands from users.

In the early days of web development, it could be a royal pain to deal with reorganizing a site in the sense of restructuring it, but FrontPage takes care of the most annoying part, fixing all the relative links within the web that have to be updated once you start moving files or even folders around.

As a web outgrows its original structure, sometimes it makes sense to designate sections of the web as subwebs to make them easier to deal with. This may also facilitate delegating some of the work to others (always an important milestone to reach).

Let's start, though, with the purely visual sense of reorganizing a web, and then go on to making fundamental changes to a site's structure.

Sorting Your Files by Date

When working on a large web, it can be easy to lose track of what files have been added or changed recently. FrontPage's Reports view offers a few easy ways to take a look.

- To see files that have been added recently, select View | Reports | Recently Added Files.
- To see files that have been changed recently, select View | Reports | Recently Changed Files.
- To see files that were added a long time ago and haven't been changed recently, select View | Reports | Older Files.

EXPERT ADVICE

To include files in hidden folders in this report, click Tools | Web Settings, click the Advanced tab, click Show Documents In Hidden Directories, and click OK.

To change what FrontPage considers an older file, click the Report Setting drop-down list box in the Reporting toolbar and choose a different number of days.

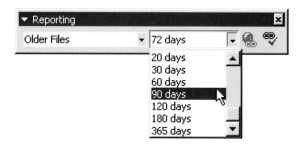

Of course, you can double-click any file listed in a report to edit it.

Moving Folders Around

You can reorganize your web very easily, more or less the same way you would reorganize your computer's desktop. That is, you can click on files and drag them into folders, or you can click on folders and drag them into other folders. FrontPage will automatically update any links that are "broken" by your move.

Setting Up Subwebs

You can change any folder in your web into a subweb for organizational purposes. Among other things, you can assign a subweb a different password or make it available to a different group of workers from the primary web. For a small web with a limited number of people working on it, it's unlikely that you'll see any real benefit from designating a section of the site as a subweb. In a large organization, however, with many different departments, particularly if some of those departments need to share access to sensitive information (think, personnel records), designating the folder assigned to each department as a separate subweb can make it easy to maintain the security standards you'd need. (We'll get to passwords and permissions later in this chapter.)

To convert a folder to a subweb, right-click on it and select Convert To Web from the menu that pops up.

CAUTION

FrontPage foolishly makes it possible for you to designate the hard drive of a computer (such as C:) as a subweb, even though that could damage the drive and render it useless. Be careful not to do this!

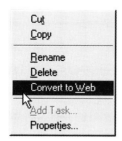

FrontPage then warns you of some of the consequences of this change of status. Click Yes.

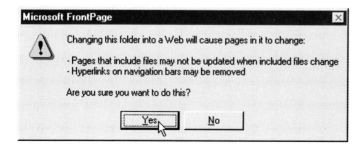

Depending on the size of the contents of the folder, it may take several minutes to complete the conversion. A subweb folder is marked with a globe symbol so you can distinguish it from an ordinary folder.

EXPERT ADVICE

You can change a subweb back to a folder by right-clicking on it and selecting Convert To Folder. As with the original conversion, this change may also require some clean-up afterward.

Protecting Your Web with Permissions

For web's that are published on the World Wide Web, there's a fairly clear distinction between the web's creator (you and your collaborators), and the web's visitors. You have access to the host server. Your visitors do not. However, on an intranet, the distinctions between creators and users might not be so clear cut. For a web that's published on a private network, some of the same people who visit (browse) the web may also require permission to edit (author) it. Some may even require permission to administer the web, although the fewer people with this level of permission the better. Administering a web includes the capability of creating new users and user groups and assigning different levels of permission to them.

Depending on the server where your web is published, you may be able to administer it through a web interface or you may be able to administer it using FrontPage itself. If your ISP offers web-based administration, then it's really up to them to explain to you how their interface works. Generally, you visit a page called something like http://*yourwebsitename*/admin/ and enter a username and password. Then you simply fill out web forms to create groups, create users, and edit permissions.

Permission to Browse, Author, or Administer

So there are three levels of permission: browse, author, and administer. A user with browse permission may visit the web and that's it. A user with author permission may make changes to the web. A user with administer permission may add or remove other users. A user or group of users may be assigned any combination of these three levels of permission.

If your host server is Microsoft's Internet Information Services (IIS), FrontPage automatically assigns administer permission to all members of the Windows NT Administrators group and the SYSTEM account.

By default, the permissions granted at the top level (the root) of your web apply to any and all subwebs below that level. You can, however, establish separate permissions for a subweb. To make any changes to permissions, users, or groups, select Tools | Security | Permissions. This brings up the Permissions dialog box for your web (see Figure 10.1).

If you're working within a subweb and want to establish permissions for the subweb different from those of its parent web, click Use Unique Permissions For This Web, and then click the Apply button.

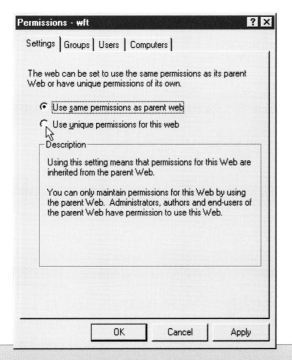

Figure 10.1: If your web is published on a host with FrontPage server extensions installed, then you can add users or groups or change permissions from within FrontPage.

Add a User

To add a new user to your web, select the User tab of the Permissions dialog box (see Figure 10.2).

Then click the Add button. This brings up the Add Users dialog box. If your host is running on an NT server, you may select a domain in the Obtain List From drop-down list, and FrontPage will obtain a list of users from that server and list them in the Names box on the left. To add a new user, type the username in the Add names box. Then choose a level of permission to assign from the choices listed at the bottom of the dialog box (see Figure 10.3). Then click OK.

If FrontPage rejects your addition, this probably means that you need to assign new users and groups directly at the server level, and you should contact the administrator of your host site on how to do that.

EXPERT ADVICE

If the Web server is a Windows NT Server running IIS (Internet Information Services), users and groups are inherited automatically from the NT setup. If you need to make changes and find that you cannot do so from within FrontPage, contact your system administrator.

Add a Group of Users

To add a new group of users to your web, select the Group tab of the Permissions dialog box. Then click the Add button. This brings up the Add Groups dialog box. To add a new group, type the group name in the Add Names box. Then choose a level of permission to assign from the choices listed at the bottom of the dialog box.

Repeat the process to Add groups with differing levels of permission.

Change Permissions for a User or Group

To change permissions for an existing User or Group, click the User or Group tab, select a specific user or group, and then click the Edit

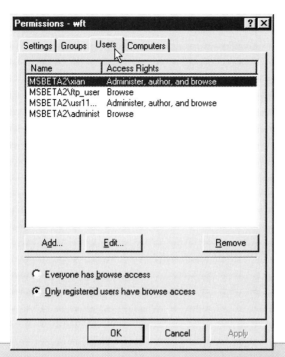

Figure 10.2: Add new users and assign their level of permission on the User tab of the Permissions dialog box.

button. In the Edit User or Edit Groups dialog box that appears, select the level of permission you'd like to assign.

Then click OK.

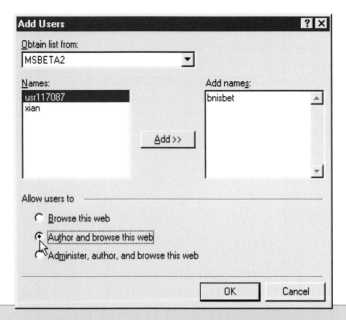

Figure 10.3: Assign a permission level to your new user or users.

Remove a User or Group

To remove an existing User or Group, click the User or Group tab, select the user or group in question, and then click the Remove button. When you're done with the Permissions dialog box, click OK.

User Self-Registration

CAUTION

Self-registration is not permitted on NT servers or any host running on an IIS server.

To monitor access to a web on an intranet, you may permit users to register themselves by creating a user registration form that will be cross-checked against the permissions you've established for users you've added. The registration form handler will save the usernames of any users who visit the web.

First, to protect the web or subweb in question, open the web, select Tools | Security | Permissions, and click Use Unique Permissions For This Web. Then click the users tab and click Only Registered Users Have

EXPERT ADVICE

Your registration form must be saved to the root web, not in the protected web or subweb.

Browse Access. Then click Add to add users (as explained in a previous section) if you have not done so already, or click OK.

To create a user registration form, first switch to page view. Then select File | New | Page. On the General tab, double-click User Registration. FrontPage generates the form page automatically (see Figure 10.4).

To activate the form, right-click on it and select Form Properties. On the Form Properties dialog box that appears, click the Options

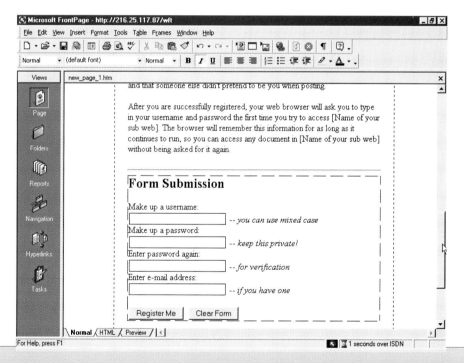

Figure 10.4: The form page automatically includes comments with instructions for you and introductory text with instructions for users. Once you've read the comments, you may delete them. You'll probably want to edit the instructions for your users.

button to bring up the Options for Registration Form Handler dialog box (see Figure 10.5).

Type the name of the web site. Click the File Results tab. Note the file name in the File Name box (or change it if you like). This is where user names of site visitors will be stored (in the _private folder of the root web). Click OK twice.

Clean up the form's supporting text, replacing bracketed words (for instance, replace [OtherWeb] with the name of the web or subweb in question). Then save the page.

Change a Password

If your web is hosted on a Unix system, or on an O'Reilly or Netscape server running on a Windows system, then users can change their own

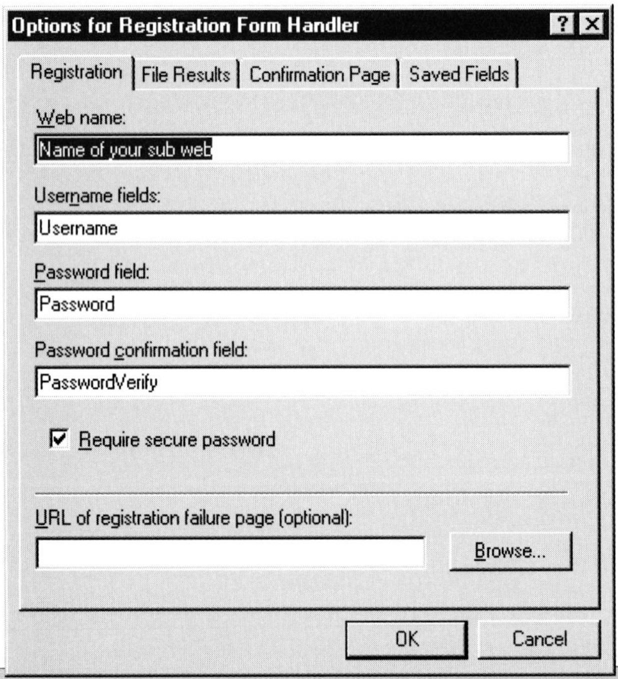

Figure 10.5: To make your registration form work, you've got to do this administrative work once.

passwords. (If the web is hosted on a Microsoft server, then passwords can only be changed by an administrator.)

To change a password, select Tools | Security | Change Password. Type the old password, press TAB, type the new password, press TAB, and type the new password again. Then click OK.

Site Maintenance and Project Management

For complicated webs or webs with several people with authoring permission, FrontPage offers a few tools to assist in the maintenance of the site. One such tool is the task list, with which you can assign tasks to specific people and track their progress so that necessary processes do not fall between the cracks. Another tool provides the capability of checking files out so that two people do not make inconsistent changes at the same time, one person's changes undoing those of another. FrontPage also makes it easy to insure that crucial pages are reviewed by whoever bears the ultimate responsibility for their content *before* they are inadvertently made public.

See "Publishing Changed Pages" in Chapter 9 for how to make simple changes to a web (such as publishing changed pages or deleting removed pages).

Completing Tasks

FrontPage's task-management tool can be a great aid in keeping track of who is supposed to be doing what and what's been done so far. If you've ever tried to manage a project with multiple participants, you know how important this can be to avoid duplication of effort, not to mention tracking those tiresome little tasks for which nobody will take responsibility. Honestly, though, with a small-scale web or very few contributors, the task system may well involve more administrative overhead than it's worth, as every significant task must be logged and updated. Regardless, I'll show you what to do and you can decide for yourself.

Create a Task

Tasks are associated with files (usually web pages, but also other types of files, such as pictures). To create one, right-click on a file icon and select Add Task.

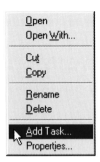

This brings up the New Task dialog box (see Figure 10.6).

View the Task List

At any point you can view all the tasks you've created in Tasks view. You may recall from earlier chapters that FrontPage sometimes creates tasks for you automatically, so there may be more tasks already listed

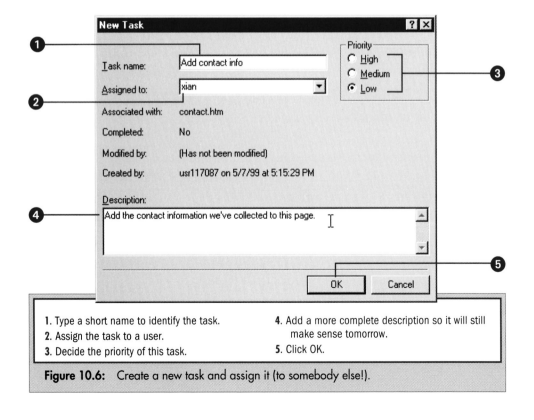

1. Type a short name to identify the task.
2. Assign the task to a user.
3. Decide the priority of this task.
4. Add a more complete description so it will still make sense tomorrow.
5. Click OK.

Figure 10.6: Create a new task and assign it (to somebody else!).

EXPERT ADVICE

To easily look at who is supposed to be doing which tasks (which can be helpful for determining whether one person is getting an unfair share of the work), just click the Assigned To button at the top of the list to resort the tasks by assignment.

than you expected. To see the existing tasks click the Tasks button in the View bar.

● Not Started	Finish regions/cascad...	xian	High	<** Page no longer in We...	Added by the FrontPage New Page di...
● In Progress	fixthis	xian	Medium	Photo Archive	fixthis
● Not Started	Soften tone	usr117087	Medium	Photo Archive	
● Not Started	Add contact info	xian	Low	contact.htm	Add the contact information we've coll...

Start Working on a Task

To start working through your assigned tasks, right-click on one and choose Start Task from the menu that pops up. This will open the file associated with the task. If it's a web page, as is usual, this simply means that the page will open in Page view. If it's a picture file, though, FrontPage will launch Image Composer or whatever other tool is associated with that file type for you.

Mark a Task as Completed

When you're ready to quit working on the file associated with a task, save it. FrontPage, ever the taskmaster, will notice you doing this and ask if you've completed the task yet.

If you click Yes, FrontPage will change the task's status to Completed. If you click No, FrontPage will change its status to In Progress (still an improvement over Not Started, don't you think?).

Another way to mark a task as completed is to right-click it in Tasks view and select Mark As Completed from the menu that pops up.

Checking Pages Out and In

You can turn on this collaboration feature by selecting Tools | Web Settings, clicking Document Check-In And Check-Out at the bottom of the General tab, and then clicking OK. Click Yes when FrontPage asks you to confirm.

One of the worst things that can happen in a collaboration is for two people to waste time working on the same problem. At best they will duplicate effort. At worst, one of them will accidentally eradicate the other's work. To help facilitate working together, FrontPage offers a system of checking files out. Once you check a file out, only you can update it. Other people will see the file as checked out. They can open and view it, but they can't save changes to it until you check the file back in.

To check a file out, right-click on it and select Check Out from the menu that pops up.

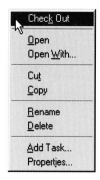

Then work on the file as long as you like, making your changes without worrying about conflicts with your colleagues. When you're done, save the page, and then right-click on its icon again and choose Check In.

EXPERT ADVICE

You can view the "checkout status" of all the files in your web by selecting View | Reports | Checkout Status.

Tracking Review Status

For all but the smallest organizations, publishing information often involves clearing it with higher-ups or people concerned with proprietary data, trade secrets, legal exposure, or other such institutional concerns. Getting an OK from the right person in this type of situation is known as "covering your behind." To help you keep track of which files must be reviewed by some high muckity-muck before publishing, and which have already been cleared, FrontPage offers a set of "review status" options and makes it possible for you to create your own.

Set the Review Status for a File

To establish that a file needs to be reviewed before it may be published, right-click on it and select Properties. In the Properties dialog box, choose the Workgroups tab (see Figure 10.7).

Later on, if you want to list all of the files in your web sorted by their review status, select View | Reports | Review Status. To change the status for a file in this Reports view, click on the file in the Review status column, click again, and then select a new status. To remove the hold on a file, just delete the contents of that cell.

Sharing Templates

When working on an elaborate web or with several collaborators, you can save a lot of effort in the long run by creating your own templates. If there is boilerplate text that you want included on all pages of a certain type, or if there are formatting choices, themes, or even standard links that you want to include on every page in some category, you can create a template with that content already included and then encourage everyone to create new files from that template in the future.

EXPERT ADVICE

To set the same review status for multiple files at once, select them all first before right-clicking on one of them.

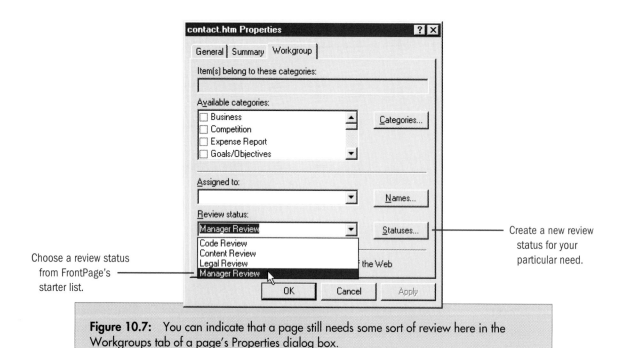

Figure 10.7: You can indicate that a page still needs some sort of review here in the Workgroups tab of a page's Properties dialog box.

Creating a Shared Template

First create the file as you would any ordinary page (see Chapter 5 for more on how to add content and formatting to a page), or open a page you've already created that contains the content or formatting or links you want in your template. When you're ready, select File | Save As. In the Save As dialog box, click the Save As Type drop-down list box, and select FrontPage Template (*.tem).

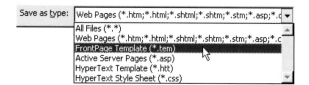

Type a file name in the File Name box and click the Save button. This brings up the Save As Template dialog box (see Figure 10.8)

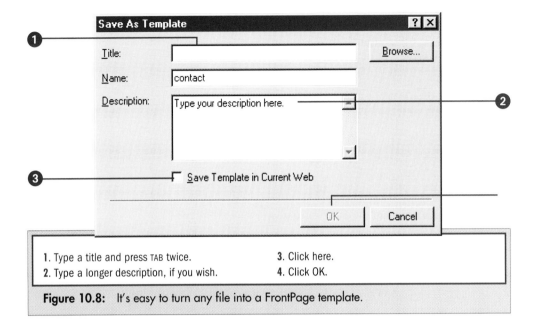

Figure 10.8: It's easy to turn any file into a FrontPage template.

Creating a New Page Based on Your Shared Template

In the future, when you want to create a new page based on the template, switch to Page view, select File | Page | New, and then double-click the Template name in the General tab of the New Page dialog box (see Figure 10.9).

Tending Your Web

Well, you've made it through a challenging course in a remarkably short period of time. By now, regardless of how busy you are, I hope you're able to get a handle on at least part of the web design, development, and publishing process. FrontPage helps a lot by automating parts of the job, but you deserve credit yourself for sticking with it and wrapping your mind around a lot of new concepts. Pat yourself on the back!

As I've implied in this chapter, web publishing is an activity that doesn't lend itself to closure. Unless you want your web to wither on the

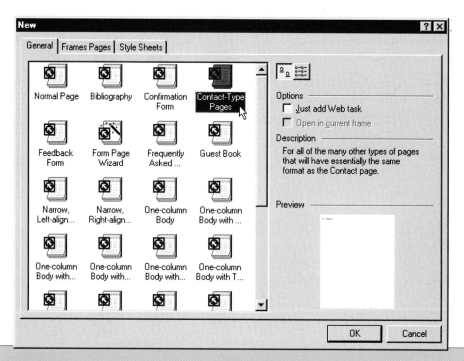

Figure 10.9: Once you've created a shared template, it appears alongside all the templates that came with FrontPage.

vine, you've got to keep at it, making improvements, responding to requests from visitors, and so on. It's a big job, but somebody's got to do it. I hope I've helped to make it all a little easier for you to grasp.

Now that I've finished writing this book, I'm going to put my money where my mouth is and put together a site to support the book using FrontPage. You can look for that site at **http://www.opublish.com/fp2k/** and I look forward to seeing you there. Oh, and if you want to check out the WildflowerTrips prototype site I developed while writing this book, you can see that at **http://www.opublish.com/fp2k/wft/**. Good luck!

Installing FrontPage

INCLUDES

- Upgrading from FrontPage 97 or 98
- Installing Office or just FrontPage
- Upgrading Internet Explorer
- Registering FrontPage

It's easy to install FrontPage (or Office) yourself, but it's easier still to have someone else do it for you! If you're the one who gets stuck with the job, this appendix will help you past any bumps you might encounter. If you have a network administrator, check with that person before proceeding. For the most part, you click OK until the process is done.

Before You Begin

How you proceed with an installation depends on several factors, specifically:

- Whether you're installing FrontPage for the first time or upgrading from a previous version
- Whether you're installing FrontPage as part of an edition of Microsoft Office 2000 or as a separate application

In the first instance, the difference may be merely a couple of clicks. In the second, there are some elements in the Office 2000 package that you will want to add to your installation, if you are installing from that package. This appendix assumes that you'll install from the Office 2000 package.

If You Are Upgrading

If you are upgrading from FrontPage 97 or 98, and you use Windows 95 or 98, you should uninstall the Microsoft Personal Web Server, or the FrontPage Personal Web Server (whichever is installed) before you install FrontPage 2000. Neither server is required any longer for creating web pages and may interfere with the installation. If you are using Windows NT, you will still need the Internet Information Server for your intranet.

If you are upgrading, you must also decide whether you want to overwrite your previous version of the program. By default it will be overwritten, but you can change that during the setup procedure.

If You Are Installing with Office 2000

If you are installing with Office 2000 and you have never installed Office 2000 before, then you should install whatever components of the Office suite you expect to use. As long as you have enough room on your hard drive, it's easier to install all the components you will use at once so that you don't have to dig up the CD every time you want to use a new feature. This appendix will simply tell you what components of FrontPage 2000 to install.

If you have already installed Office 2000, but have not installed FrontPage 2000, you may either run the setup program from the CD, Or, from the Control Panel choose Add/Remove Programs, and choose whatever edition of Office 2000 you have installed from the list. Click Add/Remove, as in Figure A.1.

From the dialog box that appears, shown in Figure A.2, choose Add Or Remove Features. From this point, you can skip to the section called "Entering Personal Information."

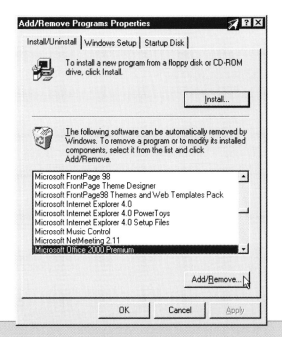

Figure A.1:   The Install/Uninstall tab of the Add/Remove Programs Properties dialog box

Figure A.2:   Click Add Or Remove Features to add FrontPage to an existing Office installation.

Performing the Installation

To begin the installation, place the installation CD in your CD-ROM drive. From the Start menu, choose Run. Use the Browse button to go to your CD-ROM drive (in most cases, this is drive D). Double-click the file called Setup.exe, and click OK. The Setup window will appear as the program searches for previous installations and examines your system. As Figure A.3 shows, a sidebar in the window lists the steps to be taken, and highlights each one as it becomes current.

Entering Personal Information

Enter your personal information in the first three fields. In the boxes along the bottom, enter the CD Key, which you will find on your CD case. Click Next or press ENTER. You will be taken to the license screen. You must accept the license agreement in order to proceed. Click on I Accept The Terms Of The License Agreement, and click Next or press ENTER. On the screen shown in Figure A.4, click Customize.

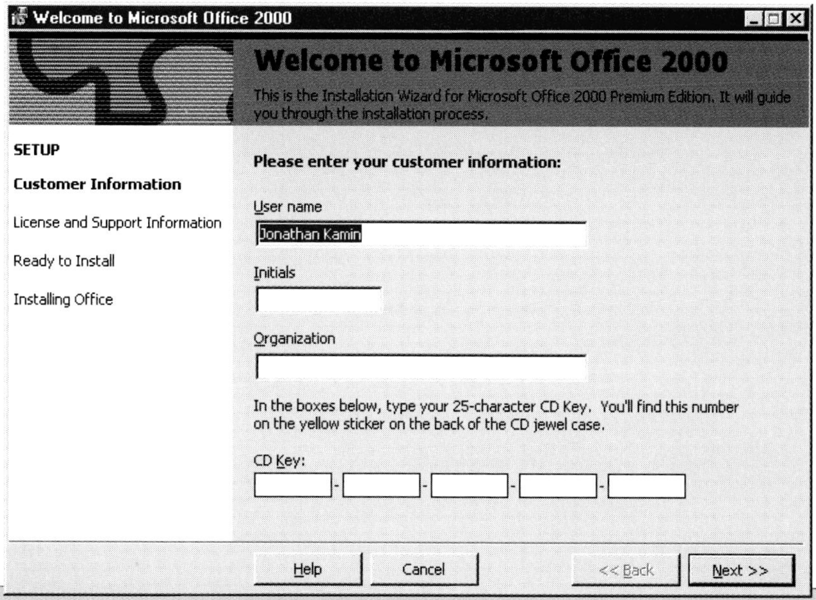

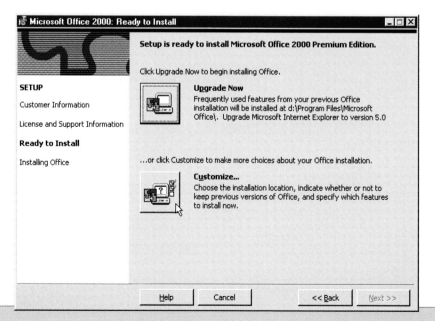

Figure A.3: Your organization name is optional, but the CD key is mandatory.

Figure A.4: Click the Customize button to choose which features to include.

Choosing a Location

The first screen displayed after you click this button allows you to choose a drive and path to which you will install Microsoft Office 2000, of which FrontPage is a component. Under most circumstances you can accept the default. If there's not enough room on drive C, and you have another drive with more room, it's perfectly acceptable to install to another drive. You can even change the name of the folder to which you install, although it's not recommended. When you've entered an acceptable installation path, click Next or press ENTER. If you chose a path to a folder containing a previous version of Office (or FrontPage), you will be warned that your old program will be overwritten. If you don't want that to happen—if you want to preserve a previous version of one or more of the programs, click the Back button, and enter a new path. Click Next when you're done.

Choosing Whether to Remove Previous Versions

At the next screen, shown in Figure A.5, the Setup program offers to remove all components of your previous versions of any Office programs you have. If you have a previous version of Office, and a separate version of FrontPage, FrontPage will be included in the list. If you're just installing or upgrading FrontPage, you should check the box labeled Keep These Programs.

Upgrading Internet Explorer

You will then be asked to upgrade to Internet Explorer 5.0, if you haven't already. You are given the choice of a Standard upgrade, which includes the web browser, Outlook Express, the Media Player, other multimedia enhancements, and some components used by other programs in Office 2000, or a Minimal upgrade which installs only the first two components. You can also choose not to upgrade. The Standard upgrade is the default. Accept it.

Choosing Components to Install

On the next screen, you see a tree diagram. This is where you choose the components to install, and how they should be installed. You have

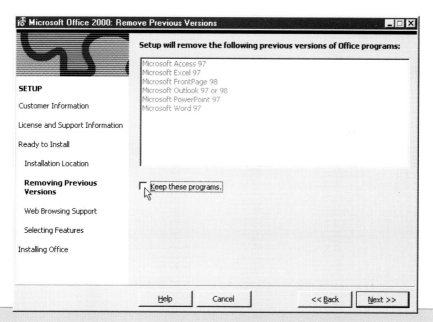

Figure A.5: Don't let Setup remove your existing Office programs unless you're upgrading them.

the option of running various components from your hard drive or from the CD.

There are at least two advantages to running from your hard drive. First, the computer reads information more quickly from a hard drive than it does from a CD. Second, you don't have to locate the CD every time you start a new process that you haven't used before.

Click on one of the drive icons with the arrow, and you see the menu shown in the following illustration. This gives you a variety of ways to install components:

- Run From My Computer means that the component will be installed on your hard drive.

- Run All From My Computer means that the component, and everything nested under it in the tree, will be installed on your hard drive. (If there are sub-components, there will be a plus sign to the left of the drive icon.)

- Run From CD places a shortcut on your system to the program on the CD, as well as placing a few files in your Windows and System folders.

- Run All From CD sets up the program so that the component and all its sub-components run directly from the CD, via a shortcut on your hard drive.

- Installed On First Use (not found on all the menus) means that the item will appear on a menu or in a dialog box, but will not be installed on your hard drive. The first time you choose the item, you will be asked for the CD so that it can be installed.

- Not Available means, "Do not install this component."

(You can also use this menu as a help system to explain the icons you see.) Click on any drive icon to change the way the attached item will be installed (see Figure A.6).

As a rule, it's easier to install things once and be done with it. For this reason, you're better off installing to your hard drive any components you expect to use.

To install FrontPage 2000, click the drive icon next to Microsoft FrontPage for Windows, and choose Run All From My Computer.

Next, click the plus sign next to Office Tools. You'll need to install several components from this list as well. First click HTML Source Editing, and choose Run All From My Computer. Scroll down the list and make sure that Office Web Components, and still further down the tree, Web Discussions and Web Publishing, are to be installed on your computer (see Figure A.7). They should be installed by default.

EXPERT ADVICE

You have the option of turning off the Office Assistant—the little animation that pops up when it thinks you're going to do something it can help with—from this list. If you don't want it, click it and choose Not Available.

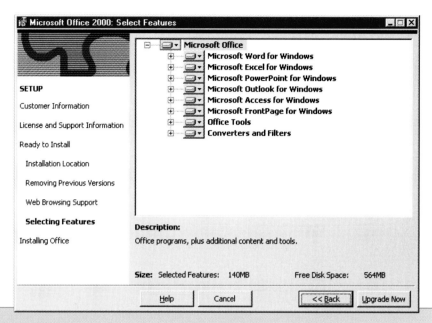

Figure A.6: Click any drive icon to change an option.

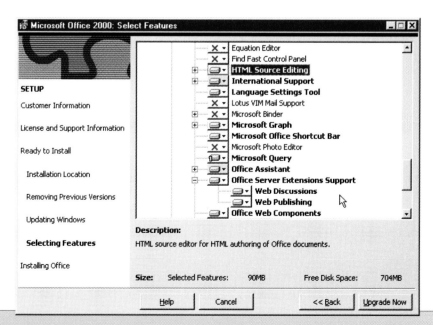

Figure A.7: Make sure all the web features will be installed.

When you're done, click Install Now or Upgrade Now, depending on whether you're doing a first installation or an upgrade. Setup checks over what you've done and begins the installation. At this point you can go clean the bathrooms, read your mail, or go out to lunch. The process probably won't be complete when you return.

When it's finished, Setup will close all open programs and wait for you to click OK to restart the computer. When you have done so, Windows shuts down and restarts. Don't take the CD out of the drive yet, because it will be needed. When the desktop appears, a progress bar indicates that Setup is continuing to install the product. When it's finished, you should see your normal desktop.

Registering the Product

To start FrontPage, click the Start button, then choose Programs | Microsoft FrontPage. You will be asked to register the product. Fill in your name in the registration form. Click Next or press ENTER and fill out your personal information. Click Next or press ENTER and you see this screen. Here you can opt out of being included on Microsoft or other mailing (probably e-mailing) lists.

Click Next or press ENTER to finish the registration process. Your default Dial-Up Connection window appears to connect you to the Internet. If you prefer, you can click Cancel and choose from the following methods of registering:

- E-mail
- Internal Fax
- External Fax or Postal Mail (i.e., printing out a form and sending it)
- Telephone

If you prefer, you can click Register Later.

If Something Goes Wrong

If something goes wrong, or if you interrupt the installation, Setup will display a warning dialog box. Click OK and then try to install the program again. If it still doesn't work, note the exact text of the error message. Assistance may be available on the Microsoft web site or from Microsoft, but you will need the exact error code.

If the installation is stopped while Setup is copying files, it will display a different dialog box asking if you want to quit. Click No to continue with Setup as usual, or click Yes to end the installation (for now). If you choose to halt the installation at this point, you'll have to repeat parts of the installation next time you install FrontPage.

Uninstalling FrontPage

If at some point you want to take FrontPage off your computer; close all programs, choose Start | Setting | Control Panel, and double-click the Add/Remove Programs icon. Then, choose Microsoft FrontPage in the lower half of the dialog box that appears, and click the Add/Remove button. (Note: if you installed as part of Office 2000 as a whole, you must select Office 2000 in the lower half of the dialog box, then choose add or remove features, and then select MS FrontPage.)

Click the Remove All button in the installation dialog box that appears. Setup asks if you're sure you want to do this. Click Yes.

Setup mysteriously tells you that it is once again checking for necessary disk space. (It needs disk space to remove files?) A dialog box reports on Setup's progress as it removes files. Setup then tells you that it is updating your system, and finally announces that FrontPage was successfully uninstalled.

You can remove FrontPage and keep other Office components if you wish.

Index

A

Absolute page positions, 177
Access database, importing, 231
Active Server Pages (ASP), 226
ActiveX controls, 207
Add/Modify FTP Locations dialog box, 249-250
Administering your site, 263-277
Animating your pages, 199-234
Announcement list, adding to a page, 259
Artwork, inserting into your web, 131
ASP extensions, 226

B

Back end (web), 9
Background image, adding to a page, 74, 151
Background sound, inserting onto a page, 154
Background spell checking, turning off, 30-31
Bad links
    checking for, 241-243
    correcting, 244
Banner Ad Manager, 205-206
Banner Ad Manager Properties dialog box, 206
Banner ads, inserting, 205-206
Bells and whistles, 157
Bevel effect (buttons), 204
Black and white, converting a picture to, 142
Blank page
    creating, 73-74
    in a predesigned web, 74
    saving, 78
Boilerplate, 74
Brainstorming web design, 5-6
Break Properties dialog box, 148

Browsers
    designing your web for, 31-33
    Office components and, 207
    previewing your work in, 122-124
Buttons (toolbar)
    adding or removing, 25
    hover buttons, 203-204
Byline, 115

C

Caption, adding to a picture, 148-149
Cascading style sheets (CSS), 107
Categories
    adding to a site map, 190-191
    assigning pages to, 189-190
    creating, 188-189
Categories Properties dialog box, 191
Cell Properties dialog box, 103
Change Folder dialog box, 80
Chart (Office component), 212-213
Child pages, adding, 177-179
Clickable area on an image map, 169
Clip Art, inserting into your web, 130
Clip Art Gallery, 130, 155
Clip Art Gallery sound clips, 155
Close button, 19
Collaboration feature, 280
Color schemes
    choosing, 151-152
    designing webs with, 151-154
Compatibility tab, Page Options dialog box, 32-33
Components. *See* FrontPage components; Office 2000
  components

Confirmation page, creating, 222
Connection speed, setting, 29
Contact-information form, 218
Content
    developing, 89-124
    filling in a table, 102
    prioritizing potential, 7-8
    unprioritized brainstormed, 6
Convert Text dialog box, 84
Converting a document into a web page, 82-84
Copying and pasting text, 96
Copyright C-in-a-circle symbol, 105
Copyright statement (dummy), 74
Corporate Presence Web, 47-51
    Folders view, 16
    home page, 15
    Navigation view, 18
    Reports view, 17
Create Hyperlink dialog box, 164, 168
Credits, adding to a picture, 148-149
Cropping a picture, 137-138
Custom style, removing from a page, 115
Custom toolbars, 26-27
Customer Support Web, 46-47, 65
Customization options, 27-35
Cutting and pasting text, 96

D

Database
    entering search criteria, 232-234
    importing, 228-231
    registering, 227-228
    sorting, 232
Database connectivity tools, 226
Database results page, 234
Database Results Wizard, 226, 228-231
Database-generated content, using, 226-234
Date-stamping a page, 105
Default Font tab, Page Options dialog box, 34
Designing a web. *See* Web design
Desktop, FrontPage icon on, 35-36
DHTML (dynamic HTML) effects, 213-215
DHTML Effects toolbar, 213
Directory for all your webs, establishing, 44-45
Discussion groups, 222-226
Discussion Web Wizard, 223-224

Document, converting into a web page, 82-84
Document check-in and check-out, 280
Domain name, getting your own, 261-262
Domain name host, getting, 262
Dotted lines, for shared borders, 74
Drawings, inserting into your web, 129
Dummy text, 74
Dynamic HTML, 213-215

E

Edit Groups dialog box, 273
E-mail address, linking to, 166
Embedded file, saving a page with, 79-81
Embedded pictures, web page with, 150
Empty web, creating, 45
Errors, checking for, 241-242
Excel database
    data formatting choices, 230
    importing, 229-231
    registering, 227-228
Exiting FrontPage, 19-20
External link, inserting, 167-168
External style sheet, creating, 116

F

Feedback from visitors, getting, 216-222
Feedback.htm with placeholders, 48
Files
    checking out, 280
    importing to your web later on, 57-59
    publishing status of, 244-247
    saving a page with embedded, 79-81
    sorting by date, 267-268
    tracking review status of, 281
    turning into FrontPage templates, 283
Files Of Type box (Select File dialog box), 83
Findability of your web, 258-262
Finding and replacing text, 97
Flipping a picture, 141
Folder for all your webs, establishing, 44-45
Folder List, 14, 16
Folders, 14
    converting to subwebs, 269
    deleting, 64
    making, 60-62

moving around, 268
naming, 63
Folders view, 16, 61, 175
Font dialog box, 108-110
Font size and button height, 204
Fonts, default, 34
Form information
saving, 219-221
validating, 221-222
Form Page Wizard, 216-218
Form Properties sheet, 218-219
Formatting
removing, 99
with style sheets, 107-114
a table, 102-103
text, 98-99
text links in a nav bar, 184
Formatting toolbar, 14
Forms, for visitors, 216-222
Frame properties dialog box, 196
Frames, 193-197
filling, 194-195
formatting, 196
sizing, 195
target (for links), 197
Frames page, creating, 194
Frames templates, 194
Frequently Asked Questions page, 48
Front end (web), 9
FrontPage
choosing components to install, 290-294
essentials, 12-20
exiting, 19-20
installing, 285-295
installing with Office 2000, 287
on Quick Launch toolbar, 37
registering, 294
removing previous versions, 290
shortcuts to, 35-37
starting, 12-13
uninstalling, 295
upgrading, 286
on Windows Start menu, 36
FrontPage components, inserting, 202-207
FrontPage icon, on Windows desktop, 35-36
FrontPage Personal Web Server, 240
FrontPage screen, 13-18

FrontPage server extensions, 240-241
FrontPage-compatible servers, 240
FTP, publishing via, 249-251
FTP address, 249
FTP sites, 250-251

G

General tab, Options dialog box, 28
GIF (Graphics Interchange Format), 128
Global formatting with style sheets, 107-114
Graphics, 125-157. *See also* Images
background, 74, 151
inserting into your web, 129
Groups
permission to add, 272-273
removing, 274

H

Heading 2 style, applying, 99
Hit counters, 257-258
Home pages, 15, 92, 94, 112
bottom border, 104
first draft, 11
flagging for search engines, 260
with nav bar, 183
Hosting, using an ISP for, 239
Hosting your own site, 239-240
Hotspots (image map), 169-171
Hover button, inserting, 203-204
HTML code/tags
editing, 13, 121-122
viewing/revealing, 30, 121
HTML (dynamic), 213-215
HTML editor, default, 13
HTTP, publishing via, 248-249
Hyperlinks. *See* Linking; Links (hyperlinks)
Hyperlinks view, 18-19, 171-172
Hyperlinks view of a hypertext story, 19

I

I-beam pointer, 14
Image (background), adding, 151
Image formats for the Web, standard, 128
Image map, creating, 169-170

Image map hotspots, 169-171
Images. *See also* Graphics
    Alternative Text for, 150
    putting text on, 149
Importing files to your web later on, 57-59
Importing a web, 52-60
    from the Internet, 53-55
    from your computer/network, 55-57
Indentation, paragraph, 111
Insertion point, 14
Installing FrontPage, 285-295
    and choosing components, 290-294
    with Office 2000, 287
Interface, 12
Internet, importing a web from, 53-55
Internet Explorer, upgrading, 290
Internet Information Server (IIS), 240
Intranet, publishing on, 251-253
ISP (Internet Service Provider), 239, 248

JPEG (Joint Photographic Experts) format, 128

Keyboard shortcuts, Screen Tips with, 27
Keywords, adding to your web, 260-261

Laying out pages, using tables for, 100-103
Line art, inserting into your web, 131
Lines, drawing, 101
Link anchor, selecting, 164
Link Style Sheet dialog box, 120
Linking
    to an e-mail address, 166
    pages, 162-175
    to a style sheet, 119-121
    to a Web address, 167-168
    within your web, 165
Links (hyperlinks), 162-175
    bold, 174
    checking for bad, 241-243
    correcting bad, 244
    deleting, 169

    image map default, 170
    inserting, 164
    light blue, 174-175
    recalculating, 172-173
    rollover effects, 173-174
    target frames for, 197
    verifying and updating, 242
    viewing, 171-172

M

Main folder for all your webs, establishing, 44-45
Maintenance, web site, 266, 277-284
Marquee Properties dialog box, 203
Marquees, inserting, 202-203
Master Category List dialog box, 189
Maximize button, 13
Menu commands, displaying hidden, 27
Microsoft Internet Information Server (IIS), 240
Microsoft Office 2000 components, inserting, 207-213
Microsoft Personal Web Server, 240
Misspellings, correcting throughout an article, 97
Modify Style dialog box, 109, 112
More Buttons button, 24
Multiple-files Properties dialog box, 246

N

Naming your folders, 63
Naming your web, 67-68
Napkins, designing your web on, 4-12
Navigation Bar Properties dialog box, 181-182
Navigation bars (nav bars), 181
    editing, 183-184
    excluding pages from, 179
    home page with, 183
    inserting on a page, 180-183
    removing, 184-185
    setting up, 175-185
Navigation buttons, 74
Navigation tree, 175, 180
Navigation view, 17-18, 176
Navigational structure of your web, 17, 159-198
Netscape window, web page in, 124
Network, importing a web from, 55-57
New Database Connection dialog box, 229
New dialog box, 75-76

New Task dialog box, 278
New web, setting up, 39-68
No frames page, setting up, 197
Normal style sheet, 116

O

ODBC Microsoft Excel Setup dialog box, 228
Office 2000 components
        Chart, 212-213
        inserting, 207-213
        Pivot Table, 213
        Spreadsheet, 208-212
One Page Web template, 45-46
Open File dialog box, 87
Open Web dialog box, 59, 250
Opening a web page, 86-88
Opening your last project at startup, 27
Options dialog box
        General tab, 28
        Reports View tab, 29
Organizing your web site, 60-64
Orienting a picture, 140-141
Orphaned pages, cleaning up, 255

P

Page elements, editing, 52
Page Options dialog box
        Compatibility tab, 32-33
        Default Font tab, 34
        Spelling, 31
Page positions, types of, 177
Page Properties dialog box, 152, 155, 188
Page transitions, 215-216
Page Transitions dialog box, 215
Page view, 14-15, 73
Page-layout, using tables, 100-103
Pages. *See* Web pages
Paragraph dialog box, 110-111
Paragraph indentation, 111
Password, changing, 276-277
Permissions, 270-277
        to add a group of users, 272-273
        to add a user, 272-273
        to browse/author/administer, 270-271
Personal Web Server (FrontPage), 240

Personal Web Server (Microsoft), 240
Personal Web template, 50, 52
Photo CDs, processing negatives into, 134
Photographs, inserting into your web, 129, 134-135
Picture dialog box, 132
Picture formats, 128-129
Picture Properties dialog box
        General tab, 146-147
        Video tab, 156
Picture toolbar, 136, 169
Pictures
        adding text to, 148-150
        captions and credits for, 148-149
        contrast and brightness, 141
        converting to another format, 146-147
        converting to black and white, 142
        cropping, 137-138
        editing, 136-141
        inserting into your web, 129-136
        orienting, 140-141
        pointing to multiple destinations, 169
        positioning, 143-145
        resampling, 140
        resizing, 138-139
        saving with a page, 150
        scheduling, 204-205
Pivot Table (Office component), 213
Placeholders, 48
Planning your web, 1-20
PNG (Portable Network Graphic), 128
Poor Richard's Web Site, 239, 258
Portals, registering at, 259-260
Position dialog box (picture), 144-145
Positioning a picture, 143-145
Predesigned page, starting with, 75-77
Preview in Browser dialog box, 122-124
Preview tab, 123
Previewing your work, 122-124
Project management, 277-283
Project Web template, 50-51
Promoting your web, 258-262
Proofreading as you go, 94-95
Properties dialog box, Workgroup tab, 247
Properties dialog box (multiple-files), 246
Protecting your web with permissions, 270-277
Publish Changed Pages Only, 255
Publish Status report, 245

Publish Web dialog box, 249
Published web
 updating, 254-255
 viewing, 256
Publishing status of files, 244-247
Publishing your web, 235-262
 and dynamic pages, 254
 for the first time, 248
 via FTP, 249-251
 via HTTP, 248-249
 on an intranet, 251-253
 parts not ready for, 244-247
 preventing a page from being published, 86

Q

Quick Launch toolbar, adding FrontPage to, 37
QuickSum button (Office spreadsheet), 210

R

Recent web pages, reopening, 88
Registering FrontPage, 294
Registering at portals, 259-260
Registration form, creating, 275-276
Relative page positions, 177
Reopening a recent web page, 88
Reorganizing your web, 267
Repeating elements in shared borders, 104-106
Reporting, 16
Reports view, 17, 242, 244
Reports View tab, Options dialog box, 29
Resampling a picture, 140
Resizing handles, 138-139
Resizing a picture, 138-139
Restore Picture button, 141
Restoring your work to a previous state, 95
Restructuring your web, 267
Review status, tracking, 281
Rollover effects (links), 173-174
Rotating a picture, 141

S

Save As dialog box, 79
Save As Template dialog box, 283

Saving
 changes before exiting, 19
 a copy of a page with Save As, 82
 form results, 219-221
 a page with an embedded file, 79-81
 a page for the first time, 78-81
 repeatedly as you work, 82
 and titling a web page, 77-82
Scanned photographic prints, 134-135
Scanner driver, 135
Schedule Picture Properties dialog box, 205
Scheduling a picture, 204-205
Screen (FrontPage), 13-18
Screen Tips, with keyboard shortcuts, 27
Scroll bars, 14
Search criteria (database), 232-234
Search engines, flagging your home page for, 260
Search page, adding to your web, 191-193
Select File dialog box, 83, 133
Select Hyperlink dialog box, 120
Server, choosing, 239-240
Server extensions, 240-241
Service provider (ISP), 239
Set Action dialog box, 81
Set Page Title dialog box, 78
Shared borders
 customer-support web with, 65
 defined, 64
 dotted lines for, 74
 repeating elements in, 104-106
 turning on, 64-67
Shared Borders dialog box, 66, 106
Sharing templates, 281-284
Shortcuts to FrontPage, 35-37
Show All, 25
Sibling pages, 177-178
Site map, 186
 adding lists of categories to, 190-191
 making, 188-191
Sites. *See* Webs
Size To Fit, 18
Slide scanners, 134
Sorting files by date, 267-268
Sound, adding to your web, 154-155
Sound clips from Clip Art Gallery, 155
Spell checking (background), turning off, 30-31
Spelling options, Page Options dialog box, 31
Spreadsheet (Office component), 208-212

Spreadsheet Property Toolbox (Office), 208-209
Standard toolbar, 14
Start menu, listing FrontPage on, 36
Starting FrontPage, 12-13
Startup, with your last project open, 27
Status bar, 14, 28-29
Style dialog box, 113
Style sheets
    adding styles to, 117-118
    creating, 116
    formatting with, 107-114
    linking pages to, 119-121
    opening, 119
    saving, 118
    stand-alone, 107
Styles
    adding to a style sheet, 117-118
    applying to text, 98-99
    changing, 107-113
    list of, 108
    making new, 114
    removing from a page, 115
    for your whole web, 115-120
Subfolders, making, 62-63
Subwebs, setting up, 268-269

T

Table of Contents Properties dialog box, 186
Table of contents for your web, 185-191
    with dummy text, 187
    page template, 187
    types of, 185-186
Table Properties dialog box, 103
Table structure, changing, 100-102
Tables, 100-103
    drawing, 100-101
    formatting, 102-103
Tags (HTML)
    editing, 13, 121-122
    viewing/revealing, 30, 121
Task list, viewing, 278-279
Task-management tools, 277
Tasks, creating, 277-279
Tasks view, 18
Templates, 43
    icons for, 43

list of, 44
    sharing, 281-284
    turning files into, 283
Text
    adding to a picture, 148-150
    applying a style to, 98-99
    corrections and changes to, 94-97
    cutting and pasting, 96
    editing, 96
    entering, 93
    finding and replacing, 97
    formatting, 98-99
    formatting with style sheets, 107-114
    proofreading as you go, 94-95
    putting on an image, 149
    working with, 93-99
Text Box Validation dialog box, 221
Text file, formatting, 84
Text links in a nav bar, formatting, 184
Themes
    changing, 153
    choosing, 152
    designing webs with, 151-154
    removing, 154
Thumbnails, creating, 142-144
Titling a web page, 78
Toolbars, 13-18, 24-27
Top-level pages, 177
Tracking access, 257-258
Tracking review status, 281
Transparent color, 142

U

Undoing big mistakes, 95
Undoing several actions at once, 95
Uninstalling FrontPage, 295
Updating and verifying links, 242
Updating your published web, 254-255
Upgrading FrontPage, 286
Upgrading Internet Explorer, 290
URL, for a local web server, 252
URL box (Create Hyperlink), 168
User Meta Variable dialog box, 261
User registration form, creating, 275-276
User self-registration, 274-276
User variables, 260

Users
    permission to add, 272-273
    permission levels for new, 274
    removing, 274

V

Validating form information, 221-222
Verify Hyperlinks dialog box, 242
Verifying links, 242
Video, adding to your web, 154-156
Video properties, setting, 156
View bar, 14
Viewing your published web, 256
Visitor feedback, getting, 216-222
Visitor numbers, tracking, 257-258

W

Web address, linking to, 167-168
Web content. *See* Content
Web design
    brainstorming, 5-6
    changing things as you go, 12
    on cocktail napkins, 4-12
    with color schemes and themes, 151-154
    home page first draft, 11
    home page mock up, 10
    iterative process, 9
    massaging structure and design, 10-12
    presentation, 9-12
    prioritizing potential content, 7-8
    sketching a skeleton, 9-10
    unprioritized content, 6
Web pages. *See also* Web design; Webs
    announcement list for, 259
    assigning to categories, 189-190
    with background sound, 154
    cleaning up orphaned, 255
    converting a document into, 82-84
    creating, 72-77
    creating while linking, 165
    date-stamping, 105
    defined, 3
    deleting, 85
    dragging to make links, 163
    with embedded pictures, 150

    excluding from navigation bars, 179
    finding when last updated, 105
    linking, 162-175
    linking to a style sheet, 119-121
    making, 69-88
    opening, 86-88
    placing navigation bars on, 180-183
    preventing from being published, 86
    publishing, 247-256
    removing, 84-86
    removing a custom style from, 115
    removing without deleting, 85-86
    reopening recent, 88
    saving blank, 78
    saving for the first time, 78-81
    saving a picture with, 150
    saving and titling, 77-82
    in 640 X 480 Netscape window, 124
    types of, 92
    using tables for layout, 100-103
    viewing underlying HTML for, 30, 121
Web picture formats, 128-129
Web server, choosing, 239-240
Web site maintenance, 266, 277-284
Web sites. *See* Webs
Web to support this book, 284
Webs. *See also* Web design; Web pages
    administering, 263-277
    adding keywords to, 260-261
    adding a search page, 191-193
    adding sound or video, 154-157
    background image and color scheme, 151-152
    bells and whistles, 157
    creating, 42-52
    designing for a browser, 31-33
    FrontPage predesigned, 46-52
    hosting, 239-240
    importing, 52-60
    inserting photographs into, 134-135
    inserting pictures into, 129-136
    ISP to host, 239
    linking within, 165
    maintaining, 266, 277-284
    naming, 67-68
    navigational structure of, 159-198
    opening, 59-60
    organizing, 60-64

personal, 50, 52
planning, 1-20
promotion and findability, 258-262
protecting with permissions, 270-277
publishing, 235-262
publishing for the first time, 248
removing pages from, 84-86
reorganizing, 267
restructuring, 267
setting up, 39-68
skeletal structure of, 175
slowing down to a crawl, 157

starting with a blank page, 73-74
starting from scratch, 45-46
style for, 115-120
table of contents for, 185-191
updating after publishing, 254-255
viewing links in, 171-172
viewing published, 256
WildflowerTrips prototype site, 284
Windows desktop, FrontPage icon on, 35-36
Windows Start menu, listing FrontPage on, 36
Wizards, 43-44
Workgroup Properties, 247

The Computer Books You Love to Read Are Even Better Than Ever!

With the release of Office 2000, Osborne presents a fresh new line of Busy People™ books...

"Well-organized and illustrated and aimed directly at working people who need to get specific jobs done quickly."
—LIBRARY JOURNAL

"Entertaining enough to be read over lunch and relaxing enough to take to bed."
—WACO TRIBUNE-HERALD

"About as far from the old dry textbook-style computer books as you can get with good navigational aids, lots of illustrations and shortcuts."
—COMPUTER LIFE

500,000+ Busy People Books Sold!

Office 2000 for Busy People
Peter Weverka
ISBN: 0-07-211857-1 $19.99

Word 2000 for Busy People
Christian Crumlish
ISBN: 0-07-211982-9 $19.99

Excel 2000 for Busy People
Ron Mansfield
ISBN: 0-07-211988-8 $19.99

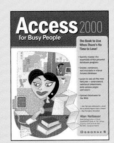

Access 2000 for Busy People
Alan Neibauer
ISBN: 0-07-211983-7 $19.99

FrontPage 2000 for Busy People
Christian Crumlish
ISBN: 0-07-211981-0 $19.99

300 Classic Blocks
for Crochet Projects

300 Classic Blocks
for Crochet Projects

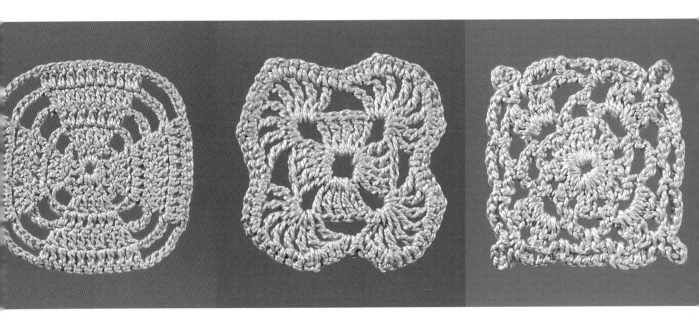

Revised Edition

Linda P. Schapper

LARK
CRAFTS

An Imprint of Sterling Publishing Co., Inc.
New York

WWW.LARKCRAFTS.COM

Editor: Susan Mowery Kieffer
Technical Editor: Karen Manthey
Art Director: Shannon Yokeley
Cover Designer: Cindy LaBreacht
Photographer: Steve Mann
Illustrator: Orrin Lundgren
Diagrams: Karen Manthey

The Library of Congress has cataloged the hardcover edition as follows:

Schäpper, Linda.
  300 classic blocks for crochet projects / Linda P. Schapper. -- Rev. ed.
    p. cm.
  Includes index.
  ISBN-13: 978-1-57990-913-0 (hbk. : alk. paper)
  ISBN-10: 1-57990-913-2 (hbk. : alk. paper)
  1. Crocheting--Patterns. I. Title. II. Title: Three hundred classic
blocks for crochet projects.
  TT820.S277 2007
  746.43'4041--dc22

                        2007046181

10 9 8 7 6 5 4 3 2 1

Published by Lark Crafts
An Imprint of Sterling Publishing Co., Inc.
387 Park Avenue South, New York, N.Y. 10016

First Paperback Edition 2011
Revised Edition
Text © 2008, Linda P. Schapper
Photography © 2008, Lark Crafts, an Imprint of Sterling Publishing Co., Inc.
Illustrations © 2008, Lark Crafts, an Imprint of Sterling Publishing Co., Inc., unless
otherwise specified
First published in 1987 by Sterling Publishing Co., Inc.

Distributed in Canada by Sterling Publishing,
c/o Canadian Manda Group, 165 Dufferin Street
Toronto, Ontario, Canada M6K 3H6

Distributed in the United Kingdom by GMC Distribution Services,
Castle Place, 166 High Street, Lewes, East Sussex, England BN7 1XU

Distributed in Australia by Capricorn Link (Australia) Pty Ltd.,
P.O. Box 704, Windsor, NSW 2756 Australia

If you have questions or comments about this book, please contact:
Lark Crafts
67 Broadway
Asheville, NC 28801
828-253-0467

Manufactured in China

ISBN 13: 978-1-57990-913-0 (hardcover) 978-1-60059-821-0 (paperback)

For information about custom editions, special sales, premium and corporate purchases, please
contact Sterling Special Sales Department at 800-805-5489 or specialsales@sterlingpub.com.

For information about desk and examination copies available to college and university professors,
requests must be submitted to academic@larkbooks.com. Our complete policy can be found
at www.larkcrafts.com.

■ Contents ■

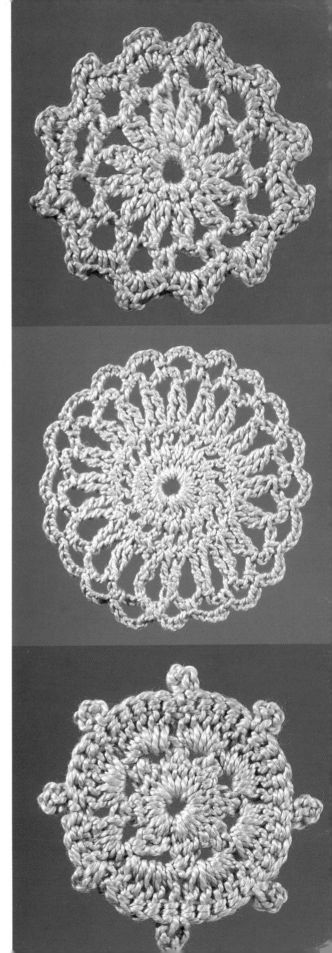

Introduction		6
Basic Stitches		7
Joining Blocks		15
International Crochet Symbols		16

Patterns

1	Single Crochets & Chains	18
2	Double Crochets & Filet	23
3	Double Crochets & Chains	36
4	Treble Crochets & Double Treble Crochets	54
5	Clusters	60
6	Bobbles	72
7	Puff Stitches	79
8	Popcorn Stitches	104
9	Post Stitches	112
10	Shells	120
11	Picots	130
12	Mixed Stitches	147
13	Triangle Blocks	170
14	Circles	176
15	Hexagons	184
16	Floral Patterns	199
17	Sculptured Blocks	222
18	Small Blocks	228
19	Sampler Blocks	232

Crochet Terms and Abbreviations	255
Acknowledgments	256
About the Author	256

▪ Introduction ▪

Very little has survived in the way of a written record about the early history of crochet. However, we believe that the craft dates back to the Stone Age, when a crude hook was used to join sections of clothing. In all probability, we adopted the French word for hook—*crochet*—as the name of the craft because the French did more than any other group to record crochet patterns.

As with many handcrafts, crochet developed and flourished, taught from generation to generation without written instructions. Patterns survived by being handed down through families. New patterns were copied by examining designs with a magnifying glass. In the 19th century, written instructions became more popular as the reading level of women improved. Instructions, however, can be often long and tedious and, although perfectly clear to the writer, frequently difficult for the crocheter.

Here in *Crochet Blocks* I provide written instructions for each pattern as well as instruction in the International Crochet Symbols system. The diagrams for these symbols are easy to read after you have memorized a few of the basic stitches. This system enables you to see the whole pattern in proportion, and it is an enjoyable experience to pick up a crochet book written for a Russian, French, or Japanese audience and be able to understand the crochet symbols. The symbols themselves look a great deal like the actual crochet stitches and, as you will see, are not at all difficult to follow.

Crochet begins with a chain, and the way the stitches are formed determines the pattern. You need only a hook, your hand, and the thread. It is a portable craft and can be done almost anywhere, and it is difficult to make a mistake that cannot be corrected immediately. Crochet is versatile. You can make lace patterns, both large and small, mimic knitting, patchwork, or weaving, and you can create any number of textile patterns.

This book focuses on blocks and includes an extensive variety of shapes and sizes. Patterns range from small to large, and from circles and squares to triangles and hexagons. Some of the patterns are sculptured, while some are in the shape of rosettes and other floral patterns.

When I first discovered crochet blocks 20 years ago, I was enchanted with the sheer number of different patterns that could be made with a simple crochet hook and the same white thread. It brought to mind all the infinite possibilities we have with our lives. The slow build up of the pattern, block-by-block, suggested to me that, with small steps, we can get through anything. A close friend had died, and I was going through a particularly sad time in my life, and crocheting the blocks was a comforting exercise. Since then, my life has gone through many highs and more lows and, all these years later, I am still enchanted by the beautiful patterns we can make with a little bit of organization and determination.

With the resurgence of interest in crochet today, it has become popular with both newcomers to the craft and veteran crocheters alike. My hope is that with this book, you, too, will discover or perhaps even rediscover the joy of crochet.

Notes for those using the written instructions
- The abbreviations used throughout are ones used in the United States. A list of basic terms used in the U.K. and Australia is on page 255.
- Learn to read the diagrams, as they are much easier to follow than the instructions. When in doubt about the written instructions, check them against the diagrams.
- To make the motifs reversible, turn at the end of each round, and work the wrong-side rows in reverse—clockwise—following the diagram. Many of the motifs were worked this way to make them reversible.
- The division of stitches into chapters is somewhat arbitrary because many of the patterns can fit into several chapters. I tried to place them where they were most typical.

■ Basic Stitches ■

SLIP KNOT

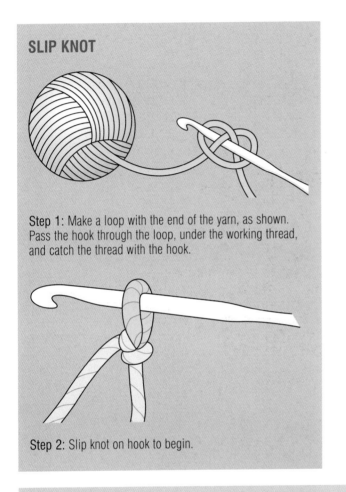

Step 1: Make a loop with the end of the yarn, as shown. Pass the hook through the loop, under the working thread, and catch the thread with the hook.

Step 2: Slip knot on hook to begin.

CHAIN (ch)

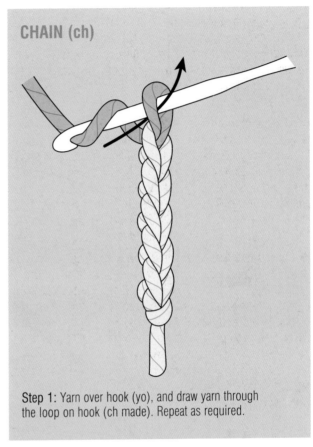

Step 1: Yarn over hook (yo), and draw yarn through the loop on hook (ch made). Repeat as required.

SLIP STITCH (sl st)

Step 1: Insert hook in designated stitch.

Step 2: Yo, draw yarn through stitch and the loop on hook (sl st made).

SINGLE CROCHET (sc)

This is a short, tight stitch.

Make a chain of desired length.
Step 1: Insert hook in designated st (2nd ch from hook for first sc).

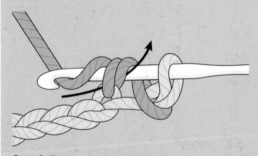

Step 2: Draw yarn through stitch.

Step 3: Yo, draw yarn through 2 loops on hook (sc made).

Step 4: Insert hook in next chain, and repeat steps to create another single crochet.

HALF DOUBLE CROCHET (hdc)

This stitch gives a lot of body and structure and resembles knitting.

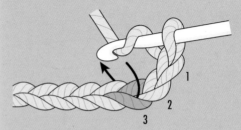

Make a chain of desired length.
Step 1: Yo, insert hook in designated st (3rd ch from hook for first hdc).

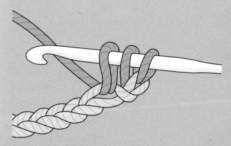

Step 2: Yo, draw through stitch (3 loops on hook).

Step 3: Yo, draw yarn through 3 loops on hook (hdc made).

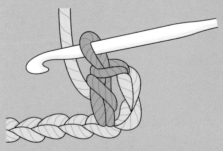

Step 4: You will have one loop left on the hook. Yo, insert hook in next ch, and repeat sequence across row.

DOUBLE CROCHET (dc)

This is perhaps the most popular and frequently used crochet stitch.

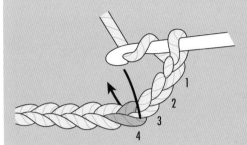

Make a chain of desired length.
Step 1: Yo, insert hook in designated st (4th ch from hook for first dc).

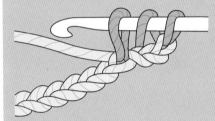

Step 2: Yo, draw through stitch (3 loops on hook).

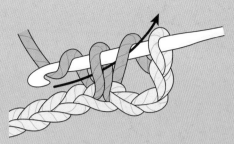

Step 3: Yo, draw yarn through first 2 loops on hook.

Step 4: Yo, draw yarn through last 2 loops on hook (dc made).

Step 5: Yo, insert hook in next st, and repeat steps to continue across row. Repeat steps 2-4 to work next dc.

TREBLE CROCHET (tr)

Make a chain of desired length.
Step 1: Yo twice, insert hook in designated st (5th ch from hook for first tr).

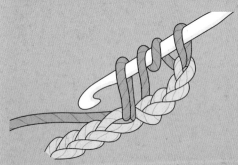

Step 2: Yo, draw through stitch (4 loops on hook).

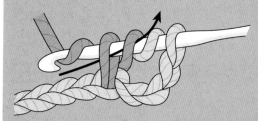

Step 3: Yo, draw yarn through 2 loops on hook (3 loops on hook).

Step 4: Yo, draw yarn through 2 loops on hook (2 loops on hook).

Step 5: Yo, draw yarn through 2 loops on hook (tr made).

Step 6: Yo twice, and repeat steps in next ch st.

BOBBLE

Can be made with 2 to 6 loops. Shown for 4 loops.

Step 1: Yo, insert hook in designated st.

Step 2: Yo, draw yarn through st and up to level of work (first loop).

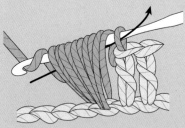

Step 3: (Yo, insert hook in same st, yo, draw yarn through st) as many times as required (3 more times for 4-looped bobble st—11 loops on hook).

Step 4: Yo, draw yarn through all loops on hook (bobble made).

PUFF STITCH

Can be made with 2 to 6 sts. Shown for 3 dc.

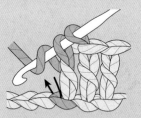

Step 1: Yo, insert hook in designated st (4th ch from hook for first puff st), yo, draw yarn through st, yo, draw yarn through 2 loops on hook (half-closed dc made—2 loops remain on hook).

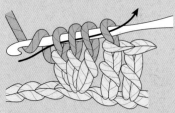

Step 2: Yo, insert hook in same st, yo, draw yarn through st, yo, draw yarn through 2 loops on hook for each additional dc required (2 more times for 3-dc puff stitch—4 loops on hook).

Step 3: Yo, draw yarn through all loops on hook (puff stitch made).

POPCORN (pop)
Can be made with 2 to 6 sts. Shown with 5 dc.

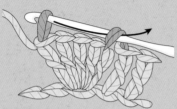

Pop on RS rows:
Step 1: Work 5 dc in designated st (4th ch from hook for first pop).

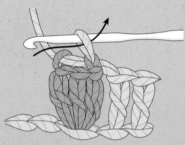

Step 2: Drop loop from hook, insert hook from front to back in top of first dc of group, pick up dropped loop, and draw through st, ch 1 tightly to secure (pop made).

Pop on WS rows:
Step 1: Work 5 dc in designated st (4th ch from hook for first pop).

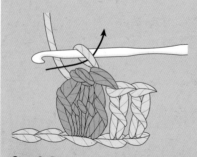

Step 2: Drop loop from hook, insert hook from back to front in top of first dc of group, pick up dropped loop, and draw through st, ch 1 tightly to secure (pop made).

CLUSTER
Shown for 4-dc cluster.

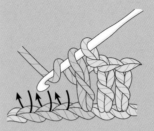

Step 1: Yo, insert hook in designated st, yo, draw yarn through st, yo, draw yarn through 2 loops on hook (half-closed dc made—2 loops remain on hook).

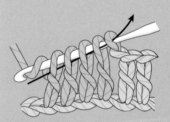

Step 2: (Yo, insert hook in next designated st, yo, draw yarn through st, yo, draw yarn through 2 loops on hook) as many times as required (3 more times for 4-dc cluster—4 half-closed dc made—5 loops on hook).

Step 3: Yo, draw yarn through all loops on hook (cluster made).

PICOT

Shown for ch-3 picot.

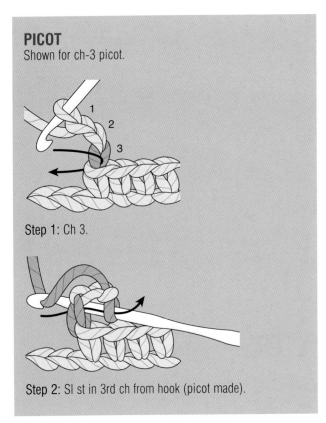

Step 1: Ch 3.

Step 2: Sl st in 3rd ch from hook (picot made).

CROSSED STITCH (CROSSED tr SHOWN)

Step 1: Skip required number of sts (skip 2 sts shown), tr in next st, ch required number of sts (ch 1 shown), working behind tr just made, tr in first skipped st.

V-STITCH (V-st), OR SHELL

A designated number of stitches (frequently worked with double crochet stitches) worked in same stitch (shown for 4-dc shell). V-sts are comprised of 2 dc (with or without a ch space). Shells can be made with 3 or more dc (with or without ch spaces).

Work 4 dc in designated st (shell made).

Y-STITCH (OPEN VERSION SHOWN)

Step 1: Work tr in designated st.

Step 2: Ch required number of sts (ch 3 shown), yo, work dc in 2 strands at center of tr just made (Y-st made).

FRONT POST DOUBLE CROCHET (FPDC)
Stitch is raised to front side of work.

Step 1: Yo, insert hook from front to back to front again, around the post of next designated st.

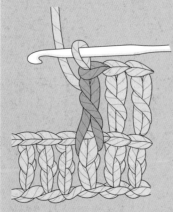

Step 2: Yo, draw yarn through st, (yo, draw yarn through 2 loops on hook) twice (FPdc made).

BACK POST DOUBLE CROCHET (BPDC)
Stitch is raised to back side of work.

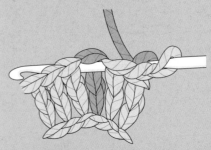

Step 1: Yo, insert hook from back to front to back again, around the post of next designated st.

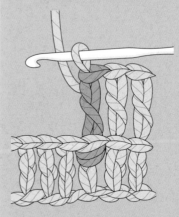

Step 2: Yo, draw yarn through st, (yo, draw yarn through 2 loops on hook) twice (BPdc made).

JOINING BLOCKS

Blocks such as squares, triangles, and hexagons, and even some other designs can be joined together directly without using a different shape to fill out the pattern. Others, such as circular or floral blocks, must be alternated, sometimes with a pattern of a different shape. This provides an opportunity to use your imagination in the selection of a complementary pattern. There is no right or wrong way. Whatever looks good to you can be used.

Illustrations © Karen Manthey

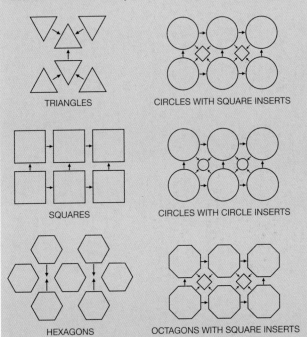

TRIANGLES

CIRCLES WITH SQUARE INSERTS

SQUARES

CIRCLES WITH CIRCLE INSERTS

HEXAGONS

OCTAGONS WITH SQUARE INSERTS

JOINING MOTIFS TOGETHER

There are several methods for joining motifs together. Sewing and crocheting are the most popular methods. Sewn seams are the least bulky, but if you prefer to avoid sewing, I've included two methods of crocheting seams.

Joinings can be worked with right sides or wrong sides facing. Worked with the wrong sides facing, the joining will stand out on the front of the piece. Placing the motifs with right sides of the motifs facing, the joining will be on the back and less noticeable. Use whichever method you prefer, just be consistent throughout.

Joinings can be worked through both loops of stitches for a sturdy join or through only the back loops of both pieces for a flexible seam. Illustrations show sewing and slip stitching through back loops of stitches and single crocheting through both loops of stitches. Always work joining stitches as loosely as the crocheted pieces to avoid tight seams that distort the fabric.

SEWN OR WHIPSTITCHED SEAMS

Place motifs together with right (or wrong) sides facing. Using a yarn needle and matching yarn, insert needle through back loop only of corner stitches of both pieces, draw yarn through and secure with a knot, *insert needle from top to bottom through the back loop 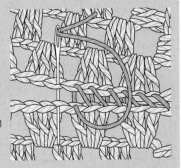 of the next stitch of each piece, then draw yarn through; repeat from * across side to be joined, to next corner stitch. Fasten off.

SLIP STITCHED SEAMS

Place motifs together with right (or wrong) sides facing. Using crochet hook and matching yarn, make a slip knot with yarn. Insert hook 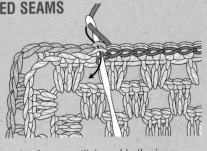 through back loop only of corner stitches of both pieces, place slip knot on hook, *insert hook through back loop of next stitch of each piece, yo, draw yarn through all three loops on hook; repeat from * across side to be joined, to next corner stitch. Fasten off.

SINGLE CROCHETED SEAMS

Place motifs together with right (or wrong) sides facing. Using crochet hook and matching yarn, make a slip knot with yarn. Insert hook through both loops of corner stitches of both pieces, place slip knot on hook, ch 1, insert hook through same two stitches, yo, draw yarn through stitches, yo, draw yarn through 2 loops on hook, *insert hook through both loops of next stitch of each piece, yo, draw yarn through stitches, yo, draw yarn through two loops on hook; repeat from * across side to be joined, to next corner stitch. Fasten off.

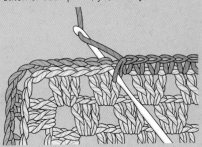

■ International Crochet Symbols ■

chain stitch (ch)	⬮	⬮⬮⬮⬮⬮
slip stitch (sl st)	•	• • • • •
single crochet (sc)	X	X X X X X
half double crochet (hdc)	T	T T T T T
double crochet (dc)	⊺	⊺ ⊺ ⊺ ⊺ ⊺
treble crochet (tr)	⫫	⫫ ⫫ ⫫ ⫫ ⫫
double treble crochet (dtr)	⫫	⫫ ⫫ ⫫ ⫫ ⫫
triple treble crochet (trtr)	⫫	⫫ ⫫ ⫫ ⫫ ⫫
Front Post double crochet (FPdc)	⌡	⌡ ⌡ ⌡ ⌡ ⌡
Back Post double crochet (BPdc)	⌐	⌐ ⌐ ⌐ ⌐ ⌐
ch-3 picot	⊶⊶	⊶⊶ ⊶⊶ ⊶⊶ ⊶⊶ ⊶⊶
ch-4 picot	⬠	⬠ ⬠ ⬠ ⬠ ⬠
3-dc popcorn (pop)	⬭	⬭ ⬭ ⬭ ⬭ ⬭
4-dc popcorn (pop)	⬭	⬭ ⬭ ⬭ ⬭ ⬭
5-dc popcorn (pop)	⬭	⬭ ⬭ ⬭ ⬭ ⬭
2-looped bobble	◡	◡ ◡ ◡ ◡ ◡
3-looped bobble	◡	◡ ◡ ◡ ◡ ◡
4-looped bobble	◡	◡ ◡ ◡ ◡ ◡
5-looped bobble	◡	◡ ◡ ◡ ◡ ◡

2-dc puff st	
3-dc puff st	
4-dc puff st	
5-dc puff st	
crossed dc	
crossed tr	
2-dc cluster	
3-dc cluster	
4-dc cluster	
5-dc cluster	
V-st	
3-dc shell	
4-dc shell	
5-dc shell	
4-dc shell with ch-2 space	
6-dc shell with ch-2 space	
working over previous rows	
Y-stitch	

.1.
Single Crochets & Chains

1 **Ch** 6 and sl st in first ch to form a ring.

Rnd 1: Ch 1, 6 sc in ring, sl st in first sc to join.

Rnd 2: Ch 1, 2 sc in each sc around, sl st in first sc to join.

Rnd 3: Ch 1, *sc in sc, 3 sc in next sc, sc in next sc; rep from * around, sl st in first sc to join.

Rnd 4: Ch 1, sc in each sc around, sl st in first sc to join.

Rnd 5: Ch 1, *sc in each of next 2 sc, 3 sc in next sc, sc in each of next 2 sc; rep from * around, sl st in first sc to join.

Rnd 3: Ch 1, *sc in each of next 3 sc, 3 sc in next sc, sc in each of next 3 sc; rep from * around, sl st in first sc to join. Fasten off.

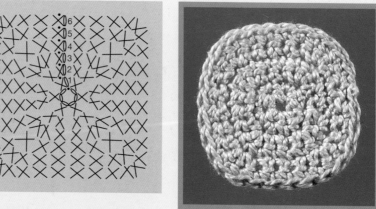
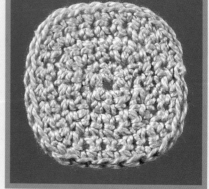

2 **Ch** 20 and sl st in first ch to form a ring.

Rnd 1: Ch 1, 36 sc in ring, sl st in first sc to join.

Rnd 2: *Ch 7, skip next 2 sc, sl st in next sc; rep from * around, ending with sl st in first sl st. Fasten off.

3 Ch 18 and sl st in first ch to form a ring.

Rnd 1: Ch 7, sl st to opposite side of ring, ch 1, 11 sc in first half of ring, 11 sc in 2nd half of ring, sl st in first sc to join. Fasten off.

4 Ch 8 and sl st in first ch to form a ring.

Rnd 1: Ch 1, 16 sc in ring, sl st in first sc to join.

Rnd 2: Ch 1, (sc, ch 5) in each sc around, sl st in first sc to join. Fasten off.

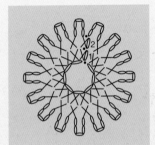

5 Ch 8 and sl st in first ch to form a ring.

Rnd 1: Ch 1, (sc, ch 2) 8 times in ring, sl st in first sc to join.

Rnd 2: Sl st in next ch-2 space, ch 1, (sc, ch 3) in each ch-2 space around, sl st in first sc to join.

Rnd 3: Sl st to center of next ch-3 loop, ch 1, (sc, ch 4) in each ch-3 loop around, sl st in first sc to join.

Rnd 4: Sl st to center of next ch-4 loop, ch 1, (sc, ch 5) in each ch-4 loop around, sl st in first sc to join. Fasten off.

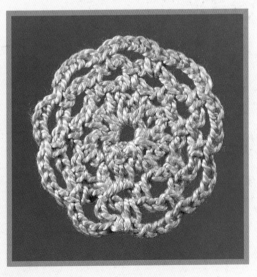

6 **Ch** 6 and sl st in first ch to form a ring.

Rnd 1: Ch 1, 12 sc in ring, sl st in first sc to join.

Rnd 2: Ch 1, (sc, ch 3) in each sc around, sl st in first sc to join.

Rnd 3: Sl st to center of next ch-3 loop, ch 1, (sc, ch 4) in each ch-3 loop around, sl st in first sc to join.

Rnd 4: Sl st to center of next ch-4 loop, ch 1, (sc, ch 5) in each ch-4 loop around, sl st in first sc to join.

Rnd 5: Sl st to center of next ch-5 loop, ch 1, (sc, ch 6) in each ch-5 loop around, sl st in first sc to join.

Rnd 6: Sl st to center of next ch-6 loop, ch 1, (sc, ch 7) in each ch-6 loop around, sl st in first sc to join. Fasten off.

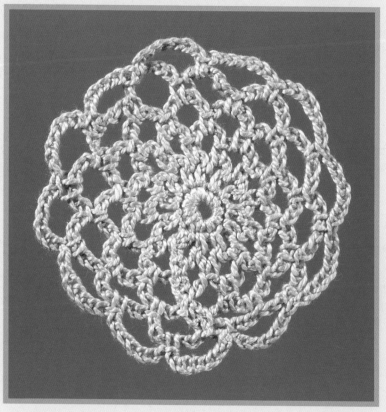

7

Ch 6 and sl st in first ch to form a ring.

Rnd 1: Ch 3 (counts as dc), 17 dc in ring, sl st in 3rd ch of beg ch to join.

Rnd 2: Ch 1, sc in first st, ch 5, skip next 2 dc, *sc in next dc, ch 5, skip next 2 dc; rep from * around, sl st in first sc to join.

Rnd 3: Ch 1, *sc in sc, ch 7, skip next loop; rep from * around, sl st in first sc to join.

Rnd 4: Ch 1, *sc in sc, ch 9, skip next loop; rep from * around, sl st in first sc to join.

Rnd 5: Ch 1, *sc in sc, ch 11, skip next loop; rep from * around, sl st in first sc to join.

Rnd 6: Ch 1, *sc in sc, ch 13, skip next loop; rep from * around, sl st in first sc to join. Fasten off.

8 Ch 6 and sl st in first ch to form a ring.

Rnd 1: Ch 1, 12 sc in ring, sl st in first sc to join.

Rnd 2: Ch 1, *sc in sc, ch 5, skip next sc; rep from * around, sl st in first sc to join.

Rnd 3: Sl st to center of first ch-5 loop, ch 1, (sc, ch 5, sc, ch 5) in each ch-5 loop around, sl st in first sc to join.

Rnd 4: Sl st to center of next ch-5 loop, ch 1, *(sc, ch 5, sc) in ch-5 loop, ch 5, sc in next ch-5 loop, ch 5; rep from * around, sl st in first sc to join.

Rnd 5: Sl st to center of next ch-5 loop, ch 1, *(sc, ch 5, sc) in ch-5 loop, (ch 5, sc) in each of next 2 ch-5 loops, ch 5; rep from * around, sl st in first sc to join.

Rnd 6: Sl st to center of next ch-5 loop, ch 1, *(sc, ch 5, sc) in ch-5 loop, (ch 5, sc) in each of next 3 ch-5 loops, ch 5; rep from * around, sl st in first sc to join. Fasten off.

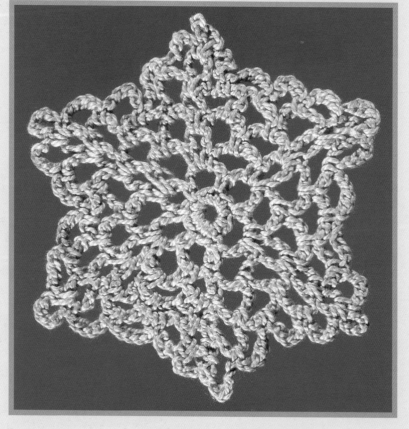

.2.
Double Crochets
& Filet

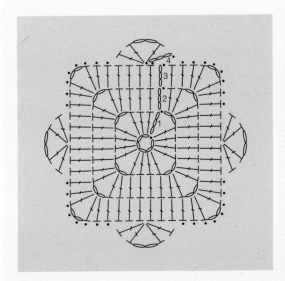

9 Ch 6 and sl st in first ch to form a ring.

Rnd 1: Ch 3 (counts as dc), 3 dc in ring, ch 2, (4 dc, ch 2) 3 times in ring, sl st in 3rd ch of beg ch to join.

Rnd 2: Ch 3 (counts as dc), dc in each of next 3 dc, *(2 dc, ch 1, 2 dc) in next ch-2 space**, dc in each of next 4 dc; rep from * around, ending last rep at **, sl st in 3rd ch of beg ch to join.

Rnd 3: Ch 3 (counts as dc), dc in each of next 5 dc, *(2 dc, ch 1, 2 dc) in next ch-2 space**, dc in each of next 8 dc; rep from * around, ending last rep at **, dc in next 2 dc, sl st in 3rd ch of beg ch to join.

Rnd 4: Sl st in next dc, sl st bet last dc and next dc, ch 3 (counts as dc), (dc, ch 2, 2 dc) in same space, *skip next 3 dc, sl st in each of next 3 dc, sl st in each of next 2 ch, sl st in each of next 3 dc**, skip next 3 dc, (2 dc, ch 2, 2 dc) bet last skipped and next dc; rep from * around, ending last rep at **, sl st in 3rd ch of beg ch to join. Fasten off.

10

Ch 6 and sl st in first ch to form a ring.

Rnd 1: Ch 3 (counts as dc), 11 dc in ring, sl st in 3rd ch of beg ch to join.

Rnd 2: Ch 4 (counts as dc, ch 1), dc in first dc, *dc in each of next 2 dc**, (dc, ch 1, dc) in next dc; rep from * around, ending last rep at **, sl st in 3rd ch of beg ch to join.

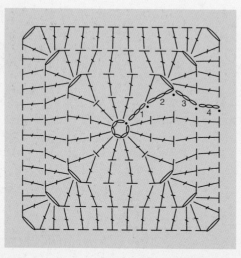

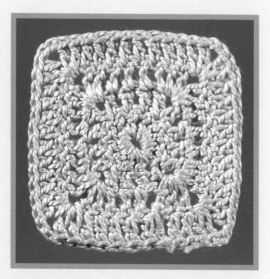

Rnd 3: Ch 3 (counts as dc), *(2 dc, ch 1, 2 dc) in next ch-1 space, dc in each of next 4 dc; rep from * around, omitting last dc, sl st in 3rd ch of beg ch to join.

Rnd 4: Ch 3 (counts as dc), dc in each of next 2 dc, *(2 dc, ch 1, 2 dc) in next ch-1 space**, dc in each of next 8 dc; rep from * around, ending last rep at **, dc in each of next 5 dc, sl st in 3rd ch of beg ch to join. Fasten off.

11

Ch 6 and sl st in first ch to form a ring.

Rnd 1: Ch 4 (counts as dc, ch 1), *4 dc in ring, ch 1, dc in ring, ch 1; rep from * twice, 4 dc in ring, ch 1, sl st in 3rd ch of beg ch to join.

Rnd 2: Ch 3 (counts as dc), (dc, ch 1, 2 dc) in first st, *skip next ch-1 space, dc in each of next 4 dc, skip next ch-1 space**, (2 dc, ch 1, 2 dc) in next dc; rep from * around, ending last rep at **, sl st in 3rd ch of beg ch to join.

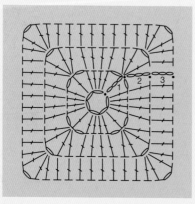

Rnd 3: Ch 3 (counts as dc), dc in next dc, *(2 dc, ch 1, 2 dc) in next ch-1 space**, dc in each of next 8 dc; rep from * around, ending last rep at **, dc in each of next 6 dc, sl st in 3rd ch of beg ch to join. Fasten off.

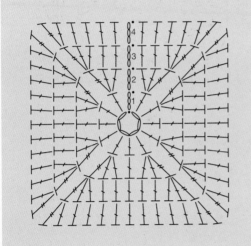

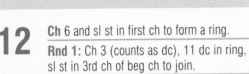

12 Ch 6 and sl st in first ch to form a ring.

Rnd 1: Ch 3 (counts as dc), 11 dc in ring, sl st in 3rd ch of beg ch to join.

Rnd 2: Ch 3 (counts as dc), *(2 dc, tr) in next dc, (tr, 2 dc) in next dc, dc in next dc; rep from * around, omitting last dc, sl st in 3rd ch of beg ch to join.

Rnd 3: Ch 3 (counts as dc), *dc in each of next 2 dc, (2 dc, tr) in next tr, (tr, 2 dc) in next tr, dc in each of next 3 dc; rep from * around, omitting last dc, sl st in 3rd ch of beg ch to join.

Rnd 4: Ch 3 (counts as dc), *dc in each of next 4 dc, (dc, tr) in next tr, (tr, dc) in next tr, dc in each of next 5 dc; rep from * around, omitting last dc, sl st in 3rd ch of beg ch to join. Fasten off.

13 Ch 3 and sl st in first ch to form a ring.

Rnd 1: Ch 8 (counts as dc, ch 5), (dc, ch 5) 3 times in ring, sl st in 3rd ch of beg ch to join. Fasten off.

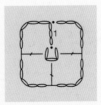

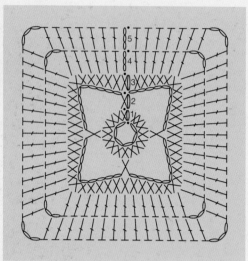

14 Ch 6 and sl st in first ch to form a ring.

Rnd 1: Ch 1, 16 sc in ring, sl st in first sc to join.

Rnd 2: Ch 1, *sc in sc, ch 10, skip next 3 sc; rep from * around, sl st in first sc to join.

Rnd 3: Ch 1, *sc in sc, 11 sc in next ch-10 loop; rep from * around, sl st in first sc to join.

Rnd 4: Ch 3 (counts as dc), *dc in each of next 5 sc, (dc, ch 3, dc) in next sc, dc in each of next 6 sc; rep from * around, omitting last dc, sl st in 3rd ch of beg ch to join.

Rnd 5: Ch 3 (counts as dc), *dc in each of next 6 dc, (dc, ch 3, dc) in next ch-3 loop, dc in each of next 7 dc; rep from * around, omitting last dc, sl st in 3rd ch of beg ch to join. Fasten off.

15 Ch 6 and sl st in first ch to form a ring.

Rnd 1: Ch 3 (counts as dc), 2 dc in ring, ch 3, (3 dc, ch 3) 3 times in ring, sl st in 3rd ch of beg ch to join.

Rnd 2: Ch 3 (counts as dc), dc in each of next 2 dc, *(dc, ch 5, dc) in next ch-3 loop**, dc in each of next 3 dc; rep from * around, ending last rep at **, sl st in 3rd ch of beg ch to join.

Rnd 3: Ch 3 (counts as dc), dc in each of next 3 dc, *(dc, ch 7, dc) in next ch-5 loop**, dc in each of next 5 dc; rep from * around, ending last rep at **, dc in next dc, sl st in 3rd ch of beg ch to join. Fasten off.

16

Ch 13 and sl st in first ch to form a ring.

Rnd 1: Ch 5 (counts as dc, ch 2), (dc, ch 5, dc, ch 2) 3 times in ring, dc in ring, ch 5, sl st in 3rd ch of beg ch to join.

Rnd 2: Ch 3 (counts as dc), *2 dc in next ch-2 space, dc in next dc, (3 dc, ch 5, 3 dc) in next ch-5 loop**, dc in next dc; rep from * around, ending last rep at **, sl st in 3rd ch of beg ch to join. Fasten off.

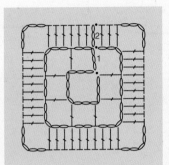

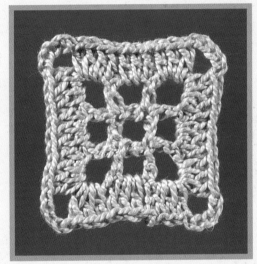

17

Ch 13 and sl st in first ch to form a ring.

Rnd 1: Ch 5 (counts as dc, ch 2), (dc, ch 5, dc, ch 2) 3 times in ring, dc in ring, ch 5, sl st in 3rd ch of beg ch to join.

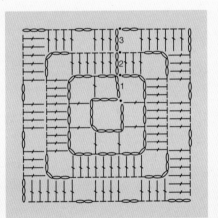

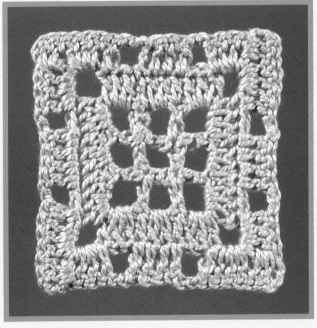

Rnd 2: Ch 3 (counts as dc), *2 dc in next ch-2 space, dc in next dc, (3 dc, ch 5, 3 dc) in next ch-5 loop**, dc in next dc; rep from * around, ending last rep at **, sl st in 3rd ch of beg ch to join.

Rnd 3: Ch 3 (counts as dc), *dc in each of next 3 dc, ch 2, skip next 2 dc, dc in next dc, 3 dc in next ch-5 loop, ch 3, 2 dc in side of last dc made, 3 dc in same ch-5 loop already holding 3 dc, dc in next dc, ch 2, skip next 2 dc**, dc in next dc; rep from * around, ending last rep at **, sl st in 3rd ch of beg ch to join. Fasten off.

18

Ch 8 and sl st in first ch to form a ring.

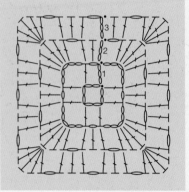

Rnd 1: Ch 4 (counts as dc, ch 1), (dc, ch 5, dc, ch 1) 3 times in ring, dc in ring, ch 5, sl st in 3rd ch of beg ch to join.

Rnd 2: Ch 3 (counts as dc), *dc in next ch-1 space, dc in next dc, ch 1, 5 dc in next ch-5 loop, ch 1**, dc in next dc; rep from * around, ending last rep at **, sl st in 3rd ch of beg ch to join.

Rnd 3: Ch 4 (counts as dc, ch 1), *skip next dc, dc in next dc, dc in next ch-1 space, dc in next dc, ch 1, skip next dc, 5 dc in next dc, ch 1, skip next dc, dc in next dc, dc in next ch-1 space**, dc in next dc; rep from * around, ending last rep at **, sl st in 3rd ch of beg ch to join. Fasten off.

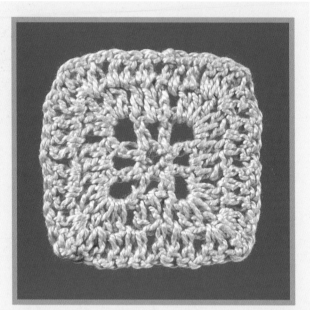

19

Ch 12 and sl st in first ch to form a ring.

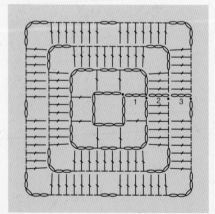

Rnd 1: Ch 8 (counts as dc, ch 5), (dc, ch 2, dc, ch 5) 3 times in ring, dc in ring, ch 2, sl st in 3rd ch of beg ch to join.

Rnd 2: Ch 3 (counts as dc), *(3 dc, ch 5, 3 dc) in next ch-5 loop, dc in next dc, 2 dc in next ch-2 space**, dc in next dc; rep from * around, ending last rep at **, sl st in 3rd ch of beg ch to join.

Rnd 3: Ch 3 (counts as dc), *dc in each of next 3 dc, (3 dc, ch 5, 3 dc) in next ch-5 loop, dc in each of next 4 dc, ch 2, skip next 2 dc**, dc in next dc; rep from * around, ending last rep at **, sl st in 3rd ch of beg ch to join. Fasten off.

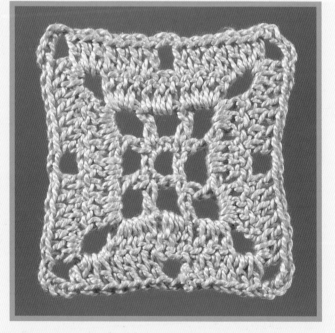

20 **Ch** 10 and sl st in first ch to form a ring.

Rnd 1: Ch 1, 16 sc in ring, sl st in first sc to join.

Rnd 2: Ch 6 (counts as dc, ch 3), *skip next sc, sc in next sc, ch 3**, skip next sc, dc in next sc, ch 3; rep from * around, ending last rep at **, sl st in 3rd ch of beg ch to join.

Rnd 3: Ch 3 (counts as dc), *4 dc in next ch-3 loop, dc in next sc, 4 dc in next ch-3 loop**, dc in next dc; rep from * around, ending last rep at **, sl st in 3rd ch of beg ch to join. Fasten off.

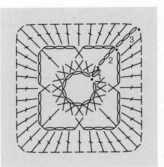

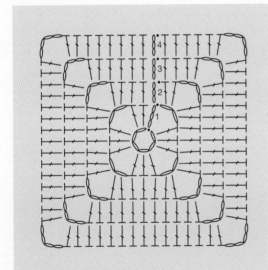

21 **Ch** 6 and sl st in first ch to form a ring.

Rnd 1: Ch 3 (counts as dc), 2 dc in ring, ch 2, (3 dc, ch 2) 3 times in ring, sl st in 3rd ch of beg ch to join.

Rnd 2: Ch 3 (counts as dc), *dc in each of next 2 dc, (2 dc, ch 4, 2 dc) in next ch-2 space, dc in next dc; rep from * around, omitting last dc, sl st in 3rd ch of beg ch to join.

Rnd 3: Ch 3 (counts as dc), *dc in each of next 4 dc, (2 dc, ch 4, 2 dc) in next ch-4 loop, dc in each of next 3 dc; rep from * around, omitting last dc, sl st in 3rd ch of beg ch to join.

Rnd 4: Ch 3 (counts as dc), *dc in each of next 6 dc, (2 dc, ch 4, 2 dc) in next ch-4 loop, dc in each of next 5 dc; rep from * around, omitting last dc, sl st in 3rd ch of beg ch to join. Fasten off.

22

Ch 6 and sl st in first ch to form a ring.

Rnd 1: Ch 6 (counts as dc, ch 3), (dc, ch 2, dc, ch 3) 3 times in ring, dc in ring, ch 2, sl st in 3rd ch of beg ch to join.

Rnd 2: Sl st in next ch-3 loop, ch 3 (counts as dc), (2 dc, ch 3, 3 dc) in same ch-3 loop, *ch 2, dc in next ch-2 space, ch 2**, (3 dc, ch 3, 3 dc) in next ch-3 loop; rep from * around, ending last rep at **, sl st in 3rd ch of beg ch to join.

Rnd 3: Ch 5 (counts as dc, ch 2), *skip next 2 dc, (3 dc, ch 3, 3 dc) in next ch-3 loop, ch 2, skip next 2 dc, dc in next dc, ch 2, skip next ch-2 space, dc in next dc, ch 2, skip next ch-2 space**, dc in next dc, ch 2; rep from * around, ending last rep at **, sl st in 3rd ch of beg ch to join.

Rnd 4: Ch 5 (counts as dc, ch 2), *skip next ch-2 space, dc in next dc, ch 2, skip next 2 dc, (3 dc, ch 3, 3 dc) in next ch-3 loop, ch 2, skip next 2 dc, dc in next dc, (ch 2, skip next ch-2 space, dc in next dc) twice, ch 2, skip next ch-2 space**, dc in next dc, ch 2; rep from * around, ending last rep at **, sl st in 3rd ch of beg ch to join.

Rnd 5: Ch 5 (counts as dc, ch 2), *skip next ch-2 space, dc in next dc, ch 2, skip next ch-2 space, dc in next dc, ch 2, skip next 2 dc, (3 dc, ch 3, 3 dc) in next ch-3 loop, ch 2, skip next 2 dc, dc in next dc, (ch 2, skip next ch-2 space, dc in next dc) 3 times, ch 2**, dc in next dc, ch 2; rep from * around, ending last rep at **, sl st in 3rd ch of beg ch to join. Fasten off.

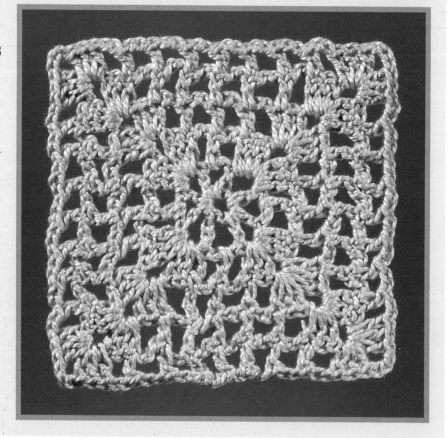

23

Ch 6 and sl st in first ch to form a ring.

Rnd 1: Ch 3 (counts as dc), 2 dc in ring, ch 3, (3 dc, ch 3) 3 times in ring, sl st in 3rd ch of beg ch to join.

Rnd 2: Ch 3 (counts as dc), dc in each of next 2 dc, *(dc, ch 1, dc, ch 1, dc) in next ch-3 loop**, dc in each of next 3 dc; rep from * around, ending last rep at **, sl st in 3rd ch of beg ch to join.

Rnd 3: Ch 3 (counts as dc), *dc in each of next 3 dc, 2 dc in next ch-1 space, ch 1, dc in next dc, ch 1, 2 dc in next ch-1 space, dc in each of next 2 dc; rep from * around, omitting last dc, sl st in 3rd ch of beg ch to join.

Rnd 4: Ch 3 (counts as dc), *dc in each of next 5 dc, 2 dc in next ch-1 space, ch 1, dc in next dc, ch 1, 2 dc in next ch-1 space, dc in each of next 4 dc; rep from * around, omitting last dc, sl st in 3rd ch of beg ch to join.

Rnd 5: Ch 3 (counts as dc), *dc in each of next 7 dc, 2 dc in next ch-1 space, ch 1, dc in next dc, ch 1, 2 dc in next ch-1 space, dc in each of next 6 dc; rep from * around, omitting last dc, sl st in 3rd ch of beg ch to join.

Rnd 6: Ch 3 (counts as dc), *dc in each of next 9 dc, 2 dc in next ch-1 space, ch 1, dc in next dc, ch 1, 2 dc in next ch-1 space, dc in each of next 8 dc; rep from * around, omitting last dc, sl st in 3rd ch of beg ch to join.

Rnd 7: Ch 3 (counts as dc), *dc in each of next 11 dc, 2 dc in next ch-1 space, ch 1, dc in next dc, ch 1, 2 dc in next ch-1 space, dc in each of next 10 dc; rep from * around, omitting last dc, sl st in 3rd ch of beg ch to join. Fasten off.

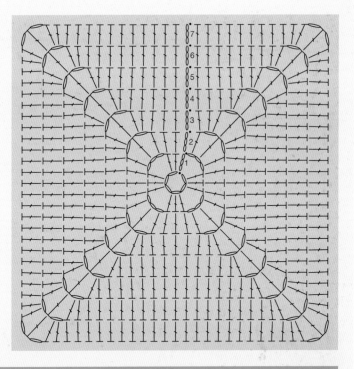

24 Ch 10 and sl st in first ch to form a ring.

Rnd 1: Ch 1, (3 sc, ch 1) 4 times in ring, sl st in first sc to join.

Rnd 2: Ch 3 (counts as dc), dc in each of next 2 sc, *ch 5, skip next ch-1 space**, dc in each of next 3 sc; rep from * around, ending last rep at **, sl st in 3rd ch of beg ch to join.

Rnd 3: Ch 3 (counts as dc), dc in each of next 2 dc, *(dc, ch 7, dc) in next ch-5 loop**, dc in each of next 3 dc; rep from * around, ending last rep at **, sl st in 3rd ch of beg ch to join.

Rnd 4: Ch 3 (counts as dc), *dc in each of next 3 dc, (4 dc, ch 3, 4 dc) in next ch-7 loop, dc in each of next 2 dc; rep from * around, omitting last dc, sl st in 3rd ch of beg ch to join.

Rnd 5: Ch 3 (counts as dc), *dc in each of next 7 dc, (2 dc, ch 3, 2 dc) in next ch-3 loop, dc in each of next 6 dc; rep from * around, omitting last dc, sl st in 3rd ch of beg ch to join. Fasten off.

25

Ch 6 and sl st in first ch to form a ring.

Rnd 1: Ch 3 (counts as dc), 2 dc in ring, ch 2, (3 dc, ch 2) 3 times in ring, sl st in 3rd ch of beg ch to join.

Rnd 2: Ch 3 (counts as dc), dc in first st, *dc in next dc, 2 dc in next dc, ch 3, skip next ch-2 space**, 2 dc in next dc; rep from * around, ending last rep at **, sl st in 3rd ch of beg ch to join.

Rnd 3: Ch 3 (counts as dc), dc in first st, *dc in each of next 3 dc, 2 dc in next dc, ch 5, skip next ch-3 loop**, 2 dc in next dc; rep from * around, ending last rep at **, sl st in 3rd ch of beg ch to join.

Rnd 4: Ch 3 (counts as dc), dc in first st, *dc in each of next 5 dc, 2 dc in next dc, ch 6, skip next ch-5 loop**, 2 dc in next dc; rep from * around, ending last rep at **, sl st in 3rd ch of beg ch to join.

Rnd 5: Ch 3 (counts as dc), dc in first st, *dc in each of next 7 dc, 2 dc in next dc, ch 8, skip next ch-6 loop**, 2 dc in next dc; rep from * around, ending last rep at **, sl st in 3rd ch of beg ch to join. Fasten off.

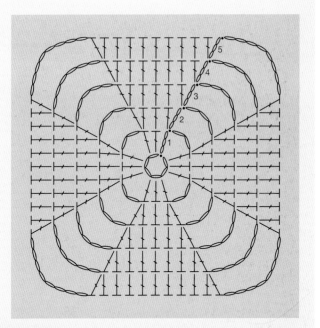

26

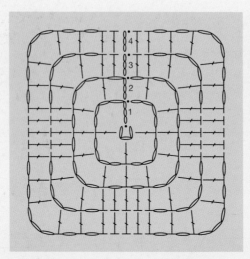

Ch 3 and sl st in first ch to form a ring.

Rnd 1: Ch 7 (counts as dc, ch 4), (dc, ch 4) 3 times in ring, sl st in 3rd ch of beg ch to join.

Rnd 2: Ch 4 (counts as dc, ch 1), *(dc, ch 3, dc) in next ch-4 loop, ch 1**, dc in next dc, ch 1; rep from * around, ending last rep at **, sl st in 3rd ch of beg ch to join.

Rnd 3: Ch 3 (counts as dc), *dc in next ch-1 space, dc in next dc, ch 1, (dc, ch 3, dc) in next ch-3 loop, ch 1, dc in next dc, dc in next ch-1 space**, dc in next dc; rep from * around, ending last rep at **, sl st in 3rd ch of beg ch to join.

Rnd 4: Ch 3 (counts as dc), *dc in each of next 2 dc, ch 1, skip next ch-1 space, dc in next dc, ch 1, (dc, ch 3, dc) in next ch-3 loop, ch 1, dc in next dc, ch 1, skip next ch-1 space, dc in next 2 dc**, dc in next dc; rep from * around, ending last rep at **, sl st in 3rd ch of beg ch to join. Fasten off.

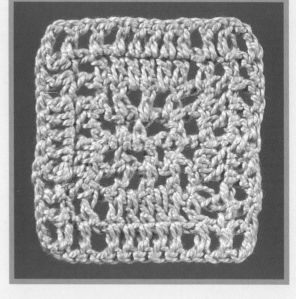

27

Ch 9 and sl st in first ch to form a ring.

Rnd 1: Ch 1, (3 sc, ch 1) 4 times in ring, sl st in first sc to join.

Rnd 2: Ch 3 (counts as dc), dc in each of next 2 sc, *ch 5, skip next ch-1 space**, dc in each of next 3 sc; rep from * around, ending last rep at **, sl st in 3rd ch of beg ch to join.

Rnd 3: Ch 3 (counts as dc), dc in each of next 2 dc, *(dc, ch 7, dc) in next ch-5 loop**, dc in each of next 3 dc; rep from * around, ending last rep at **, sl st in 3rd ch of beg ch to join.

Rnd 4: Ch 3 (counts as dc), dc in each of next 3 dc, *(4 dc, ch 3, 4 dc) in next ch-7 loop**, dc in each of next 5 dc; rep from * around, ending last rep at **, dc in next dc sl st in 3rd ch of beg ch to join. Fasten off.

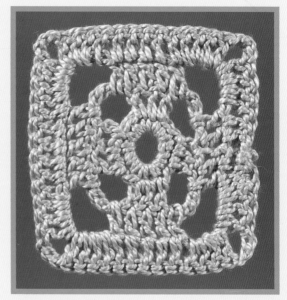

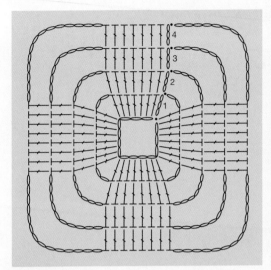

28 Ch 14 and sl st in first ch to form a ring.

Rnd 1: Ch 3 (counts as dc), 7 dc in ring, ch 2, (8 dc, ch 2) 3 times in ring, sl st in 3rd ch of beg ch to join.

Rnd 2: Ch 3 (counts as dc), dc in each of next 7 dc, *ch 6, skip next ch-2 space**, dc in each of next 8 dc; rep from * around, ending last rep at **, sl st in 3rd ch of beg ch to join.

Rnd 3: Ch 3 (counts as dc), dc in each of next 7 dc, *ch 10, skip next ch-6 loop**, dc in each of next 8 dc; rep from * around, ending last rep at **, sl st in 3rd ch of beg ch to join.

Rnd 4: Ch 3 (counts as dc), dc in each of next 7 dc, *ch 14, skip next ch-10 loop**, dc in each of next 8 dc; rep from * around, ending last rep at **, sl st in 3rd ch of beg ch to join. Fasten off.

.3.
Double Crochets & Chains

29 Ch 6 and sl st in first ch to form a ring.

Rnd 1: Ch 3 (counts as dc), 11 dc in ring, sl st in 3rd ch of beg ch to join.

Rnd 2: Ch 4 (counts as dc, ch 1), (dc, ch 1) in each dc around, sl st in 3rd ch of beg ch to join.

Rnd 3: Ch 3 (counts as dc), *skip next ch-1 space, dc in next dc, 6 dc in next ch-1 space, dc in next dc, skip next ch-1 space**, dc in next dc; rep from * around, ending last rep at **, sl st in 3rd ch of beg ch to join. Fasten off.

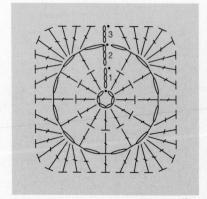

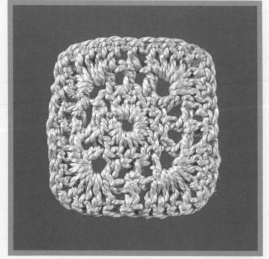

30 Ch 4 and sl st in first ch to form a ring.

Rnd 1: Ch 3 (counts as dc), 2 dc in ring, ch 2, (3 dc, ch 2) 3 times in ring, sl st in 3rd ch of beg ch to join.

Rnd 2: Ch 3 (counts as dc), dc in each of next 2 dc, *5 dc in next ch-2 space**, dc in each of next 3 dc; rep from * around, ending last rep at **, sl st in 3rd ch of beg ch to join.

Rnd 3: Ch 1, *([sc, ch 1] bet next 2 dc) 5 times, (sc, ch 2, sc) in next dc, ch 1, ([sc, ch 1] bet next 2 dc) 3 times; rep from * around, sl st in first sc to join. Fasten off.

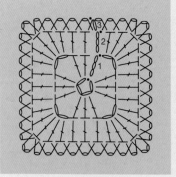

31

Ch 6 and sl st in first ch to form a ring.

Rnd 1: Ch 3 (counts as dc), 15 dc in ring, sl st in 3rd ch of beg ch to join.

Rnd 2: Ch 1, *sc in dc, ch 3, skip next dc; rep from * around, sl st in first sc to join.

Rnd 3: Sl st in first ch-3 loop, ch 3 (counts as dc), dc in same ch-3 loop, *(3 dc, ch 3, 3 dc) in next ch-3 loop**, 2 dc in next ch-3 loop; rep from * around, ending last rep at **, sl st in 3rd ch of beg ch to join.

Rnd 4: Ch 1, sc in first 5 dc, *3 sc in next ch-3 loop**, sc in each of next 8 dc; rep from * around, ending last rep at **, sc in each of next 3 dc, sl st in first sc to join. Fasten off.

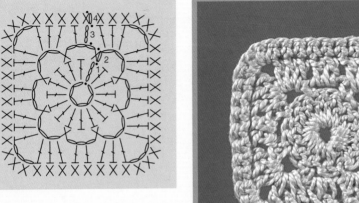

32

Ch 6 and sl st in first ch to form a ring.

Rnd 1: Ch 3 (counts as dc), 11 dc in ring, sl st in 3rd ch of beg ch to join.

Rnd 2: Ch 1, (sc, ch 3) in each dc around, sl st in first sc to join.

Rnd 3: Sl st in first ch-3 loop, ch 3 (counts as dc), dc in same ch-3 loop, *2 dc in next ch-3 loop, (3 dc, ch 3, 3 dc) in next ch-3 loop**, 2 dc in next ch-3 loop; rep from * around, ending last rep at **, sl st in 3rd ch of beg ch to join.

Rnd 4: Ch 1, sc in first 7 dc, *3 sc in next ch-3 loop**, sc in each of next 10 dc; rep from * around, ending last rep at **, sc in each of next 3 dc, sl st in first sc to join. Fasten off.

33

Ch 6 and sl st in first ch to form a ring.

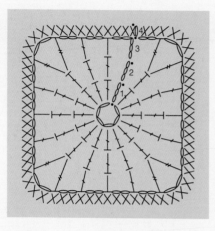

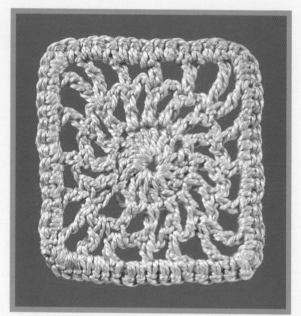

Rnd 1: Ch 3 (counts as dc), 15 dc in ring, sl st in 3rd ch of beg ch to join.

Rnd 2: Ch 3 (counts as dc), dc in each dc around, sl st in 3rd ch of beg ch to join.

Rnd 3: Ch 5 (counts as dc, ch 2), *hdc in next dc, ch 2, dc in next dc, ch 2, (tr, ch 2, tr) in next dc, ch 2**, dc in next dc, ch 2; rep from * around, ending last rep at **, sl st in 3rd ch of beg ch to join.

Rnd 4: Ch 1, *sc in dc, 2 sc in next ch-2 space, sc in next hdc, 2 sc in next ch-2 space, sc in next dc, 2 sc in next ch-2 space, sc in next tr, 3 sc in next ch-2 space, sc in next tr, 2 sc in next ch-2 space; rep from * around, sl st in first sc to join. Fasten off.

34

Ch 6 and sl st in first ch to form a ring.

Rnd 1: Ch 6 (counts as dc, ch 3), (dc, ch 3) 7 times in ring, sl st in 3rd ch of beg ch to join.

Rnd 2: Sl st in next ch-3 loop, ch 3 (counts as dc), 3 dc in same ch-3 loop, ch 2, (4 dc, ch 2) in each ch-3 loop around, sl st in 3rd ch of beg ch to join.

Rnd 3: Ch 5 (counts as dc, ch 2), (6 dc, ch 2) in each of next 7 ch-2 spaces, 5 dc in last ch-2 space, sl st in 3rd ch of beg ch to join.

Rnd 4: Sl st in next ch-2 space, ch 1, *sc in ch-2 space, ch 3, skip next 3 dc, sc bet last skipped and next dc, ch 3, sc in next ch-2 space, ch 3, skip next 3 dc, (2 dc, ch 3, 2 dc) bet last skipped and next dc, ch 3; rep from * around, sl st in first sc to join. Fasten off.

35

Ch 6 and sl st in first ch to form a ring.

Rnd 1: Ch 3 (counts as dc), 15 dc in ring, sl st in 3rd ch of beg ch to join.

Rnd 2: Ch 4 (counts as dc, ch 1), (dc, ch 1) in each dc around, sl st in 3rd ch of beg ch to join.

Rnd 3: Ch 3 (counts as dc), *2 dc in next ch-1 space**, dc in next dc; rep from * around, ending last rep at **, sl st in 3rd ch of beg ch to join.

Rnd 4: Ch 1, *sc in dc, ch 3, skip next 2 dc, sc in next dc, ch 2, skip next 2 dc, sc in next dc, ch 5, skip next 2 dc, sc in next dc, ch 2, skip next 2 dc; rep from * around, sl st in first sc to join.

Rnd 5: Sl st in next ch-3 loop, ch 3 (counts as dc), 4 dc in same ch-3 loop, *sc in next ch-2 space, (5 dc, ch 3, 5 dc) in next ch-5 loop, sc in next ch-2 space**, 5 dc in next ch-3 loop; rep from * around, ending last rep at **, sl st in 3rd ch of beg ch to join. Fasten off.

36

Ch 10 and sl st in first ch to form a ring.

Rnd 1: Ch 1, (sc, ch 10) 11 times in ring, sc in ring, ch 4, dtr in in first sc to join and form last loop.

Rnd 2: Ch 2 (counts as hdc), 2 hdc in same loop, *3 hdc in next ch-10 loop, (3 dc, ch 2, 3 dc) in next ch-10 loop**, 3 hdc in next ch-10 loop; rep from * around, ending last rep at **, sl st in 2nd ch of beg ch to join. Fasten off.

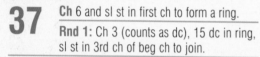

37 **Ch** 6 and sl st in first ch to form a ring.

Rnd 1: Ch 3 (counts as dc), 15 dc in ring, sl st in 3rd ch of beg ch to join.

Rnd 2: Ch 5 (counts as dc, ch 2), (dc, ch 2) in each dc around, sl st in 3rd ch of beg ch to join.

Rnd 3: Sl st in next ch-2 space, ch 1, sc in same ch-2 space, ch 2, (sc, ch 2) in each of next 2 ch-2 spaces, *(2 dc, ch 3, 2 dc) in next ch-2 space, ch 2**, (sc, ch 2) in each of next 4 ch-2 spaces; rep from * around, ending last rep at **, sl st in first sc to join.

Rnd 4: Sl st in next ch-2 space, ch 1, sc in same ch-2 space, ch 2, (sc, ch 2) in each of next 2 ch-2 spaces, *(2 dc, ch 3, 2 dc) in next ch-3 space, ch 2**, (sc, ch 2) in each of next 4 ch-2 spaces; rep from * around, ending last rep at **, sc in next ch-2 space, ch 2, sl st in first sc to join.

Rnd 5: Sl st in next ch-2 space, ch 3 (counts as dc), dc in same ch-2 space, ch 1, (2 dc, ch 1) in each of next 2 ch-2 spaces, *(3 dc, ch 2, 3 dc) in next ch-3 loop, ch 1**, (2 dc, ch 1) in each of next 5 ch-2 spaces; rep from * around, ending last rep at **, (2 dc, ch 1) in each of next 2 ch-2 spaces, sl st in 3rd ch of beg ch to join. Fasten off.

38

Ch 8 and sl st in first ch to form a ring.

Rnd 1: Ch 3 (counts as dc), 2 dc in ring, *ch 5, 3 dc in ring; rep from * 6 times, ch 3, tr in 3rd ch of beg ch to join and form last loop.

Rnd 2: Ch 3 (counts as dc), (2 dc, ch 3, 3 dc) in same loop, ch 7, *skip next ch-5 loop, (3 dc, ch 3, 3 dc) in next ch-5 loop, ch 7; rep from * around, skip next ch-5 loop, sl st in 3rd ch of beg ch to join.

Rnd 3: Ch 3 (counts as dc), *dc in each of next 2 dc, (2 dc, ch 2, 2 dc) in next ch-3 loop, dc in each of next 3 dc, ch 7 skip next ch-7 loop**, dc in next dc; rep from * around, ending last rep at **, sl st in 3rd ch of beg ch to join. Fasten off.

39

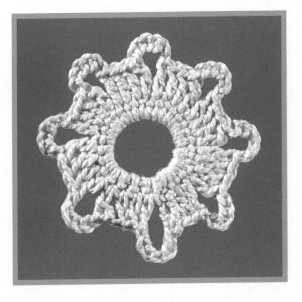

Ch 16 and sl st in first ch to form a ring.

Rnd 1: Ch 1, 32 sc in ring, sl st in first sc to join.

Rnd 2: Ch 3 (counts as dc), dc in each of next 3 sc, ch 6, *dc in each of next 4 sc, ch 6; rep from * around, sl st in 3rd ch of beg ch to join. Fasten off.

40 Ch 6 and sl st in first ch to form a ring.

Rnd 1: Ch 3 (counts as dc), 4 dc in ring, *ch 11, 5 dc in ring; rep from * twice, ch 5, trtr in 3rd ch of beg ch to join and form last loop.

Rnd 2: Ch 3 (counts as dc), (2 dc, ch 3, 3 dc) in same loop, ch 10, *(3 dc, ch 3, 3 dc) in next ch-11 loop, ch 10; rep from * around, sl st in 3rd ch of beg ch to join.

Rnd 3: Ch 3 (counts as dc), *dc in each of next 2 dc, (3 dc, ch 3, 3 dc) in next ch-3 loop, dc in each of next 3 dc, ch 5, sl st in next ch-10 loop, ch 5**, dc in next dc; rep from * around, ending last rep at **, sl st in 3rd ch of beg ch to join. Fasten off.

41 Ch 6 and sl st in first ch to form a ring.

Rnd 1: Ch 3 (counts as dc), 13 dc in ring, sl st in 3rd ch of beg ch to join.

Rnd 2: Ch 7 (counts as dc, ch 4), (dc, ch 4) in each dc around, sl st in 3rd ch of beg ch to join.

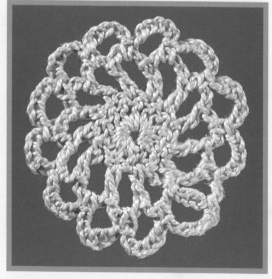

Rnd 3: Sl st to center of next ch-4 loop, ch 1, (sc, ch 6) in in each ch-4 loop around, sl st in first sc to join. Fasten off.

42

Center Square:

Ch 17.

Row 1: Dc in 8th ch from hook, *ch 2, skip next 2 ch, dc in next ch; rep from * across, turn.

Rows 2-4: Ch 5 (counts as dc, ch 2), skip next ch-2 space, (dc, ch 2) in each of next 3 dc, dc in 3rd ch of turning ch, turn.

Edging:

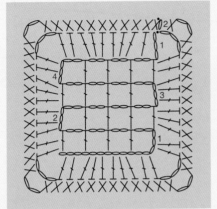

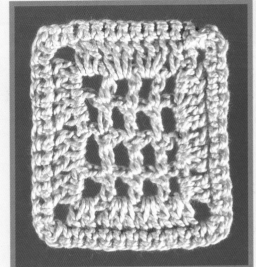

Rnd 1: Ch 3 (counts as dc), working across top edge of Center Square, dc in next ch-2 space, *3 dc in each of next 2 ch-2 spaces, (2 dc, ch 3, 2 dc) in next corner loop, working across side edge of Center Square, 3 dc in each of next 2 row-end sts**, (2 dc, ch 3, 2 dc) in next corner loop; rep from * to ** once, 2 dc in next row-end st of corner, ch 3, sl st in 3rd ch of beg ch to join.

Rnd 2: Ch 1, *sc in each of next 10 dc, (sc, ch 2, sc) in next ch-3 loop; rep from * around, sl st in first sc to join. Fasten off.

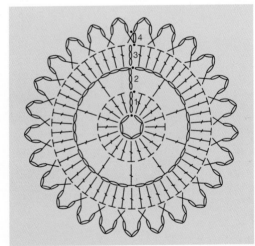

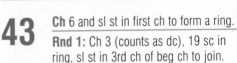

43

Ch 6 and sl st in first ch to form a ring.

Rnd 1: Ch 3 (counts as dc), 19 sc in ring, sl st in 3rd ch of beg ch to join.

Rnd 2: Ch 6 (counts as dc, ch 3), skip next dc, *dc in next dc, ch 3, skip next dc; rep from * around, sl st in 3rd ch of beg ch to join.

Rnd 3: Ch 3 (counts as dc), *4 dc in next ch-3 loop**, dc in next dc; rep from * around, ending last rep at **, sl st in 3rd ch of beg ch to join.

Rnd 4: Ch 1, *sc in dc, ch 4, skip next dc; rep from * around, sl st in first sc to join. Fasten off.

44

Ch 10 and sl st in first ch to form a ring.

Rnd 1: Ch 3 (counts as dc), dc in ring, (ch 5, 2 dc) 9 times in ring, ch 2, dc in 3rd ch of beg ch to join and form last loop.

Rnd 2: Ch 1, (sc, ch 5) in each loop around, sl st in first sc to join.

Rnd 3: Ch 1, 6 sc in each ch-5 loop around, sl st in first sc to join.

Rnd 4: Ch 1, *sc in sc, ch 6, skip next 2 sc; rep from * around, sl st in first sc to join.

Rnd 5: Sl st to center of next ch-6 loop, ch 1, (sc, ch 7) in each ch-6 loop around, sl st in first sc to join.

Rnd 6: Sl st to center of next ch-7 loop, ch 1, (sc, ch 7, 3 dc) in each ch-7 loop around, sl st in first sc to join. Fasten off.

45

Ch 8 and sl st in first ch to form a ring.

Rnd 1: Ch 3 (counts as dc), 2 dc in ring, *ch 7, 3 dc in ring; rep from * 6 times, ch 3, tr in 3rd ch of beg ch to join and form last loop.

Rnd 2: Ch 3 (counts as dc), (2 dc, ch 3, 3 dc) in same loop, ch 7, *(3 dc, ch 3, 3 dc) in next ch-7 loop, ch 7; rep from * around, sl st in 3rd ch of beg ch to join.

Rnd 3: Ch 3 (counts as dc), *dc in each of next 2 dc, (2 dc, ch 2, 2 dc) in next ch-3 loop, dc in each of next 3 dc, ch 7**, dc in next dc; rep from * around, ending last rep at **, sl st in 3rd ch of beg ch to join.

Rnd 4: Ch 3 (counts as dc), *dc in each of next 4 dc, (2 dc, ch 2, 2 dc) in next ch-2 space, dc in each of next 5 dc, ch 4, sc over next next 3 ch-7 loops in 3 rnds below, ch 4**, dc in next dc; rep from * around, ending last rep at **, sl st in 3rd ch of beg ch to join. Fasten off.

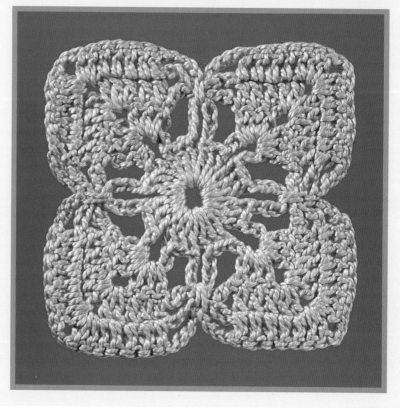

46 *2-dc cluster:*
Yo, insert hook in next st, yo, draw yarn through st, yo, draw yarn through 2 loops on hook, skip next ch-3 loop, yo, insert hook in next st, yo, draw yarn through st, yo, draw yarn through 2 loops on hook, yo, draw yarn through 3 loops on hook.

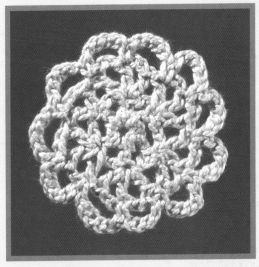

Ch 6 and sl st in first ch to form a ring.

Rnd 1: Ch 6 (counts as dc, ch 3), (dc, ch 3) 5 times in ring, sl st in 3rd ch of beg ch to join.

Rnd 2: Ch 5 (counts as dc, ch 2), work 2-dc cluster, working first half-closed dc in first st, skip next ch-3 loop, work 2nd half-closed dc in next dc, yo, complete cluster, ch 2, *dc in same dc already holding 2nd leg of last cluster, ch 2, work 2-dc cluster, working first half-closed dc in same dc holding last dc, skip next ch-3 loop, work 2nd half-closed dc in next dc, yo, complete cluster, ch 2; rep from * around, sl st in 3rd ch of beg ch to join.

Rnd 3: Ch 1, *sc in dc, ch 5, skip next ch-2 space, sc in next cluster, ch 5; rep from * around, sl st in first sc to join. Fasten off.

47

Ch 6 and sl st in first ch to form a ring.

Rnd 1: Ch 4 (counts as dc, ch 1), (dc, ch 1) 13 times in ring, sl st in 3rd ch of beg ch to join.

Rnd 2: Sl st in next ch-1 space, ch 5 (counts as dc, ch 2), (dc, ch 2) in each ch-1 space around, sl st in 3rd ch of beg ch to join.

Rnd 3: Sl st in first ch-2 space, ch 3 (counts as dc), 2 dc in same ch-2 space, ch 1, (3 dc, ch 1) in each ch-2 space around, sl st in 3rd ch of bet ch to join.

Rnd 4: Turn, sl st in next ch-1 space, ch 1, turn, (sc, ch 6) in each ch-1 space around, sl st in first sc to join.

Rnd 5: Sl st to center of next ch-6 loop, ch 1, (sc, ch 6) in each ch-1 space around, sl st in first sc to join.

Rnd 6: Sl st in next ch-6 loop, ch 1, 6 sc in each ch-6 loop around, sl st in first sc to join. Fasten off.

48

Ch 10 and sl st in first ch to form a ring.

Rnd 1: Ch 3 (counts as dc), 23 dc in ring, sl st in 3rd ch of beg ch to join.

Rnd 2: Ch 4 (counts as dc, ch 1), (dc, ch 1) in each dc around, sl st in 3rd ch of beg ch to join.

Rnd 3: Sl st in next ch-1 space, ch 10 (counts as tr, ch 6), ch 6, skip next ch-1 space, *tr in next ch-1 space, ch 6, skip next ch-1 space; rep from * around, sl st in 4th ch of beg ch to join.

Rnd 4: Ch 1, *sc in tr, ch 3, (dc, ch 2, dc) in next ch-6 loop, ch 3; rep from * around, sl st in first sc to join.

Rnd 5: Ch 1, *sc in sc, ch 2, skip next ch-3 loop, dc in next dc, ch 2, dc in next ch-2 space, ch 2, dc in next dc, ch 2; rep from * around, sl st in first sc to join. Fasten off.

49

Ch 6 and sl st in first ch to form a ring.

Rnd 1: Ch 4 (counts as dc, ch 1), (dc, ch 1) 11 times in ring, sl st in 3rd ch of beg ch to join.

Rnd 2: Sl st in next ch-1 space, ch 1, (sc, ch 5) in each ch-1 space around, sl st in first sc to join.

Rnd 3: Sl st to center of next ch-5 loop, ch 1, (sc, ch 6) in each ch-5 loop around, sl st in first sc to join.

Rnd 4: Sl st to center of next ch-6 loop, ch 1, (sc, ch 7) in each ch-6 loop around, sl st in first sc to join.

Rnd 5: Sl st to center of next ch-7 loop, ch 3 (counts as dc), (dc, ch 2, 2 dc) in same ch-7 loop, *ch 3, (dc, ch 5, dc) in next ch-7 loop, ch 3**, (2 dc, ch 2, 2 dc) in next ch-7 loop; rep from * around, ending last rep at **, sl st in 3rd ch of beg ch to join. Fasten off.

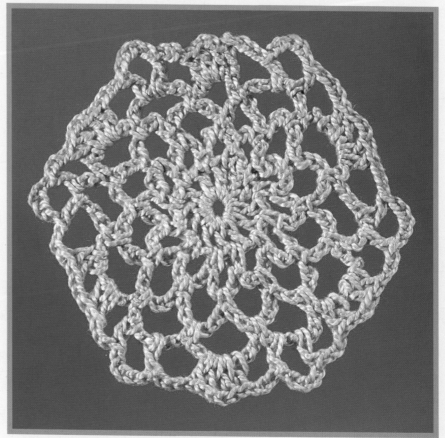

50

Ch 6 and sl st in first ch to form a ring.

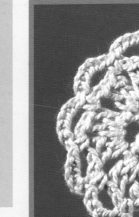

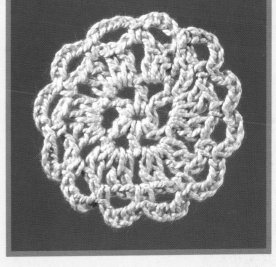

Rnd 1: Ch 6 (counts as dc, ch 3), (dc, ch 3) 5 times in ring, sl st in 3rd ch of beg ch to join.

Rnd 2: Sl st in next ch-3 loop, ch 3 (counts as dc), (dc, ch 2, 2 dc) in same ch-3 loop, ch 2, *(2 dc, ch 2, 2 dc) in next ch-3 loop, ch 2; rep from * around, sl st in 3rd ch of beg ch to join.

Rnd 3: Sl st to next ch-2 space, ch 1, (sc, ch 5) in in each ch-2 space around, sl st in first sc to join. Fasten off.

51

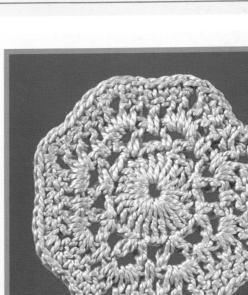

Ch 6 and sl st in first ch to form a ring.

Rnd 1: Ch 3 (counts as dc), 23 sc in ring, sl st in 3rd ch of beg ch to join.

Rnd 2: Ch 5 (counts as dc, ch 2), dc in first st, ch 1, skip next 2 dc, *(dc, ch 2, dc) in next dc, ch 1, skip next 2 dc; rep from * around, sl st in 3rd ch of beg ch to join.

Rnd 3: Sl st in next ch-2 space, ch 3 (counts as dc), (dc, ch 2, 2 dc) in same ch-2 space, dc in next ch-1 space, *(2 dc, ch 2, 2 dc) in next ch-2 space, dc in next ch-1 space; rep from * around, sl st in 3rd ch of beg ch to join.

Rnd 4: Ch 1, sc in first 2 dc, *2 sc in next ch-2 space**, sc in each of next 5 dc; rep from * around, ending last rep at **, sc in each of last 3 dc, sl st in first sc to join. Fasten off.

52

Ch 6 and sl st in first ch to form a ring.

Rnd 1: Ch 4 (counts as dc, ch 1), (dc, ch 1) 15 times in ring, sl st in 3rd ch of beg ch to join.

Rnd 2: Sl st in next ch-1 space, ch 3 (counts as dc), dc in same ch-1 space, ch 2, (2 dc, ch 2) in each ch-1 space around, sl st in 3rd ch of beg ch to join.

Rnd 3: Ch 3 (counts as dc), dc in same st, dc in next dc, ch 7, skip next ch-2 space, *2 dc in next dc, dc in next dc, ch 7, skip next ch-2 space; rep from * around, sl st in 3rd ch of bet ch to join.

Rnd 4: Sl st in next dc, ch 1, *sc in dc, ch 3, sc in next ch-7 loop, ch 3, skip next dc; rep from * around, sl st in first sc to join.

Rnd 5: Ch 1, *sc in sc, ch 3, skip next ch-3 loop, (sc, ch 5, sc) in next sc, ch 3, skip next ch-3 loop; rep from * around, sl st in first sc to join. Fasten off.

53

Ch 6 and sl st in first ch to form a ring.

Rnd 1 (RS): Ch 1, (2 sc, ch 12) 8 times in ring, sl st in first sc to join. Fasten off.

Rnd 2: With RS facing rejoin yarn in any ch-12 loop, ch 3 (counts as dc), (2 dc, ch 3, 3 dc) in same ch-12 loop, *ch 2, 3 dc in next ch-12 loop, ch 2**, (3 dc, ch 3, 3 dc) in next ch-12 loop; rep from * around, ending last rep at **, sl st in 3rd ch of beg ch to join.

Rnd 3: Sl st to next ch-3 loop, ch 3 (counts as dc), (2 dc, ch 3, 3 dc) in same ch-3 loop, *ch 2, (3 dc, ch 2) in each of next 2 ch-2 spaces**, (3 dc, ch 3, 3 dc) in next ch-3 loop; rep from * around, ending last rep at **, sl st in 3rd ch of beg ch to join.

Rnd 4: Ch 3 (counts as dc), dc in each of next 2 dc, *(2 dc, ch 2, 2 dc) in next ch-3 loop, (dc in each of next 3 dc, 2 dc in next ch-2 space) 3 times**, dc in each of next 3 dc; rep from * around, ending last rep at **, sl st in 3rd ch of beg ch to join. Fasten off.

.4.
Treble Crochets & Double Treble Crochets

54 **Ch** 8.

Row 1: Tr in 5th ch from hook, tr in each of next 3 ch, *ch 4, 4 tr around the post of last tr made; rep from * twice, sl st in 4th ch of beg ch to join. Fasten off.

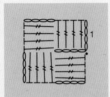

55 **Ch** 8 and sl st in first ch to form a ring.

Rnd 1: Ch 5 (counts as dtr), 3 dtr in ring, ch 5, (4 dtr, ch 5) 3 times in ring, sl st in 5th ch of beg ch to join. Fasten off.

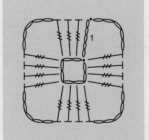

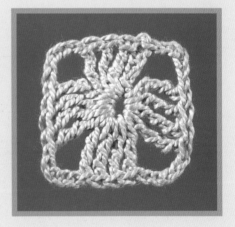

56

Ch 15 and sl st in first ch to form a ring.

Rnd 1: Ch 4 (counts as tr), 4 tr in ring, ch 7, (5 tr, ch 7) 3 times in ring, sl st in 4th ch of beg ch to join. Fasten off.

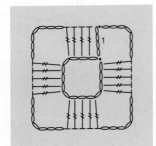

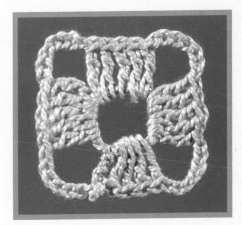

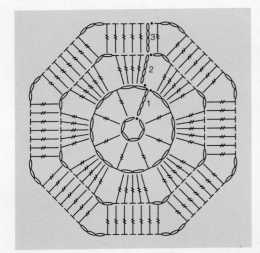

57

Ch 6 and sl st in first ch to form a ring.

Rnd 1: Ch 6 (counts as tr, ch 2), (tr, ch 2) 7 times in ring, sl st in 4th ch of beg ch to join.

Rnd 2: Sl st in next ch-2 space, ch 4 (counts as tr), 4 tr in same space, ch 2, (5 tr, ch 2) in each ch-2 space around, sl st in 4th ch of beg ch to join.

Rnd 3: Ch 4 (counts as tr), tr in each of next 4 tr, *(tr, ch 3, tr) in next ch-2 space**, tr in each of next 5 tr; rep from * around, ending last rep at **, sl st in 4th ch of beg ch to join. Fasten off.

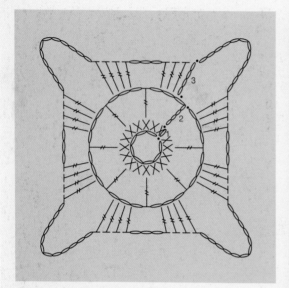

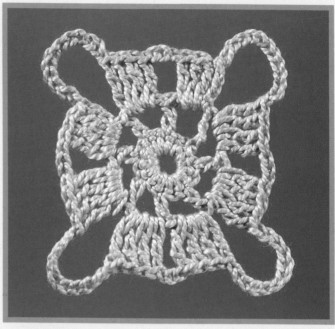

58 Ch 8 and sl st in first ch to form a ring.

Rnd 1: Ch 1, 16 sc in ring, sl st in first sc to join.

Rnd 2: Ch 7 (counts as tr, ch 3), skip next sc, *tr in next sc, ch 3, skip next sc; rep from * around, sl st in 4th ch of beg ch to join.

Rnd 3: Sl st in next ch-3 loop, ch 4 (counts as tr), 3 tr in same ch-3 loop, *ch 3, 4 tr in next ch-3 loop, ch 12**, 4 tr in next ch-3 loop; rep from * around, ending last rep at **, sl st in 4th ch of beg ch to join. Fasten off.

59 Ch 6 and sl st in first ch to form a ring.

Rnd 1: Ch 4 (counts as dc, ch 1), (4 dc, ch 1) 3 times in ring, 3 dc in ring, sl st in 3rd ch of beg to join.

Rnd 2: Sl st in next ch-1 space, ch 3 (counts as dc), (2 dc, ch 2, 3 dc) in same ch-1 space, (3 dc, ch 2, 3 dc) in each ch-1 space around, sl st in 3rd ch of beg ch to join.

Rnd 3: Sl st to next ch-2 space, ch 4 (counts as tr), (3 tr, ch 3, 4 tr) in same ch-2 space, (4 tr, ch 3, 4 tr) in each ch-2 space around, sl st in 4th ch of beg ch to join.

Rnd 4: Ch 1, *sc in each of next 4 tr, 3 sc in next ch-3 loop, sc in each of next 4 tr; rep from * around, sl st in first sc to join. Fasten off.

60

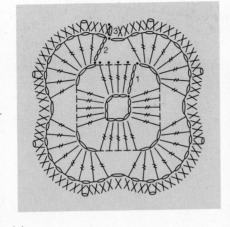

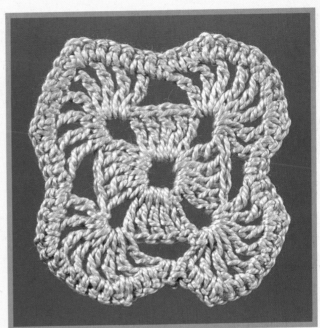

Ch 10 and sl st in first ch to form a ring.

Rnd 1: Ch 4 (counts as tr), 4 tr in ring, ch 3, (5 tr, ch 3) 3 times in ring, sl st in 4th ch of beg ch to join.

Rnd 2: Sl st to next ch-3 loop, ch 5 (counts as tr, ch 1), (tr, ch 1) 7 times in same ch-2 space, (tr, ch 1) 8 times in each ch-3 loop around, sl st in 4th ch of beg ch to join.

Rnd 3: Ch 1, *sc in tr, sc in next ch-1 space, sc in next tr, (sc, ch 1, sc) in next ch-1 space, (sc in next tr, sc in next ch-1 space) 3 times, sc in next tr, (sc, ch 1, sc) in next ch-1 space, (sc in next tr, sc in next ch-1 space) twice; rep from * around, sl st in first sc to join. Fasten off.

61

Ch 16 and sl st in first ch to form a ring.

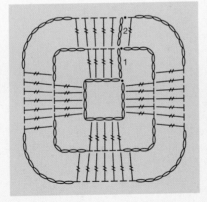

Rnd 1: Ch 4 (counts as tr), 4 tr in ring, ch 7, (5 tr, ch 7) 3 times in ring, sl st in 4th ch of beg ch to join.

Rnd 2: Ch 4 (counts as tr), *tr in each of next 4 tr, (tr, ch 9, tr) in next ch-7 loop**, tr in next tr; rep from * around, ending last rep at **, sl st in 4th ch of beg ch to join. Fasten off.

62

Ch 10 and sl st in first ch to form a ring.

Rnd 1: Ch 4 (counts as tr), 3 tr in ring, ch 7, (4 tr, ch 7) 3 times in ring, sl st in 4th ch of beg ch to join.

Rnd 2: Ch 1, *sc in each of next 4 tr, 6 sc in next ch-7 loop; rep from * around, sl st in first sc to join.

Rnd 3: Ch 4 (counts as tr), tr in each of next 6 sc, *(tr, ch 5, tr) bet next 2 sc**, tr in each of next 10 sc; rep from * around, ending last rep at **, tr in each of next 3 sc, sl st in 4th ch of beg ch to join.

Rnd 4: Ch 1, *sc in each of next 8 tr, 6 sc in next ch-5 loop, sc in each of next 4 tr; rep from * around, sl st in first sc to join.

Rnd 5: Ch 4 (counts as tr), tr in each of next 10 sc, *3 tr bet next 2 sc**, tr in each of next 18 sc; rep from * around, ending last rep at **, tr in each of next 7 sc, sl st in 4th ch of beg ch to join. Fasten off.

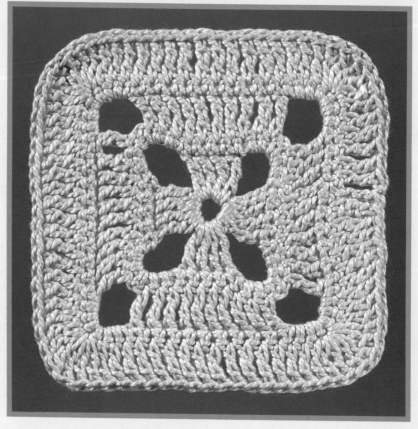

63

Ch 6 and sl st in first ch to form a ring.

Rnd 1: Ch 3 (counts as dc), 15 dc in ring, sl st in 3rd ch of beg ch to join.

Rnd 2: Ch 4 (counts as tr), 6 tr in same st, *skip next dc, dc in next dc, skip next dc**, 7 tr in next dc; rep from * around, ending last rep at **, sl st in 4th ch of beg ch to join.

Rnd 3: Sl st in each of next 3 tr, ch 5 (counts as tr, ch 1), (tr, ch 1) 6 times in same tr, *5 tr in next ch-3 loop, ch 1**, skip next 3 tr, (tr, ch 1) 7 times in next tr; rep from * around, ending last rep at **, sl st in 4th ch of beg ch to join. Fasten off.

.5.
Clusters

64 *4-tr cluster:* (Yo [twice], insert hook in next st, yo, draw yarn through st, [yo, draw yarn through 2 loops on hook] twice) 4 times, yo, draw yarn through 5 loops on hook.

5-tr cluster: (Yo [twice], insert hook in next st, yo, draw yarn through st, [yo, draw yarn through 2 loops on hook] twice) 5 times, yo, draw yarn through 6 loops on hook.

Ch 6 and sl st in first ch to form a ring.

Rnd 1: Ch 3 (counts as dc), dc in ring, ch 2, (2 dc, ch 2) 5 times in ring, sl st in 3rd ch of beg ch to join.

Rnd 2: Sl st to next ch-2 space, ch 4 (counts as tr), 4 tr in same ch-2 space, ch 3, (5 tr, ch 3) in each ch-2 space around, sl st in 4th ch of beg ch to join.

Rnd 3: Ch 4 (counts as tr), 4-tr cluster worked across next 4 tr, *ch 4, (sc, ch 7, sc) in next ch-3 loop, ch 4**, 5-tr cluster worked across next 5 tr; rep from * around, ending last rep at **, sl st in first cluster to join. Fasten off.

65

4-tr cluster: (Yo [twice], insert hook in next st, yo, draw yarn through st, [yo, draw yarn through 2 loops on hook] twice) 4 times, yo, draw yarn through 5 loops on hook.

Ch 8 and sl st in first ch to form a ring.

Rnd 1: Ch 1, (sc, ch 3, 4 tr, ch 3) 4 times in ring, sl st in first sc to join.

Rnd 2: Sl st to top of first ch-3 loop, ch 1, *sc in ch-3 loop, ch 3, 4-tr cluster worked across next 4 tr, ch 3, sc in next ch-3 loop, ch 2; rep from * around, sl st in first sc to join.

Rnd 3: Sl st to first cluster, *ch 4, skip next ch-3 loop, working over ch-2 space in last rnd, work (dc, ch 2, dc) in next corresponding sc 2 rnds below, ch 4, skip next ch-3 loop, sl st in next cluster; rep from * around, ending with sl st in first sl st to join.

Rnd 4: Ch 1, *2 sc in ch-4 loop, (4 dc, ch 3, 4 dc) in next ch-2 space, 2 sc in next ch-4 loop; rep from * around, sl st in first sc to join. Fasten off.

66

Y-st: Tr in next space, 2 dc in 2 strands at center of tr just made.

2-dc cluster: (Yo, insert hook in next st, yo, draw yarn through st, yo, draw yarn through 2 loops on hook) twice, yo, draw yarn through 3 loops on hook.

3-dc cluster: (Yo, insert hook in next st, yo, draw yarn through st, yo, draw yarn through 2 loops on hook) 3 times, yo, draw yarn through 4 loops on hook.

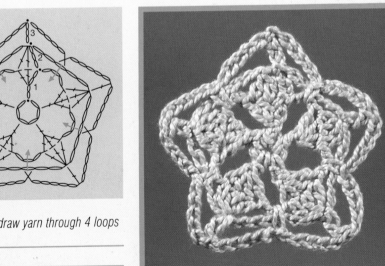

Ch 6 and sl st in first ch to form a ring.

Rnd 1: Ch 4, 2 dc in 3rd ch from hook (counts as first Y-st), ch 3, (Y-st, ch 3) 4 times in ring, sl st in 4th ch of beg ch to join.

Rnd 2: Ch 3, 2 dc cluster worked across next 2 dc, ch 5, skip next ch-3 loop, *3-dc cluster worked across next 3 sts of Y-st, ch 5, skip next ch-3 loop; rep from * around, sl st in first cluster to join.

Rnd 3: Ch 8 (counts as dc, ch 5), *sc in over next 2 loops in 2 rnds below, ch 5**, dc in next cluster, ch 5; rep from * around, ending last rep at **, sl st in 3rd ch of beg ch to join. Fasten off.

67

Y-st: *Tr in next space, 2 dc in 2 strands at center of tr just made.*

2-dc cluster: *(Yo, insert hook in next st, yo, draw yarn through st, yo, draw yarn through 2 loops on hook) twice, yo, draw yarn through 3 loops on hook.*

3-dc cluster: *(Yo, insert hook in next st, yo, draw yarn through st, yo, draw yarn through 2 loops on hook) 3 times, yo, draw yarn through 4 loops on hook.*

Ch 6 and sl st in first ch to form a ring.

Rnd 1: Ch 4, 2 dc in 3rd ch from hook (counts as first Y-st), ch 3, (Y-st, ch 3) 5 times in ring, sl st in 4th ch of beg ch to join.

Rnd 2: Ch 3, 2 dc cluster worked across next 2 dc, ch 5, skip next ch-3 loop, *3-dc cluster worked across next 3 sts of Y-st, ch 5, skip next ch-3 loop; rep from * around, sl st in first cluster to join.

Rnd 3: Ch 8 (counts as dc, ch 5), *sc in over next 2 loops in 2 rnds below, ch 5**, dc in next cluster, ch 5; rep from * around, ending last rep at **, sl st in 3rd ch of beg ch to join. Fasten off.

68

2-dc cluster: *(Yo, insert hook in next st, yo, draw yarn through st, yo, draw yarn through 2 loops on hook) twice, yo, draw yarn through 3 loops on hook.*

3-dc cluster: *(Yo, insert hook in next st, yo, draw yarn through st, yo, draw yarn through 2 loops on hook) 3 times, yo, draw yarn through 4 loops on hook.*

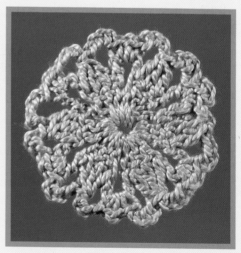

Ch 6 and sl st in first ch to form a ring.

Rnd 1: Ch 3 (counts as dc), 2 dc in ring, ch 5, (3 dc, ch 5) 5 times in ring, sl st in 3rd ch of beg ch to join.

Rnd 2: Ch 3 (counts as dc), 2-dc cluster worked across next 2 dc, *ch 4, (sc, ch 1, sc) in next ch-5 loop, ch 4**, 3-dc cluster worked across next 3 dc; rep from * around, ending last rep at **, sl st in first cluster to join. Fasten off.

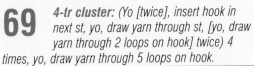

69 *4-tr cluster:* (Yo [twice], insert hook in next st, yo, draw yarn through st, [yo, draw yarn through 2 loops on hook] twice) 4 times, yo, draw yarn through 5 loops on hook.

5-tr cluster: (Yo [twice], insert hook in next st, yo, draw yarn through st, [yo, draw yarn through 2 loops on hook] twice) 5 times, yo, draw yarn through 6 loops on hook.

Picot: Ch 4, sl st in 4th ch from hook.

Ch 6 and sl st in first ch to form a ring.

Rnd 1: Ch 3 (counts as dc), dc in ring, ch 2, (2 dc, ch 2) 5 times in ring, sl st in 3rd ch of beg ch to join.

Rnd 2: Sl st to next ch-2 space, ch 4 (counts as tr), 4 tr in same ch-2 space, ch 3, (5 tr, ch 3) in each ch-2 space around, sl st in 4th ch of beg ch to join.

Rnd 3: Ch 4 (counts as tr), 4-tr cluster worked across next 4 tr, picot, *ch 4, (sc, ch 8, sc) in next ch-3 loop, ch 4**, 5-tr cluster worked across next 5 tr, picot; rep from * around, ending last rep at **, sl st in first cluster to join. Fasten off.

70

6-dc cluster: *(Yo, insert hook in next st, yo, draw yarn through st, yo, draw yarn through 2 loops on hook) 6 times, yo, draw yarn through 7 loops on hook.*

7-dc cluster: *(Yo, insert hook in next st, yo, draw yarn through st, yo, draw yarn through 2 loops on hook) 7 times, yo, draw yarn through 8 loops on hook.*

Ch 11 and sl st in first ch to form a ring.

Rnd 1: Ch 3 (counts as dc), 4 dc in ring, ch 9, (5 dc, ch 9) 3 times in ring, sl st in 3rd ch of beg ch to join.

Rnd 2: Ch 3 (counts as dc), dc in first st, *dc in each of next 3 dc, 2 dc in next dc, ch 2, (3 dc, ch 5, 3 dc) in next ch-9 loop, ch 2**, 2 dc in next dc; rep from * around, ending last rep at **, sl st in 3rd ch of beg ch to join.

Rnd 3: Ch 3 (counts as dc), 6-dc cluster worked across next 6 dc, *ch 4, skip next ch-2 space, (dc, ch 3, 2 dc, ch 2, 2 dc, ch 3, dc) in next ch-5 loop, ch 4, skip next ch-2 space**, 7-dc cluster worked across next 7 dc; rep from * around, ending last rep at **, sl st in first cluster to join.

Rnd 4: Ch 1, *sc in cluster, 3 sc in next ch-4 loop, sc in next dc, 3 sc in next ch-3 loop, sc in each of next 2 dc, 3 sc in next ch-2 space, sc in each of next 2 dc, 3 sc in next ch-3 loop, sc in next dc, 3 sc in next ch-4 loop; rep from * around, sl st in first sc to join.

Rnd 5: Ch 1, *sc in each of next 11 sc, 2 sc in next sc, sc in each of next 10 sc; rep from * around, sl st in first sc to join. Fasten off.

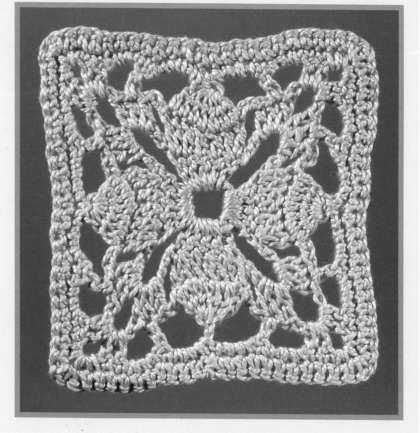

71

4-dc cluster: *(Yo, insert hook in next st, yo, draw yarn through st, yo, draw yarn through 2 loops on hook) 4 times, yo, draw yarn through 5 loops on hook.*

5-dc cluster: *(Yo, insert hook in next st, yo, draw yarn through st, yo, draw yarn through 2 loops on hook) 5 times, yo, draw yarn through 6 loops on hook.*

3-dc puff st: *(Yo, insert hook in next space, yo, draw yarn through space, yo, draw yarn through 2 loops on hook) 3 times in same space, yo, draw yarn through 4 loops on hook.*

4-dc puff st: *(Yo, insert hook in next space, yo, draw yarn through space, yo, draw yarn through 2 loops on hook) 4 times in same space, yo, draw yarn through 5 loops on hook.*

Ch 10 and sl st in first ch to form a ring.

Rnd 1: Ch 3 (counts as dc), 4 dc in ring, ch 2, (5 dc, ch 2) 5 times in ring, sl st in 3rd ch of beg ch to join.

Rnd 2: Ch 3 (counts as dc), 4-dc cluster worked across next 4 dc, ch 6, dc in next ch-2 space, ch 6**, 5-dc cluster worked across next 5 dc; rep from * around, ending last rep at **, sl st in first cluster to join.

Rnd 3: Sl st to center of first ch-6 loop, ch 1, (2 sc, ch 6) in each ch-6 loop around, sl st in first sc to join.

Rnd 4: Sl st to next ch-6 loop, ch 3 (counts as dc), (3-dc puff st, ch 9, 4-dc puff st) in same ch-6 loop, (4-dc puff st, ch 9, 4-dc puff st) in each ch-6 loop around, sl st in first puff st to join. Fasten off.

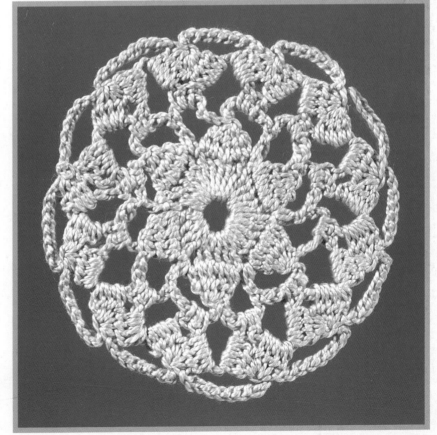

72

3-dc cluster: (Yo, insert hook in next st, yo, draw yarn through st, yo, draw yarn through 2 loops on hook) 3 times, yo, draw yarn through 4 loops on hook.

4-dc cluster: (Yo, insert hook in next st, yo, draw yarn through st, yo, draw yarn through 2 loops on hook) 4 times, yo, draw yarn through 5 loops on hook.

Puff st: (Yo, insert hook in next st, yo, draw yarn through st, yo, draw yarn through 2 loops on hook) 3 times in same st, yo, draw yarn through 4 loops on hook.

Ch 6 and sl st in first ch to form a ring.

Rnd 1: Ch 3 (counts as dc), 15 dc in ring, sl st in 3rd ch of beg ch to join.

Rnd 2: Ch 3 (counts as dc), dc in each of next 3 dc, ch 7, *dc in each of next 4 dc, ch 7; rep from * around, sl st in 3rd ch of beg ch to join.

Rnd 3: Ch 3 (counts as dc), 3-dc cluster worked across next 3 dc, *ch 5, (dc, ch 5, dc) in center ch of next ch-7 loop, ch 5**, 4-dc cluster worked across next 4 dc; rep from * around, ending last rep at **, sl st in first cluster to join.

Rnd 4: Ch 1, *sc in cluster, ch 3, skip next ch-5 loop, puff st in next dc, ch 5 (puff st, ch 5, puff st, ch 5, puff st) in next ch-5 loop, ch 5, puff st in next dc, ch 3; rep from * around, sl st in first sc to join. Fasten off.

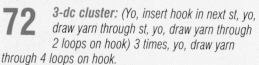

73

2-tr clus-ter: (Yo [twice], insert hook in next st, yo, draw yarn through st, [yo, draw yarn through 2 loops on hook] twice) twice, yo, draw yarn through 3 loops on hook.

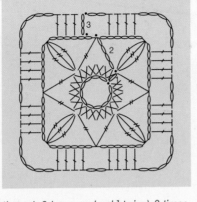

3-tr puff st: (Yo [twice], insert hook in next st, yo, draw yarn through st, [yo, draw yarn through 2 loops on hook] twice) 3 times in same st, yo, draw yarn through 4 loops on hook.

Ch 11 and sl st in first ch to form a ring.

Rnd 1: Ch 1, 20 sc in ring, sl st in first sc to join.

Rnd 2: Ch 4 (counts as tr), skip next 4 sc, tr in next sc, ch 6, *3-tr puff st in same sc holding last tr, ch 6**, 2-tr cluster, working first half-closed tr in same sc holding last puff st, skip next 4 sc, work 2nd half-closed tr in next sc, yo, complete cluster; rep from * around, ending last rep at **, sl st in 4th ch of beg ch to join.

Rnd 3: Sl st in next ch-6 loop, ch 3 (counts as dc), 3 dc in same ch-6 loop, *ch 6, 4 dc in next ch-6 loop, ch 2**, 4 dc in next ch-6 loop; rep from * around, ending last rep at **, sl st in 3rd ch of beg ch to join. Fasten off.

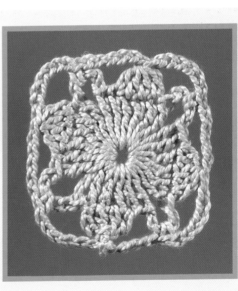

74

3-tr cluster: (Yo [twice], insert hook in next st, yo, draw yarn through st, [yo, draw yarn through 2 loops on hook] twice) 3 times, yo, draw yarn through 4 loops on hook.

4-tr cluster: (Yo [twice], insert hook in next st, yo, draw yarn through st, [yo, draw yarn through 2 loops on hook] twice) 4 times, yo, draw yarn through 5 loops on hook.

Ch 6 and sl st in first ch to form a ring.

Rnd 1: Ch 4 (counts as tr), 5 tr in ring, ch 5, (6 tr, ch 5) 3 times in ring, sl st in 4th ch of beg ch to join.

Rnd 2: Sl st in next tr, ch 4 (counts as tr), 3-tr cluster worked across next 3 tr, ch 6, sc in next ch-5 loop, ch 6, skip next tr**, 4-tr cluster worked across next 4 tr; rep from * around, ending last rep at **, sl st in first cluster to join. Fasten off.

75

2-dc cluster: (Yo, insert hook in next st, yo, draw yarn through st, yo, draw yarn through 2 loops on hook) twice, yo, draw yarn through 3 loops on hook.

3-dc cluster: (Yo, insert hook in next st, yo, draw yarn through st, yo, draw yarn through 2 loops on hook) 3 times, yo, draw yarn through 4 loops on hook.

Ch 10 and sl st in first ch to form a ring.

Rnd 1: Ch 3 (counts as dc), 23 dc in ring, sl st in 3rd ch of beg ch to join.

Rnd 2: Ch 3 (counts as dc), dc in next dc, ch 3, *2-dc cluster worked across next 2 dc, ch 3; rep from * around, sl st in 3rd ch of beg ch to join.

Rnd 3: Ch 3 (counts as dc), *4 dc in next ch-3 loop**, dc in next cluster; rep from * around, ending last rep at **, sl st in 3rd ch of beg ch to join.

Rnd 4: Ch 3 (counts as dc), 2-dc cluster worked across next 2 dc, *ch 7, skip next 2 dc**, 3-dc cluster worked across next 3 dc; rep from * around, ending last rep at **, sl st in first cluster to join.

Rnd 5: Ch 3 (counts as dc), *7 dc in next ch-7 loop**, dc in next cluster; rep from * around, ending last rep at **, sl st in 3rd ch of beg ch to join. Fasten off.

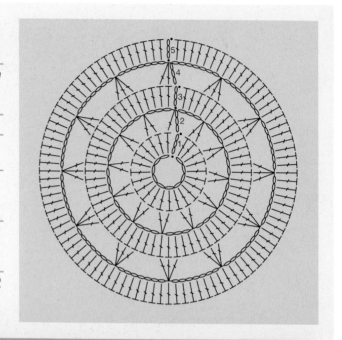

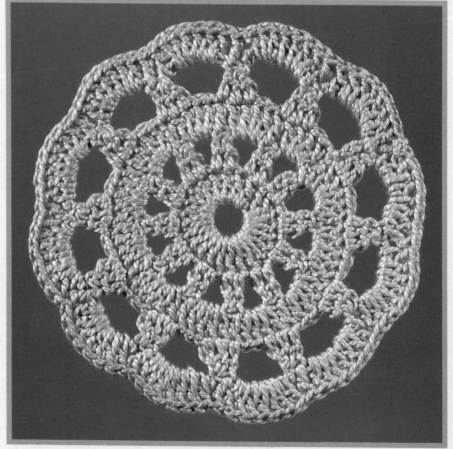

76

2-dtr puff st: *(Yo [3 times], insert hook in next space, yo, draw yarn through space, [yo, draw yarn through 2 loops on hook] 3 times) twice in same space, yo, draw yarn through 3 loops on hook.*

Ch 8 and sl st in first ch to form a ring.

Rnd 1: Ch 5 (counts as dtr), dtr in ring, ch 1, (2-dtr puff st, ch 1) 15 times in ring, sl st in 5th ch of beg ch to join.

Rnd 2: Sl st in next ch-1 space, ch 1, sc in same ch-1 space, ch 3, sc in next ch-1 space, ch 3, *(2 dc, ch 3, 2 dc) in next ch-1 space, ch 3**, (sc, ch 3) in each of next 3 ch-1 spaces; rep from * around, ending last rep at **, sc in next ch-1 space, ch 3, sl st in first sc to join.

Rnd 3: Sl st in next ch-3 loop, ch 3 (counts as dc), 2 dc in same ch-3 loop, ch 2, *skip next ch-3 loop, (3 dc, ch 2, 3 dc) in next ch-3 loop, ch 2, skip next ch-3 loop**, (3 dc, ch 2) in each of next 2 ch-3 loops; rep from * around, ending last rep at **, 3 dc in next ch-3 loop, ch 2, sl st in 3rd ch of beg ch to join.

Rnd 4: Sl st to next ch-2 space, ch 3 (counts as dc), 2 dc in same ch-2 space, ch 2, *(3 dc, ch 2, 3 dc) in next ch-2 space, ch 2**, (3 dc, ch 2) in each of next 3 ch-2 spaces; rep from * around, ending last rep at **, (3 dc, ch 2) in each of next 2 ch-2 spaces, sl st in 3rd ch of beg to join.

Rnd 5: Sl st to next ch-2 space, ch 3 (counts as dc), 2 dc in same ch-2 space, *(3 dc, ch 2, 3 dc) in next ch-2 space**, 3 dc in each of next 4 ch-2 spaces; rep from * around, ending last rep at **, 3 dc in each of next 3 ch-2 spaces, sl st in 3rd ch of beg to join. Fasten off.

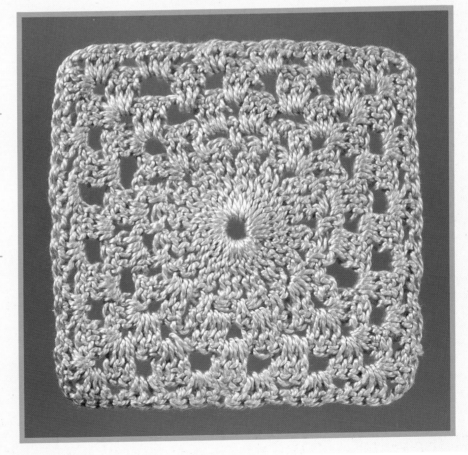

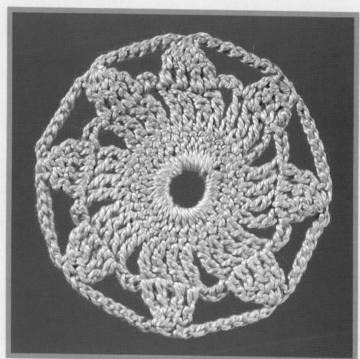

77

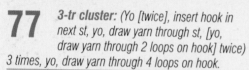

3-tr cluster: *(Yo [twice], insert hook in next st, yo, draw yarn through st, [yo, draw yarn through 2 loops on hook] twice) 3 times, yo, draw yarn through 4 loops on hook.*

4-tr cluster: *(Yo [twice], insert hook in next st, yo, draw yarn through st, [yo, draw yarn through 2 loops on hook] twice) 4 times, yo, draw yarn through 5 loops on hook.*

Ch 10 and sl st in first ch to form a ring.

Rnd 1: Ch 3 (counts as dc), 31 dc in ring, sl st in 3rd ch of beg ch to join.

Rnd 2: Ch 4 (counts as tr), tr in each of next 3 dc, ch 3, *tr in each of next 4 dc, ch 3; rep from * around, sl st in 4th ch of beg ch to join.

Rnd 3: Ch 4 (counts as tr), 3-tr cluster worked across next 3 tr, ch 8, skip next ch-3 loop, *4-tr cluster worked across next 4 tr, ch 8, skip next ch-3 loop; rep from * around, sl st in first cluster to join. Fasten off.

78

3-dtr puff st: (Yo [3 times], insert hook in next space, yo, draw yarn through space, [yo, draw yarn through 2 loops on hook] 3 times) 3 times in same space, yo, draw yarn through 4 loops on hook.

4-dtr puff st: *(Yo [3 times], insert hook in next space, yo, draw yarn through space, [yo, draw yarn through 2 loops on hook] 3 times) 4 times in same space, yo, draw yarn through 5 loops on hook.*

4-tr puff st: *(Yo [twice], insert hook in next space, yo, draw yarn through space, [yo, draw yarn through 2 loops on hook] twice) 4 times in same space, yo, draw yarn through 5 loops on hook.*

Ch 6 and sl st in first ch to form a ring.

Rnd 1: Ch 5 (counts as dtr), 3-dtr puff st in ring, ch 5, (4-dtr puff st, ch 5) 9 times in ring, sl st in first puff st to join.

Rnd 2: Ch 1, *sc in puff st, ch 4, 4-tr puff st in next ch-5 loop, ch 4; rep from * around, sl st in first sc to join. Fasten off.

.6.
Bobbles

79 *4-looped bobble:* (Yo, insert hook in next st, yo, draw yarn through st and up to level of work) 4 times in same st, yo, draw yarn through 9 loops on hook.

5-looped bobble: (Yo, insert hook in next st, yo, draw yarn through st and up to level of work) 5 times in same st, yo, draw yarn through 11 loops on hook.

Ch 6 and sl st in first ch to form a ring.

Rnd 1: Ch 4 (counts as dc, ch 1), (dc, ch 1) 11 times in ring, sl st in 3rd ch of beg ch to join.

Rnd 2: Ch 3, 4-looped bobble in first st, ch 3, *5-looped bobble in next dc, ch 2, skip next ch-1 space, 5-looped bobble in next dc, ch 3, skip next ch-1 space**, 5-looped bobble in next dc, ch 3, skip next ch-1 space; rep from * around, ending last rep at **, sl st in first bobble to join.

Rnd 3: Sl st in next ch-3 loop, ch 1, *(sc, ch 2, sc) in each of next 3 loops, ch 3; rep from * around, sl st in first sc to join.

Rnd 4: Sl st in next ch-2 space, ch 1, *3 sc in each of next 3 ch-2 spaces, (hdc, 3 dc, hdc) in next ch-3 loop; rep from * around, sl st in first sc to join. Fasten off.

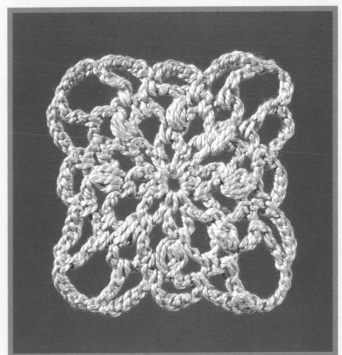

80 3-looped bobble: (Yo, insert hook in next st, yo, draw yarn through st and up to level of work) 3 times in same st, yo, draw yarn through 7 loops on hook.

Ch 6 and sl st in first ch to form a ring.

Rnd 1: Ch 1, (sc, ch 5) 8 times in ring, sl st in first sc to join.

Rnd 2: Sl st to center of next ch-5 loop, ch 1, (sc, ch 5) in each ch-5 loop around, around, sl st in first sc to join.

Rnd 3: Sl st to center of next ch-5 loop, ch 1, *sc in ch-5 loop, ch 3, 3-looped bobble in next sc, ch 3; rep from * around, sl st in first sc to join.

Rnd 4: Sl st to center of next ch-3 loop, ch 1, *(sc, ch 5) in each of next 2 ch-3 loops, (tr, ch 5) in each of next 2 ch-3 loops; rep from * around, sl st in first sc to join. Fasten off.

81

3-looped bobble:
(Yo, insert hook in next space, yo, draw yarn through space and up to level of work) 3 times in same space, yo, draw yarn through 7 loops on hook.

4-looped bobble: (Yo, insert hook in next space, yo, draw yarn through space and up to level of work) 4 times in same space, yo, draw yarn through 9 loops on hook.

Ch 6 and sl st in first ch to form a ring.

Rnd 1: Ch 4 (counts as dc, ch 1), (dc, ch 1) 11 times in ring, sl st in 3rd ch of beg ch to join.

Rnd 2: Sl st in next ch-1 space, ch 3, 3-looped bobble in same ch-1 space, ch 2, *4-looped bobble in next ch-1 space, ch 3, tr in next dc, ch 3, 4-looped bobble in next ch-1 space, ch 2**, 4-looped bobble in next ch-1 space; rep from * around, ending last rep at **, sl st in first bobble to join.

Rnd 3: Ch 1, *sc in bobble, ch 2, skip next ch-2 space, 4 dc in next ch-3 loop, ch 2, tr in next tr, ch 2, 4 dc in next ch-3 loop, ch 2; rep from * around, sl st in first sc to join. Fasten off.

82

2-looped bobble: (Yo, insert hook in next space, yo, draw yarn through space and up to level of work) twice in same space, yo, draw yarn through 5 loops on hook.

3-looped bobble: (Yo, insert hook in next space, yo, draw yarn through space and up to level of work) 3 times in same space, yo, draw yarn through 7 loops on hook.

Ch 6 and sl st in first ch to form a ring.

Rnd 1: Ch 5 (counts as tr, ch 1), (tr, ch 1) 11 times in ring, sl st in 4th ch of beg ch to join.

Rnd 2: Sl st in next ch-1 space, ch 3, 2-looped puff st in same ch-1 space, ch 1, (3-looped puff st, ch 1, 3 looped puff st, ch 1) in each of next 11 ch-1 spaces, 3-looped bobble in first ch-1 space, ch 1, sl st in first bobble to join.

Rnd 3: Sl st in next ch-1 space, ch 1, *sc in ch-1 space, ch 1, hdc in next ch-1 space, ch 1, dc in next ch-1 space, ch 1, (dc, ch 1, dc) in next ch-1 space, ch 1, dc in next ch-1 space, ch 1, hdc in next ch-1 space, ch 1; rep from * around, sl st in first sc to join. Fasten off.

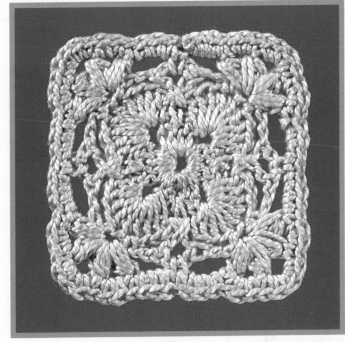

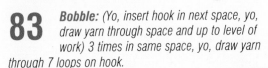

83 ***Bobble:*** *(Yo, insert hook in next space, yo, draw yarn through space and up to level of work) 3 times in same space, yo, draw yarn through 7 loops on hook.*

Ch 6 and sl st in first ch to form a ring.

Rnd 1: Ch 3 (counts as dc), 3 dc in ring, ch 2, (4 dc, ch 2) 3 times in ring, sl st in 3rd ch of beg ch to join.

Rnd 2: Sl st in next dc, ch 1, *sc bet next 2 dc, 9 dc in next ch-2 space, skip next 2 dc; rep from * around, sl st in first sc to join.

Rnd 3: Sl st in next dc, ch 5 (counts as dc, ch 2), working behind ch-5 beg ch, skip 1 sc to the right, dc in next dc to the right, *ch 2, skip next 3 dc, sc bet next 2 dc, ch 2, sc bet next 2 dc, ch 2, skip next 5 sts**, dc in next dc, ch 2, working behind last dc made, skip next sc to the right, dc in next dc to the right (crossed dc made); rep from * around, ending last rep at **, sl st in 3rd ch of beg ch to join.

Rnd 4: Sl st in next ch-2 space, ch 1, *sc in ch-2 space, ch 3, skip next ch-2 space, (bobble, ch 2, bobble, ch 3, bobble, ch 2, bobble) in next ch-2 space, ch 3, skip next ch-2 space; rep from * around, sl st in first sc to join.

Rnd 5: Ch 1, *sc in sc, 3 sc in next ch-3 loop, sc in next bobble, 2 sc in next ch-2 space, sc in next bobble, 3 sc in next ch-3 loop, sc in next bobble, 2 sc in next ch-2 space, sc in next bobble, 3 sc in next ch-3 loop; rep from * around, sl st first sc to join. Fasten off.

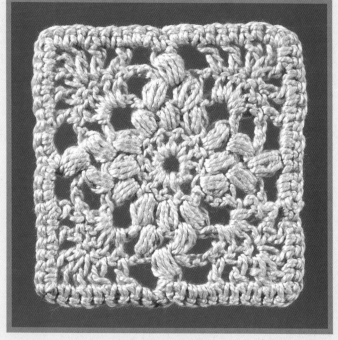

84 *3-looped bobble:* (Yo, insert hook in next st, yo, draw yarn through st and up to level of work) 3 times in same st, yo, draw yarn through 7 loops on hook.

4-looped bobble: (Yo, insert hook in next st, yo, draw yarn through st and up to level of work) 4 times in same st, yo, draw yarn through 9 loops on hook.

Ch 6 and sl st in first ch to form a ring.

Rnd 1: Ch 3 (counts as dc), 11 dc in ring, sl st in 3rd ch of beg ch to join.

Rnd 2: Ch 3, 3-looped bobble in same st, *ch 1, 4-looped bobble in next dc, ch 1, 4-looped bobble in next dc, ch 5**, 4-looped bobble in next dc; rep from * around, ending last rep at **, sl st in first bobble to join.

Rnd 3: Sl st in next ch-1 space, ch 3, 3-looped bobble in same ch-1 space, *ch 1, 4-looped bobble in next ch-1 space, ch 2, 5 dc in next ch-5 loop, ch 2**, 4-looped bobble in next ch-1 space; rep from * around, ending last rep at **, sl st in first bobble to join.

Rnd 4: Sl st in next ch-1 space, ch 3, 3-looped bobble in same ch-1 space, *ch 3, skip next ch-2 space, (dc, ch 1) in each of next 2 dc, (dc, ch 1, dc, ch 1, dc) in next dc, (ch 1, dc) in each of next 2 dc, ch 3**, 4-looped bobble in next ch-1 space; rep from * around, ending last rep at **, sl st in first bobble to join.

Rnd 5: Ch 1, *sc in bobble, 3 sc in next ch-3 loop, (sc in next dc, sc in next ch-1 space) 3 times, 3 sc in next dc, (sc in next ch-1 space, sc in next dc) 3 times, 3 sc in next ch-3 loop; rep from * around, sl st in first sc to join. Fasten off.

85

Bobble: *(Yo, insert hook in next space, yo, draw yarn through space and up to level of work) 4 times in same space, yo, draw yarn through 9 loops on hook.*

Ch 6 and sl st in first ch to form a ring.

Rnd 1: Ch 3 (counts as dc), 2 dc in ring, ch 3, (3 dc, ch 3) 3 times in ring, sl st in 3rd ch of beg ch to join.

Rnd 2: Ch 3 (counts as dc), dc in each of next 2 dc, *ch 1, (bobble, ch 4, bobble) in next ch-4 loop, ch 1**, dc in each of next 3 dc; rep from * around, ending last rep at **, sl st in 3rd ch of beg ch to join.

Rnd 3: Ch 3 (counts as dc), dc in each of next 2 dc, *skip next ch-1 space, dc in next bobble, ch 1, (bobble, ch 5, bobble) in next ch-4 loop, ch 1, dc in next bobble, skip next ch-1 space**, dc in each of next 3 dc; rep from * around, ending last rep at **, sl st in 3rd ch of beg ch to join.

Rnd 4: Ch 3 (counts as dc), dc in each of next 3 dc, *skip next ch-1 space, dc in next bobble, ch 1, (bobble, ch 5, bobble) in next ch-5 loop, ch 1, dc in next bobble, skip next ch-1 space**, dc in each of next 5 dc; rep from * around, ending last rep at **, dc in next dc, sl st in 3rd ch of beg ch to join.

Rnd 5: Ch 3 (counts as dc), dc in each of next 4 dc, *skip next ch-1 space, dc in next bobble, ch 1, (bobble, ch 5, bobble) in next ch-5 loop, ch 1, dc in next bobble, skip next ch-1 space**, dc in each of next 7 dc; rep from * around, ending last rep at **, dc in each of next 2 dc, sl st in 3rd ch of beg ch to join. Fasten off.

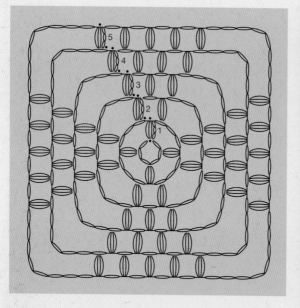
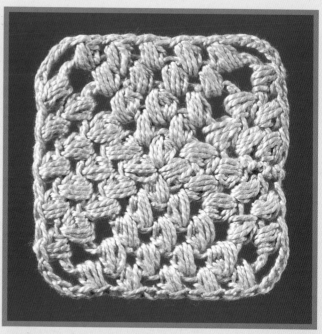

86

3-looped bobble: *(Yo, insert hook in next space, yo, draw yarn through space and up to level of work) 3 times in same space, yo, draw yarn through 7 loops on hook.*

4-looped bobble: *(Yo, insert hook in next space, yo, draw yarn through space and up to level of work) 4 times in same space, yo, draw yarn through 9 loops on hook.*

Ch 6 and sl st in first ch to form a ring.

Rnd 1: Ch 3 (counts as dc), 3-looped bobble in ring, ch 3, (4-looped bobble, ch 3) 3 times in ring, sl st in first bobble to join.

Rnd 2: Sl st in next ch-3 loop, ch 3, (3-looped bobble, ch 4, 4-looped bobble) in same ch-4 loop, ch 1, (4-looped bobble, ch 4, 4-looped bobble, ch 1) in each ch-4 loop around, sl st in first bobble to join.

Rnd 3: Sl st in next ch-3 loop, ch 3, (3-looped bobble, ch 6, 4-looped bobble) in same ch-4 loop, *ch 1, 4-looped bobble in next ch-1 space, ch 1**, (4-looped bobble, ch 6, 4-looped bobble) in next ch-4 loop; rep from * around, ending last rep at **, sl st in first bobble to join.

Rnd 4: Sl st in next ch-3 loop, ch 3, (3-looped bobble, ch 7, 4-looped bobble) in same ch-6 loop, *(ch 1, 4-looped bobble) in each of next 2 ch-1 spaces, ch 1**, (4-looped bobble, ch 7, 4-looped bobble) in next ch-6 loop; rep from * around, ending last rep at **, sl st in first bobble to join.

Rnd 5: Sl st in next ch-3 loop, ch 3, (3-looped bobble, ch 8, 4-looped bobble) in same ch-7 loop, *(ch 1, 4-looped bobble) in each of next 3 ch-1 spaces, ch 1**, (4-looped bobble, ch 8, 4-looped bobble) in next ch-7 loop; rep from * around, ending last rep at **, sl st in first bobble to join. Fasten off.

.7.
Puff Stitches

87

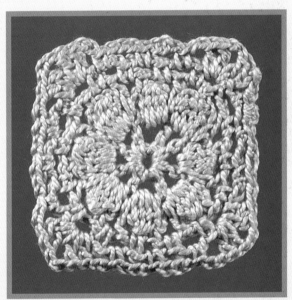

3-dc puff st: (Yo, insert hook in next space, yo, draw yarn through space, draw yarn through 2 loops on hook) 3 times in same space, yo, draw yarn through 4 loops on hook.

4-dc puff st: (Yo, insert hook in next space, yo, draw yarn through space, draw yarn through 2 loops on hook) 4 times in same space, yo, draw yarn through 5 loops on hook.

Ch 6 and sl st in first ch to form a ring.

Rnd 1: Ch 5 (counts as dc, ch 2), (dc, ch 2) 7 times in ring, sl st in 3rd ch of beg ch to join.

Rnd 2: Sl st in next ch-2 space, ch 3 (counts as dc), 3-dc puff st in same ch-2 space, ch 5, (4-dc puff st, ch 5) in each ch-2 space around, sl st in first puff st to join.

Rnd 3: Ch 1, *sc in puff st, ch 2, working over next ch-5 loop, dc in next corresponding dc 2 rnds below, ch 2; rep from * around, sl st in first sc to join.

Rnd 4: Sl st in next ch-2 space, ch 1, (sc, ch 3) in each ch-2 space around, sl st in first sc to join.

Rnd 5: Sl st in next ch-3 loop, ch 3 (counts as dc), (dc, ch 2, 2 dc) in same ch-3 loop, *ch 2, (sc, ch 3) in each of next 2 ch-3 loops, sc in next ch-3 loop, ch 2**, (2 dc, ch 2, 2 dc) in next ch-3 loop; rep from * around, ending last rep at **, sl st in 3rd ch of beg ch to join. Fasten off.

88

2-dc puff st: (Yo, insert hook in next space, yo, draw yarn through space, draw yarn through 2 loops on hook) twice in same space, yo, draw yarn through 3 loops on hook.

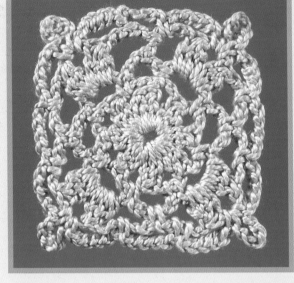

3-dc puff st: (Yo, insert hook in next space, yo, draw yarn through space, draw yarn through 2 loops on hook) 3 times in same space, yo, draw yarn through 4 loops on hook.

Ch 6 and sl st in first ch to form a ring.

Rnd 1: Ch 3 (counts as dc), 2-dc puff st in ring, ch 3, (3-dc puff st, ch 3) 7 times in ring, sl st in first puff st to join.

Rnd 2: Sl st in next ch-3 loop, ch 1, (sc, ch 5) in each ch-3 loop around, sl st in first sc to join.

Rnd 3: Sl st to center of next ch-5 loop, ch 3 (counts as dc), (2-dc puff st, ch 3, 3-dc puff st) in same ch-5 loop, *ch 5, sc in next ch-5 loop, ch 5**, (3-dc puff st, ch 3, 3-dc puff st) in next ch-5 loop; rep from * around, ending last rep at **, sl st in first puff st to join.

Rnd 4: Sl st to next ch-3 loop, ch 1, *(sc, ch 5, sc) in ch-3 loop, ch 5, (sc, ch 5) in each of next 2 ch-5 loops; rep from * around, sl st in first sc to join. Fasten off.

89

3-dc puff st: *(Yo, insert hook in next space, yo, draw yarn through space, draw yarn through 2 loops on hook) 3 times in same space, yo, draw yarn through 4 loops on hook.*

4-dc puff st: *(Yo, insert hook in next space, yo, draw yarn through space, draw yarn through 2 loops on hook) 4 times in same space, yo, draw yarn through 5 loops on hook.*

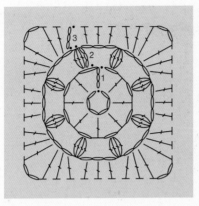

Ch 6 and sl st in first ch to form a ring.

Rnd 1: Ch 4 (counts as dc, ch 1), (dc, ch 1) 7 times in ring, sl st in 3rd ch of beg ch to join.

Rnd 2: Sl st in next ch-1 space, ch 3 (counts as dc), 3-dc puff st in same ch-1 space, ch 3, (4-dc puff st, ch 3) in each ch-1 space around, sl st in first puff st to join.

Rnd 3: Sl st in next ch-3 loop, ch 3 (counts as dc), (2 dc, ch 2, 3 dc) in same ch-3 loop, *3 dc in next ch-3 loop**, (3 dc, ch 2, 3 dc) in next ch-3 loop; rep from * around, ending last rep at **, sl st in 3rd ch of beg ch to join. Fasten off.

90

2-tr puff st: *(Yo [twice], insert hook in next st, yo, draw yarn through st, [draw yarn through 2 loops on hook] twice) twice in same st, yo, draw yarn through 3 loops on hook.*

3-tr puff st: *(Yo [twice], insert hook in next st, yo, draw yarn through st, [draw yarn through 2 loops on hook] twice) 3 times in same st, yo, draw yarn through 4 loops on hook.*

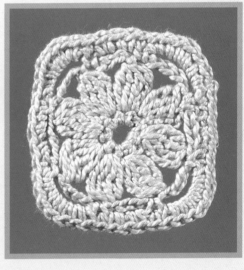

Ch 6 and sl st in first ch to form a ring.

Rnd 1: Ch 1, 8 sc in ring, sl st in first sc to join.

Rnd 2: Ch 4 (counts as tr), 2-tr puff st in first sc, ch 4, (3-tr puff st, ch 4) in each sc around, sl st in 4th ch of beg ch to join.

Rnd 3: Ch 1, *sc in puff st, ch 3, skip next ch-4 loop, sc in next puff st, ch 5, skip next ch-4 loop; rep from * around, sl st in first sc to join.

Rnd 4: Sl st in next ch-3 loop, ch 1, *3 sc in ch-3 loop, 7 sc in next ch-5 loop; rep from * around, sl st in first sc to join. Fasten off.

91

2-dc puff st: (Yo, insert hook in next st, yo, draw yarn through st, draw yarn through 2 loops on hook) twice in same st, yo, draw yarn through 3 loops on hook.

3-dc puff st: (Yo, insert hook in next st, yo, draw yarn through st, draw yarn through 2 loops on hook) 3 times in same st, yo, draw yarn through 4 loops on hook.

Ch 6 and sl st in first ch to form a ring.

Rnd 1: Ch 1, 8 sc in ring, sl st in first sc to join.

Rnd 2: Ch 1, (sc, ch 1) in each sc around, sl st in first sc to join.

Rnd 3: Ch 3 (counts as dc), 2-dc puff st in same sc, ch 2, *3-dc puff st in next ch-1 space, ch 2**, 3-dc puff st in next sc, ch 2; rep from * around, ending last rep at **, sl st in first puff st to join.

Rnd 4: Ch 1, (sc, ch 3) in each of first 2 puff sts, *(sc, ch 6, sc) in next puff st, ch 3**, (sc, ch 3) in each of next 3 puff sts; rep from * around, ending last rep at **, sc in next puff st, ch 3, sl st in first sc to join. Fasten off.

92

Puff st: (Yo, insert hook in next st, yo, draw yarn through st, draw yarn through 2 loops on hook) 3 times in same st, yo, draw yarn through 4 loops on hook.

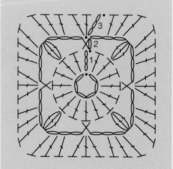

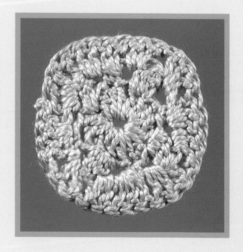

Ch 6 and sl st in first ch to form a ring.

Rnd 1: Ch 3 (counts as dc), 15 dc in ring, sl st in 3rd ch of beg ch to join.

Rnd 2: Ch 1, *sc in dc, ch 3, skip next dc, puff st in next dc, ch 3, skip next dc; rep from * around, sl st in first sc to join.

Rnd 3: Ch 3 (counts as dc), 2 dc in same sc, *3 dc in each of next 2 ch-3 loops**, 3 dc in next sc; rep from * around, ending last rep at **, sl st in 3rd ch of beg ch to join. Fasten off.

93

Puff st: (Yo, insert hook in next space, yo, draw yarn through space, draw yarn through 2 loops on hook) twice in same space, yo, draw yarn through 3 loops on hook.

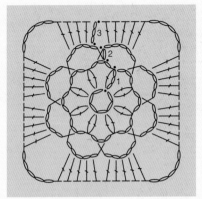

Ch 6 and sl st in first ch to form a ring.

Rnd 1: Ch 3 (counts as dc), dc in ring, ch 3, (puff st, ch 3) 7 times in ring, sl st in 3rd ch of beg ch to join.

Rnd 2: Sl st in next ch-3 loop, ch 1, (sc, ch 5) in each ch-3 loop around, sl st in first sc to join.

Rnd 3: Sl st in next ch-5 loop, ch 3 (counts as dc), 4 dc in same ch-5 loop, *ch 5, 5 dc in next ch-5 loop**, 5 dc in next ch-5 loop; rep from * around, ending last rep at **, sl st in 3rd ch of beg ch to join. Fasten off.

94

3-dc puff st: (Yo, insert hook in next space, yo, draw yarn through space, draw yarn through 2 loops on hook) 3 times in same space, yo, draw yarn through 4 loops on hook.

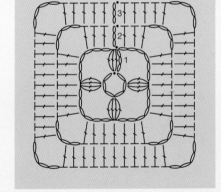

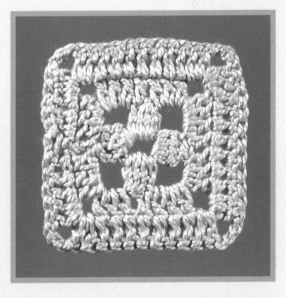

4-dc puff st: (Yo, insert hook in next space, yo, draw yarn through space, draw yarn through 2 loops on hook) 4 times in same space, yo, draw yarn through 5 loops on hook.

Ch 6 and sl st in first ch to form a ring.

Rnd 1: Ch 3 (counts as dc), 3-dc puff st in ring, ch 6, (4-dc puff st, ch 6) 3 times in ring, sl st in first puff st to join.

Rnd 2: Ch 3 (counts as dc), *(3 dc, ch 4, 3 dc) in next ch-6 loop**, dc in next puff st; rep from * around, ending last rep at **, sl st in first sc to join.

Rnd 3: Ch 3 (counts as dc), dc in each of next 3 dc, *(2 dc, ch 4, 2 dc) in next ch-4 loop**, dc in each of next 7 dc; rep from * around, ending last rep at **, dc in each of next 3 dc, sl st in 3rd ch of beg ch to join. Fasten off.

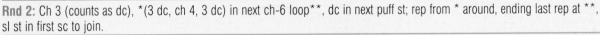

95

2-tr puff st:
(Yo [twice], insert hook in next st, yo, draw yarn through st, [draw yarn through 2 loops on hook] twice) twice in same st, yo, draw yarn through 3 loops on hook.

Rnd 1: (Ch 4, 2-tr puff st in 4th ch from hook) 4 times, sl st in ch at base of first puff st to join.

Rnd 2: Ch 1, *sc bet 2 puff sts, ch 11, skip next ch-4 loop; rep from * around, sl st in first sc to join.

Rnd 3: Ch 3 (counts as dc), *(6 dc, ch 3, 6 dc) in next ch-11 loop**, dc in next sc; rep from * around, ending last rep at **, sl st in 3rd ch of beg ch to join. Fasten off.

96

2-dc puff st: (Yo, insert hook in next space, yo, draw yarn through space, draw yarn through 2 loops on hook) twice in same space, yo, draw yarn through 3 loops on hook.

3-dc puff st: (Yo, insert hook in next space, yo, draw yarn through space, draw yarn through 2 loops on hook) 3 times in same space, yo, draw yarn through 4 loops on hook.

Ch 6 and sl st in first ch to form a ring.

Rnd 1: Ch 4 (counts as dc, ch 1), (dc, ch 1) 11 times in ring, sl st in 3rd ch of beg ch to join.

Rnd 2: Sl st in next ch-1 space, ch 3 (counts as dc), 2-dc puff st in same ch-1 space, ch 3, (3-dc puff st, ch 3) in each ch-1 space around, sl st in first puff st to join.

Rnd 3: Sl st in next ch-3 loop, ch 1, (sc, ch 5) in each ch-3 loop around, sl st in first sc to join.

Rnd 4: Sl st to the center of next ch-5 loop, ch 1, *sc in ch-5 loop, ch 1, (5 dc, ch 3, 5 dc) in next ch-5 loop, ch 1, sc in next ch-5 loop, ch 5; rep from * around, sl st in first sc to join. Fasten off.

97

2-dc puff st: (Yo, insert hook in next space, yo, draw yarn through space, draw yarn through 2 loops on hook) twice in same space, yo, draw yarn through 3 loops on hook.

3-dc puff st: (Yo, insert hook in next space, yo, draw yarn through space, draw yarn through 2 loops on hook) 3 times in same space, yo, draw yarn through 4 loops on hook.

Ch 6 and sl st in first ch to form a ring.

Rnd 1: Ch 3 (counts as dc), 2-dc puff st in ring, ch 2, (3-dc puff st, ch 2) 7 times in ring, sl st in first puff st to join.

Rnd 2: Sl st in next ch-2 space, ch 3 (counts as dc), 2 dc in same ch-2 space, *ch 2, (3-dc puff st, ch 3, 3-dc puff st) in next ch-2 space, ch 2**, 3 dc in next ch-2 space; rep from * around, ending last rep at **, sl st in 3rd ch of beg ch to join.

Rnd 3: Ch 3 (counts as dc), dc in each of next 2 dc, *2 dc in next ch-2 space, ch 2, (3-dc puff st, ch 3, 3-dc puff st) in next ch-3 loop, ch 2, 2 dc in next ch-2 space**, dc in each of next 3 dc; rep from * around, ending last rep at **, sl st in 3rd ch of beg ch to join.

Rnd 4: Ch 3 (counts as dc), dc in each of next 4 dc, *2 dc in next ch-2 space, ch 2, (3-dc puff st, ch 3, 3-dc puff st) in next ch-3 loop, ch 2, 2 dc in next ch-2 space**, dc in each of next 7 dc; rep from * around, ending last rep at **, dc in each of next 2 dc, sl st in 3rd ch of beg ch to join.

Rnd 5: Ch 3 (counts as dc), dc in each of next 6 dc, *2 dc in next ch-2 space, ch 2, (3-dc puff st, ch 3, 3-dc puff st) in next ch-3 loop, ch 2, 2 dc in next ch-2 space**, dc in each of next 9 dc; rep from * around, ending last rep at **, dc in each of next 4 dc, sl st in 3rd ch of beg ch to join. Fasten off.

98

2-dc puff st: *(Yo, insert hook in next space, yo, draw yarn through space, draw yarn through 2 loops on hook) twice in same space, yo, draw yarn through 3 loops on hook.*

3-dc puff st: *(Yo, insert hook in next space, yo, draw yarn through space, draw yarn through 2 loops on hook) 3 times in same space, yo, draw yarn through 4 loops on hook.*

Ch 6 and sl st in first ch to form a ring.

Rnd 1: Ch 3 (counts as dc), 2-dc puff st in ring, ch 1, 3-dc puff st in ring, ch 5, *3-dc puff st in ring, ch 1, 3-dc puff st in ring, ch 5; rep from * twice, sl st in first puff st to join.

Rnd 2: Sl st in next ch-1 space, ch 3 (counts as dc), 2 dc in same ch-1 space, *ch 1, (3-dc puff st, ch 5, 3-dc puff st) in next ch-5 loop, ch 1**, 3 dc in next ch-1 space; rep from * around, ending last rep at **, sl st in 3rd ch of beg ch to join.

Rnd 3: Ch 3 (counts as dc), dc in each of next 2 dc, *dc in next ch-1 space, ch 2, (3-dc puff st, ch 5, 3-dc puff st) in next ch-5 loop, ch 2, dc in next ch-1 space**, dc in each of next 3 dc; rep from * around, ending last rep at **, sl st in 3rd ch of beg ch to join.

Rnd 4: Ch 3 (counts as dc), dc in each of next 3 dc, *dc in next ch-2 space, ch 2, (3-dc puff st, ch 6, 3-dc puff st) in next ch-5 loop, ch 2, dc in next ch-2 space**, dc in each of next 5 dc; rep from * around, ending last rep at **, dc in next dc, sl st in 3rd ch of beg ch to join.

Rnd 5: Ch 3 (counts as dc), dc in each of next 4 dc, *dc in next ch-2 space, ch 2, (3-dc puff st, ch 6, 3-dc puff st) in next ch-6 loop, ch 2, dc in next ch-2 space**, dc in each of next 7 dc; rep from * around, ending last rep at **, dc in each of next 2 dc, sl st in 3rd ch of beg ch to join. Fasten off.

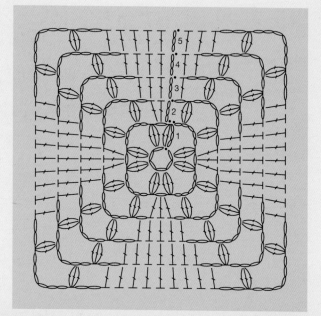

99

2-dc puff st: (Yo, insert hook in next space, yo, draw yarn through space, draw yarn through 2 loops on hook) twice in same space, yo, draw yarn through 3 loops on hook.

3-dc puff st: (Yo, insert hook in next space, yo, draw yarn through space, draw yarn through 2 loops on hook) 3 times in same space, yo, draw yarn through 4 loops on hook.

Ch 6 and sl st in first ch to form a ring.

Rnd 1: Ch 1, 12 sc in ring, sl st in first sc to join.

Rnd 2: Ch 3 (counts as dc), dc in next sc, ch 3, *dc in each of next 2 sc, ch 3; rep from * around, sl st in 3rd ch of beg ch to join.

Rnd 3: Sl st to next ch-3 loop, ch 3 (counts as dc), (2-dc puff st, ch 4, 3-dc puff st) in same ch-3 loop, ch 4, *(3-dc puff st, ch 4, 3-dc puff st) in next ch-3 loop, ch 4; rep from * around, sl st in first puff st to join.

Rnd 4: Sl st in next ch-4 loop, ch 1, (2 sc, ch 3, 2 sc) in each ch-4 loop around, sl st in first sc to join. Fasten off.

100

Ch 6 and sl st in first ch to form a ring.

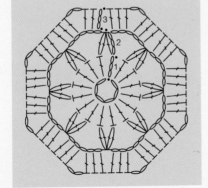

Rnd 1: Ch 3 (counts as dc), 15 dc in ring, sl st in 3rd ch of beg ch to join.

Rnd 2: Ch 3 (counts as dc), 3-dc cluster, working first half-closed dc in same st as beg ch, work next 2 half-closed dc in next dc, yo, complete cluster, ch 5, *4-dc cluster, working first 2 half-closed dc in next dc, work next 2 half-closed dc in next dc, yo, complete cluster, ch 5; rep from * around, sl st in first cluster to join.

Rnd 3: Sl st in next ch-5 loop, ch 3 (counts as dc), (2 dc, ch 2, 3 dc) in same loop, (3 dc, ch 2, 3 dc) in each ch-5 loop around, sl st in 3rd ch of beg ch to join. Fasten off.

101

3-tr puff st: *(Yo [twice], insert hook in next space, yo, draw yarn through space, [yo, draw yarn through 2 loops on hook] twice) 3 times in same space, yo, draw yarn through 4 loops on hook.*

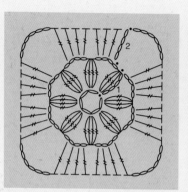

4-tr puff st: *(Yo [twice], insert hook in next space, yo, draw yarn through space, [yo, draw yarn through 2 loops on hook] twice) 4 times in same space, yo, draw yarn through 5 loops on hook.*

Ch 6 and sl st in first ch to form a ring.

Rnd 1: Ch 4 (counts as tr), 3-tr puff st in ring, ch 4, (4-tr puff st, ch 4) 7 times in ring, sl st in first puff st to join.

Rnd 2: Sl st in next ch-4 loop, ch 4 (counts as tr), 3 tr in same loop, *4 tr in next ch-4 loop, ch 6**, 4 tr in next ch-4 loop; rep from * around, ending last rep at **, sl st in 4th ch of beg ch to join. Fasten off.

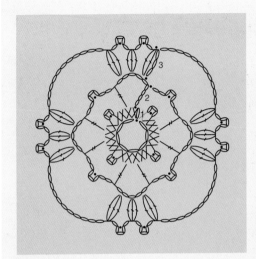

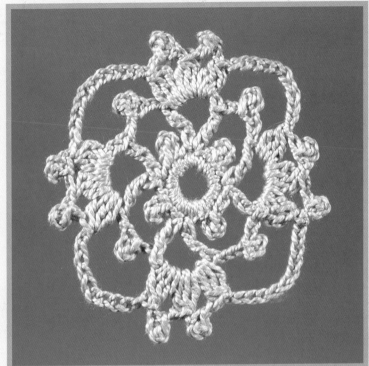

102

Picot: Ch 3, sl st in 3rd ch from hook.

2-dc puff st: (Yo, insert hook in next space, yo, draw yarn through space, draw yarn through 2 loops on hook) twice in same space, yo, draw yarn through 3 loops on hook.

3-dc puff st: (Yo, insert hook in next space, yo, draw yarn through space, draw yarn through 2 loops on hook) 3 times in same space, yo, draw yarn through 4 loops on hook.

Ch 8 and sl st in first ch to form a ring.

Rnd 1: Ch 1, (4 sc, picot, sc) 4 times in ring, sl st in first sc to join.

Rnd 2: Ch 9 (counts as tr, ch 5), tr in next sc, *ch 2, picot, ch 2**, tr in next sc, ch 5, tr in next sc; rep from * around, ending last rep at **, sl st in 4th ch of beg ch to join.

Rnd 3: Sl st to next ch-5 loop, ch 3 (counts as dc), (2-dc puff st, ch 1, picot, ch 1, 3-dc puff st, ch 1, picot, ch 1, 3-dc puff st) in same ch-5 loop, ch 11, *(3-dc puff st, ch 1, picot, ch 1, 3-dc puff st, ch 1, picot, ch 1, 3-dc puff st) in next ch-5 loop, ch 11; rep from * around, sl st in first puff st to join. Fasten off.

103

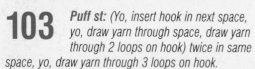

Puff st: (Yo, insert hook in next space, yo, draw yarn through space, draw yarn through 2 loops on hook) twice in same space, yo, draw yarn through 3 loops on hook.

Ch 6 and sl st in first ch to form a ring.

Rnd 1: Ch 1, 12 sc in ring, sl st in first sc to join.

Rnd 2: Ch 3 (counts as dc), dc in first sc, ch 3, (puff st, ch 3) in each sc around, sl st in 3rd ch of beg ch to join.

Rnd 3: Sl st in next ch-3 loop, ch 1, (sc, ch 4) in each loop around, sl st in first sc to join.

Rnd 4: Sl st in first ch-4 loop, ch 1, (2 sc, ch 3, 2 sc) in each ch-4 loop around, sl st in first sc to join. Fasten off.

104

3-tr puff st: *(Yo [twice], insert hook in next space, yo, draw yarn through space, [yo, draw yarn through 2 loops on hook] twice) 3 times in same space, yo, draw yarn through 4 loops on hook.*

2-dc puff st: *(Yo, insert hook in next space, yo, draw yarn through space, draw yarn through 2 loops on hook) twice in same space, yo, draw yarn through 3 loops on hook.*

3-dc puff st: *(Yo, insert hook in next space, yo, draw yarn through space, draw yarn through 2 loops on hook) 3 times in same space, yo, draw yarn through 4 loops on hook.*

Ch 6 and sl st in first ch to form a ring.

Rnd 1: Ch 4 (counts as dc, ch 1), (dc, ch 1) 7 times in ring, sl st in 3rd ch of beg ch to join.

Rnd 2: Ch 5 (counts as dc, ch 2), *dc in next ch-1 space, ch 2**, dc in next dc, ch 2; rep from * around, ending last rep at **, sl st in 3rd ch of beg ch to join.

Rnd 3: Ch 3 (counts as dc), 2 dc in next ch-2 space, *dc in next dc, 2 dc in next ch-2 space; rep from * around, sl st in 3rd ch of beg ch to join.

Rnd 4: Ch 6 (counts as dc, ch 3), skip next 2 dc, *dc in next dc, ch 3, skip next 2 dc; rep from * around, sl st in 3rd ch of beg ch to join.

Rnd 5: Sl st in next ch-3 loop, ch 3 (counts as dc), 2 dc in same loop, *ch 1, 3 dc in next ch-3 loop, ch 1, 3 dc in next ch-3 loop, ch 2, (3-tr puff st, ch 3, 3-tr puff st, ch 3, 3-tr puff st) in next ch-3 loop, ch 2**, 3 dc in next ch-3 loop; rep from * around, ending last rep at **, sl st in 3rd ch of beg ch to join.

Rnd 6: Sl st to next ch-1 space, ch 3 (counts as dc), 2-dc puff st in same space, *ch 3, (3-dc puff st, ch 3) in each of next 2 spaces, (3-tr puff st, ch 3, 3-tr puff st, ch 3) in each of next 2 ch-3 loops, 3-dc puff st in next ch-3 loop, ch 3**, 3-dc puff st in next ch-3 loop; rep from * around, ending last rep at **, sl st in first puff st to join. Fasten off.

105

2-dc puff st: *(Yo, insert hook in next space, yo, draw yarn through space, draw yarn through 2 loops on hook) twice in same space, yo, draw yarn through 3 loops on hook.*

3-tr puff st: *(Yo [twice], insert hook in next st, yo, draw yarn through st, [yo, draw yarn through 2 loops on hook] twice) 3 times in same st, yo, draw yarn through 4 loops on hook.*

4-tr puff st: *(Yo [twice], insert hook in next st, yo, draw yarn through st, [yo, draw yarn through 2 loops on hook] twice) 4 times in same st, yo, draw yarn through 5 loops on hook.*

Picot: *Ch 4, sl st in 4th ch from hook.*

Ch 6 and sl st in first ch to form a ring.

Rnd 1: Ch 3 (counts as dc), dc in ring, ch 3, (2-dc puff st, ch 3) 9 times in ring, sl st in 3rd ch of beg ch to join.

Rnd 2: Ch 4 (counts as tr), 3-tr puff st in first dc, ch 5, *(4-tr puff st, ch 5) in each puff st around, sl st in first puff st to join.

Rnd 3: Sl st in next ch-5 loop, ch 1, (3 sc, picot, 3 sc) in each ch-5 loop around, sl st in first sc to join. Fasten off.

106

2-dc puff st: (Yo, insert hook in next space, yo, draw yarn through space, draw yarn through 2 loops on hook) twice in same space, yo, draw yarn through 3 loops on hook.

3-dc puff st: (Yo, insert hook in next space, yo, draw yarn through space, draw yarn through 2 loops on hook) 3 times in same space, yo, draw yarn through 4 loops on hook.

Ch 6 and sl st in first ch to form a ring.

Rnd 1: Ch 3 (counts as dc), 2-dc puff st in ring, ch 3, (3-dc puff st, ch 3) 7 times in ring, sl st in first puff st to join.

Rnd 2: Sl st in next ch-3 loop, ch 1, (sc, ch 5) in each ch-3 loop around, sl st in first sc to join.

Rnd 3: Sl st in next ch-5 loop, ch 1, 5 sc in each ch-5 loop around, sl st in first sc to join.

Rnd 4: Sl st in each of next 2 sc, ch 1, *sc in sc, ch 7, skip next 4 sc; rep from * around sl st in first sc to join.

Rnd 5: Sl st in next ch-7 loop, ch 1, (4 sc, ch 3, 4 sc) in each ch-7 loop around, sl st in first sc to join. Fasten off.

107

2-dc puff st: *(Yo, insert hook in next space, yo, draw yarn through space, draw yarn through 2 loops on hook) twice in same space, yo, draw yarn through 3 loops on hook.*

3-dc puff st: *(Yo, insert hook in next space, yo, draw yarn through space, draw yarn through 2 loops on hook) 3 times in same space, yo, draw yarn through 4 loops on hook.*

Ch 6 and sl st in first ch to form a ring.

Rnd 1: Ch 3 (counts as dc), 15 dc in ring, sl st in 3rd ch of beg ch to join.

Rnd 2: Ch 5 (counts as dc, ch 2), skip first st, (dc, ch 2) in each dc around, sl st in 3rd ch of beg ch to join.

Rnd 3: Sl st in next ch-2 space, ch 3 (counts as dc), 2-dc puff st in first ch-2 space, ch 5, (3-dc puff st, ch 5) in each ch-2 space around, sl st in first puff st to join.

Rnd 4: Sl st to center of first ch-5 loop, ch 1, (sc, ch 5) in each ch-5 loop around sl st in first sc to join. Fasten off.

108

3-tr puff st: (Yo [twice], insert hook in next space, yo, draw yarn through space, [yo, draw yarn through 2 loops on hook] twice) 3 times in same space, yo, draw yarn through 4 loops on hook.

4-tr puff st: (Yo [twice], insert hook in next space, yo, draw yarn through space, [yo, draw yarn through 2 loops on hook] twice) 4 times in same space, yo, draw yarn through 5 loops on hook.

Ch 10 and sl st in first ch to form a ring.

Rnd 1: Ch 4 (counts as tr), 27 tr in ring, sl st in 4th ch of beg ch to join.

Rnd 2: Ch 1, sc in first st, ch 5, skip next tr, *sc in next tr, ch 5, skip next tr; rep from * around, sl st in first sc to join.

Rnd 3: Sl st to center of first ch-5 loop, ch 4 (counts as tr), 3-tr puff st in first ch-5 loop, ch 7, (4-tr puff st, ch 7) in each ch-5 loop around, sl st in first puff st to join. Fasten off.

109

3-dc puff st: (Yo, insert hook in next space, yo, draw yarn through space, draw yarn through 2 loops on hook) 3 times in same space, yo, draw yarn through 4 loops on hook.

4-dc puff st: (Yo, insert hook in next space, yo, draw yarn through space, draw yarn through 2 loops on hook) 4 times in same space, yo, draw yarn through 4 loops on hook.

Ch 10 and sl st in first ch to form a ring.

Rnd 1: Ch 4 (counts as tr), tr in ring, ch 2, (2 tr, ch 2) 11 times in ring, sl st in 4th ch of beg ch to join.

Rnd 2: Sl st to next ch-2 space, ch 3 (counts as dc), 3-dc puff st in first ch-2 space, ch 8, (4-dc puff st, ch 8) in each ch-2 space around, sl st in first puff st to join.

Rnd 3: Sl st to center of first ch-8 loop, ch 1, (sc, ch 7) in each ch-8 loop around, sl st in first sc to join. Fasten off.

110

2-tr puff st: (Yo [twice], insert hook in next space, yo, draw yarn through space, [yo, draw yarn through 2 loops on hook] twice) twice in same space, yo, draw yarn through 3 loops on hook.

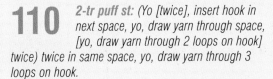

3-dc puff st: (Yo, insert hook in next space, yo, draw yarn through space, draw yarn through 2 loops on hook) 3 times in same space, yo, draw yarn through 4 loops on hook.

4-dc puff st: (Yo, insert hook in next space, yo, draw yarn through space, draw yarn through 2 loops on hook) 4 times in same space, yo, draw yarn through 4 loops on hook.

Ch 9 and sl st in first ch to form a ring.

Rnd 1: Ch 4 (counts as tr), tr in ring, ch 2, (2-tr puff st, ch 2) 11 times in ring, sl st in 4th ch of beg ch to join.

Rnd 2: Sl st in next ch-2 space, ch 3 (counts as dc), 3-dc puff st in first ch-2 space, ch 5, (4-dc puff st, ch 5) in each ch-2 space around, sl st in first puff st to join.

Rnd 3: Sl st to center of first ch-5 loop, ch 1, (sc, ch 7) in each ch-5 loop around, sl st in first sc to join. Fasten off.

111

2-tr puff st: *(Yo [twice], insert hook in next space, yo, draw yarn through space, [yo, draw yarn through 2 loops on hook] twice) twice in same space, yo, draw yarn through 3 loops on hook.*

3-tr puff st: *(Yo [twice], insert hook in next space, yo, draw yarn through space, [yo, draw yarn through 2 loops on hook] twice) 3 times in same space, yo, draw yarn through 4 loops on hook.*

Ch 10 and sl st in first ch to form a ring.

Rnd 1: Ch 4 (counts as tr), 2-tr puff st in ring, ch 6, (3-tr puff st, ch 6) 7 times in ring, sl st in first puff st to join.

Rnd 2: Sl st to center of first ch-6 loop, ch 4 (counts as tr), (2-tr puff st, ch 5, 3-tr puff st) in first ch-6 loop, *ch 6, (sc, ch 5, 3-tr puff st) in next ch-6 loop; ch 6**, (3-tr puff st, ch 5, 3-tr puff st) in next ch-6 loop; rep from * around, ending last rep at **, sl st in first puff st to join. Fasten off.

112

Ch 8 and sl st in first ch to form a ring.

Rnd 1: Ch 3 (counts as dc), 19 dc in ring, sl st in 3rd ch of beg ch to join.

Rnd 2: Ch 4 (counts as dc, ch 1), skip next dc, *dc bet last skipped and next dc, ch 1, skip next dc; rep from * around, ending with (dc, ch 1) in space bet last dc and beg ch, sl st in 3rd ch of beg ch to join.

Rnd 3: Ch 3 (counts as dc), skip next ch-1 space, dc in next dc, ch 5, *work 2-dc cluster, working first half-closed dc in same dc holding last dc, skip next ch-1 space, work 2nd half-closed dc in next dc, yo, complete cluster, ch 5; rep from * around, sl st in 3rd ch of beg ch to join.

Rnd 4: Sl st to center of first ch-5 loop, ch 1, (sc, ch 5) in each ch-5 loop around, sl st in first sc to join. Fasten off.

113

2-tr puff st: *(Yo [twice], insert hook in next space, yo, draw yarn through space, [yo, draw yarn through 2 loops on hook] twice) twice in same space, yo, draw yarn through 3 loops on hook.*

3-tr puff st: *(Yo [twice], insert hook in next space, yo, draw yarn through space, [yo, draw yarn through 2 loops on hook] twice) 3 times in same space, yo, draw yarn through 4 loops on hook.*

5-tr puff st: *(Yo [twice], insert hook in next space, yo, draw yarn through space, [yo, draw yarn through 2 loops on hook] twice) 5 times in same space, yo, draw yarn through 6 loops on hook.*

Ch 8 and sl st in first ch to form a ring.

Rnd 1: Ch 6 (counts as dc, ch 3), (dc, ch 3) 7 times in ring, sl st in 3rd ch of beg ch to join.

Rnd 2: Sl st in first ch-3 loop, ch 4 (counts as tr), (2-tr puff st, ch 5, 3-tr puff st) in first ch-3 loop, ch 5, (3-tr puff st, ch 5, 3-tr puff st, ch 5) in each ch-3 loop around, sl st in first puff st to join.

Rnd 3: Sl st in next ch-5 loop, ch 1, (sc, ch 4, 5-tr puff st) in first ch-5 loop, *ch 5, 5-tr puff st in next ch-5 loop, ch 5**, (sc, ch 4, 5-tr puff st) in next ch-5 loop; rep from * around, ending last rep at **, sl st in first sc to join. Fasten off.

114

3-tr puff st: (Yo [twice], insert hook in next space, yo, draw yarn through space, [yo, draw yarn through 2 loops on hook] twice) 3 times in same space, yo, draw yarn through 4 loops on hook.

4-tr puff st: (Yo [twice], insert hook in next space, yo, draw yarn through space, [yo, draw yarn through 2 loops on hook] twice) 4 times in same space, yo, draw yarn through 5 loops on hook.

Ch 6 and sl st in first ch to form a ring.

Rnd 1: Ch 3 (counts as dc), 13 dc in ring, sl st in 3rd ch of beg ch to join.

Rnd 2: Ch 10 (counts as dtr, ch 5), skip first st, (dtr, ch 5) in each dc around, sl st in 5th ch of beg ch to join.

Rnd 3: Sl st to center of next ch-5 loop, ch 4 (counts as tr), 3-tr puff st in first ch-5 loop, ch 5, (4-tr puff st, ch 5) in each ch-5 loop around, sl st in first puff st to join.

Rnd 4: Sl st to center of first ch-5 loop, ch 3 (counts as dc), 2 dc in first ch-5 loop, ch 5, (3 dc, ch 5) in each ch-5 loop around, sl st in 3rd ch of beg ch to join. Fasten off.

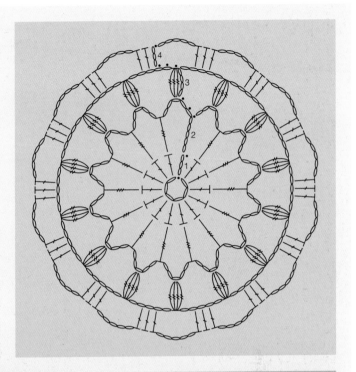

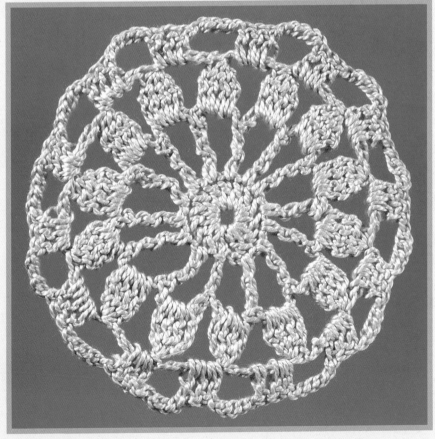

115

2-dc puff st:
(Yo, insert hook in next st or space, yo, draw yarn through st or space, draw yarn through 2 loops on hook) twice in same st or space, yo, draw yarn through 3 loops on hook.

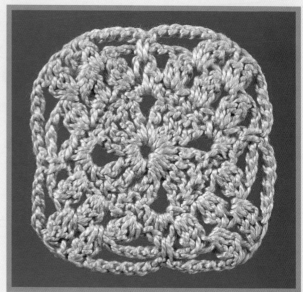

3-dc puff st: *(Yo, insert hook in next st or space, yo, draw yarn through st or space, draw yarn through 2 loops on hook) 3 times in same st or space, yo, draw yarn through 4 loops on hook.*

Ch 6 and sl st in first ch to form a ring.

Rnd 1: Ch 4 (counts as tr), 3 tr in ring, ch 2, (4 tr, ch 2) 3 times in ring, sl st in 4th ch of beg ch to join.

Rnd 2: Ch 1, sc in first 4 sts, *(2 sc, ch 2, 2 sc) in next ch-2 space**, sc in each of next 4 tr; rep from * around, ending last rep at **, sl st in first sc to join.

Rnd 3: Ch 3 (counts as dc), 2-dc puff st in first sc, *(ch 1, skip next sc, 3-dc puff st in next sc) twice, ch 7, skip next (sc, ch 2, 2 sc)**, 3-dc puff st in next sc; rep from * around, ending last rep at **, sl st in first puff st to join.

Rnd 4: Sl st in next ch-1 space, ch 3 (counts as dc), 2-dc puff st in first ch-1 space, *ch1, 3-dc puff st in next ch-1 space, ch 6, sc in next ch-7 loop, ch 6**, 3-dc puff st in next ch-1 space; rep from * around, ending last rep at **, sl st in first puff st to join. Fasten off.

116

2-dc puff st: (Yo, insert hook in next st or space, yo, draw yarn through st or space, draw yarn through 2 loops on hook) twice in same st or space, yo, draw yarn through 3 loops on hook.

Ch 6 and sl st in first ch to form a ring.

Rnd 1: Ch 1, 12 sc in ring, sl st in first sc to join.

Rnd 2: Ch 3 (counts as dc), dc in first sc, ch 3, (2-dc puff st, ch 3) in each dc around, sl st in 3rd ch of beg ch to join.

Rnd 3: Sl st in first ch-3 loop, ch 1, (sc, ch 4) in each ch-3 loop around, sl st in first sc to join.

Rnd 4: Sl st in next ch-4 loop, ch 1, (2 sc, ch 3, 2 sc) in each ch-4 loop around, sl st in first sc to join.

Rnd 5: Sl st in next sc, sl st in next ch-3 loop, ch 3 (counts as dc), (dc, ch 4, 2-dc puff st) in first ch-3 loop, (2-dc puff st, ch 3, 2-dc puff st) in each ch-3 loop around, sl st in 3rd ch of beg ch to join.

Rnd 6: Sl st in next ch-4 loop, ch 1 (2 sc, ch 3, 2 sc) in each ch-4 loop around, sl st in first sc to join. Fasten off.

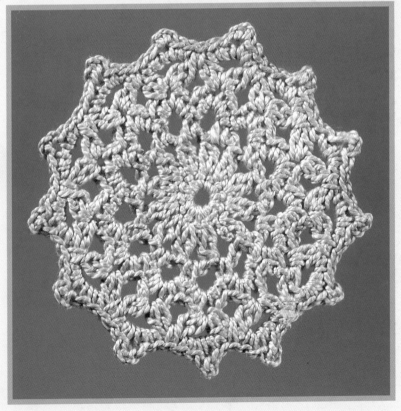

.8.
Popcorn Stitches

117 *Beginning popcorn (beg pop):* Ch 3 (counts as dc), 4 dc in same space, drop loop from hook, insert hook from front to back in 3rd ch of beg ch, place dropped loop on hook, draw loop through st.

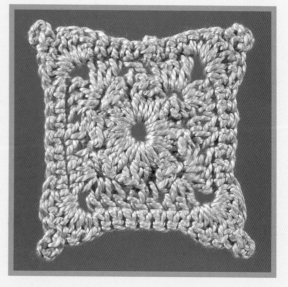

Popcorn (pop): 5 dc in same space, drop loop from hook, insert hook from front to back in first dc of 5-dc group, place dropped loop on hook, draw loop through st.

Picot: Ch 3, sl st in 3rd ch from hook.

Ch 6 and sl st in first ch to form a ring.

Rnd 1: Beg pop in ring, ch 3, (pop, ch 3) 7 times in ring, sl st in first pop to join.

Rnd 2: Sl st in first ch-3 loop, ch 3 (counts as dc), dc in first ch-3 loop, *(3 dc, ch 3, 3 dc) in next ch-3 loop**, 2 dc in next ch-3 loop; rep from * around, ending last rep at **, sl st in 3rd ch of beg ch to join.

Rnd 3: Ch 1, sc in first 5 sts, *(hdc, 2 dc, picot, 2 dc, hdc) in next ch-3 loop**, sc in each of next 8 dc; rep from * around, ending last rep at **, sc in each of next 3 dc, sl st in 3rd ch of beg ch to join. Fasten off.

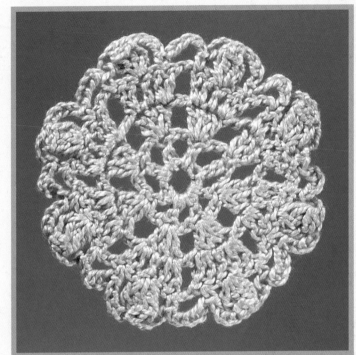

118 *Popcorn (pop): 4 dc in same st, drop loop from hook, insert hook from front to back in first dc of 4-dc group, place dropped loop on hook, draw loop through st.*

Ch 6 and sl st in first ch to form a ring.

Rnd 1: Ch 5 (counts as dc, ch 2), (dc, ch 2) 7 times in ring, sl st in 3rd ch of beg ch to join.

Rnd 2: Ch 3 (counts as dc), 2 dc in first st, ch 2, skip next ch-2 space, *3 dc in next dc, ch 2, skip next ch-2 space; rep from * around, sl st in 3rd ch of beg ch to join.

Rnd 3: Ch 3 (counts as dc), dc in first st, *dc in next dc, 2 dc in next dc, ch 2, skip next ch-2 space**, 2 dc in next dc; rep from * around, ending last rep at **, sl st in 3rd ch of beg ch to join.

Rnd 4: Ch 1, *sc in dc, ch 4, skip next dc, pop in next dc, ch 4, skip next dc, sc in next dc, ch 5, skip next ch-2 space; rep from * around, sl st in first sc to join. Fasten off.

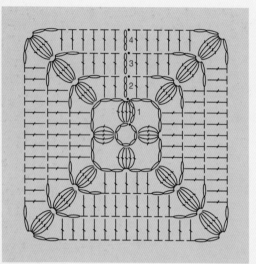

119

Beginning popcorn (beg pop): Ch 3 (counts as dc), 4 dc in same space, drop loop from hook, insert hook from front to back in 3rd ch of beg ch, place dropped loop on hook, draw loop through st.

Popcorn (pop): 5 dc in same space, drop loop from hook, insert hook from front to back in first dc of 5-dc group, place dropped loop on hook, draw loop through st.

Ch 8 and sl st in first ch to form a ring.

Rnd 1: Beg pop in ring, ch 5, (pop, ch 5) 3 times in ring, sl st in first pop to join.

Rnd 2: Ch 3 (counts as dc), *(2 dc, ch 2, pop, ch 2, 2 dc) in next ch-5 loop**, dc in next pop; rep from * around, ending last rep at **, sl st in 3rd ch of beg ch to join.

Rnd 3: Ch 3 (counts as dc), dc in each of next 2 dc, *2 dc in next ch-2 space, ch 2, pop in next pop, ch 2, 2 dc in next ch-2 space**, dc in each of next 5 dc; rep from * around, ending last rep at **, dc in each of next 2 dc, sl st in 3rd ch of beg ch to join.

Rnd 4: Ch 3 (counts as dc), dc in each of next 4 dc, *2 dc in next ch-2 space, ch 2, pop in next pop, ch 2, 2 dc in next ch-2 space**, dc in each of next 9 dc; rep from * around, ending last rep at **, dc in each of next 4 dc, sl st in 3rd ch of beg ch to join. Fasten off.

120

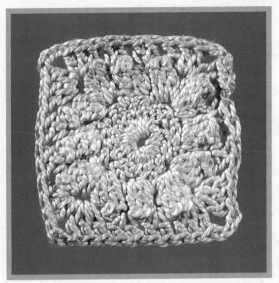

Beginning pop-corn (beg pop):
*Ch 3 (counts as dc),
3 dc in same space,
drop loop from
hook, insert hook
from front to back
in 3rd ch of beg ch,
place dropped loop
on hook, draw loop
through st.*

Popcorn (pop): *4
dc in same space,
drop loop from hook, insert hook from front to back in first dc of 4-dc
group, place dropped loop on hook, draw loop through st.*

Ch 6 and sl st in first ch to form a ring.

Rnd 1: Ch 3 (counts as dc), 15 dc in ring, sl st in 3rd ch of beg ch to join.

Rnd 2: Ch 1, sc in first st, ch 3, skip next dc, *sc in next dc, ch 3, skip next dc; rep from * around, sl st in first sc to join.

Rnd 3: Sl st in next ch-3 loop, beg pop in same ch-3 loop, *ch 1, (pop, ch 3, pop) in next ch-3 loop, ch 1**, pop in next ch-3 loop; rep from * around, ending last rep at **, sl st in first pop to join.

Rnd 4: Sl st in next ch-1 space, ch 3 (counts as dc), dc in same ch-1 space, *ch 1, (3 dc, ch 3, 3 dc) in next ch-3 loop, ch 1, 2 dc in next ch-1 space, ch 1**, 2 dc in next ch-1 space; rep from * around, ending last rep at **, sl st in 3rd ch of beg ch to join. Fasten off.

121

Beginning popcorn (beg pop):
Ch 3 (counts as dc), 4 dc in same st,
drop loop from hook, insert hook from
front to back in 3rd ch of beg ch, place dropped loop
on hook, draw loop through st.

Popcorn (pop): 5 dc in same st, drop loop from
hook, insert hook from front to back in first dc of
5-dc group, place dropped loop on hook, draw loop
through st.

Ch 12 and sl st in first ch to form a ring.

Rnd 1: Ch 3 (counts as dc), 4 dc in ring, ch 2, (5
dc, ch 2) 3 times in ring, sl st in 3rd ch of beg ch
to join.

Rnd 2: Ch 3 (counts as dc), dc in each of next 4 dc,
*(dc, ch 3, dc) in next ch-3 loop**, dc in each of
next 5 dc; rep from * around, ending last rep at **,
sl st in 3rd ch of beg ch to join.

Rnd 3: Ch 3 (counts as dc), *pop in next dc, dc in
next dc, pop in next dc, dc in each of next 2 dc, (dc,
ch 3, dc) in next ch-3 loop**, dc in each of next 2
dc; rep from * around, ending last rep at **, dc in
next dc, sl st in 3rd ch of beg ch to join.

Rnd 4: Ch 3 (counts as dc), dc in each
of next 6 sts, *(dc, ch 4, dc) in next ch-
3 loop**, dc in each of next 9 dc; rep
from * around, ending last rep at **, dc
in each of next 2 dc, sl st in 3rd ch of
beg ch to join.

Rnd 5: Beg pop in first st, *(dc in next
dc, pop in next dc) twice, dc in each of
next 3 dc, (dc, ch 4, dc) in next ch-4
loop, dc in each of next 3 dc**, pop in
next dc; rep from * around, ending last
rep at **, sl st in first pop to join.

Rnd 6: Ch 3 (counts as dc), dc in each
of next 8 sts, *(dc, ch 5, dc) in next ch-
4 loop**, dc in each of next 13 sts; rep
from * around, ending last rep at **, dc
in each of next 4 dc, sl st in 3rd ch of
beg ch to join. Fasten off.

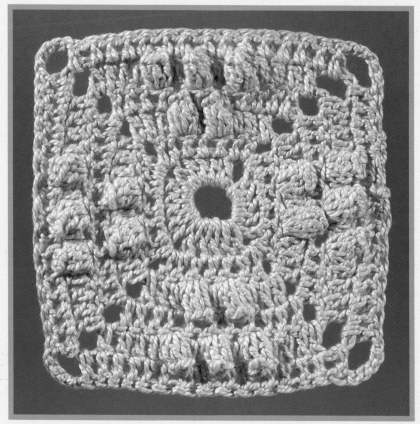

122

Beginning popcorn (beg pop): Ch 3 (counts as dc), 4 dc in same space, drop loop from hook, insert hook from front to back in 3rd ch of beg ch, place dropped loop on hook, draw loop through st.

Popcorn (pop): 5 dc in same space, drop loop from hook, insert hook from front to back in first dc of 5-dc group, place dropped loop on hook, draw loop through st.

Ch 10 and sl st in first ch to form a ring.

Rnd 1: Beg pop in ring, ch 1, *pop in ring, ch 4**, pop in ring, ch 1; rep from * twice, rep from * to ** once, sl st in first pop to join.

Rnd 2: Ch 5 (counts as dc, ch 2), skip next ch-1 space, *dc in next pop, ch 2, (pop, ch 4, pop) in next ch-4 loop, ch 2**, dc in next pop, ch 2; rep from * around, ending last rep at **, sl st in 3rd ch of beg ch to join.

Rnd 3: Ch 5 (counts as dc, ch 2), skip next ch-2 space, *dc in next dc, ch 2, skip next ch-2 space, dc in next pop, ch 2, (pop, ch 4, pop) in next ch-4 loop, ch 2, dc in next pop, ch 2, skip next ch-2 space**, dc in next dc, ch 2; rep from * around, ending last rep at **, sl st in 3rd ch of beg ch to join.

Rnd 4: Ch 5 (counts as dc, ch 2), skip next ch-2 space, *(dc in next dc, ch 2, skip next ch-2 space) twice, dc in next pop, ch 2, (pop, ch 4, pop) in next ch-4 loop, ch 2, dc in next pop, ch 2, skip next ch-2 space, dc in next dc, ch 2, skip next ch-2 space**, dc in next dc, ch 2, skip next ch-2 space; rep from * around, ending last rep at **, sl st in 3rd ch of beg ch to join.

Rnd 5: Ch 5 (counts as dc, ch 2), skip next ch-2 space, *(dc in next dc, ch 2, skip next ch-2 space) 3 times, dc in next pop, ch 2, (pop, ch 4, pop) in next ch-4 loop, ch 2, dc in next pop, ch 2, skip next ch-2 space, (dc in next dc, ch 2, skip next ch-2 space) twice**, dc in next dc, ch 2, skip next ch-2 space; rep from * around, ending last rep at **, sl st in 3rd ch of beg ch to join. Fasten off.

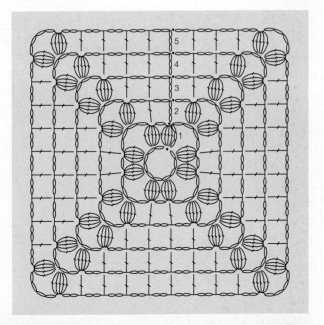

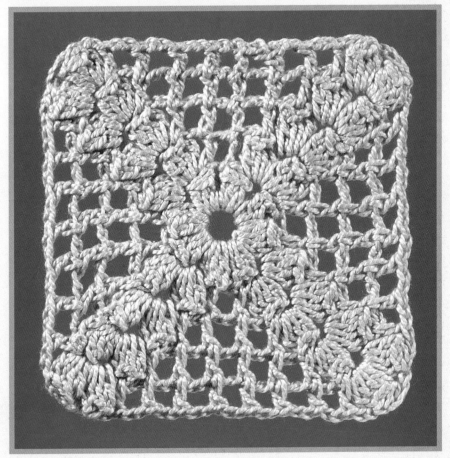

123

Beginning popcorn (beg pop): Ch 3 (counts as dc), 3 dc in same st, drop loop from hook, insert hook from front to back in 3rd ch of beg ch, place dropped loop on hook, draw loop through st.

Popcorn (pop): 4 dc in same st, drop loop from hook, insert hook from front to back in first dc of 4-dc group, place dropped loop on hook, draw loop through st.

Ch 8 and sl st in first ch to form a ring.

Rnd 1: Ch 4 (counts as dc, ch 1), (dc, ch 1) 15 times in ring, sl st in 3rd ch of beg ch to join.

Rnd 2: Sl st in next ch-1 space, beg pop in first ch-1 space, ch 1, (pop, ch 1) in each ch-1 space around, sl st in first pop to join.

Rnd 3: Sl st in next ch-1 space, ch 3 (counts as dc), (dc, ch 3, 2 dc) in first ch-1 space, *ch 3, (sc, ch 3) in each of next 3 ch-1 spaces**, (2 dc, ch 3, 2 dc) in next ch-1 space; rep from * around, ending last rep at **, sl st in 3rd ch of beg ch to join.

Rnd 4: Sl st to next ch-3 loop, ch 3 (counts as dc), (3 dc, ch 2, 4 dc) in first ch-3 loop, *ch 2, skip next ch-3 loop, (4 dc, ch 2) in each of next 2 ch-3 loops, skip next ch-3 loop**, (4 dc, ch 2, 4 dc) in next ch-3 loop; rep from * around, ending last rep at **, sl st in 3rd ch of beg ch to join.

Rnd 5: Sl st to next ch-2 space, ch 3 (counts as dc), (2 dc, ch 2, 3 dc) in first ch-2 space, *(3 dc, ch 2) in each of next 3 ch-2 spaces** (3 dc, ch 2, 3 dc) in next ch-2 space; rep from * around, ending last rep at **, sl st in 3rd ch of beg ch to join.

Rnd 6: Sl st to next ch-2 space, ch 3 (counts as dc), (2 dc, ch 2, 3 dc) in first ch-2 space, *3 dc in each of next 4 ch-2 spaces** (3 dc, ch 2, 3 dc) in next ch-2 space; rep from * around, ending last rep at **, sl st in 3rd ch of beg ch to join. Fasten off.

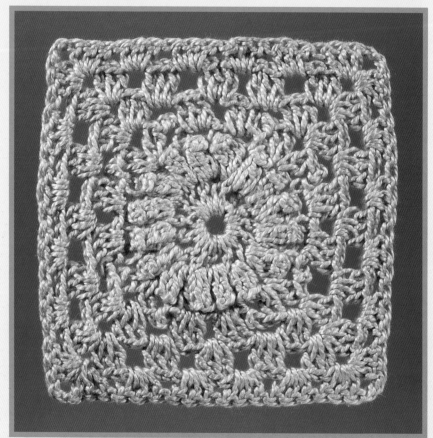

124

Beginning popcorn (beg pop): Ch 3 (counts as dc), 4 dc in same space, drop loop from hook, insert hook from front to back in 3rd ch of beg ch, place dropped loop on hook, draw loop through st.

Popcorn (pop): 5 dc in same space, drop loop from hook, insert hook from front to back in first dc of 5-dc group, place dropped loop on hook, draw loop through st.

Ch 6 and sl st in first ch to form a ring.

Rnd 1: Ch 3 (counts as dc), 15 dc in ring, sl st in 3rd ch of beg ch to join.

Rnd 2: Ch 5 (counts as dc, ch 2), (dc, ch 2) in each dc around, sl st in 3rd ch of beg ch to join.

Rnd 3: Sl st in first ch-2 space, beg pop in first ch-2 space, *ch 7, (pop, ch 5) in each of next 3 ch-2 spaces**, pop in next ch-2 space; rep from * around, ending last rep at **, sl st in first pop to join.

Rnd 4: Sl st to center of next ch-7 loop, ch 3 (counts as dc), (3 dc, ch 3, 4 dc) in first ch-7 loop, *ch 2, dc in next ch-5 loop, ch 2, (dc, ch 2, dc) in next ch-5 loop, ch 2, dc in next ch-5 loop, ch 2**, (4 dc, ch 3, 4 dc) in next ch-7 loop; rep from * around, ending last rep at **, sl st in 3rd ch of beg ch to join.

Rnd 5: Ch 3 (counts as dc), *dc in each of next 3 dc, (3 dc, ch 3, 3 dc) in next ch-3 loop, dc in each of next 4 dc, (ch 2, dc) in each of next 5 dc; rep from * around, omitting last dc, sl st in 3rd ch of beg ch to join.

Rnd 6: Ch 5 (counts as dc, ch 2), skip next 2 dc, *dc in each of next 4 dc, (3 dc, ch 3, 3 dc) in next ch-3 loop, dc in each of next 4 dc, ch 2, skip next 2 dc, (dc, ch 2) in each of next 5 dc**, dc in next dc, ch 2, skip next 2 dc; rep from * around, ending last rep at **, sl st in 3rd ch of beg ch to join. Fasten off.

.9.
Post Stitches

125

Ch 6 and sl st in first ch to form a ring.

Rnd 1: Ch 3 (counts as dc), 15 dc in ring, sl st in 3rd ch of beg ch to join.

Rnd 2: Ch 1, *sc in dc, 8 dc in next dc, sc in next dc, ch 3, skip next dc; rep from * around, sl st in first sc to join.

Rnd 3: Ch 1, *sc in sc, ch 3, skip next 8 dc, sc in next sc, (2 dc, ch 3, 2 dc) in next ch-3 loop; rep from * around, sl st in first sc to join.

Rnd 4: Sl st in next ch-3 loop, ch 2 (counts as hdc), (5 dc, hdc) in first ch-3 loop, *ch 1, skip next dc, sc in next dc, ch 2, dc in next ch-3 loop, ch 2, sc in next dc, ch 1**, (hdc, 5 dc, hdc) in next ch-3 loop; rep from * around, ending last rep at **, sl st in 2nd ch of beg ch to join.

Rnd 5: Sl st in each of next 3 dc, ch 1, *sc in dc, ch 1, 2 dc in next ch-1 space, 4 dc in each of next 2 ch-2 spaces, 2 dc in next ch-1 space; ch 1; rep from * around, sl st in first sc to join. Fasten off.

126

Front post double crochet (FPdc): Yo, insert hook from front to back to front again around the post of next st, yo, draw yarn through st, (yo, draw yarn through 2 loops on hook) twice.

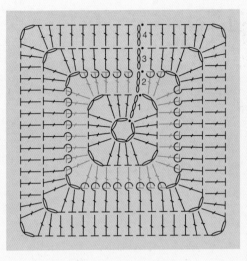

Ch 6 and sl st in first ch to form a ring.

Rnd 1: Ch 3 (counts as dc), 3 dc in ring, ch 2, (4 dc, ch 2) 3 times in ring, sl st in 3rd ch of beg ch to join.

Rnd 2: Ch 3 (counts as dc), dc in each of next 3 dc, *(2 dc, ch 2, dc) in next ch-2 space**, dc in each of next 4 dc; rep from * around, ending last rep at **, sl st in 3rd ch of beg ch to join.

Rnd 3: Ch 3 (counts as dc), *FPdc in each of next 5 dc, (2 dc, ch 2, 2 dc) in next ch-2 space, FPdc in each of next 3 dc; rep from * around, omitting last FPdc, sl st in 3rd ch of beg ch to join.

Rnd 4: Ch 3 (counts as dc), dc in each of next 7 dc, *(2 dc, ch 2, 2 dc) in next ch-2 space, dc in each of next 5 dc; rep from * around, omitting last dc, sl st in 3rd ch of beg ch to join. Fasten off.

127

Picot: Ch 3, sl st in 3rd ch from hook.

Front post treble crochet (FPtr): Yo (twice), insert hook from front to back to front again around the post of next st, yo, draw yarn through st, (yo, draw yarn through 2 loops on hook) 3 times.

Ch 6 and sl st in first ch to form a ring.

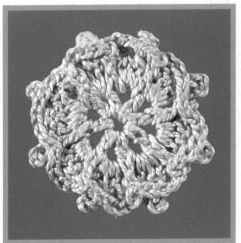

Rnd 1: Ch 5 (counts as dc, ch 2), (dc, ch 2) 7 times in ring, sl st in 3rd ch of beg ch to join.

Rnd 2: Ch 3 (counts as dc), *(2 dc, picot, dc) in next ch-2 space**, dc in next dc; rep from * around, ending last rep at **, sl st in 3rd ch of beg ch to join.

Rnd 3: Ch 1, *sc in dc, FPtr around the post of next corresponding dc 2 rnds below, ch 5, skip next (2 dc, picot, dc) in current row; rep from * around, sl st in first sc to join. Fasten off.

128

3-dc puff st: *(Yo, insert hook in next space, yo, draw yarn through space, draw yarn through 2 loops on hook) 3 times in same space, yo, draw yarn through 4 loops on hook.*

4-dc puff st: *(Yo, insert hook in next space, yo, draw yarn through space, draw yarn through 2 loops on hook) 4 times in same space, yo, draw yarn through 4 loops on hook.*

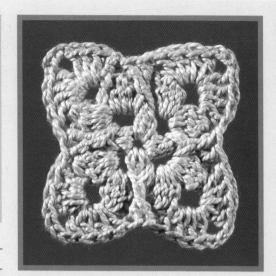

Ch 6 and sl st in first ch to form a ring.

Rnd 1: Ch 3 (counts as dc), 2 dc in ring, ch 2, (3 dc, ch 2) 3 times in ring, sl st in 3rd ch of beg ch to join.

Rnd 2: Sl st to next ch-2 space, ch 3 (counts as dc), (3-dc puff st, ch 5, 4-dc puff st) in first ch-2 space, ch 3, *(4-dc puff st, ch 5, 4-dc puff st) in next ch-2 space, ch 3; rep from * around, sl st in 3rd ch of beg ch to join.

Rnd 3: Sl st in next ch-5 loop, ch 3 (counts as dc), (3 dc, ch 3, 4 dc) in first ch-5 loop, *working over next ch-3 loop, work 2 tr in center dc 2 rnds below**, (4 dc, ch 3, 4 dc) in next ch-5 loop; rep from * around, ending last rep at **, sl st in 3rd ch of beg ch to join. Fasten off.

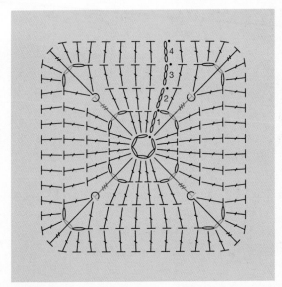

129

Front post treble crochet (FPtr): *Yo (twice), insert hook from front to back to front again around the post of next st, yo, draw yarn through st, (yo, draw yarn through 2 loops on hook) 3 times.*

Ch 6 and sl st in first ch to form a ring.

Rnd 1: Ch 3 (counts as dc), 3 dc in ring, ch 3, (4 dc, ch 3) 3 times in ring, sl st in 3rd ch of beg ch to join.

Rnd 2: Ch 3 (counts as dc), *dc in each of next 3 dc, dc in next ch-3 loop, working over ch-3 loop, dtr in center ring, dc in same ch-3 loop in Rnd 1**, dc in next dc; rep from * around, ending last rep at **, sl st in 3rd ch of beg ch to join.

Rnd 3: Ch 3 (counts as dc), *dc in each of next 4 dc, (dc, ch 3, dc) in next dtr, dc in each of next 2 dc; rep from * around, omitting last dc, sl st in 3rd ch of beg ch to join.

Rnd 4: Ch 3 (counts as dc), *dc in each of next 5 dc, 2 dc in next ch-3 loop, working over ch-3 loop, FPtr in corresponding dtr 2 rnds below, 2 dc in same ch-3 loop in Rnd 3**, dc in each of next 3 dc; rep from * around, omitting last dc, sl st in 3rd ch of beg ch to join. Fasten off.

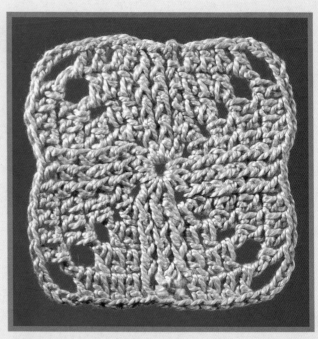

130

Front post double crochet (FPdc): *Yo, insert hook from front to back to front again around the post of next st, yo, draw yarn through st, (yo, draw yarn through 2 loops on hook) twice.*

Ch 6 and sl st in first ch to form a ring.

Rnd 1: Ch 3 (counts as dc), 2 dc in ring, ch 3, (3 dc, ch 3) 3 times in ring, sl st in 3rd ch of beg ch to join.

Rnd 2: Ch 3 (counts as dc), FPdc in each of next 2 dc, *(dc, ch 4, dc) in next ch-3 loop**, FPdc in each of next 3 dc; rep from * around, ending last rep at **, sl st in 3rd ch of beg ch to join.

Rnd 3: Ch 3 (counts as dc), FPdc in each of next 2 dc, *dc in next dc, (dc, ch 4, dc) in next ch-4 loop, dc in next dc**, FPdc in each of next 3 dc; rep from * around, ending last rep at **, sl st in 3rd ch of beg ch to join.

Rnd 4: Ch 3 (counts as dc), FPdc in each of next 2 dc, *dc in each of next 2 dc, (dc, ch 5, dc) in next ch-4 loop, dc in each of next 2 dc**, FPdc in each of next 3 dc; rep from * around, ending last rep at **, sl st in 3rd ch of beg ch to join.

Rnd 5: Ch 3 (counts as dc), *dc in each of next 5 dc, (dc, ch 5, dc) in next ch-5 loop, dc in each of next 4 dc; rep from * around, omitting last dc, sl st in 3rd ch of beg ch to join. Fasten off.

131

Front post double crochet (FPdc): *Yo, insert hook from front to back to front again around the post of next st, yo, draw yarn through st, (yo, draw yarn through 2 loops on hook) twice.*

Ch 6 and sl st in first ch to form a ring.

Rnd 1: Ch 3 (counts as dc), 2 dc in ring, ch 3, (3 dc, ch 3) 3 times in ring, sl st in 3rd ch of beg ch to join.

Rnd 2: Ch 3 (counts as dc), *FPdc around the post of next dc, 2 dc in next dc, ch 4, skip next ch-3 loop**, 2 dc in next dc; rep from * around, ending last rep at **, sl st in 3rd ch of beg ch to join.

Rnd 3: Ch 3 (counts as dc), *FPdc around the post of next dc, dc in next dc, 2 dc in next dc, ch 4, skip next ch-4 loop, 2 dc in next dc**, dc in next dc; rep from * around, ending last rep at **, sl st in 3rd ch of beg ch to join.

Rnd 4: Ch 3 (counts as dc), *FPdc around the post of next dc, dc in each of next 2 dc, 2 dc in next dc, ch 5, skip next ch-4 loop, 2 dc in next dc**, dc in each of next 2 dc; rep from * around, ending last rep at **, dc in next dc, sl st in 3rd ch of beg ch to join.

Rnd 5: Ch 3 (counts as dc), *FPdc around the post of next dc, dc in each of next 3 dc, 2 dc in next dc, ch 5, skip next ch-5 loop, 2 dc in next dc**, dc in each of next 3 dc; rep from * around, ending last rep at **, dc in each of next 2 dc, sl st in 3rd ch of beg ch to join. Fasten off.

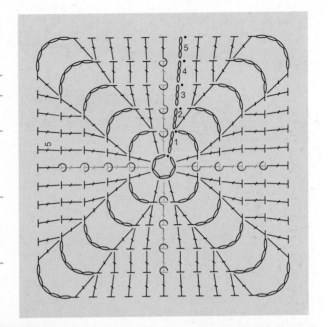

132

Front post double crochet (FPdc): Yo, insert hook from front to back to front again around the post of next st, yo, draw yarn through st, (yo, draw yarn through 2 loops on hook) twice.

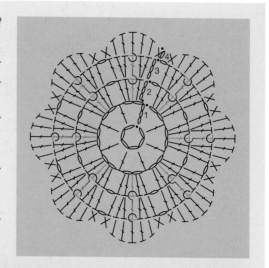

Ch 6 and sl st in first ch to form a ring.

Rnd 1: Ch 5 (counts as dc, ch 2), (dc, ch 2) 7 times in ring, sl st in 3rd ch of beg ch to join.

Rnd 2: Sl st in next ch-2 space, ch 3 (counts as dc), 4 dc in first ch-2 space, ch 1, (5 dc, ch 1) in each ch-2 space around, sl st in 3rd ch of beg ch to join.

Rnd 3: Ch 3 (counts as dc), *2 dc in next dc, FPdc around the post of next dc, 2 dc in next dc, dc in next dc, ch 1, skip next ch-1 space**, dc in next dc; rep from * around, ending last rep at **, sl st in 3rd ch of beg ch to join.

Rnd 4: Ch 1, *sc in dc, hdc in next dc, dc in next dc, FPdc around the post of next dc, dc in next dc, hdc in next dc, sc in next dc, skip next ch-1 space; rep from * around, sl st in first sc to join. Fasten off.

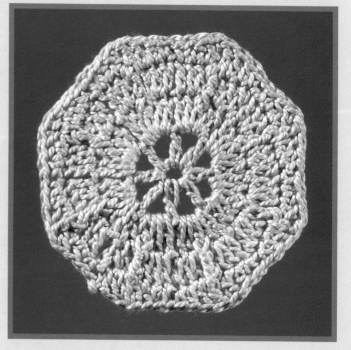

133

Back post double crochet (BPdc): *Yo, insert hook from back to front to back again around the post of next st, yo, draw yarn through st, (yo, draw yarn through 2 loops on hook) twice.*

Beginning popcorn (beg pop): *Ch 3 (counts as dc), 4 dc in same st, drop loop from hook, insert hook from front to back in 3rd ch of beg ch, place dropped loop on hook, draw loop through st.*

Popcorn (pop): *5 dc in same st, drop loop from hook, insert hook from front to back in first dc of 5-dc group, place dropped loop on hook, draw loop through st.*

Ch 6 and sl st in first ch to form a ring.

Rnd 1: Ch 3 (counts as dc), 3 dc in ring, ch 2, (4 dc, ch 2) 3 times in ring, sl st in 3rd ch of beg ch to join.

Rnd 2: Ch 3 (counts as dc), *dc in each of next 3 dc, (2 dc, ch 2, 2 dc) in next ch-2 space**, dc in next dc; rep from * around, ending last rep at **, sl st in 3rd ch of beg ch to join.

Rnd 3: Ch 3 (counts as dc), *BPdc in each of of next 5 dc, (2 dc, ch 2, 2 dc) in next ch-2 space**, BPdc in each of of next 3 dc; rep from * around, ending last rep at **, BPdc in each of of next 2 dc, sl st in 3rd ch of beg ch to join.

Rnd 4: Beg pop in first st, *dc in each of next 2 dc, (pop in next dc, dc in next dc) twice, dc in next dc, (2 dc, ch 2, 2 dc) in next ch-2 space, dc in each of next 2 dc, pop in next dc, dc in next dc**, pop in next dc; rep from * around, ending last rep at **, sl st in 3rd ch of beg ch to join.

Rnd 5: Ch 3 (counts as dc), *dc in each of next 9 sts, (2 dc, ch 2, 2 dc) in next ch-2 space**, dc in each of next 7 sts; rep from * around, ending last rep at **, dc in each of next 6 sts, sl st in 3rd ch of beg ch to join. Fasten off.

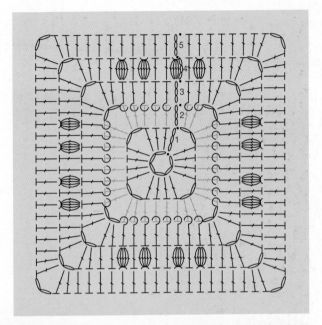

.10.
Shells

134 Ch 6 and sl st in first ch to form a ring.

Rnd 1: Ch 3 (counts as dc), 15 dc in ring, sl st in 3rd ch of beg ch to join.

Rnd 2: Ch 1, *sc in dc, skip next dc, 7 dc in next dc, skip next dc; rep from * around, sl st in first sc to join.

Rnd 3: Ch 3 (counts as dc), (dc, ch 3, 2 dc) in first sc, *ch 3, skip next 3 dc, sc in next dc, ch 3, skip next 3 dc**, (2 dc, ch 3, 2 dc) in next sc; rep from * around, ending last rep at **, sl st in 3rd ch of beg ch to join. Fasten off.

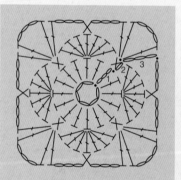

135 Ch 6 and sl st in first ch to form a ring.

Rnd 1: Ch 4 (counts as dc, ch 1), (dc, ch 1) 7 times in ring, sl st in 3rd ch of beg ch to join.

Rnd 2: Sl st in next ch-1 space, ch 3 (counts as dc), 2 dc in first ch-1 space, ch 1, (3 dc, ch 1) in each ch-1 space around, sl st in 3rd ch of beg ch to join.

Rnd 3: Sl st to next ch-1 space, ch 3 (counts as dc), 2 dc in first ch-1 space, *ch 1, (3 dc, ch 3, 3 dc) in next ch-1 space, ch 1**, 3 dc in next ch-1 space; rep from * around, ending last rep at **, sl st in 3rd ch of beg ch to join. Fasten off.

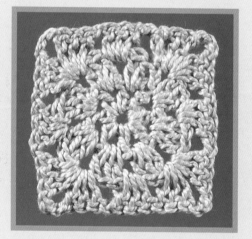

136

Ch 6 and sl st in first ch to form a ring.

Rnd 1: Ch 3 (counts as dc), dc in ring, ch 2, (2 dc, ch 2) 7 times in ring, sl st in 3rd ch of beg ch to join.

Rnd 2: Sl st to next ch-2 space, ch 3 (counts as dc), (dc, ch 2, 2 dc) in first ch-2 space, (2 dc, ch 2, 2 dc) in each ch-2 space around, sl st in 3rd ch of beg ch to join.

Rnd 3: Sl st to next ch-2 space, ch 3 (counts as dc), (2 dc, ch 3, 3 dc) in first ch-2 space, (3 dc, ch 3, 3 dc) in each ch-2 space around, sl st in 3rd ch of beg ch to join.

Rnd 4: Sl st to next ch-3 loop, ch 3 (counts as dc), (3 dc, ch 5, 4 dc) in first ch-3 loop, (4 dc, ch 5, 4 dc) in each ch-3 loop around, sl st in 3rd ch of beg ch to join. Fasten off.

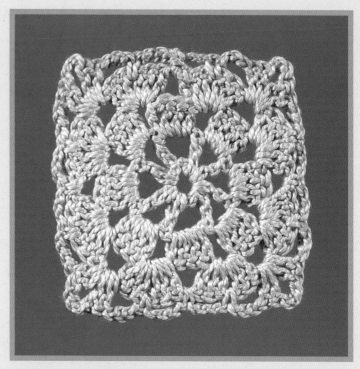

137 Ch 6 and sl st in first ch to form a ring.

Rnd 1: Ch 6 (counts as dc, ch 3), (dc, ch 3) 7 times in ring, sl st in 3rd ch of beg ch to join.

Rnd 2: Sl st in next ch-3 loop, ch 3 (counts as dc), 3 dc in first ch-3 loop, ch 1, (4 dc, ch 1) in each ch-3 loop around, sl st in 3rd ch of beg ch to join.

Rnd 3: Sl st to next ch-1 space, ch 3 (counts as dc), 5 dc in first ch-1 space, ch 1, (6 dc, ch 1) in each ch-1 space around, sl st in 3rd ch of beg ch to join.

Rnd 4: Turn, sl st in next ch-1 space, turn, ch 3 (counts as dc), (dc, ch 3, 2 dc) in first ch-1 space, *ch 3, skip next 3 dc, sc bet last skipped and next dc, ch 3, sc in next ch-1 space, ch 3, skip next 3 dc, sc bet last skipped and next dc, ch 3**, (2 dc, ch 3, 2 dc) in next ch-1 space; rep from * around, ending last rep at **, sl st in 3rd ch of beg ch to join. Fasten off.

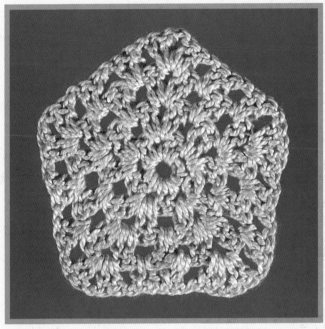

138

Ch 6 and sl st in first ch to form a ring.

Rnd 1: Ch 3 (counts as dc), dc in ring, ch 1 (2 dc, ch 1) 4 times in ring, sl st in 3rd ch of beg ch to join.

Rnd 2: Sl st to next ch-1 space, ch 3 (counts as dc), (dc, ch 1, 2 dc) in first ch-1 space, ch 1, (2 dc, ch 1, 2 dc, ch 1) in each ch-1 space around, sl st in 3rd ch of beg ch to join.

Rnd 3: Sl st to next ch-1 space, ch 3 (counts as dc), (dc, ch 1, 2 dc) in first ch-1 space, *ch 1, 2 dc in next ch-1 space, ch 1**, (2 dc, ch 1, 2 dc) in next ch-1 space; rep from * around, ending last rep at **, sl st in 3rd ch of beg ch to join.

Rnd 4: Sl st to next ch-1 space, ch 3 (counts as dc), (dc, ch 1, 2 dc) in first ch-1 space, *(ch 1, 2 dc) in each of next 2 ch-1 spaces, ch 1**, (2 dc, ch 1, 2 dc) in next ch-1 space; rep from * around, ending last rep at **, sl st in 3rd ch of beg ch to join. Fasten off.

139

Ch 6 and sl st in first ch to form a ring.

Rnd 1: Ch 3 (counts as dc), 15 dc in ring, sl st in 3rd ch of beg ch to join.

Rnd 2: Ch 1, *sc in dc, skip next dc, 5 hdc in next dc, skip next dc; rep from * around, sl st in first sc to join.

Rnd 3: Ch 3 (counts as dc), 6 dc in first sc, *skip next 2 hdc, sc in next hdc, skip next 2 hdc**, 7 dc in next sc; rep from * around, ending last rep at **, sl st in 3rd ch of beg ch to join.

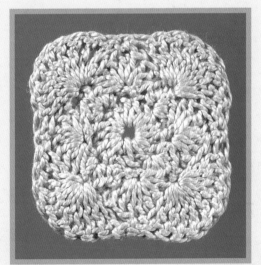

Rnd 4: Sl st in each of next 3 dc, ch 1, *sc in dc, skip next 3 dc, 9 tr in next sc, skip next 3 dc; rep from * around, sl st in first sc to join. Fasten off.

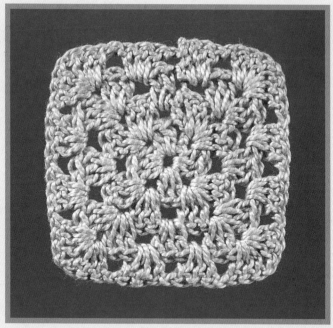

140 Ch 6 and sl st in first ch to form a ring.

Rnd 1: Ch 3 (counts as dc), 2 dc in ring, ch 1, (3 dc, ch 1) 3 times in ring, sl st in 3rd ch of beg ch to join.

Rnd 2: Sl st to next ch-1 space, ch 3 (counts as dc), (2 dc, ch 1, 3 dc) in first ch-1 space, ch 1, (3 dc, ch 1, 3 dc, ch 1) in each ch-1 space around, sl st in 3rd ch of beg ch to join.

Rnd 3: Sl st to next ch-1 space, ch 3 (counts as dc), (2 dc, ch 1, 3 dc) in first ch-1 space, *ch 1, 3 dc in next ch-1 space, ch 1**, (3 dc, ch 1, 3 dc) in next ch-1 space; rep from * around, ending last rep at **, sl st in 3rd ch of beg ch to join.

Rnd 4: Sl st to next ch-1 space, ch 3 (counts as dc), (2 dc, ch 1, 3 dc) in first ch-1 space, *(ch 1, 3 dc) in each of next 2 ch-1 spaces, ch 1**, (3 dc, ch 1, 3 dc) in next ch-1 space; rep from * around, ending last rep at **, sl st in 3rd ch of beg ch to join. Fasten off.

 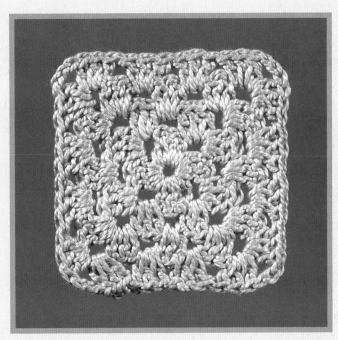

141 **Ch** 6 and sl st in first ch to form a ring.

Rnd 1: Ch 3 (counts as dc), 2 dc in ring,
ch 3, (3 dc, ch 3) 3 times in ring, sl st in 3rd ch of beg ch to join.

Rnd 2: Sl st to next ch-3 loop, ch 3 (counts as dc), (2 dc, ch 3, 3 dc) in first ch-3 loop, ch 1, (3 dc, ch 3, 3 dc, ch 1) in each ch-3 loop around, sl st in 3rd ch of beg ch to join.

Rnd 3: Sl st to next ch-3 loop, ch 3 (counts as dc), (2 dc, ch 3, 3 dc) in first ch-3 loop, *ch 1, 3 dc in next ch-1 space, ch 1**, (3 dc, ch 3, 3 dc) in next ch-3 loop; rep from * around, ending last rep at **, sl st in 3rd ch of beg ch to join.

Rnd 4: Sl st to next ch-3 loop, ch 3 (counts as dc), (2 dc, ch 3, 3 dc) in first ch-3 loop, *(ch 1, 3 dc) in each of next 2 ch-1 spaces, ch 1**, (3 dc, ch 3, 3 dc) in next ch-3 loop; rep from * around, ending last rep at **, sl st in 3rd ch of beg ch to join. Fasten off.

142

Ch 6 and sl st in first ch to form a ring.

Rnd 1: Ch 3 (counts as dc), 2 dc in ring, ch 2, (3 dc, ch 2) 3 times in ring, sl st in 3rd ch of beg ch to join.

Rnd 2: Sl st to next ch-3 loop, ch 3 (counts as dc), (2 dc, ch 2, 3 dc) in first ch-2 space, ch 2, (3 dc, ch 2, 3 dc, ch 2) in each ch-2 space around, sl st in 3rd ch of beg ch to join.

Rnd 3: Ch 3 (counts as dc), *dc in each of next 2 dc, (3 dc, ch 2, 3 dc) in next ch-2 space, dc in each of next 3 dc, 2 dc in next ch-2 space**, dc in next dc; rep from * around, ending last rep at **, sl st in 3rd ch of beg ch to join.

Rnd 4: Sl st in each of next 2 dc, ch 3 (counts as dc), 2 dc in same dc, skip next 3 dc, *(3 dc, ch 2, 3 dc) in next ch-2 space, skip next 3 dc, 3 dc in next dc, skip next 2 dc, 3 dc in next dc, skip next 3 dc**, 3 dc in next dc; rep from * around, ending last rep at **, sl st in 3rd ch of beg ch to join.

Rnd 5: Ch 3 (counts as dc), *dc in each of next 5 dc, (2 dc, ch 2, 2 dc) in next ch-2 space, dc in each of next 10 dc; rep from * around, omitting last dc, sl st in 3rd ch of beg ch to join.

Rnd 6: Ch 1, sc in each st around, working 2 sc in each corner ch-2 space, sl st in first sc to join. Fasten off.

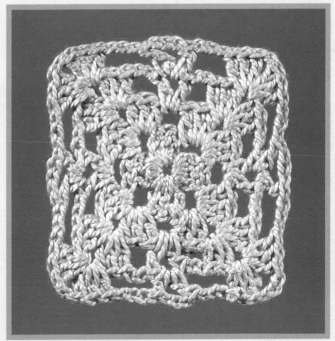

143 Ch 6 and sl st in first ch to form a ring.

Rnd 1: Ch 3 (counts as dc), 2 dc in ring, ch 3, (3 dc, ch 3) 3 times in ring, sl st in 3rd ch of beg ch to join.

Rnd 2: Sl st to next ch-3 loop, ch 3 (counts as dc), (2 dc, ch 1, 3 dc) in first ch-3 loop, ch 2, (3 dc, ch 1, 3 dc, ch 2) in each ch-3 loop around, sl st in 3rd ch of beg ch to join.

Rnd 3: Sl st to next ch-1 space, ch 3 (counts as dc), (2 dc, ch 1, 3 dc) in first ch-1 space, *ch 2, (dc, ch 2, dc) in next ch-2 space, ch 2**, (3 dc, ch 1, 3 dc) in next ch-1 space; rep from * around, ending last rep at **, sl st in 3rd ch of beg ch to join.

Rnd 4: Sl st to next ch-1 space, ch 3 (counts as dc), (2 dc, ch 1, 3 dc) in first ch-1 space, *ch 3, skip next ch-2 space, (dc, ch 3, dc) in next ch-2 space, ch 3, skip next ch-2 space**, (3 dc, ch 1, 3 dc) in next ch-1 space; rep from * around, ending last rep at **, sl st in 3rd ch of beg ch to join. Fasten off.

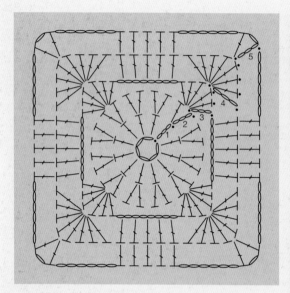

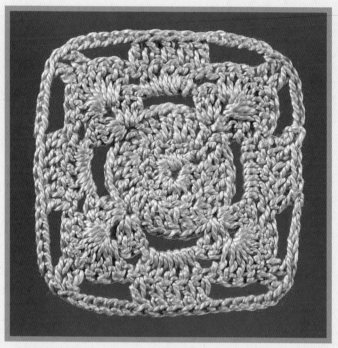

144 Ch 6 and sl st in first ch to form a ring.

Rnd 1: Ch 3 (counts as dc), 11 dc in ring, sl st in 3rd ch of beg ch to join.

Rnd 2: Ch 3 (counts as dc), dc in first dc, 2 dc in each dc around, sl st in 3rd ch of beg ch to join.

Rnd 3: Sl st bet first and 2 dc, ch 3 (counts as dc), 5 dc bet first 2 dc, *ch 8, skip next 6 dc**, 6 dc bet last skipped and next dc; rep from * around, ending last rep at **, sl st in 3rd ch of beg ch to join.

Rnd 4: Sl st in each of next 2 dc, sl st bet next 2 dc, ch 3 (counts as dc), 7 dc in same space bet 2 dc, * 5 dc in next ch-8 loop**, skip next 3 dc, 8 dc bet last skipped and next dc; rep from * around, ending last rep at **, sl st in 3rd ch of beg ch to join.

Rnd 5: Sl st in each of next 3 dc, sl st bet next 2 dc, ch 4 (counts as dc, ch 1), dc in same space bet 2 dc, *ch 6, skip next 4 dc, dc in each of next 5 dc, ch 6, skip next 4 dc**, (dc, ch 1, dc) bet last skipped and next dc; rep from * around, ending last rep at **, sl st in 3rd ch of beg ch to join. Fasten off.

145

Ch 6 and sl st in first ch to form a ring.

Rnd 1: Ch 3 (counts as dc), 2 dc in ring, ch 1, (3 dc, ch 1) 4 times in ring, sl st in 3rd ch of beg ch to join.

Rnd 2: Sl st to next ch-1 space, ch 1, (sc, ch 3, sc, ch 3) in each ch-1 space around, sl st in first sc to join.

Rnd 3: Sl st in next ch-3 loop, ch 3 (counts as dc), (2 dc, ch 1, 3 dc) in first ch-3 loop, *ch 1, 3 dc in next ch-3 loop, ch 1**, (3 dc, ch 1, 3 dc) in next ch-3 loop; rep from * around, ending last rep at **, sl st in 3rd ch of beg ch to join.

Rnd 4: Sl st to next ch-1 space, ch 1, *(sc, ch 3, sc) in ch-1 corner space, (ch 3, sc) in each of next 2 ch-1 spaces, ch 3; rep from * around, sl st in 3rd ch of beg ch to join.

Rnd 5: Sl st in next ch-3 loop, ch 3 (counts as dc), (2 dc, ch 1, 3 dc) in first ch-3 loop, *(ch 1, 3 dc) in each of next 3 ch-3 loops, ch 1**, (3 dc, ch 1, 3 dc) in next ch-3 loop; rep from * around, ending last rep at **, sl st in 3rd ch of beg ch to join.

Rnd 6: Sl st to next ch-1 space, ch 1, *(sc, ch 3, sc) in ch-1 corner space, (ch 3, sc) in each of next 4 ch-1 spaces, ch 3; rep from * around, sl st in 3rd ch of beg ch to join.

Rnd 7: Sl st in next ch-3 loop, ch 3 (counts as dc), (2 dc, ch 1, 3 dc) in first ch-3 loop, *(ch 1, 3 dc) in each of next 5 ch-3 loops, ch 1**, (3 dc, ch 1, 3 dc) in next ch-3 loop; rep from * around, ending last rep at **, sl st in 3rd ch of beg ch to join. Fasten off.

.11.
Picots

146

Picot: Ch 4, sl st in 4th ch from hook.

Ch 12 and sl st in first ch to form a ring.

Rnd 1: Ch 5 (counts as dc, ch 2), *dc in ring, ch 5, dc in ring, ch 2; rep from * twice, dc in ring, ch 5, sl st in 3rd ch of beg ch to join.

Rnd 2: Ch 1, *sc in dc, 2 sc in next ch-2 space, sc in next dc, ch 3, picot, ch 3, skip next ch-5 loop; rep from * around, sl st in first sc to join. Fasten off.

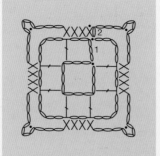

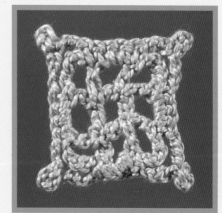

147

Picot: Ch 4, sl st in 4th ch from hook.

Ch 6 and sl st in first ch to form a ring.

Rnd 1: Ch 3 (counts as dc), 15 dc in ring, sl st in 3rd ch of beg ch to join.

Rnd 2: Ch 1, (sc, picot) in each dc around, sl st in 3rd ch of beg ch to join. Fasten off.

148

Picot: Ch 4, sl st in 4th ch from hook.

Ch 8 and sl st in first ch to form a ring.

Rnd 1: Ch 1, 16 sc in ring, sl st in first sc to join.

Rnd 2: Ch 1, *sc in sc, picot, skip next sc; rep from * around, sl st in first sc to join. Fasten off.

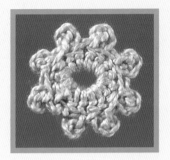

149

Picot: Ch 5, sl st in 5th ch from hook.

Ch 9 and sl st in first ch to form a ring.

Rnd 1: Ch 1, 16 sc in ring, sl st in first sc to join.

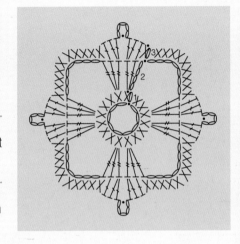

Rnd 2: Ch 4 (counts as tr), 2 tr in first sc, *3 tr in next sc, ch 7, skip next 2 sc**, 3 tr in next sc; rep from * around, ending last rep at **, sl st in 4th ch of beg ch to join.

Rnd 3: Ch 1, *sc in tr, dc in next tr, 2 dc in next tr, picot, 2 dc in next tr, dc in next tr, sc in next tr, 8 sc in next ch-7 loop; rep from * around, sl st in first sc to join. Fasten off.

150

Picot: Ch 4, sl st in 4th ch from hook.

Ch 6 and sl st in first ch to form a ring.

Rnd 1: Ch 1, 16 sc in ring, sl st in first sc to join.

Rnd 2: Ch 3 (counts as dc), skip first sc, dc in each sc around, sl st in 3rd ch of beg ch to join.

Rnd 3: Ch 1, (sc, picot) in each dc around, sl st in first sc to join. Fasten off.

151

*Picot:
Ch 4, sl
st in 4th
ch from hook.*

Ch 6 and sl st in first ch to form a ring.

Rnd 1: Ch 4 (counts as dc, ch 1), (dc, ch 1) 7 times in ring, sl st in 3rd ch of beg ch to join.

Rnd 2: Sl st in next ch-1 space, ch 1, (sc, picot, sc) in first ch-1 space, (ch 1, sc, picot, sc) in each of next 7 ch-1 spaces, sc in first sc to join.

Rnd 3: Ch 8 (counts as dc, ch 5), skip next (sc, picot, sc), (dc, ch 5) in each ch-1 space around, sl st in 3rd ch of beg ch to join.

Rnd 4: Ch 1, *sc in dc, 8 sc in next ch-5 loop; rep from * around, sl st in first sc to join. Fasten off.

152

Ch-3 picot: Ch 3, sl st in 3rd ch from hook.

Ch-4 picot: Ch 4, sl st in 4th ch from hook.

Ch 8 and sl st in first ch to form a ring.

Rnd 1: Ch 3 (counts as dc), 23 dc in ring, sl st in 3rd ch of beg ch to join.

Rnd 2: Ch 4 (counts as dc, ch 1), (dc, ch 1) in each dc around, sl st in 3rd ch of beg ch to join.

Rnd 3: Sl st in first ch-1 space, ch 1, *sc in ch-1 space, ch 2, dc in next ch-1 space, ch-3 picot, sl st in last dc made, ch-4 picot, sl st in last dc made, ch-3 picot, sl st in last dc made, ch 2; rep from * around, sl st in first sc to join. Fasten off.

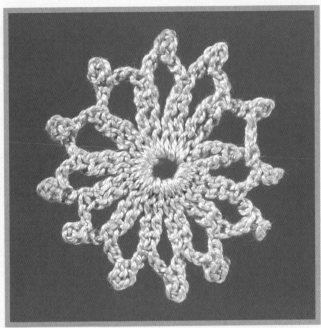

153

Picot: Ch 4, sl st in 4th ch from hook.

Ch 6 and sl st in first ch to form a ring.

Rnd 1: Ch 3 (counts as dc), 15 dc in ring, sl st in 3rd ch of beg ch to join.

Rnd 2: Ch 4 (counts as dc, ch 1), skip first st, (dc, ch 1) in each dc around, sl st in 3rd ch of beg ch to join.

Rnd 3: Sl st in next ch-1 space, ch 3 (counts as dc), 2 dc in first ch-1 space, 3 dc in each ch-1 space around, sl st in 3rd ch of beg ch to join.

Rnd 4: Sl st in each of next 2 dc, sl st bet next 2 dc, ch 1, sc bet same 2 dc, ch 3, *skip next 3 dc, sc bet last skipped and next dc, ch 3; rep from * around, skip next 3 dc, sl st in first sc to join.

Rnd 5: Ch 1, *sc in sc, (sc, picot, sc) in next ch-3 loop; rep from * around, sl st in first sc to join. Fasten off.

154

Picot: Ch 3, sl st in 3rd ch from hook.

Ch 6 and sl st in first ch to form a ring.

Rnd 1: Ch 1, 12 sc in ring, sl st in first sc to join.

Rnd 2: Ch 3 (counts as dc), dc in first sc, ch 3, skip next sc, *puff st in next sc, ch 3, ch 3, skip next sc; rep from * around, sl st in 3rd ch of beg ch to join.

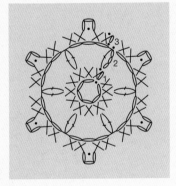

Rnd 3: Sl st in next ch-3 loop, ch 1, (2 sc, picot, 2 sc) in each ch-3 loop around, sl st in first sc to join. Fasten off.

155

Picot: *Ch 5, sl st in 5th ch from hook.*

Ch 10 and sl st in first ch to form a ring.

Rnd 1: Ch 3 (counts as dc), 23 dc in ring, sl st in 3rd ch of beg ch to join.

Rnd 2: *Ch 11, sl st in 5th ch from hook to form a ring, (picot, sl st) 5 times in ring just made, ch 6, skip next 3 dc, sl st in next dc; rep from * around, ending with last sl st in first sl st to join. Fasten off.

156

Picot: *Ch 3, sl st in 3rd ch from hook.*

Ch 6 and sl st in first ch to form a ring.

Rnd 1: Ch 3 (counts as dc), 11 dc in ring, sl st in 3rd ch of beg ch to join.

Rnd 2: *Ch 4, picot, ch 3, sl st in next dc; rep from * around, ending with last sl st in first sl st to join. Fasten off.

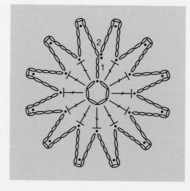

157

Picot: Ch 4, sl st in 4th ch from hook.

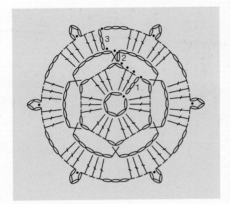

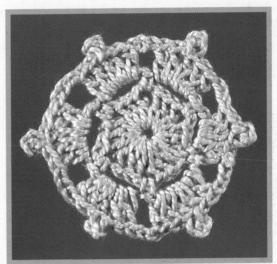

Ch 6 and sl st in first ch to form a ring.

Rnd 1: Ch 3 (counts as dc), 2 dc in ring, ch 2, (3 dc, ch 2) 5 times in ring, sl st in 3rd ch of beg ch to join.

Rnd 2: Sl st to next ch-2 space, ch 1, (sc, ch 5) in each ch-2 space around, sl st in first sc to join.

Rnd 3: Sl st in next ch-5 loop, ch 3 (counts as dc), (2 dc, picot, 3 dc) in first ch-5 loop, ch 3, (3 dc, picot, 3 dc, ch 3) in each ch-5 loop around, sl st in 3rd ch of beg ch to join. Fasten off.

158

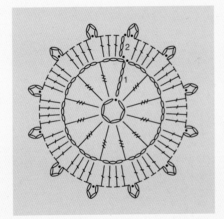

Picot: Ch 4, sl st in 4th ch from hook.

Ch 6 and sl st in first ch to form a ring.

Rnd 1: Ch 8 (counts as dtr, ch 3), (dtr, ch 3) 11 times in ring, sl st in 5th ch of beg ch to join.

Rnd 2: Sl st in next ch-3 loop, ch 3 (counts as dc), 3 dc in first ch-3 loop, picot, (4 dc, picot) in each ch-3 loop around, sl st in 3rd ch of beg ch to join. Fasten off.

159

2-dc puff st: (Yo, insert hook in next space, yo, draw yarn through space, draw yarn through 2 loops on hook) twice in same space, yo, draw yarn through 3 loops on hook.

3-dc puff st: (Yo, insert hook in next space, yo, draw yarn through space, draw yarn through 2 loops on hook) 3 times in same space, yo, draw yarn through 4 loops on hook.

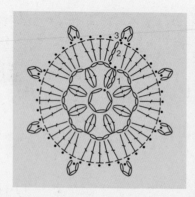

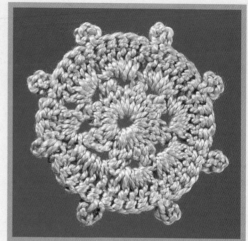

Picot: Ch 4, sl st in 4th ch from hook.

Ch 6 and sl st in first ch to form a ring.

Rnd 1: Ch 3 (counts as dc), 2-dc puff st in ring, ch 3, (3-dc puff st, ch 3) 7 times in ring, sl st in first puff st to join.

Rnd 2: Sl st in next ch-3 loop, ch 3 (counts as dc), 4 dc in first ch-3 loop, 5 dc in each ch-3 loop around, sl st in 3rd ch of beg ch to join.

Rnd 3: Sl st in each of next 4 dc, picot, *sl st in each of next 5 dc, picot; rep from * around, sl st in first sl st to join. Fasten off.

160

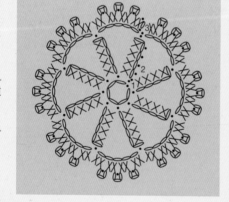

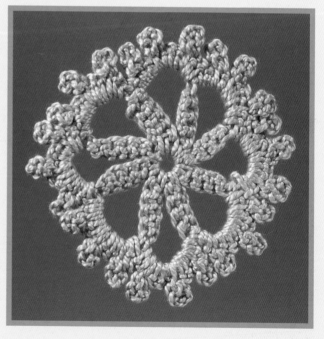

Picot: Ch 3, sl st in 3rd ch from hook.

Ch 6 and sl st in first ch to form a ring.

Rnd 1: *Ch 5, sc in 2nd ch from hook, sc in each of next 3 ch, sl st in ring; rep from * 7 times, ending with last sl st in first sl st to join (8 spokes made).

Rnd 2: Sl st in each of next 5 ch sts, (ch 5, sl st) in tip of each spoke around, ending with last sl st in first sl st to join.

Rnd 3: Sl st in next ch-5 loop, ch 1, *(2 sc, picot, 2 sc, picot, 2 sc, picot, 2 sc) in each ch-5 loop round, sl st in first sc to join. Fasten off.

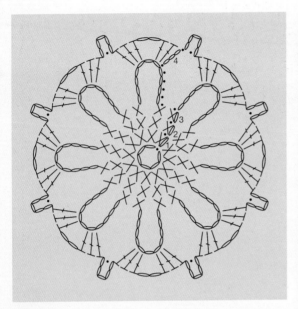

161

Picot: Ch 5, sl st in 5th ch from hook.

Ch 6 and sl st in first ch to form a ring.

Rnd 1: Ch 1, 12 sc in ring, sl st in first sc to join.

Rnd 2: Ch 1, *sc in each of next 2 sc, 2 sc in next sc; rep from * around, sl st in first sc to join.

Rnd 3: Ch 1, *sc in each of next 2 sc, ch 11; rep from * around, sl st in first sc to join.

Rnd 4: Sl st in next sc, sl st to center of next ch-11 loop, ch 3 (counts as dc), (2 dc, ch 2, 3 dc) in first ch-11 loop, picot, (3 dc, ch 2, 3 dc, picot) in each ch-11 loop around, sl st in 3rd ch of beg ch to join. Fasten off.

162

Puff st:
(Yo [3 times], insert hook in next space, yo, draw yarn through space, [yo, draw yarn through 2 loops on hook] 3 times) twice in same space, yo, draw yarn through 3 loops on hook.

Picot: Ch 3, sl st in 3rd ch from hook.

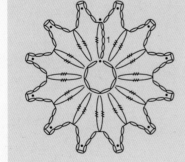

Ch 8 and sl st in first ch to form a ring.

Rnd 1: Ch 5 (counts as dtr), dtr in ring, ch 2, picot, ch 2, *puff st in ring, ch 2, picot, ch 2; rep from * 10 times, sl st in 5th ch of beg ch to join. Fasten off.

163

Picot: Ch 3, sl st in 3rd ch from hook.

Ch 8 and sl st in first ch to form a ring.

Rnd 1: Ch 3 (counts as dc), 2 dc in ring, ch 2, picot, ch 2, *3 dc in ring, ch 2, picot, ch 2; rep from * 5 times, sl st in 3rd ch of beg ch to join.

Rnd 2: Sl st in next dc, ch 1, *sc in dc, ch 10, skip next (dc, ch 2, picot, ch 2, dc); rep from * around, sl st in first sc to join. Fasten off.

164

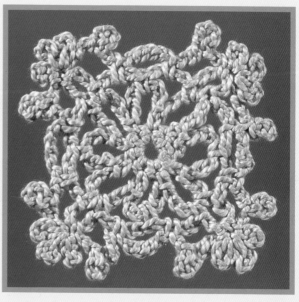

Ch-4 picot: Ch 4, sl st in 4th ch from hook.

Ch-5 picot: Ch 5, sl st in 5th ch from hook.

Ch 6 and sl st in first ch to form a ring.

Rnd 1: Ch 1, 8 sc in ring, sl st in first sc to join.

Rnd 2: Ch 1, (sc, ch 8) in each sc around, sl st in first sc to join.

Rnd 3: Sl st to center of next ch-8 loop, ch 1, *sc in ch-8 loop, ch 4, (sc, ch 5, sc) in next ch-8 loop, ch 4; rep from * around, sl st in first sc to join.

Rnd 4: Sl st to center of first ch-4 loop, ch 1, *sc in ch-4 loop, ch 2, ch-4 picot, ch 2, sc in next ch-5 loop, ch-4 picot, sl st in last sc made, ch-5 picot, sl st in last sc made, ch-4 picot, sl st in last sc made, ch 2, ch-4 picot, ch 2, sc in next ch-4 loop, ch 5; rep from * around, sl st in first sc to join. Fasten off.

165

Ch-3 picot: Ch 3, sl st in 3rd ch from hook.

Ch-4 picot: Ch 4, sl st in 4th ch from hook.

Ch-5 picot: Ch 5, sl st in 5th ch from hook.

Ch 6 and sl st in first ch to form a ring.

Rnd 1: Ch 3 (counts as dc), 2 dc in ring, ch-4 picot, (3 dc, ch-4 picot) 7 times in ring, sl st in 3rd ch of beg ch to join.

Rnd 2: Sl st in next dc, ch 8 (counts as dc, ch 5), skip next (dc, picot, dc), *dc in next dc, ch 5, skip next (dc, picot, dc); rep from * around, sl st in 3rd ch of beg ch to join.

Rnd 3: Ch 1, *sc in dc, ch 5, sc in next ch-5 loop, ch 5; rep from * around, sl st in first sc to join.

Rnd 4: Sl st to center of first ch-5 loop, ch 1, *sc in ch-5 loop, ch 2, (dc, ch-3 picot, dc, ch-5 picot, dc, ch-3 picot, dc) in next ch-5 loop, ch 2; rep from * around, sl st in first sc to join. Fasten off.

166

Picot: Ch 4, sl st in 4th ch from hook.

Ch 6 and sl st in first ch to form a ring.

Rnd 1: (Ch 3, dc, ch 3, sl st) 8 times in ring.

Rnd 2: Sl st to top of first ch-3 loop, ch 3 (counts as dc), 2-dc cluster, working first half-closed dc in next dc, work 2nd half-closed dc in next ch-3 loop, yo, complete cluster, ch 6, 3-dc cluster worked across next (ch-3 loop, dc, ch-3 loop), ch 6; rep from * around, sl st in 3rd ch of beg ch to join.

Rnd 3: Ch 1, *sc in next cluster, 6 sc in next ch-6 loop; rep from * around, sl st in first sc to join.

Rnds 4-5: Ch 1, sc in each sc around, sl st in first sc to join.

Rnd 6: Ch 1, sc in first 4 sc, *picot, sc in each of next 7 sc; rep from * 6 times, picot, sc in each of last 3 sc, sl st in first sc to join. Fasten off.

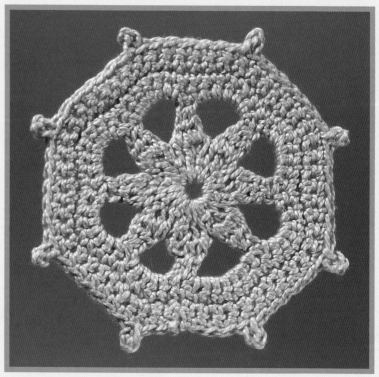

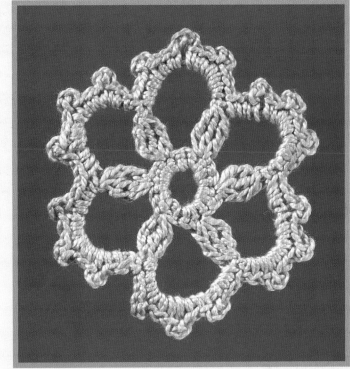

167

2-tr puff st: *(Yo [twice], insert hook in next st, yo, draw yarn through st, [yo, draw yarn through 2 loops on hook] twice) twice in same st, yo, draw yarn through 3 loops on hook.*

3-tr puff st: *(Yo [twice], insert hook in next st, yo, draw yarn through st, [yo, draw yarn through 2 loops on hook] twice) 3 times in same st, yo, draw yarn through 4 loops on hook.*

Picot: *Ch 3, sl st in 3rd ch from hook.*

Ch 10 and sl st in first ch to form a ring.

Rnd 1: Ch 1, 18 sc in ring, sl st in first sc to join.

Rnd 2: Ch 4 (counts as tr), 2-tr puff st in first sc, ch 10, skip next 2 sc, *3-tr puff st in next sc, ch 10, skip next 2 sc; rep from * around, sl st in first puff st to join.

Rnd 3: Sl st in next ch-10 loop, ch 1, (3 sc, picot, 3 sc, picot, 3 sc, picot, 3 sc) in each ch-10 loop around, sl st in first sc to join. Fasten off.

168

Picot: Ch 4, sl st in 4th ch from hook.

Ch 6 and sl st in first ch to form a ring.

Rnd 1: Ch 1, 12 sc in ring, sl st in first sc to join.

Rnd 2: Ch 6 (counts as dc, ch 3), skip next sc, *dc in next sc, ch 3, skip next sc; rep from * around, sl st in 3rd ch of beg ch to join.

Rnd 3: Sl st in next ch-3 loop, ch 1, (sc, hdc, 3 dc, hdc, sc) in each ch-3 loop around, sl st in first sc to join.

Rnd 4: Sl st in each of next 3 sts, ch 1, *sc in center dc of shell, ch 10, skip next 6 sts; rep from * around, sl st in first sc to join.

Rnd 5: Sl st in next ch-10 loop, ch 1, (5 sc, picot, 5 sc) in each ch-10 loop around, sl st in first sc to join. Fasten off.

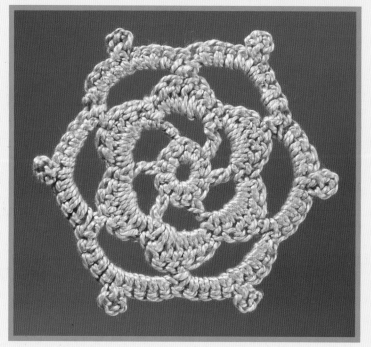

169

Picot: *Ch 3, sl st in 3rd ch from hook.*

Ch 6 and sl st in first ch to form a ring.

Rnd 1: Ch 1, (sc, ch 7) 8 times in ring, sl st in first sc to join.

Rnd 2: Sl st to center of first ch-6 loop, ch 1, (sc, ch 5) in each ch-6 loop around, sl st in first sc to join.

Rnd 3: Ch 1, *sc in sc, ch 3, (dc, ch 3, dc) in next ch-3 loop, ch 3; rep from * around, sl st in first sc to join.

Rnd 4: Ch 1, *sc in sc, ch 3, skip next ch-3 loop, (dc, picot) 5 times in next ch-3 loop, dc in same ch-3 loop, ch 3, skip next ch-3 loop; rep from * around, sl st in first sc to join. Fasten off.

170

Picot: Ch 3, sl st in 3rd ch from hook.

Ch 13 and sl st in first ch to form a ring.

Rnd 1 (RS): Ch 1, 25 sc in ring, sl st in first sc to join.

Rnd 2: Ch 1, *sc in sc, ch 6, skip next 4 sc; rep from * around, sl st in first sc to join.

Rnd 3: Sl st in next ch-6 loop, ch 1, (sc, hdc, dc, 4 tr, dc, hdc, sc) in each ch-6 loop around, sl st in first sc to join.

Rnd 4: Sl st in each of next 2 sts, ch 1, *sc in dc, picot, ch 5, picot, skip next 4 sts; rep from * around, sl st in first sc to join. Fasten off.

Rnd 5: With RS facing, join yarn in center of any ch-5 loop, ch 1, (sc, ch 9) in each ch-5 loop around, sl st in first sc to join.

Rnd 6: Sl st in next ch-9 loop, ch 1, (3 sc, picot, 3 sc, picot, 3 sc, picot, 3 sc) in each ch-9 loop around, sl st in first sc to join. Fasten off.

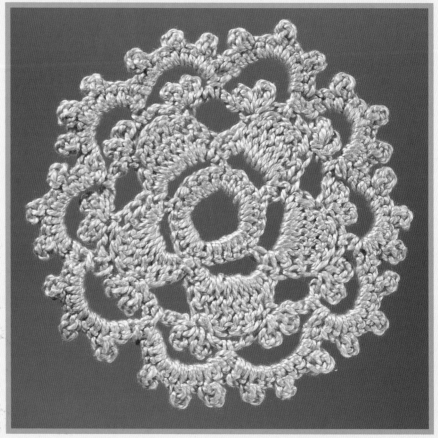

171

Picot: Ch 3, sl st in 3rd ch from hook.

Ch 12 and sl st in first ch to form a ring.

Rnd 1: Ch 4 (counts as tr), 4 tr in ring, ch 2, (5 tr, ch 2) 5 times in ring, sl st in 4th ch of beg ch to join.

Rnd 2: Sl st to next ch-2 space, ch 1, (2 sc, ch 9) in each ch-2 space around, sl st in first sc to join.

Rnd 3: Sl st to next ch-9 loop, ch 1, 13 sc in each ch-9 loop around, sl st in first sc to join.

Rnd 4: Sl st in each of next 3 sc, ch 1, *sc in each of next 7 sc, ch 9, skip next 6 sc; rep from * around, sl st in first sc to join.

Rnd 5: Ch 1, *sc in each of next 7 sc, (sc, picot, [2 sc, picot] 4 times, sc) in next ch-9 loop; rep from * around, sl st in first sc to join. Fasten off.

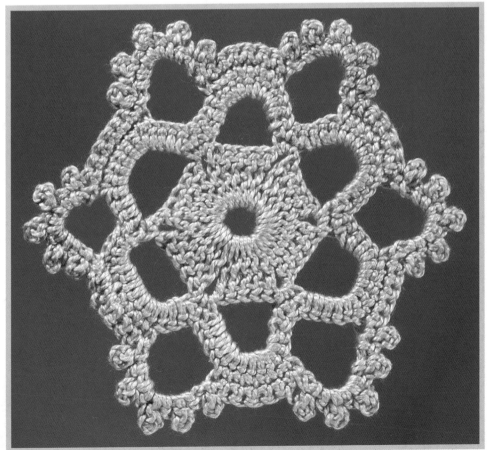

172

Picot: Ch 3, sl st in 3rd ch from hook.

Ch 14 and sl st in first ch to form a ring.

Rnd 1: Ch 1, 18 sc in ring, sl st in first sc to join.

Rnd 2: Ch 1, *sc in sc, ch 18, skip next 5 sc; rep from * around, sl st in first sc to join.

Rnd 3: Sl st in next ch-18 loop, ch 1, 18 sc in each ch-18 loop around, sl st in first sc to join.

Rnd 4: Ch 1, *sc in sc, ch 3, skip next sc; rep from * around, sl st in first sc to join.

Rnd 5: Sl st to center of next ch-3 loop, ch 1, (sc, ch 4) in each ch-3 loop around, sl st in first sc to join.

Rnd 6: Sl st in next ch-4 loop, ch 1, 4 sc in each ch-4 loop around, sl st in first sc to join.

Rnd 7: Ch 1, *sc in each of next 4 sc, picot; rep from * around, sl st in first sc to join. Fasten off.

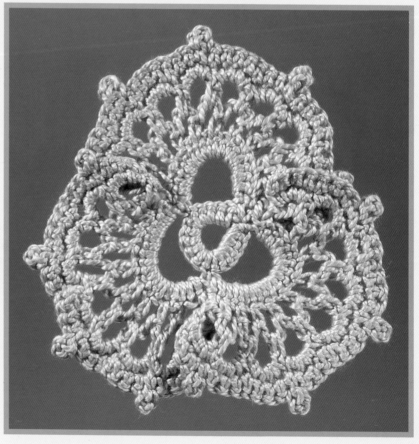

.12.
Mixed Stitches

173

Ch 6 and sl st in first ch to form a ring.

Rnd 1: Ch 3 (counts as dc), 3 dc in ring, (ch 3, 4 dc) 3 times in ring, ch 1, hdc in 3rd ch of beg ch to join.

Rnd 2: (Ch 10, sl st) in each ch-3 loop around, ending with last sl st in hdc at end of Rnd 1 to join.

Rnd 3: Ch 1, *sc in sl st, 12 sc in next ch-11 loop; rep from * around, sl st in first sc to join.

Rnd 4: Sl st in each of next 3 sc, ch 1, *sc in each of next 8 sc, ch 5, skip next 5 sc; rep from * around, sl st in first sc to join.

Rnd 5: Sl st in next sc, ch 1, *sc in each of next 6 sc, ch 5, 4 dc in next ch-5 loop, ch 5, skip next sc; rep from * around, sl st in first sc to join. Fasten off.

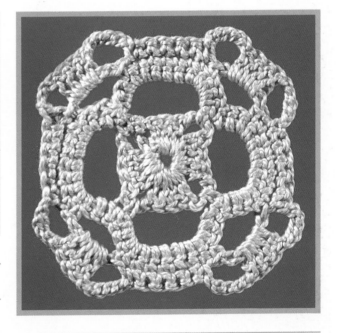

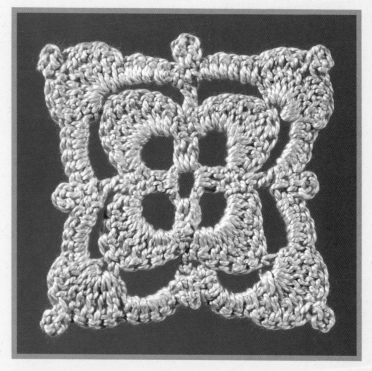

174

Picot: Ch 4, sl st in 4th ch from hook.

Ch 8 and sl st in first ch to form a ring.

Rnd 1: Ch 3 (counts as dc), dc in ring, ch 6, (2 dc, ch 6) 3 times in ring, sl st in 3rd ch of beg ch to join.

Rnd 2: Ch 1, *sc in each of next 2 dc, (sc, hdc, 2 dc, 3 tr, 2 dc, hdc, sc) in next ch-6 loop; rep from * around, sl st in first sc to join.

Rnd 3: Sl st bet first 2 sc, ch 9 (counts as dc, ch 6), *skip next 6 sts, sc in next tr, ch 6, skip next 6 sts**, dc bet last skipped and next sc; rep from * around, ending last rep at **, sl st in 3rd ch of beg ch to join.

Rnd 4: Sl st in next ch-6 loop, ch 1, *6 sc in ch-6 loop, (4 dc, picot, 4 dc) in next sc, 6 sc in next ch-6 loop, picot; rep from * around, sl st in first sc to join. Fasten off.

175

Picot: Ch 4, sl st in 4th ch from hook.

Ch 8 and sl st in first ch to form a ring.

Rnd 1: Ch 1, 12 sc in ring, sl st in first sc to join.

Rnd 2: Ch 7 (counts as tr, ch 3), tr in first sc, ch 5, skip next 2 sc, *(tr, ch 3, tr) in next sc, ch 5, skip next 2 sc; rep from * around, sl st in 4th ch of beg ch to join.

Rnd 3: Sl st to next ch-5 loop, ch 3 (counts as dc), (4 dc, picot, 4 dc, picot, 5 dc) in first ch-5 loop, (5 dc, picot, 4 dc, picot, 5 dc) in each ch-5 loop around, sl st in 3rd ch of beg ch to join. Fasten off.

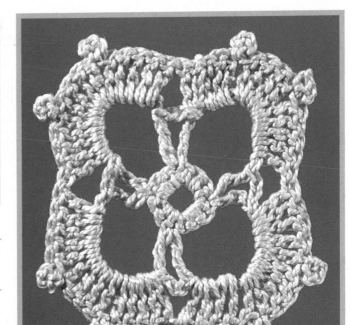

176

Ch 6 and sl st in first ch to form a ring.

Rnd 1: Ch 3 (counts as dc), 15 dc in ring, sl st in 3rd ch of beg ch to join.

Rnd 2: Ch 3 (counts as dc), dc in next dc, ch 2, *dc in each of next 2 dc, ch 2; rep from * around, sl st in 3rd ch of beg ch to join.

Rnd 3: Sl st in next dc, ch 3 (counts as dc), *2 dc in next ch-2 space, dc in next dc, ch 3**, dc in next dc; rep from * around, ending last rep at **, sl st in 3rd ch of beg ch to join.

Rnd 4: Ch 2 (counts as hdc), *hdc in each of next 3 dc, 4 hdc in next ch-3 loop**, hdc in next dc; rep from * around, ending last rep at **, sl st in 2nd ch of beg ch to join. Fasten off.

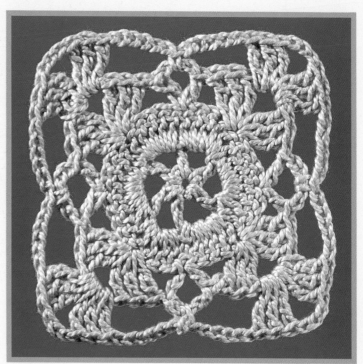

177

Ch 6 and sl st in first ch to form a ring.

Rnd 1: Ch 6 (counts as dc, ch 3), (dc, ch 3) 5 times in ring, sl st in 3rd ch of beg ch to join.

Rnd 2: Ch 3 (counts as dc), *5 dc in next ch-3 loop, (dc in next dc, 4 dc in next ch-3 loop) twice*, dc in next dc; rep from * to * once, sl st in 3rd ch of beg ch to join.

Rnd 3: Ch 8 (counts as dc, ch 5), dc in first st, *skip next 3 dc, (3 tr, ch 3, 3 tr) in next dc, skip next 3 dc**, (dc, ch 5, dc) in next dc; rep from * around, ending last rep at **, sl st in 3rd ch of beg ch to join.

Rnd 4: Sl st to center of next ch-5 loop, ch 1, *sc in ch-5 loop, ch 6, (3 tr, ch 3, 3 tr) in next ch-3 loop, ch 6; rep from * around, sl st in first sc to join. Fasten off.

178

Ch 10 and sl st in first ch to form a ring.

Rnd 1: Ch 4 (counts as tr), 6 tr in ring, ch 4, (7 tr, ch 4) 3 times in ring, sl st in 4th ch of beg ch to join.

Rnd 2: Ch 1, *sc in each of next 7 tr, 3 sc in next ch-3 loop; rep from * around, sl st in first sc to join.

Rnd 3: Sl st in next sc, ch 5 (counts as dc, ch 2), (skip next sc, dc in next sc, ch 2) 3 times, *(dc, ch 2, dc) in next sc, ch 2, dc in next sc**, (ch 2, skip next sc, dc in next sc) 4 times; rep from * around, ending last rep at **, ch 2, sl st in 3rd ch of beg ch to join.

Rnd 4: Sl st in next ch-2 space, ch 1, (sc, ch 5) in each ch-2 space around, sl st in first sc to join.

Rnd 5: Sl st to center of first ch-5 loop, ch 1, (sc, ch 5) in each ch-5 loop around, sl st in first sc to join. Fasten off.

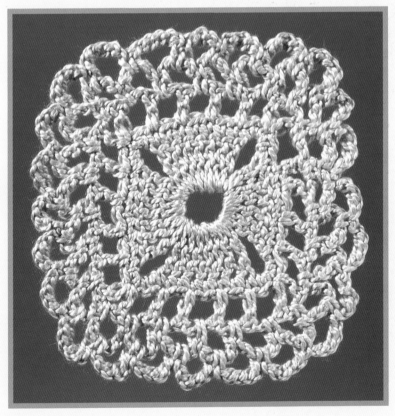

179

Picot: Ch 4, sl st in 4th ch from hook.

Ch 8 and sl st in first ch to form a ring.

Rnd 1: Ch 6 (counts as dc, ch 3), (dc, ch 3) 7 times in ring, sl st in 3rd ch of beg ch to join.

Rnd 2: Sl st in next ch-3 loop, ch 1, (sc, hdc, 3 dc, hdc, sc) in each ch-3 loop around, sl st in first sc to join.

Rnd 3: Sl st in each of next 3 sts, ch 1, *sc in center dc of shell, ch 2, skip next 3 sts, (dc, ch 3, dc) bet last skipped and next sc, ch 2, skip next 3 sts, sc in next dc, ch 6, skip next 6 sts; rep from * around, sl st in first sc to join.

Rnd 4: Sl st to next ch-3 loop, ch 1, *sc in ch-3 loop, ch 4, skip next ch-2 space, (3 dc, ch 3, 3 dc) in next ch-6 loop, ch 4, skip next ch-2 space; rep from * around, sl st in first sc to join.

Rnd 5: Ch 1, *sc in sc, picot, ch 4, skip next ch-4 loop, dc in each of next 3 dc, ch 2, picot, ch 2, skip next ch-3 loop dc in each of next 3 dc, ch 4, skip next ch-4 loop; rep from * around, sl st in first sc to join. Fasten off.

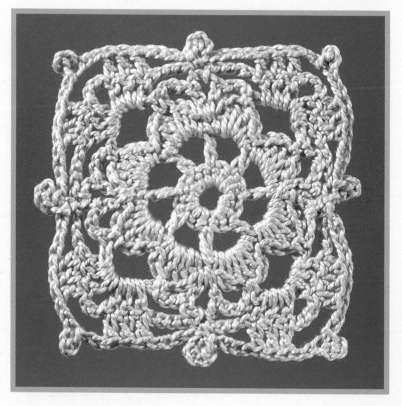

180

Ch 10 and sl st in first ch to form a ring.

Rnd 1: Ch 1, 24 sc in ring, sl st in first sc to join.

Rnd 2: Ch 1, *sc in sc, ch 8, skip next 5 sc; rep from * around, sl st in first sc to join.

Rnd 3: Ch 1, *sc in sc, 9 sc in next ch-8 loop; rep from * around, sl st in first sc to join.

Rnd 4: Ch 1, *sc in each of next 5 sc, (sc, ch 1, sc) in next sc, sc in each of next 4 sc; rep from * around, sl st in first sc to join.

Rnd 5: Sl st in next sc, ch 4 (counts as dc, ch 1), skip next sc, *dc in next sc, ch 1, skip next 2 sc, (dc, ch 3, dc) in next ch-1 space, ch 1, skip next 2 sc, (dc in next sc, ch 1, skip next sc) 3 times; rep from * around, omitting last (dc, ch 1), sl st in first sc to join.

Rnd 6: Ch 1, *(sc in dc, sc in next ch-1 space) twice, sc in next dc, (sc, ch 1, sc) in next ch-3 loop, (sc in next dc, sc in next ch-1 space) 3 times; rep from * around, sl st in first sc to join.

Rnd 7: Sl st in next sc, ch 4 (counts as dc, ch 1), skip next sc, *dc in next sc, ch 1, skip next sc, dc in next sc, ch 1, (dc, ch 2, dc) in next ch-1 space, ch 1, dc in next sc, ch 1, (skip next sc, dc in next sc, ch 1) 4 times; around, omitting last (dc, ch 1), sl st in 3rd ch of beg ch to join.

Rnd 8: Ch 1, *(sc in dc, sc in next ch-1 space) 3 times, sc in next dc, (sc, ch 1, sc) in next ch-2 space, (sc in next dc, sc in next ch-1 space) 5 times; rep from * around, sl st in first sc to join. Fasten off.

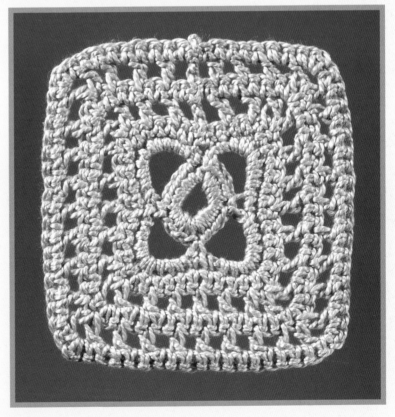

181

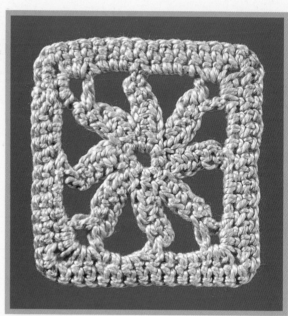

Ch 6 and sl st in first ch to form a ring.

Rnd 1 (RS): Ch 1, *sc in ring, ch 5, sc in 2nd ch from hook, sc in next ch, hdc in each of next 2 ch; rep from * 7 times, sl st in first sc to join (8 petals made). Fasten off.

Rnd 2: With RS facing, join yarn in the tip of any petal, *ch 4, (dc, ch 2, dc) in tip of next petal, ch 4, sl st in tip of next petal; rep from * around, ending with last sl st in first sl st to join.

Rnd 3: Ch 1, *sc in sl st, 4 sc in next ch-4 loop, sc in next dc, 3 sc in next ch-2 space, sc in next dc, 4 sc in next ch-4 loop; rep from * around, sl st in first sc to join.

Rnd 4: Ch 1, sc in each of next 7 sc, (sc, ch 1, sc) in next sc, sc in each of next 6 sc; rep from * around, sl st in first sc to join. Fasten off.

182

Center Square:

Ch 20.

Row 1 (RS): Dc in 8th ch from hook, *ch 2, skip next 2 ch, dc in next ch; rep from * 3 times, turn.

Row 2: Ch 5 (counts as dc, ch 2), skip next ch-2 space, (dc, ch 2) in each of next 4 dc, dc in 5th ch of turning ch, turn.

Rows 3-5: Ch 5 (counts as dc, ch 2), skip next ch-2 space, (dc, ch 2) in each of next 4 dc, dc in 3rd ch of turning ch, turn. Fasten off.

Border:

Rnd 1: With RS facing, join yarn in upper right-hand corner loop, ch 3 (counts as dc), 9 dc in corner loop, *2 dc in each of next 3 ch-2 spaces, 10 dc in next corner loop, working across side edge of Center Square, 2 dc in each of next 3 row-end sts*, 10 dc in next corner loop; rep from * to * once, sl st in 3rd ch of beg ch to join.

Rnd 2: Ch 3, skip next 3 dc, sl st in each of next 2 dc, ch 3, skip next 3 dc, sl st in next dc, ch 7, skip next 6 dc, sl st in next dc; rep from * around, ending with last sl st in first sl st to join.

Rnd 3: *Turn*, sl st in next ch-7 loop, *turn*, ch 7 (counts as tr, ch 3), *skip next ch-3 loop, sl st bet next 2 sl sts, ch 3, skip next ch-3 loop, (tr, ch 1) 11 times in next ch-7 loop**, tr in same ch-7 loop; rep from * around, ending last rep at **, sl st in 4th ch of beg ch to join. Fasten off.

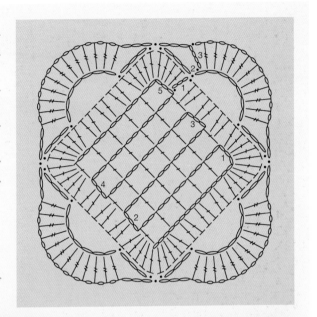

183

2-dc puff st: *(Yo, insert hook in next st, yo, draw yarn through st, draw yarn through 2 loops on hook) twice in same st, yo, draw yarn through 3 loops on hook.*

3-tr puff st: *(Yo [twice], insert hook in next st, yo, draw yarn through st, [yo, draw yarn through 2 loops on hook] twice) 3 times in same st, yo, draw yarn through 4 loops on hook.*

Ch 6 and sl st in first ch to form a ring.

Rnd 1: Ch 5 (counts as dc, ch 2), (dc, ch 2) 7 times in ring, sl st in 3rd ch of beg ch to join.

Rnd 2: Ch 7 (counts as dc, ch 4), 2-dc puff st in 5th ch from hook, skip next ch-2 space, *dc in next dc, ch 4, 2-dc puff st in last dc made, skip next ch-2 space; rep from * around, sl st in 3rd ch of beg ch to join.

Rnd 3: Ch 1, *sc in dc, ch 3, skip next ch-4 loop, (3-tr puff st, ch 4, 3-tr puff st, ch 4, 3-tr puff st) in next dc, ch 3; rep from * around, sl st in first sc to join.

Rnd 4: Sl st in next ch-3 loop, ch 1, *4 sc in ch-3 loop, 4 sc in next ch-4 loop, ch 2, 4 sc in next ch-4 loop, 4 sc in next ch-3 loop; rep from * around, sl st in first sc to join.

Rnd 5: Ch 4 (counts as tr), *tr in each of next 2 sc, dc in each of next 5 sc, (2 dc, ch 2, 2 dc) in next ch-2 space, dc in each of next 5 sc, tr in each of next 4 sc; rep from * around, omitting last tr, sl st in 4th ch of beg ch to join. Fasten off.

184

2-dc puff st: *(Yo, insert hook in next space, yo, draw yarn through space, draw yarn through 2 loops on hook) twice in same space, yo, draw yarn through 3 loops on hook.*

3-dc puff st: *(Yo, insert hook in next space, yo, draw yarn through space, draw yarn through 2 loops on hook) 3 times in same space, yo, draw yarn through 4 loops on hook.*

Picot: *Ch 4, sl st in 4th ch from hook.*

Ch 8 and sl st in first ch to form a ring.

Rnd 1: Ch 3 (counts as dc), 2-dc puff st in ring, *ch 1, 3-dc puff st in ring, ch 3, 3-dc puff st in ring; rep from * twice, ch 1, 3-dc puff st in ring, ch 3, sl st in 3rd ch of beg ch to join.

Rnd 2: Sl st in next ch-1 space, ch 3 (counts as dc), (dc, ch 2, 2 dc) in first ch-1 space, *ch 2, (2-dc puff st, ch 3, 2-dc puff st) in next ch-3 loop, ch 2**, (2 dc, ch 2, 2 dc) in next ch-2 space; rep from * around, ending last rep at **, sl st in 3rd ch of beg ch to join.

Rnd 3: Sl st in next ch-2 space, ch 3 (counts as dc), (dc, ch 2, 2 dc) in first ch-2 space, *ch 4, skip next ch-2 space, (2-dc puff st, ch 3, 2-dc puff st) in next ch-3 loop, ch 4, skip next ch-2 space**, (2 dc, ch 2, 2 dc) in next ch-2 space; rep from * around, ending last rep at **, sl st in 3rd ch of beg ch to join.

Rnd 4: Sl st in next ch-2 space, ch 3 (counts as dc), (dc, picot, 2 dc) in first ch-2 space, *ch 5, skip next ch-4 loop, (2-dc puff st, ch 5, 2-dc puff st) in next ch-3 loop, ch 5, skip next ch-4 loop**, (2 dc, picot, 2 dc) in next ch-2 space; rep from * around, ending last rep at **, sl st in 3rd ch of beg ch to join. Fasten off.

185

Ch 6 and sl st in first ch to form a ring.

Rnd 1: Ch 8 (counts as dc, ch 5), (dc, ch 5) 4 times in ring, sl st in 3rd ch of beg ch to join.

Rnd 2: Ch 1, *sc in dc, 9 sc in next ch-5 loop; rep from * around, sl st in first sc to join.

Rnd 3: Ch 1, *sc in sc, ch 9, skip next 9 sc; rep from * around, sl st in first sc to join.

Rnd 4: Ch 1, *sc in sc, 16 sc in next ch-9 loop; rep from * around, sl st in first sc to join.

Rnd 5: Ch 1, *sc in sc, ch 12, skip next 16 sc; rep from * around, sl st in first sc to join.

Rnd 6: Ch 1, *sc in sc, 20 sc in next ch-12 loop; rep from * around, sl st in first sc to join. Fasten off.

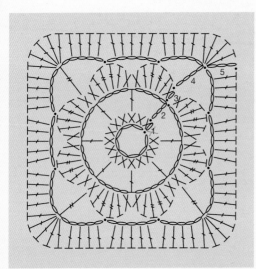

186

Ch 8 and sl st in first ch to form a ring.

Rnd 1: Ch 1, 16 sc in ring, sl st in first sc to join.

Rnd 2: Ch 7 (counts as dc, ch 4), skip next sc, *dc in next sc, ch 4, skip next sc; rep from * around, sl st in 3rd ch of beg ch to join.

Rnd 3: Sl st in next ch-4 loop, ch 1, (sc, dc, 2 tr, dc, sc) in each ch-4 loop around, sl st in first sc to join.

Rnd 4: Ch 9 (counts as tr, ch 5), *skip next 2 sts, sl st bet last skipped and next tr, ch 5, skip next 6 sts, sl st bet last skipped and next tr, ch 5, skip next 3 sts**, tr in next sc, ch 5; rep from * around, ending last rep at **, sl st in 4th ch of beg ch to join.

Rnd 5: Ch 3 (counts as dc), 4 dc in first st, *4 dc in next ch-5 loop, 5 dc in next ch-5 loop, 4 dc in next ch-5 loop**, 5 dc in next tr; rep from * around, sl st in 3rd ch of beg ch to join. Fasten off.

187

Ch 6 and sl st in first ch to form a ring.

Rnd 1: Ch 3 (counts as dc), 2 dc in ring, ch 4, (3 dc, ch 4) 5 times in ring, sl st in 3rd ch of beg ch to join.

Rnd 2: Ch 4 (counts as tr), 2 tr bet first 2 tr, *tr in next tr, 2 tr bet same tr and next tr, tr in next tr, ch 4, skip next ch-4 loop**, tr in next tr, 2 tr bet same tr and next tr; rep from * around, ending last rep at **, sl st in 4th ch of beg ch to join.

Rnd 3: Ch 4 (counts as tr), tr bet first 2 tr, *tr bet next 2 tr, tr in next tr, ch 4, skip next tr, tr in next tr, tr bet same tr and next tr, tr bet next 2 tr, tr in next tr, ch 5, skip next ch-4 loop**, tr in next tr, tr bet same tr and next tr; rep from * around, ending last rep at **, sl st in 4th ch of beg ch to join. Fasten off.

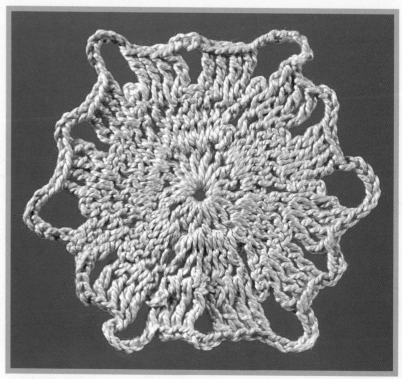

188

Ch 9 and sl st in first ch to form a ring.

Rnd 1: Ch 6 (counts as dc, ch 3), (dc, ch 3) 9 times in ring, sl st in 3rd ch of beg ch to join.

Rnd 2: Sl st in next ch-3 loop, ch 3 (counts as dc), 3 dc in first ch-3 loop, ch 2, (4 dc, ch 2) in each ch-3 loop around, sl st in 3rd ch of beg ch to join.

Rnd 3: Sl st to next ch-2 space, ch 3 (counts as dc), 4 dc in first ch-2 space, ch 3, (5 dc, ch 3) in each ch-2 space around, sl st in 3rd ch of beg ch to join.

Rnd 4: Sl st to next ch-3 loop, ch 1, (sc, ch 9) in each ch-3 loop around, sl st in first sc to join.

Rnd 5: Sl st in next ch-9 loop, ch 1, 11 sc in each ch-9 loop around, sl st in first sc to join.

Rnd 6: Ch 1, sc in each sc around, sl st in first sc to join. Fasten off.

189

2-dc puff st: (Yo, insert hook in next space, yo, draw yarn through space, draw yarn through 2 loops on hook) twice in same space, yo, draw yarn through 3 loops on hook.

3-dc puff st: (Yo, insert hook in next st or space, yo, draw yarn through st or space, draw yarn through 2 loops on hook) 3 times in same st or space, yo, draw yarn through 4 loops on hook.

Picot: Ch 4, sl st in 4th ch from hook.

Ch 6 and sl st in first ch to form a ring.

Rnd 1: Ch 1, 12 sc in ring, sl st in first sc to join.

Rnd 2: Ch 1, *sc in sc, ch 3, skip next 2 sc; rep from * around, sl st in first sc to join.

Rnd 3: Ch 1, *sc in sc, (hdc, 3 dc, hdc) in next ch-3 loop; rep from * around, sl st in first sc to join.

Rnd 4: Sl st in each of next 3 sts, ch 1, *sc in dc, ch 5, skip next 5 sts; rep from * around, sl st in first sc to join.

Rnd 5: Sl st in next ch-5 loop, ch 1, (sc, hdc, 5 dc, hdc, sc) in each ch-5 loop around, sl st in first sc to join.

Rnd 6: Sl st in each of next 4 sts, ch 1, *sc in dc, ch 4, skip next 4 sts, working over last rnd, 3-dc puff st in next corresponding sc 2 rnds below, ch 4, skip next 4 sts; rep from * around, sl st in first sc to join.

Rnd 7: Sl st in next ch-4 loop, ch 3 (counts as dc), (2-dc puff st, ch 2, 3-dc puff st) in first ch-4 loop, ch 3, *sc in next puff st, ch 3, (3-dc puff st, ch 2, 3-dc puff st) in next ch-4 loop, ch 2**, (3-dc puff st, ch 2, 3-dc puff st) in next ch-4 loop, ch 3; rep from * around, ending last rep at **, sl st in first puff st to join.

Rnd 8: Ch 1, *sc in puff st, (sc, picot, sc) in next ch-2 space, sc in next puff st, ch 3, skip next ch-3 loop, tr in next sc, picot, ch 3, skip next ch-3 loop, sc in next puff st, (sc, picot, sc) in next ch-2 space, sc in next puff st, (sc, picot, sc) in next ch-2 space; rep from * around, sl st in first sc to join. Fasten off.

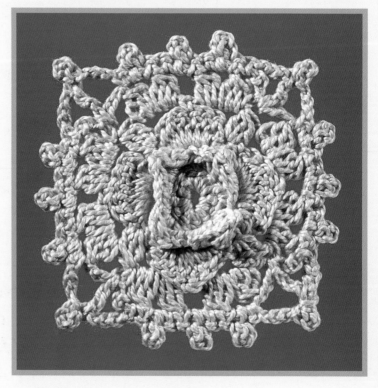

190

Puff st: *(Yo, insert hook in next space, yo, draw yarn through space, draw yarn through 2 loops on hook) twice in same space, yo, draw yarn through 3 loops on hook.*

Ch 6 and sl st in first ch to form a ring.

Rnd 1: Ch 3 (counts as dc), dc in ring, ch 2, (puff st, ch 2) 11 times in ring, sl st in 3rd ch of beg ch to join.

Rnd 2: Sl st in next ch-2 space, ch 1, *(sc, ch 9, sc) in ch-2 space, ch 5, sc in next ch-2 space, ch 5; rep from * around, sl st in first sc to join.

Rnd 3: Sl st in next ch-9 loop, ch 3 (counts as dc), (6 dc, ch 3, 7 dc) in first ch-9 loop, *sc in next ch-5 loop, ch 5, sc in next ch-5 loop**, (7 dc, ch 3, 7 dc) in next ch-9 loop; rep from * around, ending last rep at **, sl st in 3rd ch of beg ch to join.

Rnd 4: Sl st to next ch-3 loop, ch 1, *sc in ch-3 loop, ch 4, 3 tr in next ch-5 loop, ch 4; rep from * around, sl st in first sc to join. Fasten off.

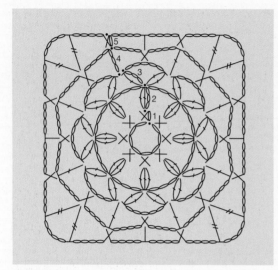

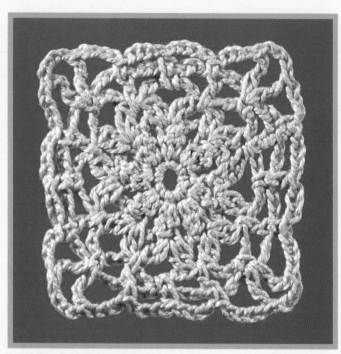

191

2-dc puff st: (Yo, insert hook in next st, yo, draw yarn through st, draw yarn through 2 loops on hook) twice in same st, yo, draw yarn through 3 loops on hook.

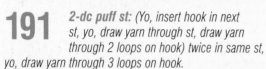

3-dc puff st: (Yo, insert hook in next st, yo, draw yarn through st, draw yarn through 2 loops on hook) 3 times in same st, yo, draw yarn through 4 loops on hook.

Ch 8 and sl st in first ch to form a ring.

Rnd 1: Ch 1, 8 sc in ring, sl st in first sc to join.

Rnd 2: Ch 3 (counts as dc), 2-dc puff st in first sc, ch 3, (3-dc puff st, ch 3) in each sc around, sl st in first puff st to join.

Rnd 3: Ch 3 (counts as dc), dc in first puff st, (2-dc puff st, ch 5, 2-dc puff st) in each of next 7 puff sts, 2-dc puff st in first puff st already holding beg ch and dc, ch 5, sl st in 3rd ch of beg ch to join.

Rnd 4: Sl st bet first dc and next puff st, ch 7 (counts as dc, ch 4), *sc in next ch-5 loop, ch 4**, dc bet next 2 puff sts, ch 4; rep from * around, ending last rep at **, sl st in first sc to join.

Rnd 5: Ch 1, *sc in dc, ch 4, skip next ch-4 loop, (tr, ch 4, tr) in next sc, ch 4, skip next ch-4 loop, sc in next dc, ch 4, skip next ch-4 loop, hdc in next sc, ch 4; rep from * around, sl st in first sc to join. Fasten off.

192

4-tr puff st: (Yo [twice], insert hook in next st, yo, draw yarn through st, [yo, draw yarn through 2 loops on hook] twice) 4 times in same st, yo, draw yarn through 5 loops on hook.

5-tr puff st: (Yo [twice], insert hook in next st, yo, draw yarn through st, [yo, draw yarn through 2 loops on hook] twice) 5 times in same st, yo, draw yarn through 6 loops on hook.

Ch 8 and sl st in first ch to form a ring.

Rnd 1: Ch 1, 12 sc in ring, sl st in first sc to join.

Rnd 2: Ch 4 (counts as tr), 4-tr puff st in first sc, ch 3, (5-tr puff st, ch 3) in each sc around, sl st in 4th ch of beg ch to join.

Rnd 3: Sl st in next ch-3 loop, ch 1, (sc, ch 5) in each ch-3 loop around, sl st in first sc to join.

Rnd 4: Sl st in next ch-5 loop, ch 5 (counts as dtr), 6 dtr in first ch-5 loop, *5 tr in each of next 2 ch-5 loop**, 7 dtr in next ch-5 loop; rep from * around, ending last rep at **, sl st in 5th ch of beg ch to join.

Rnd 5: Ch 1, sc in each st around, sl st in first sc to join. Fasten off.

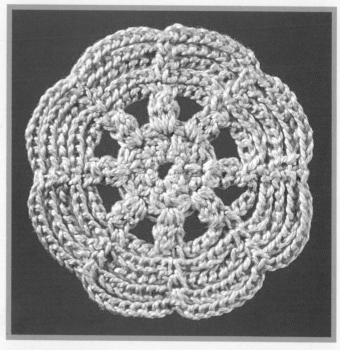

193

2-dc puff st: (Yo, insert hook in next space, yo, draw yarn through space, draw yarn through 2 loops on hook) twice in same space, yo, draw yarn through 3 loops on hook.

3-dc puff st: (Yo, insert hook in next space, yo, draw yarn through space, draw yarn through 2 loops on hook) 3 times in same space, yo, draw yarn through 4 loops on hook.

Ch 6 and sl st in first ch to form a ring.

Rnd 1: Ch 1, 8 sc in ring, sl st in first sc to join.

Rnd 2: Ch 3 (counts as dc), dc in next sc, ch 1, *2-dc cluster, working first half-closed dc in same sc as last dc made, work 2nd half-closed dc in next sc, yo, complete cluster, ch 1; rep from * around, ending with last half-closed dc of last cluster in first sc, sl st in 3rd ch of beg ch to join.

Rnd 3: Sl st in next ch-1 space, ch 3 (counts as dc), 2-dc puff st in first ch-1 space, ch 5, (3-dc puff st, ch 5) in each ch-1 space around, sl st in first puff st to join.

Rnd 4: Ch 1, (sc, ch 6) in each puff st around, sl st in first sc to join.

Rnd 5: Ch 1, (sc, ch 7) in each sc around, sl st in first sc to join.

Rnd 6: Ch 1, (sc, ch 8) in each sc around, sl st in first sc to join.

Rnd 7: Ch 1, (sc, ch 9) in each sc around, sl st in first sc to join. Fasten off.

194

2-dc puff st: *(Yo, insert hook in next space, yo, draw yarn through space, draw yarn through 2 loops on hook) twice in same space, yo, draw yarn through 3 loops on hook.*

3-dc puff st: *(Yo, insert hook in next space, yo, draw yarn through space, draw yarn through 2 loops on hook) 3 times in same space, yo, draw yarn through 4 loops on hook.*

Ch 6 and sl st in first ch to form a ring.

Rnd 1: Ch 1, 8 sc in ring, sl st in first sc to join.

Rnd 2: Ch 3 (counts as dc), dc in next sc, ch 1, *2-dc cluster, working first half-closed dc in same sc as last dc made, work 2nd half-closed dc in next sc, yo, complete cluster, ch 1; rep from * around, ending with last half-closed dc of last cluster in first sc, sl st in 3rd ch of beg ch to join.

Rnd 3: Sl st in next ch-1 space, ch 3 (counts as dc), 2-dc puff st in first ch-1 space, ch 5, (3-dc puff st, ch 5) in each ch-1 space around, sl st in puff st to join.

Rnd 4: Ch 1, (sc, ch 6) in each puff st around, sl st in first sc to join.

Rnd 5: Ch 1, (sc, ch 7) in each sc around, sl st in first sc to join.

Rnd 6: Ch 1, (sc, ch 8) in each sc around, sl st in first sc to join.

Rnd 7: Ch 1, (sc, ch 9) in each sc around, sl st in first sc to join.

Rnd 8: Ch 1, *sc in sc, (2 sc, ch 5, 2 sc) in next ch-9 loop; rep from * around, sl st in first sc to join.

Rnd 9: Turn, sl st in each of next 2 sc, turn, ch 4 (counts as tr), 4-tr cluster worked across next 4 sc, *ch 9, dc in next ch-5 loop, ch 9**, 5-tr cluster worked across next 5 sc; rep from * around, ending last rep at **, sl st in 4th ch of beg ch to join. Fasten off.

195

Picot: Ch 4, sl st in 4th ch from hook.

Ch 6 and sl st in first ch to form a ring.

Rnd 1: Ch 3 (counts as dc), 11 dc in ring, sl st in 3rd ch of beg ch to join.

Rnd 2: Sl st bet first 2 sts, ch 4 (counts as tr), tr bet first 2 sts, ch 1, *2 tr bet next 2 dc, ch 1; rep from * around, sl st in 4th ch of beg ch to join.

Rnd 3: Sl st to next ch-1 space, ch 1, *sc in ch-1 space, ch 6, sc in next ch-1 space, ch 9, sc in next ch-1 space, ch 6; rep from * around, sl st in first sc to join.

Rnd 4: Sl st in next ch-6 loop, ch 1, *(5 sc, picot, 5 sc) in ch-5 loop, 17 dc in next ch-9 loop, (5 sc, picot, 5 sc) in next ch-5 loop; rep from * around, sl st in first sc to join. Fasten off.

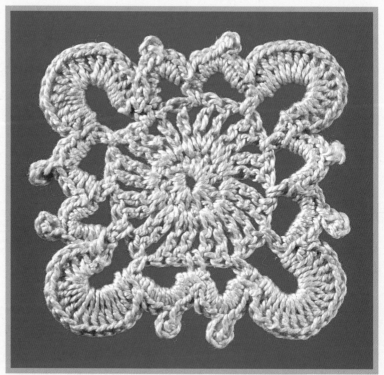

196

Ch 6 and sl st in first ch to form a ring.

Rnd 1: Ch 1, 16 sc in ring, sl st in first sc to join.

Rnd 2: Ch 8 (counts as tr, ch 4), skip next sc, *tr in next sc, ch 4, skip next sc; rep from * around, sl st in 4th ch of beg ch to join.

Rnd 3: Ch 1, 6 sc in each ch-4 loop around, sl st in first sc to join.

Rnd 4: Ch 1, sc in first sc, ch 11, skip next 4 sc, *sc bet last skipped and next sc, ch 11, skip next 5 sc; rep from * around, sl st in first sc to join.

Rnd 5: Ch 1, 13 sc in each ch-11 loop around, sl st in first sc to join.

Rnd 6: Ch 1, sc in sc, ch 5, skip next 5 sc, * sc in next sc, ch 5, skip next 6 sc **, sc bet last skipped and next sc, ch 5, skip next 6 sc; rep from * around, ending last repeat at **, sl st in first sc to join.

Rnd 7: Ch 1, 6 sc in each ch-5 loop around, sl st in first sc to join. Fasten off.

.13.
Triangle Blocks

197

Ch 6 and sl st in first ch to form a ring.

Rnd 1: Ch 3 (counts as dc), 3 dc in ring, ch 7, (4 dc, ch 7) twice in ring, sl st in 3rd ch of beg ch to join.

Rnd 2: Ch 3 (counts as dc), dc in each of next 3 dc, *(dc, ch 7, dc) in next ch-7 loop**, dc in each of next 4 dc; rep from * around, ending last rep at **, sl st in 3rd ch of beg ch to join.

Rnd 3: Ch 1, *sc in each of next 5 dc, 7 sc in next ch-7 loop, sc in next dc; rep from * around, sl st in first sc to join. Fasten off.

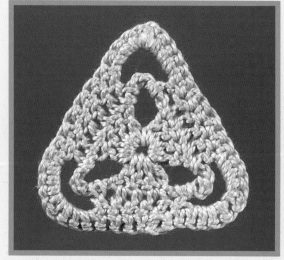

198

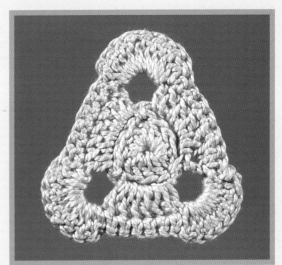

Ch 6 and sl st in first ch to form a ring.

Rnd 1: Ch 3 (counts as dc), 14 dc in ring, sl st in 3rd ch of beg ch to join.

Rnd 2: Ch 1, *sc in dc, ch 6, skip next 4 dc; rep from * around, sl st in first sc to join.

Rnd 3: Sl st in next ch-6 loop, ch 3 (counts as dc), 6 dc in first ch-6 loop, ch 4, (7 dc, ch 4) in each of next 2 ch-6 loops, sl st in 3rd ch of beg ch to join.

Rnd 4: Ch 1, *sc in each of next 7 dc, 9 dc in next ch-4 loop; rep from * around, sl st in first sc to join. Fasten off.

199

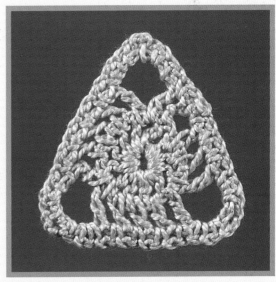

Ch 6 and sl st in first ch to form a ring.

Rnd 1: Ch 4 (counts as dc, ch 1), (dc, ch 1) 11 times in ring, sl st in 3rd ch of beg ch to join.

Rnd 2: Sl st in next ch-1 space, ch 4 (counts as dc, ch 1), *(tr, ch 7, tr) in next ch-1 space, ch 1, (dc, ch 1) in each of next 3 loops; rep from * around, omitting last (dc, ch 1), sl st in 3rd ch of beg ch to join.

Rnd 3: Sl st in next ch-1 space, ch 1, sc in first ch-1 space, ch 1, *(sc, ch 1, sc, ch 3, sc, ch 1, sc) in next ch-7 loop, ch 1, (sc, ch 1) in each of next 4 ch-1 spaces; rep from * around, omitting last (sc, ch 1), sl st in first sc to join. Fasten off.

200

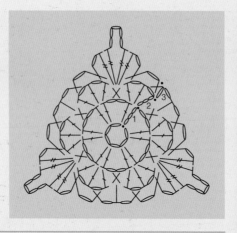

Ch 6 and sl st in first ch to form a ring.

Rnd 1: Ch 3 (counts as dc), dc in ring, ch 2, (2 dc, ch 2) 5 times in ring, sl st in 3rd ch of beg ch to join.

Rnd 2: Ch 4 (counts as dc, ch 1), dc bet first 2 sts, ch 1, dc in next dc, sc in next ch-2 space, *dc in next dc, ch 1, dc bet same dc and next dc, ch 1, dc in next dc, sc in next ch-2 space; rep from * around, sl st in 3rd ch of beg ch to join.

Rnd 3: Ch 1, *sc in next ch-1 space, ch 1, skip next ch-1 space, sc in next dc, (2 tr, ch 5, 2 tr) in next sc, sc in next dc, ch 1, skip next dc, sc in next ch-1 space, ch 1, skip next dc, hdc in next sc, ch 1; rep from * around, sl st in first sc to join. Fasten off.

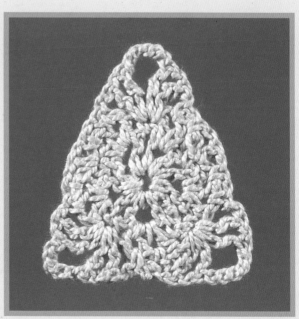

201

2-dc puff st: *(Yo, insert hook in next st, yo, draw yarn through st, draw yarn through 2 loops on hook) twice in same st, yo, draw yarn through 3 loops on hook.*

3-dc puff st: *(Yo, insert hook in next st, yo, draw yarn through st, draw yarn through 2 loops on hook) 3 times in same st, yo, draw yarn through 4 loops on hook.*

Ch 6 and sl st in first ch to form a ring.

Rnd 1: Ch 10 (counts as dc, ch 7), *dc in ring, ch 3, dc in ring, ch 7; rep from * once, dc in ring, ch 3, sl st in 3rd ch of beg ch to join.

Rnd 2: Sl st in next ch-7 loop, ch 3 (counts as dc), (3 dc, ch 7, 4 dc) in same ch-7 loop, *3 dc in next ch-3 loop**, (4 dc, ch 7, 4 dc) in next ch-7 loop; rep from * around, ending last rep at **, sl st in 3rd ch of beg ch to join.

Rnd 3: Ch 3 (counts as dc), 2-dc puff st in same st, *ch 3, (4 dc, ch 7, 4 dc) in next ch-7 loop, ch 3, skip next 3 dc, 3-dc puff st in next dc, ch 3, skip next dc, sc in next dc, ch 3, skip next dc**, 3-dc puff st in next dc; rep from * around, ending last rep at **, sl st in first puff st to join. Fasten off.

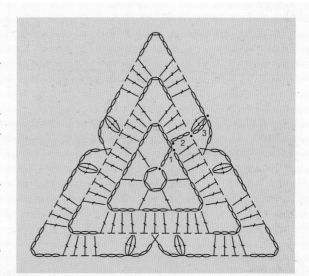

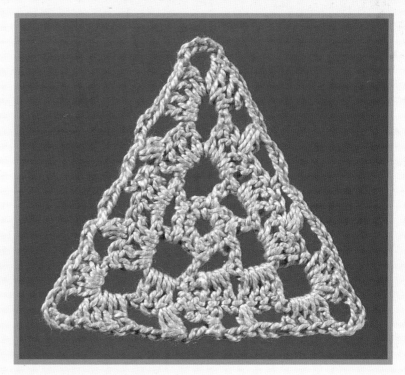

202

Ch 6 and sl st in first ch to form a ring.

Rnd 1: Ch 3 (counts as dc), 3 dc in ring, ch 4, (4 dc, ch 4) twice in ring, sl st in 3rd ch of beg ch to join.

Rnd 2: Ch 3 (counts as dc), dc in each of next 3 dc, *(dc, ch 5, dc) in next ch-4 loop**, dc in each of next 4 dc; rep from * around, ending last rep at **, sl st in 3rd ch of beg ch to join.

Rnd 3: Ch 3 (counts as dc), dc in each of next 4 dc, *(dc, ch 6, dc) in next ch-5 loop**, dc in each of next 6 dc; rep from * around, ending last rep at **, dc in next dc, sl st in 3rd ch of beg ch to join.

Rnd 4: Ch 3 (counts as dc), dc in each of next 5 dc, *(dc, ch 7, dc) in next ch-6 loop**, dc in each of next 8 dc; rep from * around, ending last rep at **, dc in each of next 2 dc, sl st in 3rd ch of beg ch to join.

Rnd 5: Ch 1, *sc in each of next 7 dc, (4 sc, ch 2, 4 sc) in next ch-7 loop**, sc in each of next 10 dc; rep from * around, ending last rep at **, sc in each of next 3 dc, sl st in first sc to join. Fasten off.

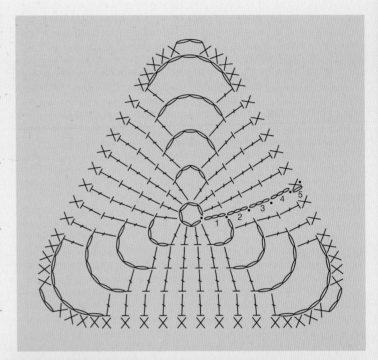

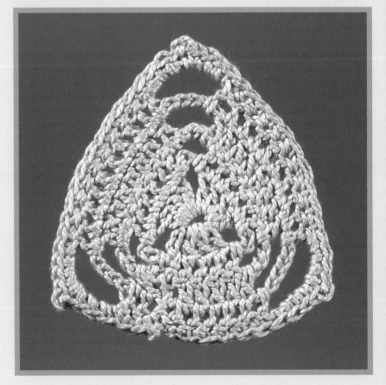

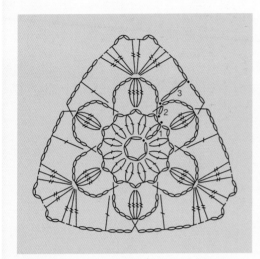

203

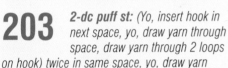

2-dc puff st: *(Yo, insert hook in next space, yo, draw yarn through space, draw yarn through 2 loops on hook) twice in same space, yo, draw yarn through 3 loops on hook.*

4-tr puff st: *(Yo [twice], insert hook in next space, yo, draw yarn through space, [yo, draw yarn through 2 loops on hook] twice) 4 times in same space, yo, draw yarn through 5 loops on hook.*

Ch 6 and sl st in first ch to form a ring.

Rnd 1: Ch 3 (counts as dc), dc in ring, ch 2, (2-dc puff st, ch 2) 11 times in ring, sl st in 3rd ch of beg ch to join.

Rnd 2: Sl st in next ch-2 space, ch 1, *sc in ch-1 space, ch 5, 4-tr puff st in next ch-2 space, ch 5; rep from * around, sl st in first sc to join.

Rnd 3: Ch 6 (counts as dc, ch 3), *skip next ch-5 loop, (3 tr, ch 3, 2 tr, ch 3, 3 tr) in next puff st, ch 3, skip next ch-5 loop, dc in next sc, ch 3, skip next ch-5 loop, sc in next puff st, ch 3, skip next ch-5 loop**, dc in next sc; rep from * around, ending last rep at **, sl st in 3rd ch of beg ch to join. Fasten off.

.14.
Circles

204
Ch 8 and sl st in first ch to form a ring.

Rnd 1: Ch 3 (counts as dc), 19 dc in ring, sl st in 3rd ch of beg ch to join. Fasten off.

205
Ch 4 and sl st in first ch to form a ring.

Rnd 1: Ch 4 (counts as dc, ch 1), (dc, ch 1) 7 times in ring, sl st in 3rd ch of beg ch to join.

Rnd 2: Sl st in next ch-1 space, ch 3 (counts as dc), 2 dc in first ch-1 space, ch 1, (3 dc, ch 1) in each ch-1 space around, sl st in 3rd ch of beg ch to join. Fasten off.

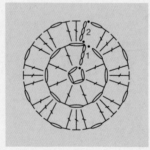

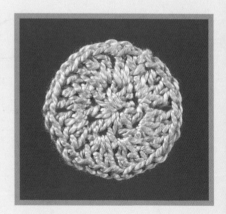

206

2-dc puff st: *(Yo, insert hook in next space, yo, draw yarn through space, draw yarn through 2 loops on hook) twice in same space, yo, draw yarn through 3 loops on hook.*

3-dc puff st: *(Yo, insert hook in next space, yo, draw yarn through space, draw yarn through 2 loops on hook) 3 times in same space, yo, draw yarn through 4 loops on hook.*

Ch 6 and sl st in first ch to form a ring.

Rnd 1: Ch 5 (counts as dc, ch 2), (dc, ch 2) 7 times in ring, sl st in 3rd ch of beg ch to join.

Rnd 2: Sl st in next ch-2 space, ch 3 (counts as dc), 2-dc puff st in first ch-2 space, ch 3, (3-dc puff st, ch 3) in each ch-2 space around, sl st in first puff st to join. Fasten off.

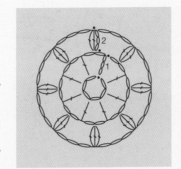 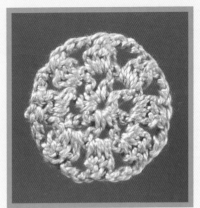

207

2-dc puff st: *(Yo, insert hook in next space, yo, draw yarn through space, draw yarn through 2 loops on hook) twice in same space, yo, draw yarn through 3 loops on hook.*

3-dc puff st: *(Yo, insert hook in next space, yo, draw yarn through space, draw yarn through 2 loops on hook) 3 times in same space, yo, draw yarn through 4 loops on hook.*

Ch 6 and sl st in first ch to form a ring.

Rnd 1: Ch 3 (counts as dc), dc in ring, ch 1, (2 dc, ch 1) 4 times in ring, sl st in 3rd ch of beg ch to join.

Rnd 2: Sl st to next ch-1 space, ch 3 (counts as dc), 2-dc puff st in first ch-1 space, ch 4, (3-dc puff st, ch 4) in each ch-1 space around, sl st in first puff st to join.

Rnd 3: Ch 1, *sc in puff st, 5 sc in next ch-4 loop; rep from * around, sl st in first sc to join. Fasten off.

208

Ch 6 and sl st in first ch to form a ring.

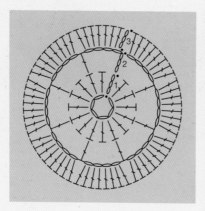

Rnd 1: Ch 3 (counts as dc), 15 dc in ring, sl st in 3rd ch of beg ch to join.

Rnd 2: Ch 7 (counts as dc, ch 4), skip next dc, *dc in next dc, ch 4, skip next dc; rep from * around, sl st in 3rd ch of beg ch to join.

Rnd 3: Sl st in next ch-4 loop, ch 3, 7 dc in first ch-4 loop, 8 dc in each ch-4 loop around, sl st in 3rd ch of beg ch to join. Fasten off.

209

2-dc puff st: *(Yo, insert hook in next space, yo, draw yarn through space, draw yarn through 2 loops on hook) twice in same space, yo, draw yarn through 3 loops on hook.*

Ch 6 and sl st in first ch to form a ring.

Rnd 1: Ch 1, 16 sc in ring, sl st in first sc to join.

Rnd 2: Ch 4 (counts as dc, ch 1), (dc, ch 1) in each sc around, sl st in 3rd ch of beg ch to join.

Rnd 3: Sl st in next ch-1 space, ch 1, 2 sc in each ch-1 space around, sl st in first sc to join.

Rnd 4: Sl st bet first and 2nd sc, ch 3 (counts as dc), dc bet first and 2nd sc, *(ch 4, skip next 3 sc, 2-dc puff st bet last skipped and next sc) 4 times, ch 4, skip next 4 sc**, 2-dc puff st bet last skipped and next sc; rep from * to ** once, sl st in 3rd ch of beg ch to join. Fasten off.

210

2-dc puff st: *(Yo, insert hook in next st, yo, draw yarn through st, draw yarn through 2 loops on hook) twice in same st, yo, draw yarn through 3 loops on hook.*

3-dc puff st: *(Yo, insert hook in next st, yo, draw yarn through st, draw yarn through 2 loops on hook) 3 times in same st, yo, draw yarn through 4 loops on hook.*

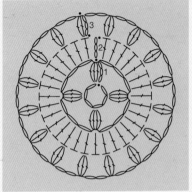

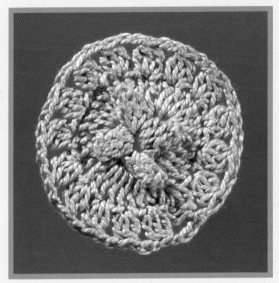

Beginning popcorn (beg pop): *Ch 3 (counts as dc), 3 dc in same st, drop loop from hook, insert hook from front to back in 3rd ch of beg ch, place dropped loop on hook, draw loop through st.*

Popcorn (pop): *4 dc in same st, drop loop from hook, insert hook from front to back in first dc of 4-dc group, place dropped loop on hook, draw loop through st.*

Ch 6 and sl st in first ch to form a ring.

Rnd 1: Beg pop in ring, ch 3, (pop, ch 3) 3 times in ring, sl st in first pop to join.

Rnd 2: Ch 3 (counts as dc), *7 dc in next ch-3 loop**, dc in next pop; rep from * around, ending last rep at **, sl st in 3rd ch of beg ch to join.

Rnd 3: Sl st in next dc, ch 3 (counts as dc), 2-dc puff st in same dc, ch 2, skip next dc, *3-dc puff st in next dc, ch 2, skip next dc; rep from * around, sl st in first puff st to join. Fasten off.

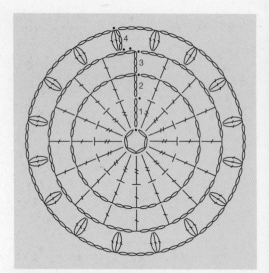

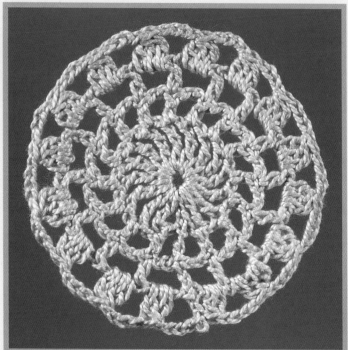

211

2-dc puff st: (Yo, insert hook in next space, yo, draw yarn through space, draw yarn through 2 loops on hook) twice in same space, yo, draw yarn through 3 loops on hook.

3-dc puff st: (Yo, insert hook in next space, yo, draw yarn through space, draw yarn through 2 loops on hook) 3 times in same space, yo, draw yarn through 4 loops on hook.

Ch 6 and sl st in first ch to form a ring.

Rnd 1: Ch 4 (counts as tr), 15 tr in ring, sl st in 4th ch of beg ch to join.

Rnd 2: Ch 5 (counts as dc, ch 2), (dc, ch 2) in each tr around, sl st in 4th ch of beg ch to join.

Rnd 3: Ch 6 (counts as dc, ch 3), skip next ch-2 space, (dc, ch 3) in each dc around, sl st in 3rd ch of beg ch to join.

Rnd 4: Sl st to center of next ch-3 loop, ch 3 (counts as dc), 2-dc puff st in first ch-3 loop, ch 4, (3-dc puff st, ch 4) in each ch-3 loop around, sl st in first puff st to join. Fasten off.

212

Ch 6 and sl st in first ch to form a ring.

Rnd 1: Ch 6 (counts as dc, ch 3), (dc, ch 3) 5 times in ring, sl st in 3rd ch of beg ch to join.

Rnd 2: Sl st in next ch-3 loop, ch 4 (counts as dc, ch 1), (dc, ch 1) 3 times in first ch-3 loop, (dc, ch 1) 4 times in each ch-3 loop around, sl st in 3rd ch of beg ch to join.

Rnd 3: Sl st in next ch-1 space, ch 10 (counts as dc, ch 7), skip next ch-1 space, *dc in next ch-1 space, ch 7, skip next ch-1 space; rep from * around, sl st in 3rd ch of beg ch to join.

Rnd 4: Sl st to center of next ch-7 loop, ch 1, sc in ch-7 loop, *ch 1, tr in next ch-7 loop, ch 3, working behind last tr made, tr in last ch-7 loop (crossed tr made), ch 1**, sc in next ch-7 loop already holding first tr of last crossed tr; rep from * around, ending last rep at **, sl st in first sc to join. Fasten off.

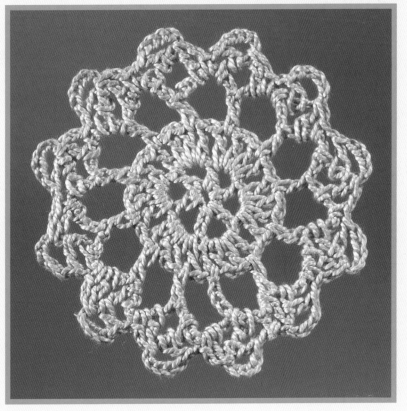

213

Ch 6 and sl st in first ch to form a ring.

Rnd 1: Ch 1, 12 sc in ring, sl st in first sc to join.

Rnd 2: Ch 5 (counts as dc, ch 2), (dc, ch 2) in each sc around, sl st in 3rd ch of beg ch to join.

Rnd 3: Ch 1, *sc in dc, skip next ch-2 space, 6 dc in next dc, skip next ch-2 space; rep from * around, sl st in first sc to join.

Rnd 4: Sl st in each of next 2 dc, ch 1, *sc in dc, ch 6, skip next 2 dc, sc in next dc, ch 6, skip next 3 sts; rep from * around, sl st in first sc to join.

Rnd 5: Ch 1, *sc in sc, 7 sc in next ch-6 loop; rep from * around, sl st in first sc to join. Fasten off.

214

Picot: Ch 4, sl st in 4th ch from hook.

Ch 6 and sl st in first ch to form a ring.

Rnd 1: Ch 3 (counts as dc), 15 dc in ring, sl st in 3rd ch of beg ch to join.

Rnd 2: Ch 5 (counts as dc, ch 2), (dc, ch 2) in each dc around, sl st in 3rd ch of beg ch to join.

Rnd 3: Ch 6 (counts as dc, ch 3), (dc, ch 3) in each dc around, sl st in 3rd ch of beg ch to join.

Rnd 4: Ch 7 (counts as dc, ch 4), (dc, ch 4) in each dc around, sl st in 3rd ch of beg ch to join.

Rnd 5: Sl st in next ch-4 loop, ch 3 (counts as dc), 4 dc in first ch-4 loop, picot, (5 dc, picot) in each ch-4 loop around, sl st in 3rd ch of beg ch to join. Fasten off.

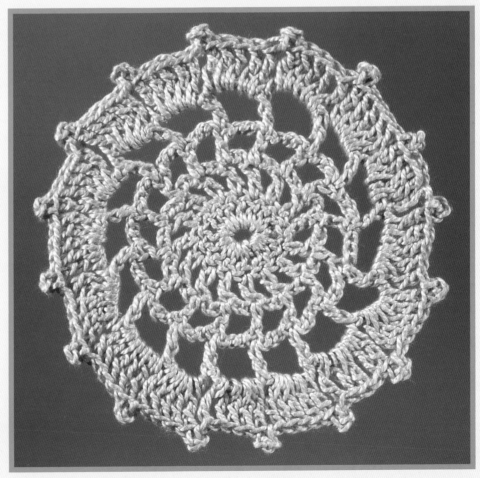

.15.
Hexagons

215

Ch 6 and sl st in first ch to form a ring.

Rnd 1: Ch 6 (counts as tr, ch 2), (tr, ch 2) 11 times in ring, sl st in 4th ch of beg ch to join.

Rnd 2: Sl st in next ch-2 space, ch 3 (counts as dc), (dc, ch 2, 2 dc) in first ch-2 space, *3 dc in next ch-2 space**, (2 dc, ch 2, 2 dc) in next ch-2 space; rep from * around, ending last rep at **, sl st in 3rd ch of beg ch to join. Fasten off.

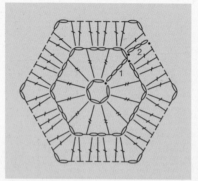

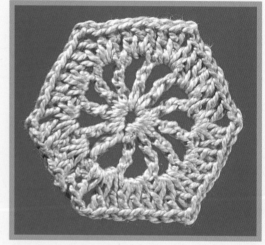

216

Ch 6 and sl st in first ch to form a ring.

Rnd 1: Ch 3 (counts as dc), 17 dc in ring, sl st in 3rd ch of beg ch to join.

Rnd 2: Ch 1, *sc in dc, ch 5, skip next 2 dc; rep from * around, sl st in first sc to join.

Rnd 3: Sl st in next ch-5 loop, ch 3 (counts as dc), (dc, ch 3, 2 dc) in first ch-5 loop, *2-dc cluster, working first half-closed dc in same ch-5 loop, work 2nd half-closed dc in next ch-5 loop, yo, complete cluster**, (2 dc, ch 3, 2 dc) in same ch-5 loop; rep from * around, ending last rep at **, sl st in 3rd ch of beg ch to join. Fasten off.

217

Ch 6 and sl st in first ch to form a ring.

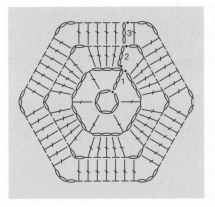

Rnd 1: Ch 6 (counts as dc, ch 3), (dc, ch 3) 5 times in ring, sl st in 3rd ch of beg ch to join.

Rnd 2: Sl st in next ch-3 loop, ch 3 (counts as dc), 4 dc in first ch-3 loop, ch 2, (5 dc, ch 2) in each ch-3 loop around, sl st in 3rd ch of beg ch to join.

Rnd 3: Ch 3 (counts as dc), dc in each of next 4 dc, *(dc, ch 3, dc) in next ch-2 space**, dc in each of next 5 dc; rep from * around, ending last rep at **, sl st in 3rd ch of beg ch to join. Fasten off.

218

Ch 6 and sl st in first ch to form a ring.

Rnd 1: Ch 3 (counts as dc), 2 dc in ring, ch 1, (3 dc, ch 1) 5 times in ring, sl st in 3rd ch of beg ch to join.

Rnd 2: Sl st to next ch-1 space, ch 3 (counts as dc), (2 dc, ch 1, 3 dc) in first ch-1 space, (3 dc, ch 1, 3 dc) in each ch-1 space around, sl st in 3rd ch of beg ch to join.

Rnd 3: Sl st to next ch-1 space, ch 3 (counts as dc), (2 dc, ch 1, 3 dc) in first ch-1 space, *skip next 3 dc, 2 dc bet last skipped and next dc**, (3 dc, ch 1, 3 dc) in next ch-1 space; rep from * around, ending last rep at **, sl st in 3rd ch of beg ch to join. Fasten off.

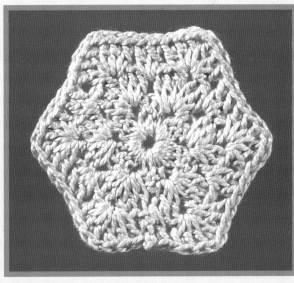

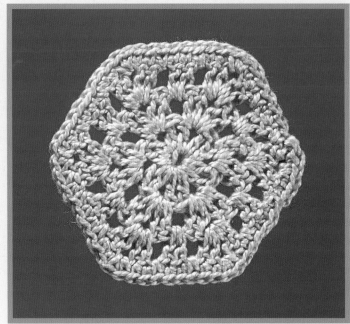

219

Ch 6 and sl st in first ch to form a ring.

Rnd 1: Ch 3 (counts as dc), dc in ring, ch 1, (2 dc, ch 1) 5 times in ring, sl st in 3rd ch of beg ch to join.

Rnd 2: Sl st to next ch-1 space, ch 3 (counts as dc), (dc, ch 1, 2 dc) in first ch-1 space, ch 1, (3 dc, ch 1, 3 dc, ch 1) in each ch-1 space around, sl st in 3rd ch of beg ch to join.

Rnd 3: Sl st to next ch-1 space, ch 3 (counts as dc), (dc, ch 1, 2 dc) in first ch-1 space, *ch 1, 2 dc in next ch-1 space, ch 1**, (2 dc, ch 1, 2 dc) in next ch-1 space; rep from * around, ending last rep at **, sl st in 3rd ch of beg ch to join.

Rnd 4: Ch 1, *sc in each of next 2 dc, 2 sc in next ch-2 space, (sc in each of next 2 dc, sc in next ch-1 space) twice; rep from * around, sl st in first sc to join. Fasten off.

220

Ch 5 and sl st in first ch to form a ring.

Rnd 1: Ch 3 (counts as dc), 11 dc in ring, sl st in 3rd ch of beg ch to join.

Rnd 2: Ch 3 (counts as dc), dc in first st, *2 dc in next dc, ch 1**, 2 dc in next dc; rep from * around, ending last rep at **, sl st in 3rd ch of beg ch to join.

Rnd 3: Ch 3 (counts as dc), dc in first st, *dc in each of next 2 dc, 2 dc in next dc, ch 2, skip next ch-1 space**, 2 dc in next dc; rep from * around, ending last rep at **, sl st in 3rd ch of beg ch to join.

Rnd 4: Ch 3 (counts as dc), dc in first st, *dc in each of next 4 dc, 2 dc in next dc, ch 3, skip next ch-2 space**, 2 dc in next dc; rep from * around, ending last rep at **, sl st in 3rd ch of beg ch to join.

Rnd 5: Ch 3 (counts as dc), dc in first st, *dc in each of next 6 dc, 2 dc in next dc, ch 4, skip next ch-3 loop**, 2 dc in next dc; rep from * around, ending last rep at **, sl st in 3rd ch of beg ch to join. Fasten off.

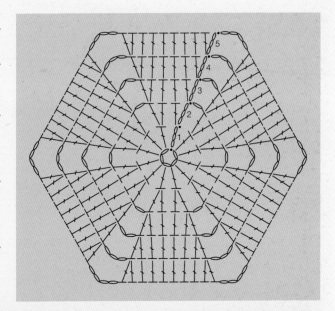

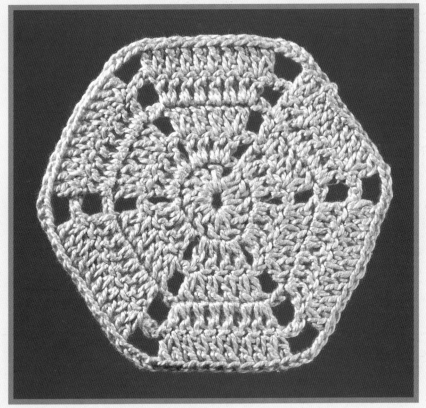

221

Beginning pop-corn (beg pop): Ch 4 (counts as tr), 4 tr in same st, drop loop from hook, insert hook from front to back in 4th ch of beg ch, place dropped loop on hook, draw loop through st.

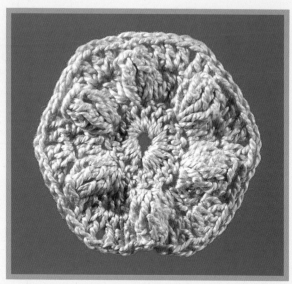

Popcorn (pop): 5 tr in same st, drop loop from hook, insert hook from front to back in first dc of 5-tr group, place dropped loop on hook, draw loop through st.

Ch 6 and sl st in first ch to form a ring.

Rnd 1: Ch 3 (counts as dc), 17 dc in ring, sl st in 3rd ch of beg ch to join.

Rnd 2: Beg pop in first st, *2 dc in each of next 2 dc**, pop in next dc; rep from * around, ending last rep at **, sl st in 3rd ch of beg ch to join.

Rnd 3: Ch 3 (counts as dc), *dc in each of next 2 dc, (dc, ch 1, dc) bet same dc and next dc, dc in each of next 2 dc**, dc in next pop; rep from * around, ending last rep at **, sl st in 3rd ch of beg ch to join. Fasten off.

222

Y-stitch (Y-st): Tr in space, 2 dc in middle of last tr made.

Ch 6 and sl st in first ch to form a ring.

Rnd 1: Ch 4 (counts as tr), 2 dc in 3rd ch from hook (counts as Y-st), ch 1, (Y-st, ch 1) 5 times in ring, sl st in 4th ch of beg ch to join.

Rnd 2: Ch 3 (counts as dc), dc in next dc, *ch 3, 2-dc cluster, working first half-closed dc in same dc as last dc made, work 2nd half-closed dc in next dc, yo, complete cluster, ch 3, skip next ch-1 space**, 2-dc cluster worked across next 2 dc; rep from * around, ending last rep at **, sl st in 3rd ch of beg ch to join.

Rnd 3: Sl st in next ch-3 loop, ch 3 (counts as dc), 2 dc in first ch-3 loop, *ch 3, working over next ch-3 loop, dc in next corresponding ch-1 space 2 rnds below, ch 3**, 3 dc in next ch-3 loop; rep from * around, ending last rep at **, sl st in 3rd ch of beg ch to join.

Rnd 4: Ch 3 (counts as dc), *(dc, ch 3, dc) in next dc, dc in next dc, 3 dc in each of next 2 ch-3 loops**, dc in next dc; rep from * around, ending last rep at **, sl st in 3rd ch of beg ch to join. Fasten off.

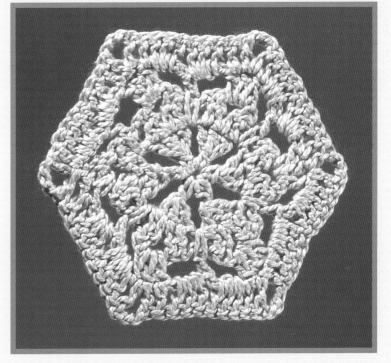

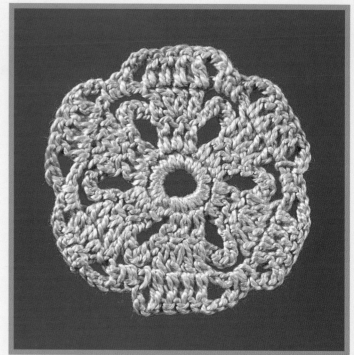

223

Ch 10 and sl st in first ch to form a ring.

Rnd 1: Ch 1, 18 sc in ring, sl st in first sc to join.

Rnd 2: Ch 3 (counts as dc), dc in each of next 2 sc, ch 6, *dc in each of next 3 sc, ch 6; rep from * around, sl st in 3rd ch of beg ch to join.

Rnd 3: Ch 3 (counts as dc), *2 dc in next dc, dc in next dc, ch 4, skip next ch-6 loop**, dc in next dc; rep from * around, ending last rep at **, sl st in 3rd ch of beg ch to join.

Rnd 4: Ch 3 (counts as dc), *dc in each of next 3 dc, ch 3, 2 sc in next ch-4 loop, ch 3**, dc in next dc; rep from * around, ending last rep at **, sl st in 3rd ch of beg ch to join. Fasten off.

224

Ch 8 and sl st in first ch to form a ring.

Rnd 1: Ch 7 (counts as dc, ch 4), (dc, ch 4) 5 times in ring, sl st in 3rd ch of beg ch to join.

Rnd 2: Ch 4 (counts as tr), *(2 tr, ch 3, 2 tr) in next ch-4 loop, tr in next dc; rep from * around, omitting last tr, sl st in 4th ch of beg ch to join.

Rnd 3: Sl st to next ch-3 loop, ch 4 (counts as tr), 4 tr in first ch-3 loop, ch 8, (5 tr, ch 8) in each ch-3 loop around, sl st in 4th ch of beg ch to join.

Rnd 4: Ch 4 (counts as tr), tr in each of next 4 tr, *ch 5, sc in next ch-8 loop, ch 5**, tr in each of next 5 tr; rep from * around, ending last rep at **, sl st in 4th ch of beg ch to join. Fasten off.

225

Ch 6 and sl st in first ch to form a ring.

Rnd 1: Ch 3 (counts as dc), 2 dc in ring, ch 1, (3 dc, ch 1) 5 times in ring, sl st in 3rd ch of beg ch to join.

Rnd 2: Sl st to next ch-1 space, ch 3 (counts as dc), 2 dc in first ch-1 space, ch 3, (3 dc, ch 3) in each ch-1 space around, sl st in 3rd ch of beg ch to join.

Rnd 3: Ch 3 (counts as dc), dc in first st, *dc in next dc, 2 dc in next dc, ch 5, skip next ch-3 loop**, 2 dc in next dc; rep from * around, ending last rep at **, sl st in 3rd ch of beg ch to join.

Rnd 4: Ch 3 (counts as dc), dc in first st, *dc in each of next 3 dc, 2 dc in next dc, ch 3, sc in next ch-5 loop, ch 3**, 2 dc in next dc; rep from * around, ending last rep at **, sl st in 3rd ch of beg ch to join.

Rnd 5: Ch 3 (counts as dc), dc in first st, *dc in each of next 5 dc, 2 dc in next dc, ch 3, (sc, ch 3) in each of next 2 ch-3 loops**, 2 dc in next dc; rep from * around, ending last rep at **, sl st in 3rd ch of beg ch to join. Fasten off.

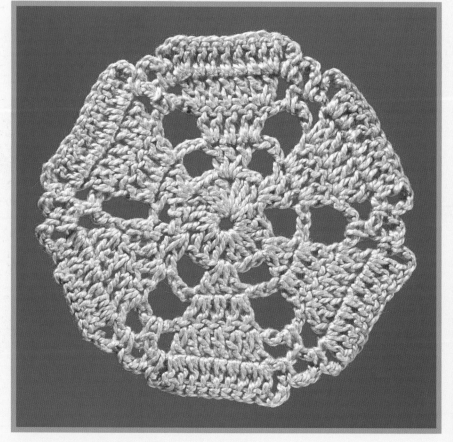

226

Ch 6 and sl st in first ch to form a ring.

Rnd 1: Ch 3 (counts as dc), 17 dc in ring, sl st in 3rd ch of beg ch to join.

Rnd 2: Ch 3 (counts as dc), 2 dc in first st, *ch 3, sc in each of next 2 dc, ch 3**, 3 dc in next dc; rep from * around, ending last rep at **, sl st in 3rd ch of beg ch to join.

Rnd 3: Sl st in next dc, ch 3 (counts as dc), (dc, ch 1, 2 dc) in same dc, *ch 2, sc in next ch-3 loop, ch 1, sc in next ch-3 loop, ch 2, skip next dc**, (2 dc, ch 1, 2 dc) in next dc; rep from * around, ending last rep at **, sl st in 3rd ch of beg ch to join.

Rnd 4: Sl st to next ch-1 space, ch 1, *sc in ch-1 space, ch 3, skip next ch-2 space, 3 dc in next ch-1 space, ch 3, skip next ch-2 space; rep from * around, sl st in first sc to join.

Rnd 5: Ch 3 (counts as dc), (dc, ch 2, 2 dc) in first sc, *ch 2, sc in next ch-3 loop, dc in each of next 3 dc, ch 2, sc in next ch-3 loop, ch 2**, (2 dc, ch 2, 2 dc) in next sc; rep from * around, ending last rep at **, sl st in 3rd ch of beg ch to join. Fasten off.

227

2-dc puff st: *(Yo, insert hook in next space, yo, draw yarn through space, draw yarn through 2 loops on hook) twice in same space, yo, draw yarn through 3 loops on hook.*

3-dc puff st: *(Yo, insert hook in next space, yo, draw yarn through space, draw yarn through 2 loops on hook) 3 times in same space, yo, draw yarn through 4 loops on hook.*

Ch 6 and sl st in first ch to form a ring.

Rnd 1: Ch 3 (counts as dc), 2-dc puff st in ring, ch 3, (3-dc puff st, ch 3) 5 times in ring, sl st in first puff st to join.

Rnd 2: Sl st in next ch-3 loop, ch 3 (counts as dc), (2-dc puff st, ch 3, 3-dc puff st) in first ch-3 loop, ch 3, *(3-dc puff st, ch 3, 3-dc puff st) in next ch-3 loop, ch 3; rep from * around, sl st in 3rd ch of beg ch to join.

Rnd 3: Sl st to center of next ch-3 loop, ch 3 (counts as dc), 2-dc puff st in first ch-3 loop, *ch 3, (3-dc puff st, ch 3, 3-dc puff st) in next ch-3 loop, ch 3**, 3-dc puff st in next ch-3 loop; rep from * around, ending last rep at **, sl st in 3rd ch of beg ch to join.

Rnd 4: Sl st in next ch-3 loop, ch 3 (counts as dc), 2 dc in first ch-3 loop, *(3 dc, ch 2, 3 dc) in next ch-3 loop**, 3 dc in each of next 2 ch-3 loops; rep from * around, ending last rep at **, 3 dc in next ch-3 loop, sl st in 3rd ch of beg ch to join.

Rnd 5: Ch 1, *sc in each of next 6 dc, 2 sc in next ch-2 space, dc in each of next 6 dc; rep from * around, sl st in first sc to join. Fasten off.

228

Puff st: *(Yo, insert hook in next st, yo, draw yarn through st, draw yarn through 2 loops on hook) twice in same st, yo, draw yarn through 3 loops on hook.*

Beginning popcorn (beg pop): *Ch 3 (counts as dc), 4 dc in same space, drop loop from hook, insert hook from front to back in 3rd ch of beg ch, place dropped loop on hook, draw loop through st.*

Popcorn (pop): *5 dc in same space, drop loop from hook, insert hook from front to back in first dc of 5-dc group, place dropped loop on hook, draw loop through st.*

Ch 6 and sl st in first ch to form a ring.

Rnd 1: Ch 1, 12 sc in ring, sl st in first sc to join.

Rnd 2: Ch 3 (counts as dc), dc in first sc, ch 3, skip next sc, *puff st in next sc, ch 3, skip next sc; rep from * around, sl st in 3rd ch of beg ch to join.

Rnd 3: Ch 1, sc in next dc, *(2 sc, ch 3, 2 sc) in next ch-3 loop**, sc in next puff st; rep from * around, ending last rep at **, sl st in first sc to join.

Rnd 4: Sl st to next ch-3 loop, beg pop in first ch-3 loop, ch 8, (pop, ch 8) in each ch-3 loop around, sl st in first pop to join.

Rnd 5: Sl st in next ch-8 loop, ch 3 (counts as dc), (4 dc, ch 3, 5 dc) in first ch-8 loop, (5 dc, ch 3, 5 dc) in each ch-8 loop around, sl st in 3rd ch of beg ch to join. Fasten off.

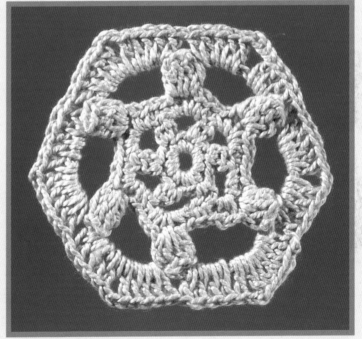

229

Beginning popcorn (beg pop): Ch 3 (counts as dc), 3 dc in same space, drop loop from hook, insert hook from front to back in 3rd ch of beg ch, place dropped loop on hook, draw loop through st.

Popcorn (pop): 4 dc in same space, drop loop from hook, insert hook from front to back in first dc of 4-dc group, place dropped loop on hook, draw loop through st.

Ch 6 and sl st in first ch to form a ring.

Rnd 1: Ch 1, 12 sc in ring, sl st in first sc to join.

Rnd 2: Ch 5 (counts as dc, ch 2), (dc, ch 2) in each sc around, sl st in 3rd ch of beg ch to join.

Rnd 3: Sl st in next ch-2 space, beg pop in first ch-2 space, ch 3, (pop, ch 3) in each ch-2 space around, sl st in first pop to join.

Rnd 4: Sl st in next ch-3 loop, ch 3 (counts as dc), 3 dc in first ch-3 loop, ch 1, (4 dc, ch 1) in each ch-3 loop around, sl st in 3rd ch of beg ch to join.

Rnd 5: Sl st to next ch-1 space, ch 3 (counts as dc), (2 dc, ch 2, 3 dc) in first ch-1 space, *ch 2, 4 dc in next ch-1 space, ch 2**, (3 dc, ch 2, 3 dc) in next ch-1 space; rep from * around, ending last rep at **, sl st in 3rd ch of beg ch to join. Fasten off.

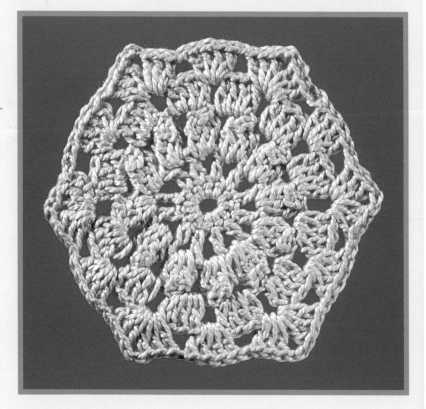

230

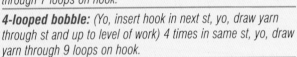

3-looped bobble: *(Yo, insert hook in next st, yo, draw yarn through st and up to level of work) 3 times in same st, yo, draw yarn through 7 loops on hook.*

4-looped bobble: *(Yo, insert hook in next st, yo, draw yarn through st and up to level of work) 4 times in same st, yo, draw yarn through 9 loops on hook.*

Ch 6 and sl st in first ch to form a ring.

Rnd 1: Ch 6 (counts as dc, ch 3), (dc, ch 3) 5 times in ring, sl st in 3rd ch of beg ch to join.

Rnd 2: Sl st to center of next ch-3 loop, ch 3 (counts as dc), 3-looped bobble in first ch-3 loop, ch 5, (4-looped bobble, ch 5) in each ch-3 loop around, sl st in first bobble to join.

Rnd 3: Sl st in next ch-5 loop, ch 3 (counts as dc), (2 dc, ch 3, 3 dc) in first ch-5 loop, (3 dc, ch 3, 3 dc) in each ch-5 loop around, sl st in 3rd ch of beg ch to join.

Rnd 4: Ch 1, *sc in each of next 3 dc, (sc, ch 2, sc) in next ch-2 space, sc in each of next 3 dc; rep from * around, sl st in first sc to join. Fasten off.

231

Ch 6 and sl st in first ch to form a ring.

Rnd 1: Ch 3 (counts as dc), 2 dc in ring, ch 3, (3 dc, ch 3) 5 times in ring, sl st in 3rd ch of beg ch to join.

Rnd 2: Sl st to next ch-3 loop, ch 5 (counts as dtr), (2 dtr, ch 2, 3 dtr) in first ch-2 space, (3 dtr, ch 2, 3 dtr) in each ch-3 loop around, sl st in 5th ch of beg ch to join.

Rnd 3: Ch 3 (counts as dc), *dc in each of next 2 dtr, (2 dc, ch 2, 2 dc) in next ch-2 space, dc in each of next 4 dtr; rep from * around, omitting last dc, sl st in 3rd ch of beg ch to join.

Rnd 4: Sl st in next dc, ch 3 (counts as dc), working behind beg ch-3 just made, dc in beg ch-3 of Rnd 3 (crossed dc made), *skip next st, dc in next st, working behind last dc made, dc in last skipped st (crossed dc made); rep from * around, sl st in 3rd ch of beg ch to join. Fasten off.

.16.
Floral Patterns

232 Ch 8 and sl st in first ch to form a ring.

Rnd 1: Ch 1, *sc in ring, ch 4, sc in 2nd ch from hook, hdc in each of next 2 ch, sc in ring, ch 6, sc in 2nd ch from hook, hdc in each of next 4 ch; rep from * 3 times, sl st in first sc to join. Fasten off.

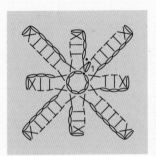 

233

Ch 10.

Row 1: Sc in 2nd ch from hook, dc in each of next 7 ch, sc in last ch.

Work now progresses in rnds.

Rnd 1: Ch 5 (counts as dc, ch 2), dc in end sc, working across opposite side of foundation ch, (ch 2, skip next ch, dc in next ch) 4 times, ch 2, (dc, ch 2, dc) in end ch, (ch 2, skip next st, dc in next st) 4 times, ch 2, sl st in 3rd ch of beg ch to join.

Rnd 2: Ch 1, *sc in dc, 3 dc in next ch-2 space; rep from * around, sl st in first sc to join. Fasten off.

234

Puff st: (Yo [twice], insert hook in next space, yo, draw yarn through space, [yo, draw yarn through 2 loops on hook] twice) twice in same space, yo, draw yarn through 3 loops on hook.

Ch 8 and sl st in first ch to form a ring.

Rnd 1: Ch 1, *sc in ring, ch 4, puff st in ring, ch 4; rep from * 4 times, sl st in first sc to join.

Rnd 2: Ch 1, *sc in sc, ch 11, skip next 2 ch-4 loops; rep from * around, sl st in first sc to join. Fasten off.

235

Ch 13 and sl st in first ch to form a ring.

Rnd 1: Ch 1, *sc in ring, ch 5, dtr in ring, ch 5, sc in ring, ch 3; rep from * ; rep from * 7 times, sl st in first sc to join. Fasten off.

236

Puff st: (Yo, insert hook in next space, yo, draw yarn through space, draw yarn through 2 loops on hook) twice in same space, yo, draw yarn through 3 loops on hook.

Picot: Ch 3, sl st in 3rd ch from hook.

Ch 6 and sl st in first ch to form a ring.

Rnd 1: Ch 3 (counts as dc), dc in ring, *ch 11, puff st in ring, ch 1, picot, ch 1, puff st in ring; rep from * 4 times, ch 11, puff st in ring, ch 1, picot, ch 1, sl st in 3rd ch of beg ch to join. Fasten off.

237

Ch 6 and sl st in first ch to form a ring.

Rnd 1: Ch 6 (counts as dc, ch 3), (dc, ch 3) 7 times in ring, sl st in 3rd ch of beg ch to join.

Rnd 2: Ch 3 (counts as dc), *4 dc in next ch-3 loop**, dc in next dc; rep from * around, ending last rep at **, sl st in 3rd ch of beg ch to join.

Rnd 3: Ch 1, *sc in dc, ch 6, sc in 2nd ch from hook, hdc in next ch, dc in next ch, tr in next ch, dtr in next ch, skip next 4 dc; rep from * around, sl st in first sc to join. Fasten off.

238

Ch 6 and sl st in first ch to form a ring.

Rnd 1: Ch 3 (counts as dc), 15 dc in ring, sl st in 3rd ch of beg ch to join.

Rnd 2: *Ch 3, skip next dc, sl st in next dc; rep from * around, ending with last sl st in first sl st to join.

Rnd 3: Sl st in next ch-3 loop, ch 3 (counts as dc), 5 dc in first ch-3 loop, 6 dc in each ch-3 loop around, sl st in 3rd ch of beg ch to join. Fasten off.

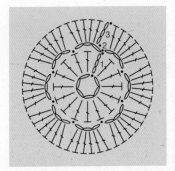

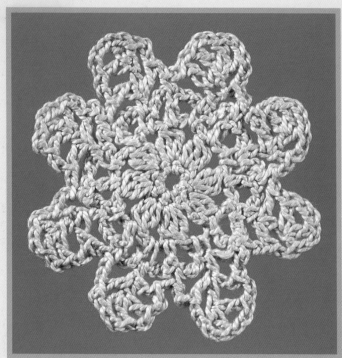

239

2-dc puff st: *(Yo, insert hook in next st, yo, draw yarn through st, draw yarn through 2 loops on hook) twice in same st, yo, draw yarn through 3 loops on hook.*

3-dc puff st: *(Yo, insert hook in next st, yo, draw yarn through st, draw yarn through 2 loops on hook) 3 times in same st, yo, draw yarn through 4 loops on hook.*

Ch 6 and sl st in first ch to form a ring.

Rnd 1: Ch 1, 8 sc in ring, sl st in first sc to join.

Rnd 2: Ch 3 (counts as dc), 2-dc puff st in first sc, ch 3, (3-dc puff st, ch 3) in each sc around, sl st in 3rd ch of beg ch to join.

Rnd 3: Ch 6 (counts as dc, ch 3), *sc in next ch-3 loop, ch 3**, dc in next puff st, ch 3; rep from * around, ending last rep at **, sl st in 3rd ch of beg ch to join.

Rnd 4: Ch 1, *sc in dc, ch 1, skip next ch-3 loop, tr in next sc, ch 2, tr in middle of last tr made, ch 2, (dc, ch 2, dc) in middle of last tr made, ch 2, dc in middle of first tr made, ch 1, skip next ch-3 loop; rep from * around, sl st in first sc to join. Fasten off.

240

Ch 10 and sl st in first ch to form a ring.

Rnd 1: Ch 3 (counts as dc), 23 dc in ring, sl st in 3rd ch of beg ch to join.

Rnd 2: Ch 6 (counts as dc, ch 3), skip next 2 dc, *dc in next dc, ch 3, skip next 2 dc; rep from * around, sl st in 3rd ch of beg ch to join.

Rnd 3: *Ch 9, sc in 2nd ch from hook, hdc in next ch, dc in next ch, tr in each of next 5 ch, skip next ch-3 loop, sl st in next dc; rep from * around, ending with last sl st in first sl st to join.

Rnd 4: Skip next ch, sc in each of next 7 ch, 3 sc in end ch, sc in each of next 7 sts, skip next tr, sl st in next sl st; rep from * around. Fasten off.

241

Puff st: (Yo, insert hook in next space, yo, draw yarn through space, draw yarn through 2 loops on hook) twice in same space, yo, draw yarn through 3 loops on hook.

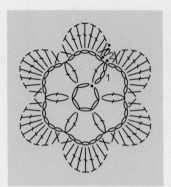

Ch 6 and sl st in first ch to form a ring.

Rnd 1: Ch 3 (counts as dc), dc in ring, ch 5, (puff st, ch 5) 5 times in ring, sl st in 3rd ch of beg ch to join.

Rnd 2: Sl st in first ch-5 loop, ch 1, (sc, hdc, 5 dc, hdc, sc) in each ch-5 loop around, sl st in first sc to join. Fasten off.

242

2-dc puff st: (Yo, insert hook in next space, yo, draw yarn through st, draw yarn through 2 loops on hook) twice in same space, yo, draw yarn through 3 loops on hook.

3-dc puff st: (Yo, insert hook in next space, yo, draw yarn through st, draw yarn through 2 loops on hook) 3 times in same space, yo, draw yarn through 4 loops on hook.

Ch 6 and sl st in first ch to form a ring.

Rnd 1: Ch 3 (counts as dc), 2-dc puff st in ring, ch 3, (3-dc puff st, ch 3) 4 times in ring, sl st in first puff st to join.

Rnd 2: Ch 1, *sc in puff st, (hdc, 3 dc, hdc) in next ch-3 loop; rep from * around, sl st in first sc to join.

Rnd 3: Ch 1, *sc in sc, ch 5, skip next 5 sts; rep from * around, sl st in first sc to join.

Rnd 4: Sl st in next ch-5 loop, ch 1, (sc, hdc, 8 dc, hdc, sc) in each ch-5 loop around, sl st in first sc to join. Fasten off.

243

Ch 8 and sl st in first ch to form a ring.

Rnd 1: Ch 4 (counts as dc, ch 1), (dc, ch 1) 11 times in ring, sl st in 3rd ch of beg ch to join.

Rnd 2: Sl st in next ch-1 space, ch 1, *sc in ch-1 space, ch 4, skip next ch-1 space; rep from * around, sl st in first sc to join.

Rnd 3: Ch 1, *sc in sc, ch 1, 4 dc in next ch-4 loop, ch 1; rep from * around, sl st in first sc to join.

Rnd 4: Ch 5 (counts as tr, ch 1), (tr, ch 1) 3 times in first sc, skip next 2 dc, sc bet last skipped and next dc, ch 1, skip next 3 sts**, (tr, ch 1) 4 times in next sc; rep from * around, ending last rep at **, sl st in first sc to join. Fasten off.

244

Picot: *Ch 3, sl st in 3rd ch from hook.*

2-dc puff st: *(Yo, insert hook in next space, yo, draw yarn through space, draw yarn through 2 loops on hook) twice in same space, yo, draw yarn through 3 loops on hook.*

3-dc puff st: *(Yo, insert hook in next space, yo, draw yarn through space, draw yarn through 2 loops on hook) 3 times in same space, yo, draw yarn through 4 loops on hook.*

Ch 8 and sl st in first ch to form a ring.

Rnd 1: Ch 3 (counts as dc), 2-dc puff st in ring, picot, ch 5, (3-dc puff st, picot, ch 5) 7 times in ring, sl st in first puff st to join.

Rnd 2: Sl st to center of next ch-5 loop, ch 1, (sc, ch 7) in each ch-5 loop around, sl st in first sc to join. Fasten off.

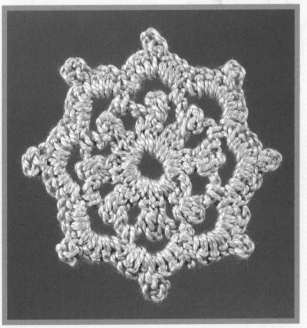

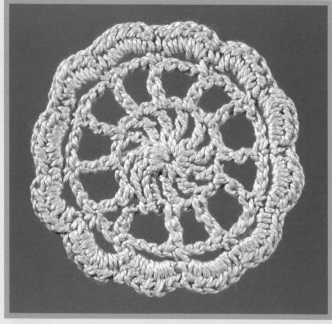

245

Ch 6 and sl st in first ch to form a ring.

Rnd 1: Ch 5 (counts as tr, ch 1), (tr, ch 1) 11 times in ring, sl st in 4th ch of beg ch to join.

Rnd 2: Ch 7 (counts as tr, ch 3), skip next ch-1 space, (tr, ch 3) in each tr around, sl st in 4th ch of beg ch to join.

Rnd 3: Ch 1, (sc, ch 4) in each tr around, sl st in first sc to join.

Rnd 4: Ch 1, *sc in sc, 5 hdc in next ch-4 loop; rep from * around, sl st in first sc to join. Fasten off.

246

Beginning popcorn (beg pop): Ch 3 (counts as dc), 4 dc in same st, drop loop from hook, insert hook from front to back in 3rd ch of beg ch, place dropped loop on hook, draw loop through st.

Popcorn (pop): 5 dc in same st, drop loop from hook, insert hook from front to back in first dc of 5-dc group, place dropped loop on hook, draw loop through st.

Ch 6 and sl st in first ch to form a ring.

Rnd 1: Ch 3 (counts as dc), 15 dc in ring, sl st in 3rd ch of beg ch to join.

Rnd 2: Beg pop in first st, ch 3, skip next dc, *pop in next dc, ch 3, skip next dc; rep from * around, sl st in first pop to join.

Rnd 3: Sl st in next ch-3 loop, ch 1, (sc, hdc, 3 dc, hdc, sc) in each ch-3 loop around, sl st in first sc to join. Fasten off.

247

2-dtr puff st: (Yo [3 times], insert hook in next space, yo, draw yarn through space, [yo, draw yarn through 2 loops on hook] 3 times) twice in same space, yo, draw yarn through 3 loops on hook.

3-dtr puff st: (Yo [3 times], insert hook in next space, yo, draw yarn through space, [yo, draw yarn through 2 loops on hook] 3 times) 3 times in same space, yo, draw yarn through 4 loops on hook.

Ch 6 and sl st in first ch to form a ring.

Rnd 1: Ch 5 (counts as dtr), 2-dtr puff st in ring, ch 7, (3-dtr puff st, ch 7) 7 times in ring, sl st in first puff st to join. Fasten off.

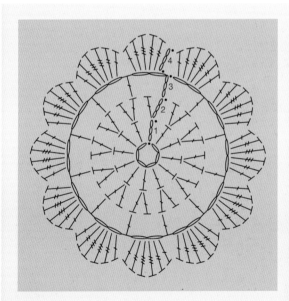

248

Ch 6 and sl st in first ch to form a ring.

Rnd 1: Ch 3 (counts as dc), 11 dc in ring, sl st in 3rd ch of beg ch to join.

Rnd 2: Ch 3 (counts as dc), dc in first st, 2 dc in each dc around, sl st in 3rd ch of beg ch to join.

Rnd 3: Ch 5 (counts as dc, ch 2), skip next dc, *dc in next dc, ch 2, skip next dc; rep from * around, sl st in 3rd ch of beg ch to join.

Rnd 4: Sl st in first ch-2 space, ch 3, (tr, 2 dtr, tr, dc) in first ch-2 space, (dc, tr, 2 dtr, tr, dc) in each ch-2 space around, sl st in 3rd ch of beg ch to join. Fasten off.

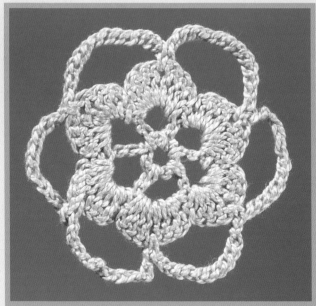

249

Ch 8 and sl st in first ch to form a ring.

Rnd 1: Ch 7 (counts as dc, ch 4), (dc, ch 4) 5 times in ring, sl st in 3rd ch of beg ch to join.

Rnd 2: Sl st in next ch-4 loop, ch 1, (sc, ch 1, 3 dc, ch 1, 3 dc, ch 1, sc) in each ch-4 loop around, sl st in first sc to join.

Rnd 3: Sl st in each of next 5 sts to ch-1 space, ch 1, *sc in ch-1 space, ch 13, skip next 10 sts; rep from * around, sl st in first sc to join. Fasten off.

250

Puff st: (Yo [twice], insert hook in next space, yo, draw yarn through space, [yo, draw yarn through 2 loops on hook] twice) 4 times in same space, yo, draw yarn through 5 loops on hook.

Ch 6 and sl st in first ch to form a ring.

Rnd 1: Ch 4 (counts as tr), 19 tr in ring, sl st in 4th ch of beg ch to join.

Rnd 2: Ch 1, *sc in tr, ch 4, skip next tr; rep from * around, sl st in first sc to join.

Rnd 3: Sl st in next ch-4 loop, ch 1, (sc, ch 4, puff st, ch 4, sc) in each ch-4 loop around, sl st in first sc to join. Fasten off.

251

Ch 6 and sl st in first ch to form a ring.

Rnd 1: Ch 3 (counts as dc), 2 dc in ring, ch 7, (3 dc, ch 7) 3 times in ring, sl st in 3rd ch of beg ch to join.

Rnd 2: Sl st in next dc, ch 1, *sc in dc, (2 dc, 3 tr, 5 dtr, 3 tr, 2 dc) in next ch-7 loop, skip next dc; rep from * around, sl st in first sc to join. Fasten off.

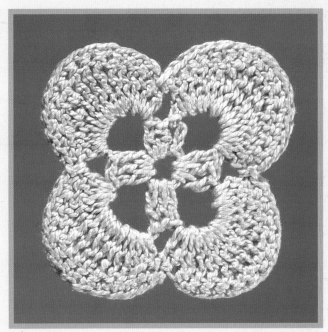

252

Ch 10 and sl st in first ch to form a ring.

Rnd 1: Ch 1, 16 sc in ring, sl st in first sc to join.

Rnd 2: Ch 1, *sc in sc, ch 6, skip next sc; rep from * around, sl st in first sc to join.

Rnd 3: Sl st in next ch-6 loop, ch 1, (sc, hdc, dc, 5 tr, dc, hdc, sc) in each ch-6 loop around, sl st in first sc to join. Fasten off.

253

Ch 8 and sl st in first ch to form a ring.

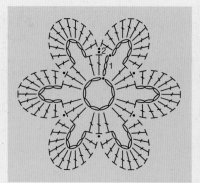

Rnd 1: Ch 3 (counts as dc), 2 dc in ring, ch 6, (3 dc, ch 6) 5 times in ring, sl st in 3rd ch of beg ch to join.

Rnd 2: Sl st in next dc, *11 dc in next ch-6 loop, skip next dc, sl st in next dc; rep from * around, ending with last sl st in first sl st to join. Fasten off.

254

Picot: Ch 4, sl st in 4th ch from hook.

Ch 6 and sl st in first ch to form a ring.

Rnd 1: Ch 1, (sc, ch 3) 12 times in ring, sl st in first sc to join.

Rnd 2: Sl st in next ch-3 loop, ch 1, (sc, ch 3) in each ch-3 loop around, sl st in first sc to join.

Rnd 3: Sl st in next ch-3 loop, ch 1, *(sc in ch-3 loop, ch 6, sc in next ch-3 loop, ch 3; rep from * around, sl st in first sc to join.

Rnd 4: Sl st in next ch-6 loop, ch 3 (counts as dc), (4 dc, picot, 5 dc) in first ch-6 loop, sc in next ch-3 loop, *(5 dc, picot, 5 dc) in next ch-6 loop, sc in next ch-3 loop; rep from * around, sl st in 3rd ch of beg ch to join. Fasten off.

255

Ch 6 and sl st in first ch to form a ring.

Rnd 1: Ch 12 (counts as tr, ch 8), (tr, ch 8) 7 times in ring, sl st in 4th ch of beg ch to join.

Rnd 2: Sl st in next ch-8 loop, ch 1, (sc, hdc, dc, 3 tr, ch 5, 3 tr, dc, hdc, sc) in each ch-8 loop around, sl st in first sc to join. Fasten off.

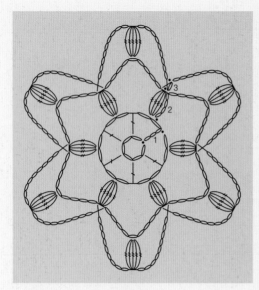

256

4-tr puff st: *(Yo [twice], insert hook in next space, yo, draw yarn through space, [yo, draw yarn through 2 loops on hook] twice) 4 times in same space, yo, draw yarn through 5 loops on hook.*

5-tr puff st: *(Yo [twice], insert hook in next space, yo, draw yarn through space, [yo, draw yarn through 2 loops on hook] twice) 5 times in same space, yo, draw yarn through 6 loops on hook.*

Ch 6 and sl st in first ch to form a ring.

Rnd 1: Ch 5 (counts as dc, ch 2), (dc, ch 2) 5 times in ring, sl st in 3rd ch of beg ch to join.

Rnd 2: Sl st in next ch-2 space, ch 4 (counts as tr), 4-tr puff st in first ch-2 space, ch 9, (5-tr puff st, ch 9) in each ch-2 space around, sl st in first puff st to join.

Rnd 3: Ch 1, *sc in puff st, ch 9, 5-tr puff st in next ch-9 loop, ch 9; rep from * around, sl st in first sc to join. Fasten off.

257

Picot: Ch 4, sl st in 4th ch from hook.

Ch 6 and sl st in first ch to form a ring.

Rnd 1: Ch 1, 16 sc in ring, sl st in first sc to join.

Rnd 2: Ch 1, *sc in each of next 2 sc, (sc, ch 10, sc) in next sc, sc in next sc; rep from * around, sl st in first sc to join.

Rnd 3: Ch 1, *sc in sc, skip next 2 sc, (2 hdc, 17 dc, 2 hdc) in next ch-10 loop, skip next 2 sc; rep from * around, sl st in first sc to join.

Rnd 4: Ch 1, *sc in sc, ch 5, skip next 5 sts, (sc in next dc, picot, ch 5, skip next 4 dc) twice, sc in next dc, picot, ch 5, skip next 5 sts; rep from * around, sl st in first sc to join. Fasten off.

258

Ch 6 and sl st in first ch to form a ring.

Rnd 1: Ch 3 (counts as dc), 15 dc in ring, sl st in 3rd ch of beg ch to join.

Rnd 2: Ch 3 (counts as dc), dc in next dc, ch 11, *dc in each of next 2 dc, ch 11; rep from * around, sl st in 3rd ch of beg ch to join.

Rnd 3: Sl st to center of next ch-11 loop, ch 3 (counts as dc), (3 dc, ch 3, 4 dc) in first ch-11 loop, (4 dc, ch 3, 4 dc) in each ch-11 loop around, sl st in 3rd ch of beg ch to join. Fasten off.

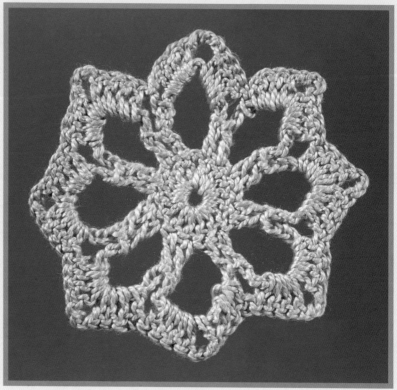

259

Picot: Ch 3, sl st in 3rd ch from hook.

Ch 6 and sl st in first ch to form a ring.

Rnd 1: Ch 3 (counts as dc), 2 dc in ring, ch 2, (3 dc, ch 2) 4 times in ring, sl st in 3rd ch of beg ch to join.

Rnd 2: Sl st to next ch-2 space, ch 1, (sc, ch 6) in each ch-2 space around, sl st in first sc to join.

Rnd 3: Ch 4 (counts as tr), *9 tr in next ch-6 loop**, tr in next sc; rep from * around, ending last rep at **, sl st in 4th ch of beg ch to join.

Rnd 4: Ch 1, *sc in each of next 2 tr, picot; rep from * around, sl st in first sc to join. Fasten off.

260

Picot: Ch 3, sl st in 3rd ch from hook.

Ch 6 and sl st in first ch to form a ring.

Rnd 1: Ch 6 (counts as dc, ch 3), (dc, ch 3) 4 times in ring, sl st in 3rd ch of beg ch to join.

Rnd 2: Sl st in next ch-3 loop, ch 3 (counts as dc), 4 dc in first ch-3 loop, ch 2, (5 dc, ch 2) in each ch-3 loop around, sl st in 3rd ch of beg ch to join.

Rnd 3: Turn, sl st in next ch-2 space, turn, ch 1, (sc, ch 10) in each ch-2 space around, sl st in first sc to join.

Rnd 4: Sl st in next ch-10 loop, ch 5 (counts as dc, ch 2), (dc, ch 2) 4 times in first ch-10 loop, (dc, ch 2) 5 times in each ch-10 loop around, sl st in 3rd ch of beg ch to join.

Rnd 5: Sl st in next ch-2 space, ch 1, (sc, picot, sc) in each ch-2 space around, sl st in first sc to join. Fasten off.

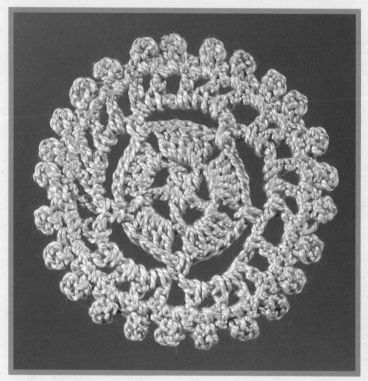

261

Ch 6 and sl st in first ch to form a ring.

Rnd 1: Ch 3 (counts as dc), 15 dc in ring, sl st in 3rd ch of beg ch to join.

Rnd 2: Ch 10 (counts as tr, ch 6), skip next dc, *tr in next dc, ch 6, skip next dc; rep from * around, sl st in 4th ch of beg ch to join.

Rnd 3: Sl st in next ch-6 loop, ch 1, (3 sc, ch 1, 3 sc, ch 1) in each ch-6 loop around, sl st in first sc to join.

Rnd 4: Sl st to next ch-1 space, ch 3 (counts as dc), (2 dc, ch 3, 3 dc) in first ch-1 space, *skip next 3 sc, sc in next ch-1 space, skip next 3 sc**, (3 dc, ch 3, 3 dc) in next ch-1 space; rep from * around, ending last rep at **, sl st in 3rd ch of beg ch to join. Fasten off.

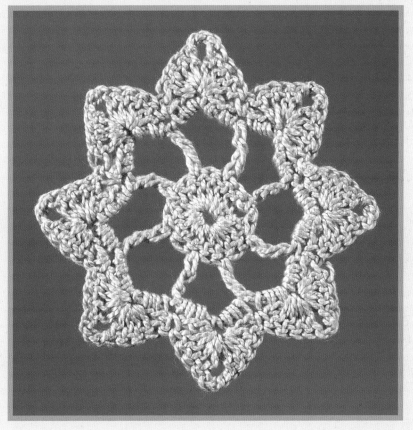

262

Picot: Ch 4, sl st in 4th ch from hook.

Ch 6 and sl st in first ch to form a ring.

Rnd 1: Ch 1, (sc, ch 7) 8 times in ring, sl st in first sc to join.

Rnd 2: Sl st to center of next ch-7 loop, ch 1, (sc, ch 4) in each ch-7 loop around, sl st in first sc to join.

Rnd 3: Sl st to center of next ch-4 loop, ch 1, (sc, picot, ch 5) in each ch-4 loop around, sl st in first sc to join.

Rnd 4: Sl st in next picot, ch 4 (counts as dc, ch 1), (dc, ch 1) 4 times in first picot, sc in next ch-5 loop, *(dc, ch 1) 5 times in next picot, sc in next ch-5 loop; rep from * around, sl st in 3rd ch of beg ch to join. Fasten off.

263

Ch 6 and sl st in first ch to form a ring.

Rnd 1: Ch 1, 8 sc in ring, sl st in first sc to join.

Rnd 2: Ch 5 (counts as dc, ch 2), (dc, ch 2) in each sc around, sl st in 3rd ch of beg ch to join.

Rnd 3: Ch 3 (counts as dc), *3 dc in next ch-2 space**, dc in next dc; rep from * around, ending last rep at **, sl st in 3rd ch of beg ch to join.

Rnd 4: Ch 1, *sc in dc, ch 11, skip next 3 dc; rep from * around, sl st in first sc to join.

Rnd 5: Sl st to center of next ch-11 loop, ch 1, (sc, ch 9) in each ch-11 loop around, sl st in first sc to join.

Rnd 6: Ch 1, *sc in sc, 9 tr in center ch of next ch-9 loop; rep from * around, sl st in first sc to join. Fasten off.

264

Ch 10 and sl st in first ch to form a ring.

Rnd 1: Ch 1, (sc, ch 10) 8 times in ring, sl st in first sc to join.

Rnd 2: Sl st to center of next ch-10 loop, ch 4 (counts as dc, ch 1), dc in first ch-10 loop, ch 5, (dc, ch 1, dc, ch 5) in each ch-10 loop around, sl st in 3rd ch of beg ch to join.

Rnd 3: Sl st in next ch-1 space, ch 3 (counts as dc), (dc, ch 2, 2 dc) in first ch-1 space, *ch 2, sc in next ch-5 loop, ch 2**, (2 dc, ch 2, 2 dc) in next ch-1 space; rep from * around, ending last rep at **, sl st in 3rd ch of beg ch to join.

Rnd 4: Sl st to next ch-2 space, ch 3 (counts as dc), (2 dc, ch 3, 3 dc) in first ch-2 space, *ch 3, skip next ch-2 space, sc in next sc, ch 3, skip next ch-2 space**, (3 dc, ch 3, 3 dc) in next ch-2 space; rep from * around, ending last rep at **, sl st in 3rd ch of beg ch to join.

Rnd 5: Sl st to next ch-3 loop, ch 3 (counts as dc), (2 dc, ch 3, 3 dc) in first ch-3 loop, *ch 4, skip next ch-3 loop, sc in next sc, ch 4, skip next ch-3 loop**, (3 dc, ch 3, 3 dc) in next ch-3 loop; rep from * around, ending last rep at **, sl st in 3rd ch of beg ch to join. Fasten off.

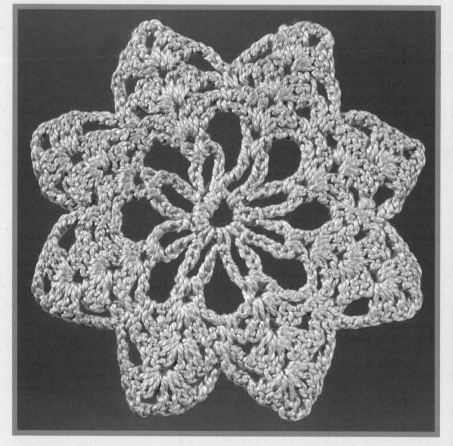

265

Ch 6 and sl st in first ch to form a ring.

Rnd 1: Ch 6 (counts as dc, ch 3), (dc, ch 3) 4 times in ring, sl st in 3rd ch of beg ch to join.

Rnd 2: Ch 1, (sc, hdc, 3 dc, hdc, sc) in each ch-5 loop around, sl st in first sc to join.

Rnd 3: Ch 1, *sc bet 2 sc, ch 5, skip next 7 sts; rep from * around, sl st in first sc to join.

Rnd 4: Ch 1, (sc, hdc, 5 dc, hdc, sc) in each ch-5 loop around, sl st in first sc to join.

Rnd 5: Ch 1, *sc bet 2 sc, ch 7, skip next 9 sts; rep from * around, sl st in first sc to join.

Rnd 6: Ch 1, (sc, hdc, 7 dc, hdc, sc) in each ch-7 loop around, sl st in first sc to join.

Rnd 7: Ch 1, *sc bet 2 sc, ch 9, skip next 11 sts; rep from * around, sl st in first sc to join.

Rnd 8: Ch 1, (sc, hdc, 9 dc, hdc, sc) in each ch-9 loop around, sl st in first sc to join. Fasten off.

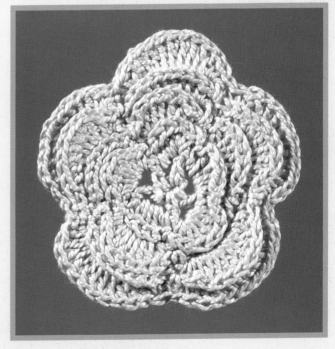

.17.

Sculptured Blocks

266 Ch 6 and sl st in first ch to form a ring.

Rnd 1: Ch 1, (sc, ch 2, 4 dc, ch 2) 4 times in ring, sl st in first sc to join.

Rnd 2: Ch 1, *sc in sc, ch 5, skip next 2 ch-2 spaces; rep from * around, sl st in first sc to join.

Rnd 3: Sl st in next ch-5 loop, ch 3 (counts as dc), (3 dc, ch 3, 4 dc) in first ch-5 loop, ch 2, (4 dc, ch 3, 4 dc, ch 2) in each ch-5 loop around, sl st in 3rd ch of beg ch to join.

Rnd 4: Sl st to next ch-3 loop, ch 3 (counts as dc), (3 dc, ch 3, 4 dc) in first ch-3 loop, *ch 1, 4 dc in next ch-2 space, ch 1**, (4 dc, ch 3, 4 dc) in next ch-3 loop; rep from * around, ending last rep at **, sl st in 3rd ch of beg ch to join. Fasten off.

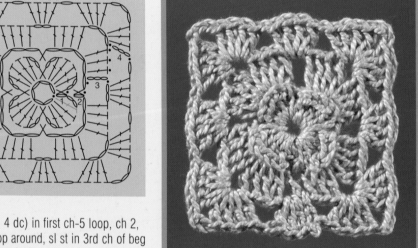

267

Ch 8 and sl st in first ch to form a ring.

Rnd 1: Ch 1, (sc, ch 2, 5 dc, ch 2) 4 times in ring, sl st in first sc to join.

Rnd 2: Ch 1, *sc in sc, ch 5, skip next 2 ch-2 spaces; rep from * around, sl st in first sc to join.

Rnd 3: Sl st in next ch-5 loop, ch 3 (counts as dc), (3 dc, ch 2, 4 dc) in first ch-5 loop, ch 2, (4 dc, ch 2, 4 dc, ch 2) in each ch-5 loop around, sl st in 3rd ch of beg ch to join.

Rnd 4: Sl st to next ch-2 space, ch 3 (counts as dc), (3 dc, ch 3, 4 dc) in first ch-2 space, *ch 1, 4 dc in next ch-2 space, ch 1**, (4 dc, ch 3, 4 dc) in next ch-2 space; rep from * around, ending last rep at **, sl st in 3rd ch of beg ch to join. Fasten off.

268

2-dc puff st: *(Yo, insert hook in next space, yo, draw yarn through space, draw yarn through 2 loops on hook) twice in same space, yo, draw yarn through 3 loops on hook.*

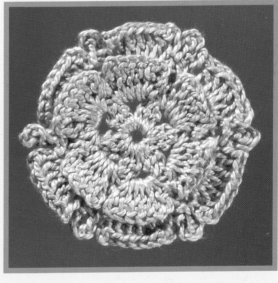

3-dc puff st: *(Yo, insert hook in next space, yo, draw yarn through space, draw yarn through 2 loops on hook) 3 times in same space, yo, draw yarn through 4 loops on hook.*

Ch 6 and sl st in first ch to form a ring.

Rnd 1: Ch 3 (counts as dc), 2-dc puff st in ring, ch 3, (3-dc puff st, ch 3) 5 times in ring, sl st in first puff st to join.

Rnd 2: Ch 1, (sc, ch 3, 4 dc, ch 3, sc) in each ch-3 loop around, sl st in first sc to join.

Rnd 3: Ch 1, *sc bet 2 sc, ch 5, skip next 2 ch-3 loops; rep from * around, sl st in first sc to join.

Rnd 4: Sl st in next ch-5 loop, ch 1, (sc, ch 3, 5 dc, ch 3, sc, ch 5) in each ch-5 loop around, sl st in first sc to join. Fasten off.

269

Ch 6 and sl st in first ch to form a ring.

Rnd 1: Ch 3 (counts as dc), 17 dc in ring, sl st in 3rd ch of beg ch to join.

Rnd 2: Ch 1, *sc in dc, ch 3, skip next 2 dc; rep from * around, sl st in first sc to join.

Rnd 3: *Ch 3, (dc, 3 tr, dc) in next ch-3 loop, ch 3, sl st in next sc; rep from * around, ending with last sl st in first sl st to join.

Rnd 4: Sl st in each of next 6 sts, *ch 9, skip next 2 ch-3 loops, skip next 2 sts, sl st in next tr; rep from * around, ending with last sl st in first sl st to join.

Rnd 5: Sl st in next ch-9 loop, ch 2 (counts as hdc), 11 hdc in first ch-9 loop, 12 hdc in each ch-9 loop around, sl st in 2nd ch of beg ch to join. Fasten off.

270

Picot: Ch 3, sl st in 3rd ch from hook.

Ch 6 and sl st in first ch to form a ring.

Rnd 1: Ch 3 (counts as dc), 15 dc in ring, sl st in 3rd ch of beg ch to join.

Rnd 2: Ch 1, *sc in dc, ch 5, skip next dc; rep from * around, sl st in first sc to join.

Rnd 3: Sl st in next ch-5 loop, ch 3 (counts as dc), (6 dc, picot, 7 dc) in first ch-5 loop, (7 dc, picot, 7 dc) in each ch-5 loop around, sl st in 3rd ch of beg ch to join.

Rnd 4: Ch 1, *working over last rnd, sc in next corresponding sc 2 rnds below, ch 5, skip next shell; rep from * around, sl st in first sc to join.

Rnd 5: Sl st in next ch-5 loop, ch 3 (counts as dc), 5 dc in first ch-5 loop, 6 dc in each ch-5 loop around, sl st in 3rd ch of beg ch to join.

Rnd 6: Sl st in next dc, ch 3 (counts as dc), (dc, ch 1, 2 dc) in first dc, skip next 2 dc, *(2 dc, ch 1, 2 dc) in next dc, skip next 2 dc; rep from * around, sl st in 3rd ch of beg ch to join. Fasten off.

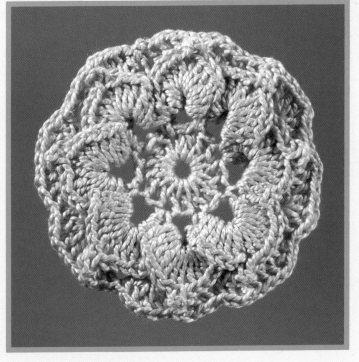

271

Ch 6 and sl st in first ch to form a ring.

Rnd 1: Ch 1, 16 sc in ring, sl st in first sc to join.

Rnd 2: Ch 6 (counts as dc, ch 3), skip next sc, *dc in next sc, ch 3, skip next sc; rep from * around, sl st in 3rd ch of beg ch to join.

Rnd 3: Ch 1, (sc, hdc, 5 dc, hdc, sc) in each ch-3 loop around, sl st in first sc to join.

Rnd 4: Ch 1, *sc bet 2 sc, ch 5, skip next 9 sts; rep from * around, sl st in first sc to join.

Rnd 5: Ch 1, (sc, hdc, 6 dc, hdc, sc) in each ch-5 loop around, sl st in first sc to join.

Rnd 6: Sl st in each of next 3 sts, ch 1, *sc in dc, ch 6, skip next 2 dc, sc in next dc, ch 6, skip next 6 sts; rep from * around, sl st in first sc to join.

Rnd 7: Sl st to center of next ch-6 loop, ch 1, *sc in ch-6 loop, (ch 6, sc) in each of next 2 ch-6 loops, ch 4, (4 dc, ch 4, 4 dc) in next ch-6 loop, ch 4; rep from * around, sl st in first sc to join. Fasten off.

272

Ch 6 and sl st in first ch to form a ring.

Rnd 1: Ch 1, 10 sc in ring, sl st in first sc to join.

Rnd 2: Ch 1, 2 sc in each sc around, sl st in first sc to join.

Rnd 3: Ch 6 (counts as tr, ch 2), (tr, ch 2) in each sc around, sl st in 4th ch of beg ch to join.

Rnd 4: Ch 1, (sc, ch 2, dc, ch 2, sc) in each ch-2 space around, sl st in first sc to join.

Rnd 5: Ch 1, *sc bet 2 sc, ch 3, skip next 2 ch-2 space; rep from * around, sl st in first sc to join.

Rnd 6: Ch 1, (sc, 3 dc, sc) in each ch-3 loop around, sl st in first sc to join.

Rnd 7: Sl st in each of next 2 sts, *ch 3, skip next 4 sts, sl st in next dc, ch 3, skip next 4 sts, (dc, ch 3, dc) in next dc, (ch 3, skip next 4 sts, sl st in next dc) twice; rep from * around, ending with last sl st in first sl st to join. Fasten off.

.18.
Small Blocks

273 Ch 20.

Row 1: Dc in 8th ch from hook, ch 2, skip next 2 ch, dc in each of next 4 ch, (ch 2, skip next 2 ch, dc in next ch) twice, turn.

Row 2: Ch 5 (counts as dc, ch 2), skip next ch-2 space, dc in next dc, 2 dc in next ch-2 space, dc in next dc, ch 5, skip next 2 dc, dc in next dc, 2 dc in next ch-2 space, dc in next dc, ch 2, skip next 2 ch of turning ch, dc in next ch of turning ch, turn.

Row 3: Ch 3 (counts as dc), 2 dc in next ch-2 space, dc in next dc, ch 5, sc in next ch-5 loop, ch 5, skip next 3 dc, dc in next dc, 2 dc in next ch-2 space of turning ch, dc in 3rd ch of turning ch, turn.

Row 4: Ch 5 (counts as dc, ch 2), skip first 3 dc, dc in next dc, 3 dc in next ch-5 loop, ch 2, 3 dc in next ch-5 loop, dc in next dc, ch 2, skip next 2 dc, dc in 3rd ch of turning ch, turn.

Row 5: Ch 5 (counts as dc, ch 2), skip next ch-2 space, dc in next dc, ch 2, skip next 2 dc, dc in next dc, 2 dc in next ch-2 space, dc in next dc, ch 2, skip next 2 dc, dc in next dc, ch 2, skip next 2 ch of turning ch, dc in 3rd ch of turning ch. Fasten off.

274

Bobble: *(Yo, insert hook in next st, yo, draw yarn through st and up to level of work) 4 times in same st, yo, draw yarn through 9 loops on hook.*

Ch 24.

Row 1: Dc in 4th ch from hook, dc in each ch across, turn.

Row 2: Ch 3 (counts as dc), dc in each of next 3 dc, *skip next dc, bobble in next dc, ch 2, skip next dc*, dc in each of next 8 dc; rep from * to * once, dc in each of next 3 dc, dc in 3rd ch of turning ch, turn.

Row 3: Ch 3 (counts as dc), dc in each of next 3 dc, *skip next ch-2 space, bobble in next bobble, ch 2*, dc in each of next 8 dc; rep from * to * once, dc in each of next 3 dc, dc in 3rd ch of turning ch, turn.

Rep Row 3 until block is 1 row less than desired depth.

Last Row: Ch 3 (counts as dc), dc in each st across, working 2 dc in each ch-2 space, ending with dc in 3rd ch of turning ch. Fasten off.

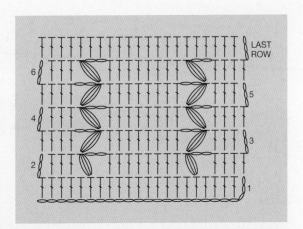

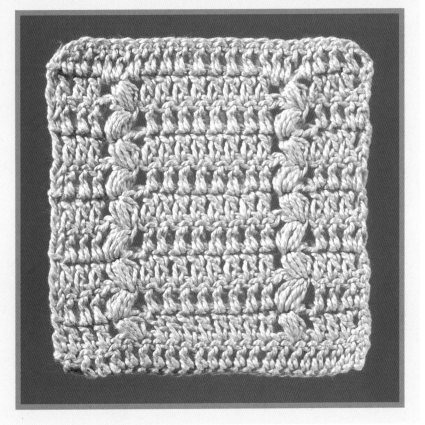

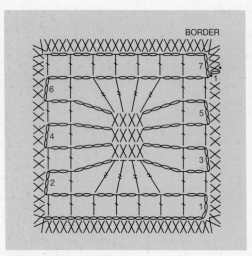

BORDER

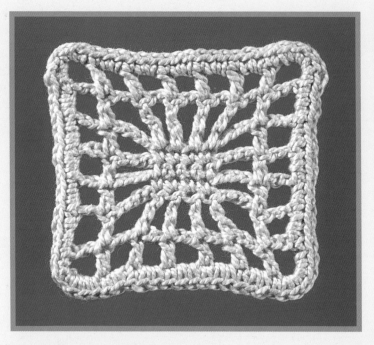

275 Ch 26.

Row 1 (RS): Dc in 8th ch from hook, *ch 2, skip next 2 ch, dc in next ch; rep from * across, turn.

Row 2: Ch 5 (counts as dc, ch 2), skip next ch-2 space, dc in next dc, ch 4, tr in each of next 4 dc, ch 4, skip next ch-2 space, dc in next dc, ch 2, skip next 2 ch of turning ch, dc in 5th ch ch of turning ch, turn.

Row 3: Ch 5 (counts as dc, ch 2), skip next ch-2 space, dc in next dc, ch 4, skip next ch-4 loop, sc in each of next 4 tr, ch 4, skip next ch-4 loop, dc in next dc, ch 2, skip next 2 ch of turning ch, dc in 3rd ch ch of turning ch, turn.

Rows 4-5: Ch 5 (counts as dc, ch 2), skip next ch-2 space, dc in next dc, ch 4, skip next ch-4 loop, sc in each of next 4 sc, ch 4, skip next ch-4 loop, dc in next dc, ch 2, skip next 2 ch of turning ch, dc in 3rd ch ch of turning ch, turn.

Row 6: Ch 5 (counts as dc, ch 2), skip next ch-2 space, dc in next dc, skip next ch-4 loop, (ch 2, tr) in each of next 4 sc, ch 2, skip next ch-4 loop, dc in next dc, ch 2, skip next 2 ch of turning ch, dc in 3rd ch ch of turning ch, turn. Fasten off.

Border

Rnd 1: With RS facing, join yarn in top right-hand corner loop, ch 1, 7 sc in corner, (sc in next dc, 2 sc in next ch-2 space) 6 times, 5 more sc in corner loop, working across side edge, work 2 sc in each row-end st across, 7 sc in next corner loop, working across bottom edge, (sc in next ch at base of dc, 2 sc in next ch-2 space) 6 times, 5 more sc in corner loop, working across side edge, work 2 sc in each row-end st across, sl st in first sc to join. Fasten off.

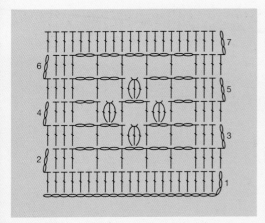

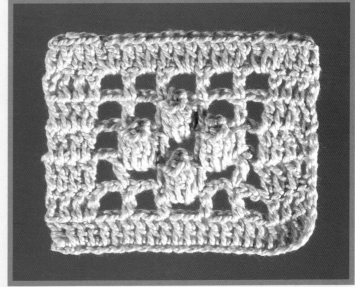

276

Popcorn (pop): 3 dc in same st, drop loop from hook, insert hook from front to back in first dc of 3-dc group, place dropped loop on hook, draw loop through st.

Ch 24.

Row 1: Dc in 4th ch from hook, dc in each ch across, turn.

Row 2: Ch 3 (counts as dc), dc in each of next 3 dc, (ch 2, skip next 2 dc, dc in next dc) 5 times, dc in each of next 2 dc, dc in 3rd ch of turning ch, turn.

Row 3: Ch 3 (counts as dc), dc in each of next 3 dc, (ch 2, skip next ch-2 space, dc in next dc) twice, pop in next next ch-2 space, dc in next dc, (ch 2, skip next ch-2 space, dc in next dc) twice, dc in each of next 2 dc, dc in 3rd ch of turning ch, turn.

Row 4: Ch 3 (counts as dc), dc in each of next 3 dc, ch 2, skip next ch-2 space, dc in next dc, pop in next next ch-2 space, dc in next dc, ch 2, skip next pop, dc in next dc, pop in next next ch-2 space, dc in next dc, ch 2, skip next ch-2 space, dc in each of next 3 dc, dc in 3rd ch of turning ch, turn.

Row 5: Ch 3 (counts as dc), dc in each of next 3 dc, ch 2, skip next ch-2 space, dc in next dc, ch 2, skip next pop, dc in next dc, pop in next next ch-2 space, dc in next dc, ch 2, skip next pop, dc in next dc, ch 2, skip next ch-2 space, dc in each of next 3 dc, dc in 3rd ch of turning ch, turn.

Row 6: Ch 3 (counts as dc), dc in each of next 3 dc, (ch 2, skip next ch-2 space or pop, dc in next dc) 5 times, dc in each of next 2 dc, dc in 3rd ch of turning ch, turn.

Row 7: Ch 3 (counts as dc), dc in each of next 3 dc, (2 dc in next ch-2 space, dc in next dc) 5 times, dc in each of next 2 dc, dc in 3rd ch of turning ch. Fasten off.

.19.
Sampler Blocks

277 **Ch** any number of sts for desired width.

Row 1: Sc in 2nd ch from hook, sc in each ch across, turn.

Row 2: Ch 1, sc in each sc across, turn.

Rep Row 2 for desired depth. Fasten off.

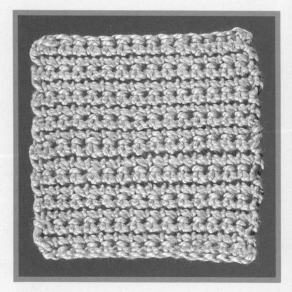

278

Ch any number of sts for desired width.

Row 1 (RS): Sc in 2nd ch from hook, sc in each ch across, turn.

Row 2: Ch 1, sc in each sc across, turn.

Rep Row 2 for desired depth. Fasten off.

Border:

Rnd 1: With RS facing, join yarn in top right-hand corner sc, ch 1, *(sc, ch 5, sc) in corner st, (ch 5, skip next st, sc in next st) across to within 2 sts of next corner, ch 5, (sc, ch 5, sc) in next corner sc, working across side edge, (ch 5, skip next row-end sc, sc in next row-end sc) across to within 2 rows of next corner; rep from * around, sl st in first sc to join. Fasten off.

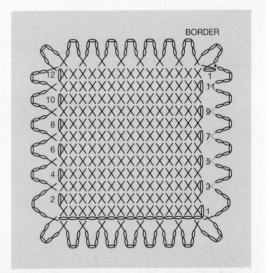

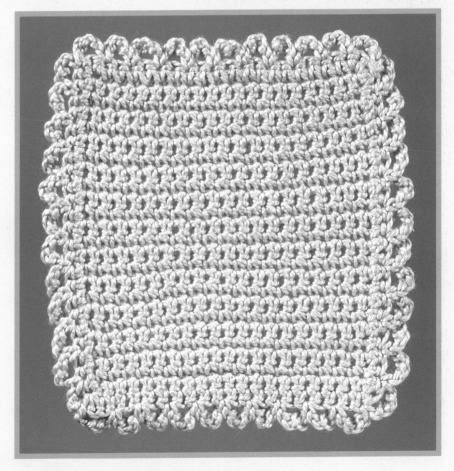

279

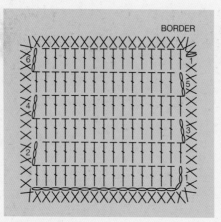

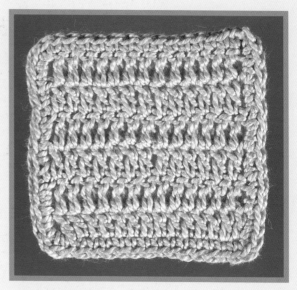

Ch any number of sts for desired width.

Row 1 (RS): Dc in 4th ch from hook, dc in each ch across, turn.

Row 2: Ch 3 (counts as dc), dc in each dc across, ending with dc in 3rd ch of turning ch, turn.

Rep Row 2 for desired depth. Fasten off.

Border:

Rnd 1: With RS facing, join yarn in top right-hand corner sc, ch 1, sc evenly around, working sc in each st, 2 sc in each row-end st, and 3 sc in each corner, sl st in first sc to join. Fasten off.

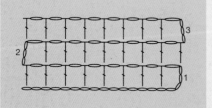

280

Ch a multiple of 2 for desired width.

Row 1: Dc in 6th ch from hook, *ch 1, skip next ch, dc in next ch; rep from * across, turn.

Row 2: Ch 4 (counts as dc, ch 1), skip next ch-1 space, *dc in next dc, ch 1, skip next ch-1 space; rep from * across to turning ch, dc in next ch of turning ch, turn.

Rep Row 2 for desired depth. Fasten off.

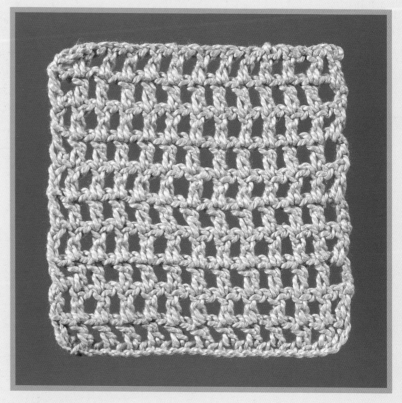

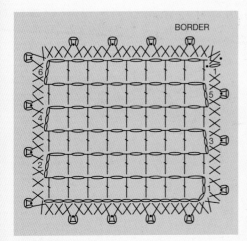

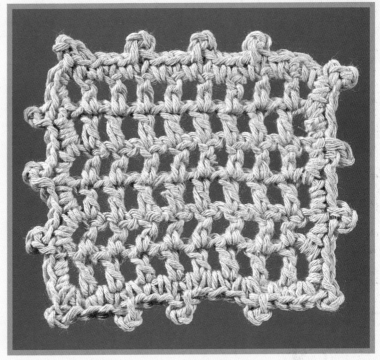

281

Picot: *Ch 3, sl st in 3rd ch from hook.*

Ch a multiple of 2 for desired width.

Row 1 (RS): Dc in 6th ch from hook, *ch 1, skip next ch, dc in next ch; rep from * across, turn.

Row 2: Ch 4 (counts as dc, ch 1), skip next ch-1 space, *dc in next dc, ch 1, skip next ch-1 space; rep from * across to turning ch, dc in next ch of turning ch, turn.

Rep Row 2 for desired depth. Fasten off.

Border:

Rnd 1: With RS facing, join yarn in top right-hand corner loop, ch 1, 3 sc in corner, sc in next ch-1 space, picot, *sc in each of next 4 sts, picot; rep from * around working 2 sc in each row-end st across side edges, maintaining picot pattern, sl st in first sc to join. Fasten off.

282

Ch a multiple of 4 plus 1 for desired width.

Row 1: Dc in 4th ch from hook, dc in next ch, *ch 1, skip next ch, dc in each of next 3 ch; rep from * across, turn.

Row 2: Ch 3 (counts as dc), dc in each of next 2 dc, *ch 1, skip next ch-1 space, dc in each of next 3 dc; rep from * across, ending with last dc in 3rd ch of turning ch, turn.

Rep Row 2 for desired depth. Fasten off.

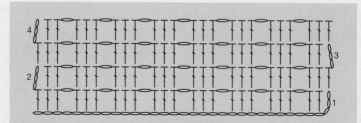

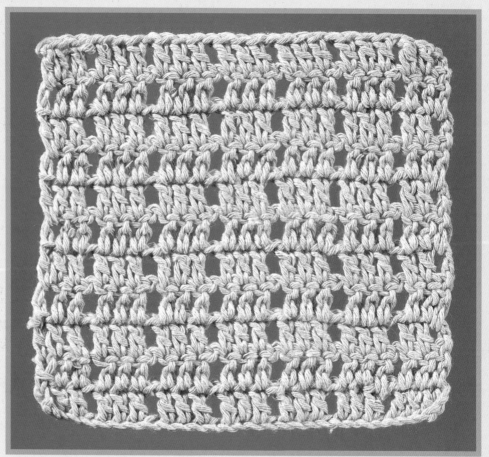

283

Ch a multiple of 4 plus 1 for desired width.

Row 1: Dc in 4th ch from hook, dc in next ch, *ch 1, skip next ch, dc in each of next 3 ch; rep from * across, turn.

Row 2: Ch 4 (counts as dc, ch 1), skip first 2 dc, *dc in next dc, dc in next ch-1 space, dc in next dc, ch 1, skip next dc; rep from * across to turning ch, dc in 3rd ch of turning ch, turn.

Rep Row 2 for desired depth. Fasten off.

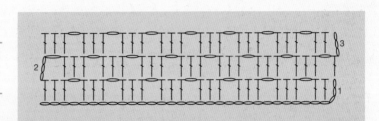

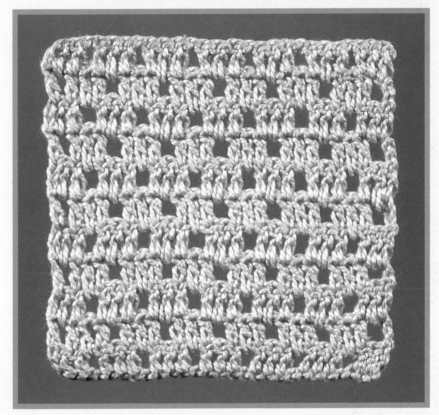

284

Ch a multiple of 2 for desired width.

Row 1: Dc in 6th ch from hook, *ch 1, skip next ch, dc in next ch; rep from * across, turn.

Row 2: Ch 3 (counts as dc), skip next ch-1 space, *2 dc in next dc, skip next ch-1 space; rep from * across to turning ch, 2 dc in next ch of turning ch, turn.

Row 3: Ch 4 (counts as dc, ch 1), skip next dc, *dc in next dc, ch 1, skip next dc; rep from * across to turning ch, dc in 3rd ch of turning ch, turn.

Rep Rows 2-3 for desired depth. Fasten off.

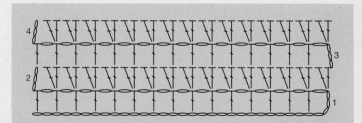

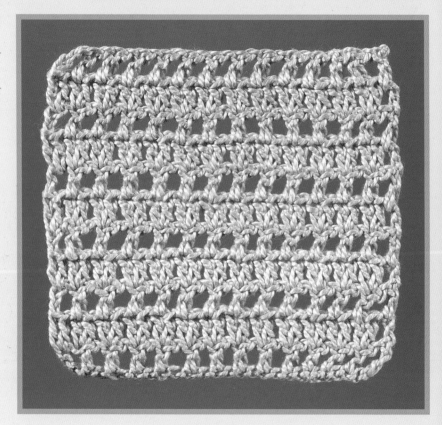

285

Ch a multiple of 8 plus 6 for desired width.

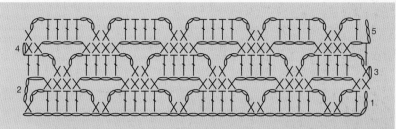

Row 1: Dc in 4th ch from hook, *ch 3, skip next ch, sc in each of next 2 ch, ch 3, skip next ch, dc in each of next 4 ch; rep from * across to within last 2 ch, ch 3, skip next ch, sc in last ch, turn.

Row 2: Ch 4 (counts as dc, ch 1), skip next ch-3 loop, *sc in each of next 4 dc, ch 4, skip next 2 ch-3 loops; rep from * across to within last 2 sts, sc in next dc, sc in 3rd ch of turning ch, turn.

Row 3: Ch 1, sc in first sc, ch 3, skip next sc, *4 dc in next ch-4 loop, ch 3, skip next sc, sc in each of next 2 sc, ch 3, skip next sc; rep from * across to turning ch, dc in ch-1 space of turning ch, dc in 3rd ch of turning ch, turn.

Row 4: Ch 1, sc in first 2 dc, *ch 4, skip next 2 ch-3 loops, sc in each of next 4 dc; rep from * across to within last ch-3 loop, ch 1, skip next ch-3 loop, dc in last sc, turn.

Row 5: Ch 3, dc in next ch-1 space, *ch 3, skip next sc, sc in each of next 2 sc, ch 3, skip next sc, 4 dc in next ch-4 loop; rep from * across to within last 2 sc, ch 3, skip next sc, sc in last sc, turn.

Rep Rows 2-5 for desired depth. Fasten off.

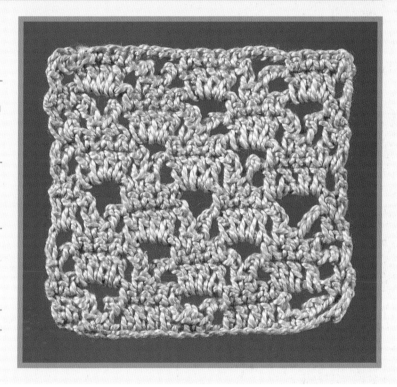

286

Ch a multiple of 10 plus 6 for desired width.

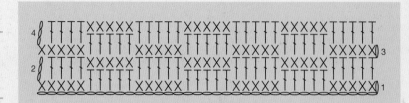

Row 1: Sc in 2nd ch from hook, sc in each of next 4 ch, *dc in each of next 5 ch, sc in each of next 5 ch; rep from * across, turn.

Row 2: Ch 3 (counts as dc), dc in each of next 4 sc, *sc in each of next 5 dc, dc in each of next 5 sc; rep from * across, turn.

Row 3: Ch 1, sc in each of first 5 dc, *dc in each of next 5 sc, sc in each of next 5 dc; rep from * across, ending with last sc in 3rd ch of turning ch, turn.

Rep Rows 2-3 for desired depth. Fasten off.

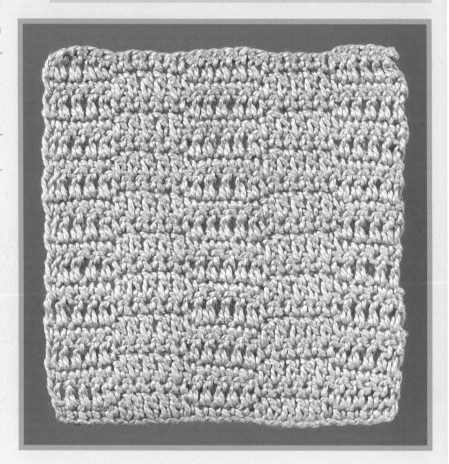

287

Ch a multiple of 2 plus 1 for desired width.

Row 1: Sc in 2nd ch from hook, sc in each ch across, turn.

Row 2: Ch 3 (counts as dc), 2 dc in next sc, *skip next sc, 2 dc in next sc; rep from * across, turn.

Row 3: Ch 3 (counts as dc), skip first 2 dc, *2 dc bet last skipped and next dc, skip next 2 dc; rep from * across to turning ch, 2 dc in 3rd ch of turning ch, turn.

Rep Row 3 for desired depth. Fasten off.

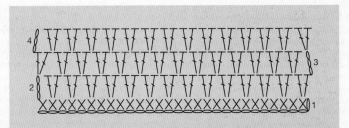

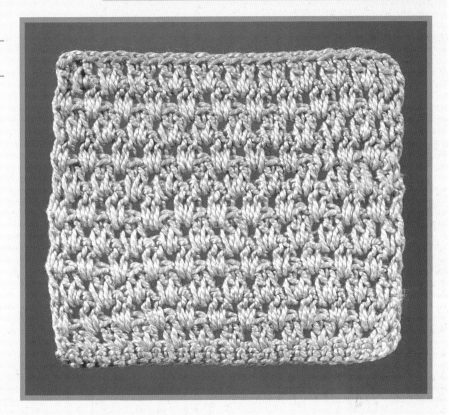

288

Ch a multiple of 4 plus 3 for desired width.

Row 1: Sc in 2nd ch from hook, sc in next ch, *ch 2, skip next 2 ch, sc in each of next 2 ch; rep from * across, turn.

Row 2: Ch 3 (counts as dc), dc in next sc, *ch 2, skip next ch-2 space, dc in each of next 2 sc; rep from * across, turn.

Row 3: Ch 1, sc in each of first 2 dc, *ch 2, skip next ch-2 space, sc in each of next 2 dc; rep from * across, ending with last sc in 3rd ch of turning ch, turn.

Rep Rows 2-3 for desired depth. Fasten off.

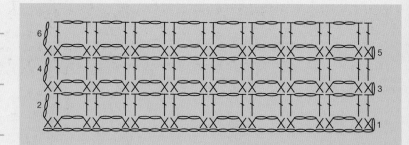

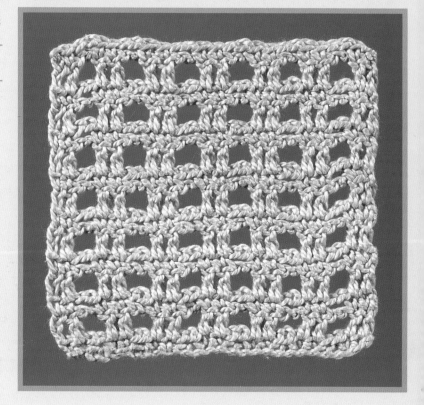

289

Ch a multiple of 6 plus 4 for desired width.

Row 1: Dc in 4th ch from hook, *ch 1, skip next 2 ch, dc in next ch, ch 1, skip next 2 ch, 3 dc in next ch; rep from * across, ending with 2 dc in last ch, turn.

Row 2: Ch 4 (counts as dc, ch 1), skip next ch-1 space, *3 dc in next dc, ch 1, skip next dc**, dc in next dc, ch 1, skip next ch-1 space; rep from * across, ending last rep at **, dc in 3rd ch of turning ch, turn.

Row 3: Ch 3, dc in first sc, *ch 1, skip next dc, dc in next dc, ch 1, skip next ch-1 space, 3 dc in next dc; rep from * across, ending with 2 dc in 3rd ch of turning ch, turn.

Rep Rows 2-3 for desired depth. Fasten off.

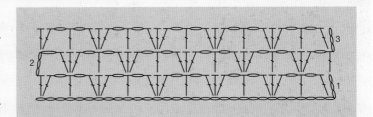

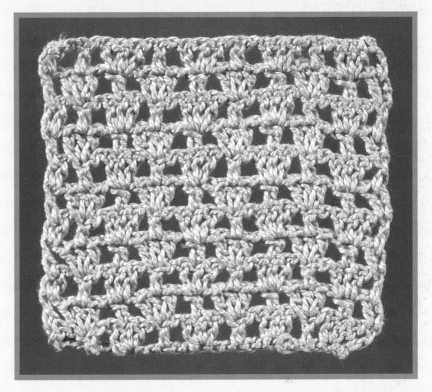

290

Ch a multiple of 3 plus 2 for desired width.

Row 1: Sc in 2nd ch from hook, *ch 2, skip next 2 ch, sc in next ch; rep from * across, turn.

Row 2: Ch 3 (counts as dc), dc in first sc, *skip next ch-2 space, 3 dc in next sc; rep from * across, ending with 2 dc in last sc, turn.

Row 3: Ch 1, sc in first dc, *ch 2, skip next 2 dc, sc in next dc; rep from * across, ending with last sc in 3rd ch of turning ch, turn.

Rep Rows 2-3 for desired depth. Fasten off.

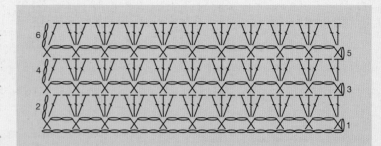

291 **Ch** a multiple of 8 plus 6 for desired width.

Row 1: Dc in 6th ch from hook, *skip next 2 ch, 5 dc in next ch, skip next 2 ch, dc in next ch, ch 1, skip next ch, dc in next ch; rep from * across, turn.

Row 2: Ch 4 (counts as dc, ch 1), skip next ch-1 space, *dc in next dc, skip next 2 dc, 5 dc in next dc, skip next 2 dc, dc in next dc, ch 1, skip next ch-1 space; rep from * across to turning ch, dc in next ch of turning ch, turn.

Rep Row 2 for desired depth. Fasten off.

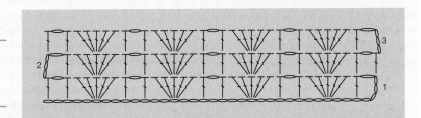

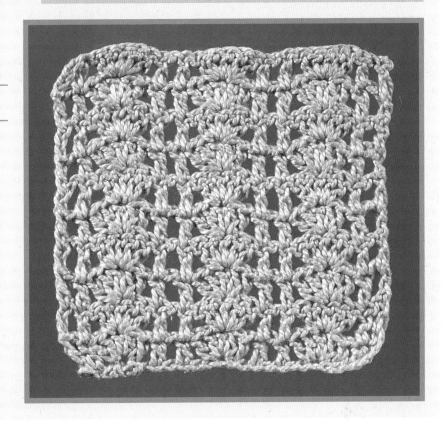

292

Ch a multiple of 4 plus 2 for desired width.

Row 1: 4 dc in 6th ch from hook, *skip next 3 ch, 4 dc in next ch; rep from * across, ending with 3 dc in last ch, turn.

Row 2: Ch 1, sc in each dc across, ending with last sc in top of turning ch, turn.

Row 3: Ch 3 (counts as dc), skip first sc, 2 dc in next sc, *skip next 3 sc, 4 dc in next sc; rep from * across to within last 2 sc, skip next sc, dc in last sc, turn.

Row 4: Ch 1, sc in each dc across, ending with last sc in 3rd ch of turning ch, turn.

Row 5: Ch 3 (counts as dc), skip first 3 sc, *4 dc in next sc, skip next 3 sc; rep from * across to within last sc, 3 dc in last sc, turn.

Rep Rows 2-5 for desired depth, ending with Row 2 of 4 of pattern. Fasten off.

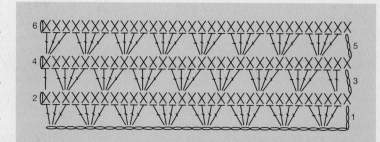

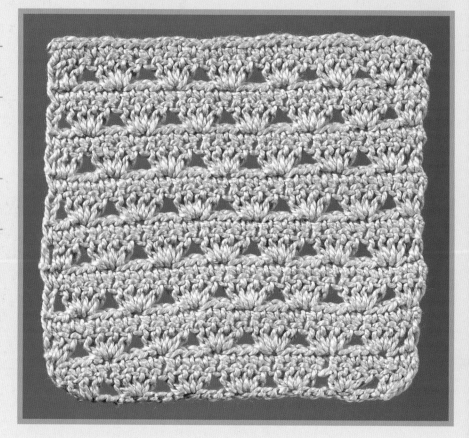

295

Ch a multiple of 8 plus 1 for desired width.

Row 1 (WS): Dc in 4th ch from hook, dc in each ch across, turn.

Row 2: Ch 3 (counts as dc), dc in each of next 2 dc, *FPdc in next dc, dc in each of next 3 dc**, ch 1, skip next dc, dc in each of next 3 dc; rep from * across, ending last rep at **, with last dc in 3rd ch of turning ch, turn.

Row 3: Ch 3 (counts as dc), dc in each of next 2 dc, *BPdc in next dc, dc in each of next 3 dc**, ch 1, skip next ch-1 space, dc in each of next 3 dc; rep from * across, ending last rep at **, with last dc in 3rd ch of turning ch, turn.

Rep Rows 2-3 for desired depth. Fasten off.

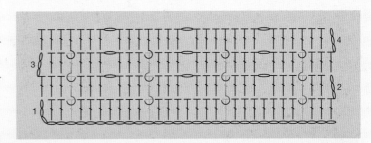

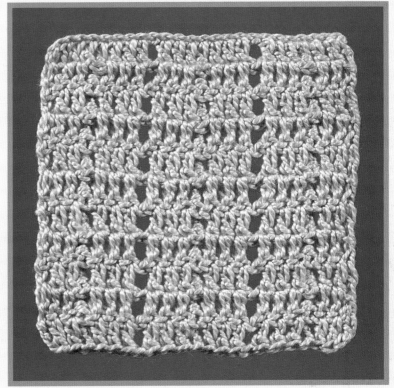

296

Ch a multiple of 12 plus 17 for desired width.

Row 1 (WS): Dc in 4th ch from hook, dc in each ch across, turn.

Row 2: Ch 3 (counts as dc), dc in each of next 2 dc, *(skip next dc, [dc, ch 1, dc] in next dc, skip next dc) 3 times**, FPdc in each of next 3 dc; rep from * across, ending last rep at **, dc in each of next 2 dc, dc in 3rd ch of turning ch, turn.

Row 3: Ch 3 (counts as dc), dc in each of next 2 dc, *(dc, ch 1, dc) in each of next 3 ch-1 spaces, skip next dc**, BPdc in each of next 3 dc; rep from * across, ending last rep at **, dc in each of next 2 dc, dc in 3rd ch of turning ch, turn.

Rep Rows 2-3 for desired depth. Fasten off.

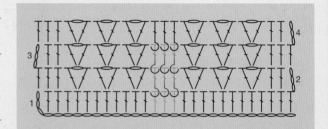

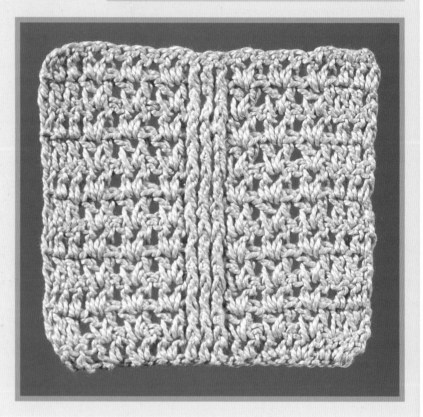

297

Ch a multiple of 3 plus 1 for desired width.

Row 1: Sc in 2nd ch from hook, sc in each ch across, turn.

Row 2: Ch 3 (counts as dc), skip first sc, *(dc, ch 1, dc) in next sc, skip next 2 sc; rep from * across to within last 2 sc, dc in next sc, ch 1, 2-dc cluster, working first half-closed dc in same sc holding last dc, work 2nd half-closed dc in last sc, yo, complete cluster, turn.

Row 3: Ch 3 (counts as dc), puff st in next ch-1 space, (ch 2, puff st) in each ch-1 space across to turning ch, dc in 3rd ch of turning ch turn.

Row 4: Ch 1, sc in first dc, sc in next puff st, *2 sc in next ch-2 space, sc in next puff st; rep from * across to turning ch, sc in 3rd ch of turning ch, turn.

Row 5: Ch 1, sc in each sc across, turn.

Rep Rows 2-5 for desired depth. Fasten off.

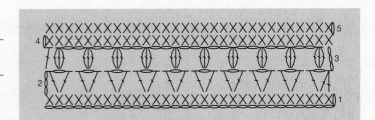

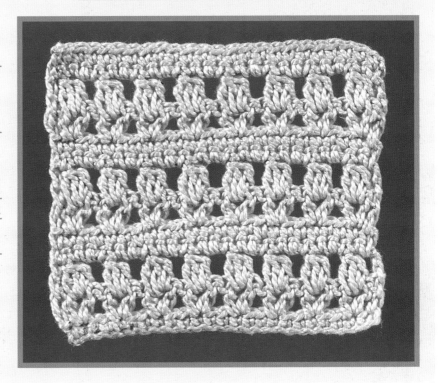

298

Ch a multiple of 4 plus 2 for desired width.

Row 1: (Sc, ch 2, 4 dc) in 2nd ch from hook, *skip next 3 ch, (sc, ch 2, 4 dc) in next ch; rep from * across to within last 4 ch, skip next 3 ch, sc in last ch, turn.

Row 2: Ch 3 (counts as dc), 2 dc in first sc, *skip next 4 dc, (sc, ch 2, 4 dc) in next ch-2 space; rep from * across to within last ch-2 space, sc in last ch-2 space, turn.

Row 3: Ch 3 (counts as dc), 2 dc in first sc, *skip next 4 dc, (sc, ch 2, 4 dc) in next ch-2 space; rep from * across to within last 3 sts, skip next 2 dc, sc in 3rd ch of turning ch, turn.

Rep Row 3 for desired depth. Fasten off.

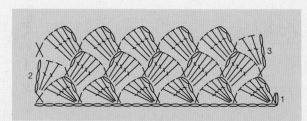

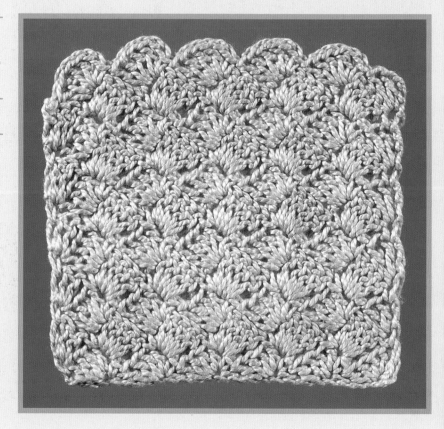

299

Ch a multiple of 4 plus 2 for desired width.

Row 1: Sc in 2nd ch from hook, *ch 3, skip next 3 ch, sc in next ch; rep from * across, turn.

Row 2: Ch 1, (sc, ch 3, 2 dc, hdc, sc) in each ch-3 loop across, turn.

Row 3: Ch 6 (counts as dc, ch 3), skip first 4 sts, sc in next ch-3 loop, (ch 3, sc) in each ch-3 loop across, turn.

Rep Rows 2-3 for desired depth. Fasten off.

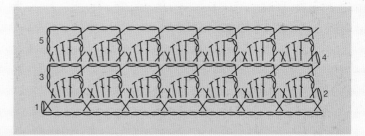

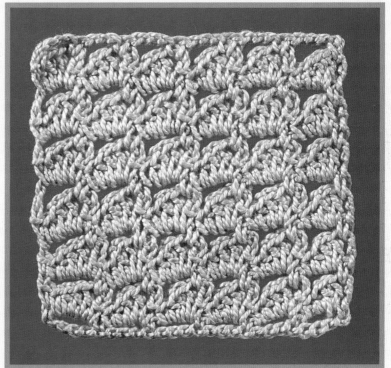

300

Popcorn (pop): 4 dc in same st, drop loop from hook, insert hook from front to back in first dc of 4-dc group, place dropped loop on hook, draw loop through st.

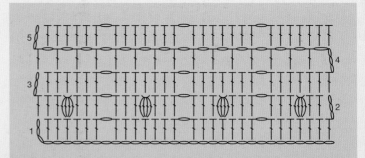

Ch a multiple of 8 plus 1 for desired width.

Row 1: Dc in 4th ch from hook, dc in each of next 5 ch, *ch 1, skip next ch, dc in each of next 7 ch; rep from * across, turn.

Row 2: Ch 3 (counts as dc), dc in each of next 2 dc, *pop in next dc, dc in each of next 3 dc**, ch 1, skip next ch-1 space, dc in each of next 3 dc; rep from * across, ending last rep at **, with last dc in 3rd ch of turning ch, turn.

Row 3: Ch 3 (counts as dc), dc in each of next 6 sts, *ch 1, skip next ch-1 space, dc in each of next 7 sts; rep from * across, ending with last dc in 3rd ch of turning ch, turn.

Row 4: Ch 4 (counts as dc, ch 1), skip first 2 dc, *dc in next dc, ch 1, skip next st; rep from * across to turning ch, dc in 3rd ch of turning ch, turn.

Row 5: Ch 3 (counts as dc), *(dc in next ch-1 space, dc in next dc) 3 times**, ch 1, skip next ch-1 space, dc in next dc; rep from * across, ending last rep at **, with last dc in 3rd ch of turning ch, turn.

Rep Rows 2-5 for desired depth. Fasten off.

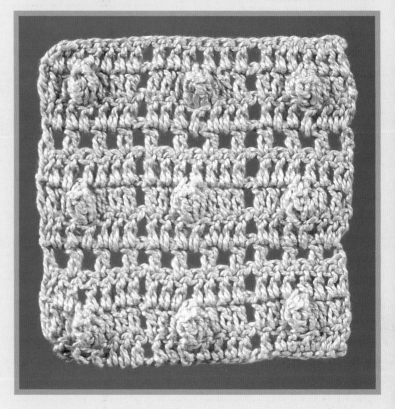

Crochet Terms and Abbreviations

Abbreviations

beg	begin, beginning		RS	right side
BPdc	back post double crochet		rnd(s)	round(s)
			sc	single crochet
ch	chain		sl st	slip stitch
dc	double crochet		st(s)	stitch(es)
dtr	double treble crochet		tr	treble crochet
FPdc	front post double crochet		trtr	triple treble crochet
			WS	wrong side
hdc	half double crochet		V-st	V-stitch
pop	popcorn		yo	yarn over
rep	repeat			

* Repeat directions following * as many times as indicated

() Repeat directions inside parentheses as many times as indicated

() Work directions inside parentheses into stitch indicated

U.S. Term	U.K./AUS Term
sl st slip st	sc single crochet
sc single crochet	dc double crochet
hdc half double crochet	htr half treble crochet
dc double crochet	tr treble crochet
tr treble crochet	dtr double treble crochet
dtr double treble crochet	trip tr or trtr triple treble crochet
trtr triple treble crochet	qtr quadruple treble crochet
rev sc reverse single crochet	rev dc reverse double crochet
yo yarn over	yoh yarn over hook

■ Acknowledgments ■

I'd like to thank Charles Nurnberg, president of Sterling Publishing Company in New York, who very kindly remembered me from 20 years ago, when I wrote my first crochet books, and gave me the wonderful opportunity of reprising them with Lark Books and passing on again these timeless techniques and my own love of crochet.

Thanks also to the Lark team who helped me through the revision of this book and who brought the entire project together—my editor Susan Kieffer, technical editor Karen Manthey, and art director Shannon Yokeley. I appreciate your dedication and vision. And, thanks to the following for their assistance with editorial details: Amanda Carestio, Dawn Dillingham, Rosemary Kast, and intern Halley Lawrence, and to the following for their assistance with production details: Jeff Hamilton, Avery Johnson, and intern Eva Reitzel.

■ About the Author ■

Linda Schapper's artistic vision is expressed in a wide range of media, from patchwork quilts and crochet, to painting and liturgical textiles, all of which are characterized by a folk-art style. She has traveled and taught extensively around the world in more than 30 countries, speaks four languages, and has had some 100 exhibits of her patchwork quilts. She has written eight books, four of them on crochet. She now divides her time between painting and writing, primarily about her liturgical work.

It's all on www.larkcrafts.com

Daily blog posts featuring needlearts, jewelry and beading, and all things crafty

Free, downloadable *projects* and *how-to videos*

Calls for artists and *book submissions*

A free *e-newsletter* announcing new and exciting books

...and a place to celebrate the *creative spirit*